Further praise for *The Suspicions of Mr Whicher:*

'A page-turning merging of scrupulous research with vivid storytelling. Full of atmosphere and striking detail, it is a triumph' *Observer*

'One of the Victorian era's most intriguing murder mysteries is given a fresh and gripping examination' *Sunday Times*

'A dramatic page-turning detective yarn of a real-life murder that inspired the birth of modern detective fiction. Kate Summerscale has brilliantly merged scrupulous archival research with vivid storytelling that reads with the pace of a Victorian thriller . . . leaves one gripped until the final paragraph' Rosie Boycott

'A thoroughly satisfying read, brilliantly researched, winningly told, and it's hard to see how this subject could have been better treated. It'll stand as a true crime classic' David Sexton, *Evening Standard*

'Fact and fiction do not so much blur as bleed into each other in *The Suspicions of Mr Whicher* . . . Summerscale accomplishes what modern genre authors hardly bother to do anymore, which is to use a murder investigation as a portal to a wider world' *New York Times*

'The best whodunit of the year – and it's all true. The fascinating story of a famous Victorian murder case and the detective who solved it has all the ingredients of a classic murder mystery . . . Agatha Christie, eat your heart out' Sebastian Shakespeare, *Tatler*

BY THE SAME AUTHOR

The Queen of Whale Cay

The SUSPICIONS of MR WHICHER

or THE MURDER at ROAD HILL HOUSE

KATE SUMMERSCALE

BLOOMSBURY

LONDON · BERLIN · NEW YORK

First published 2008
This paperback edition published 2009

Bloomsbury Publishing Plc, 36 Soho Square, London W1D 3QY

www.bloomsbury.com

www.mrwhicher.com

Bloomsbury Publishing, London, New York and Berlin

A CIP catalogue record for this book is available from the British Library

ISBN 978 1 4088 0614 2

10 9 8 7 6 5 4 3 2 1

Typeset by Hewer Text UK Ltd, Edinburgh
Printed in Great Britain by Clays Ltd, St Ives plc

To my sister, Juliet

'Do you feel an uncomfortable heat at the pit of your stomach, sir? and a nasty thumping at the top of your head? Ah! not yet? It will lay hold of you . . . I call it the detective-fever'

From *The Moonstone* (1868), by Wilkie Collins

CONTENTS

PART THREE: THE UNRAVELLING

INTRODUCTION

This is the story of a murder committed in an English country house in 1860, perhaps the most disturbing murder of its time. The search for the killer threatened the career of one of the first and greatest detectives, inspired a 'detective-fever' throughout England, and set the course of detective fiction. For the family of the victim, it was a murder of unusual horror, which threw suspicion on almost everyone within the house. For the country as a whole, the murder at Road Hill became a kind of myth – a dark fable about the Victorian family and the dangers of detection.

A detective was a recent invention. The first fictional sleuth, Auguste Dupin, appeared in Edgar Allan Poe's 'The Murders in the rue Morgue' in 1841, and the first real detectives in the English-speaking world were appointed by the London Metropolitan Police the next year. The officer who investigated the murder at Road Hill House – Detective-Inspector Jonathan Whicher of Scotland Yard – was one of the eight men who formed this fledgling force.

The Road Hill case turned everyone detective. It riveted the people of England, hundreds of whom wrote to the newspapers, to the Home Secretary and to Scotland Yard with their solutions. It helped shape the fiction of the 1860s and beyond, most obviously Wilkie Collins' *The Moonstone*, which was described by T.S. Eliot as the first and best of all English detective novels. Whicher was the inspiration for that story's cryptic Sergeant Cuff, who has influenced nearly every detective hero since. Elements of the case surfaced in Charles Dickens' last, unfinished novel, *The Mystery of Edwin Drood*. And although Henry James's terrifying novella

The Turn of the Screw was not directly inspired by the Road Hill murder – James said he based it on an anecdote told to him by the Archbishop of Canterbury – it was alive with the eerie doubts and slippages of the case: a governess who might be a force for good or evil, the enigmatic children in her charge, a country house steeped in secrets.

A Victorian detective was a secular substitute for a prophet or a priest. In a newly uncertain world, he offered science, conviction, stories that could organise chaos. He turned brutal crimes – the vestiges of the beast in man – into intellectual puzzles. But after the investigation at Road Hill the image of the detective darkened. Many felt that Whicher's inquiries culminated in a violation of the middle-class home, an assault on privacy, a crime to match the murder he had been sent to solve. He exposed the corruptions within the household: sexual transgression, emotional cruelty, scheming servants, wayward children, insanity, jealousy, loneliness and loathing. The scene he uncovered aroused fear (and excitement) at the thought of what might be hiding behind the closed doors of other respectable houses. His conclusions helped to create an era of voyeurism and suspicion, in which the detective was a shadowy figure, a demon as well as a demi-god.

Everything we know about Road Hill House is determined by the murder that took place there on 30 June 1860. The police and magistrates turned up hundreds of details of the building's interior – handles, latches, footprints, nightclothes, carpets, hotplates – and of its inhabitants' habits. Even the interior of the victim's body was exposed to the public with an unflinching, forensic candour that now seems startling.

Because each piece of information that has come down to us was given in answer to an investigator's question, each is the mark of a suspicion. We know who called at the house on 29 June because one of the callers might have been the killer. We know when the house's lantern was fixed because it might have illuminated the path to the scene of the murder. We know how the lawn was cut because a scythe might have served as the weapon. The resulting portrait of life in Road Hill House is hungrily attentive, but it is also incomplete: the investigation into the killing was like a torch swung round onto sudden movements, into corners and up stairwells. Everyday domestic events were lit with possible meanings. The ordinary was made sinister. The method of the murder seeped into the gathering detail, in the witnesses' repeated references to hard and soft surfaces, such as knives and cloths, and to openings and closings, incisions and bolts.

For as long as the crime went unsolved, the inhabitants of Road Hill House were cast variously as suspects, conspirators, victims. The whole of the secret that Whicher guessed at did not emerge until many years after all of them had died.

This book is modelled on the country-house murder mystery, the form that the Road Hill case inspired, and uses some of the devices of detective fiction. The content, though, aims to be factual. The main sources are the government and police files on the murder, which are held in the National Archives at Kew, south-west London, and the books, pamphlets, essays and newspaper pieces published about the case in the 1860s, which can be found in the British Library. Other sources include maps, railway timetables, medical textbooks, social histories and police memoirs. Some descriptions of buildings and landscapes are from personal observation. Accounts of the weather conditions are from press reports, and the dialogue is from testimony given in court.

In the later stages of the story the characters disperse – notably to London, the city of the detectives, and to Australia, a land of exiles – but most of the action of the book takes place in an English village over one month in the summer of 1860.

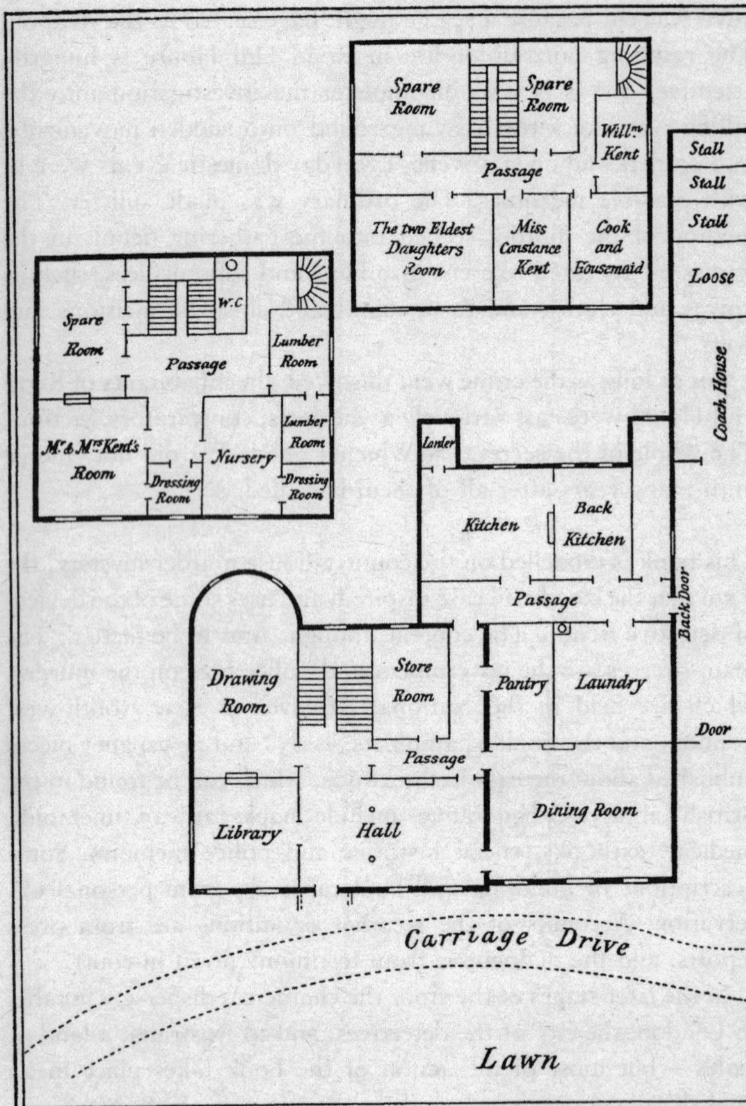
Spare Room
Spare Room
Will.m Kent
Passage
The two Eldest Daughters Room
Miss Constance Kent
Cook and Housemaid
Stall
Stall
Stall
Loose
Coach House
Spare Room
W.C
Lumber Room
Passage
Mr & Mrs Kent's Room
Dressing Room
Nursery
Lumber Room
Dressing Room
Larder
Kitchen
Back Kitchen
Passage
Back Door
Drawing Room
Store Room
Pantry
Laundry
Door
Passage
Library
Hall
Dining Room
Carriage Drive
Lawn

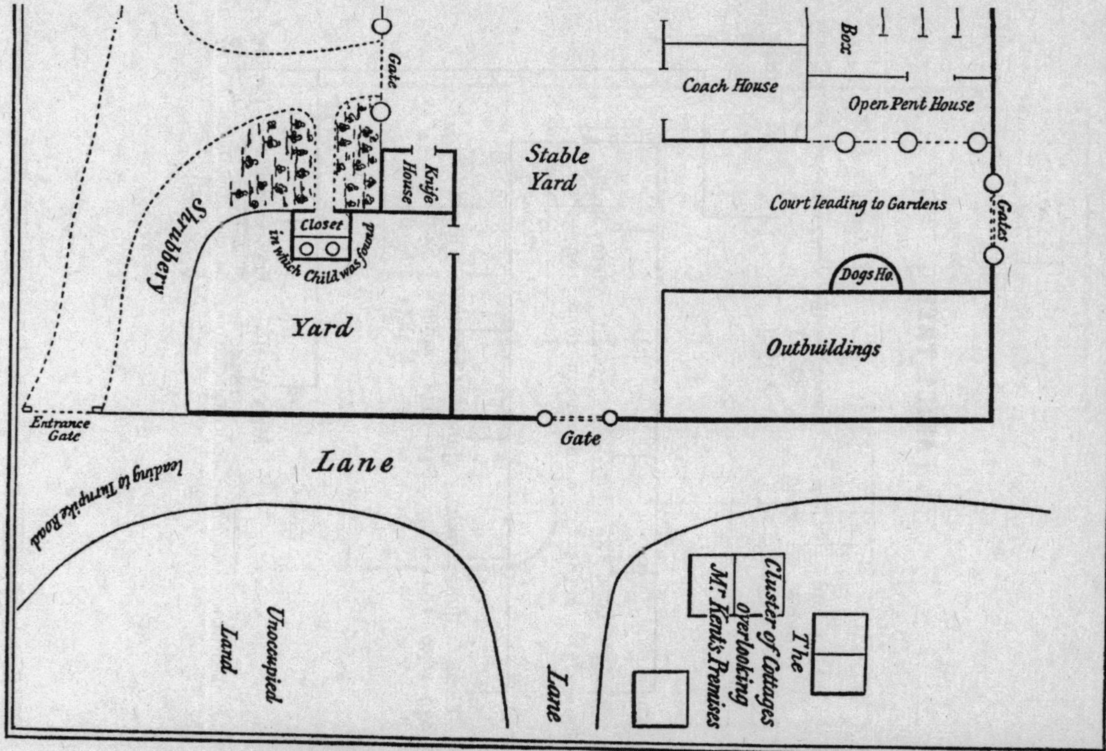
Gate
Shrubbery
Closet
in which Child was found
Knife House
Stable Yard
Coach House
Box
Open Pent House
Court leading to Gardens
Gates
Dogs Ho.
Yard
Outbuildings
Entrance Gate
Gate
Lane
leading to Turnpike Road
Unoccupied Land
Lane
The Cluster of Cottages overlooking Mr. Kent's Premises

FAMILY TREE

Mary Ann Windus 1808–1852 *(1) m.* 1829 Samuel Saville KENT *b.* 1801 *(2) m.* 1853 Mary Drewe Pratt *b.* 1820

- Children of the first marriage (1829):
  - Thomas 1830–1831
  - Mary Ann *b.* 1831
  - Elizabeth *b.* 1832
  - Edward 1835–1858
  - Henry Saville 1837–1838
  - Ellen 1839–1839
  - John Saville 1841–1841
  - Julia 1842–1842
  - Constance Emily *b.* 1844
  - William Saville *b.* 1845
- Children of the second marriage (1853):
  - Mary Amelia *b.* 1855
  - Francis Saville *b.* 1856
  - Eveline *b.* 1858

LIST OF CHARACTERS

AT ROAD HILL HOUSE

Samuel Kent, sub-inspector of factories, aged 59 in June 1860
Mary Kent, *née* Pratt, Samuel's second wife, 40
Mary Ann Kent, daughter of Samuel Kent's first marriage, 29
Elizabeth Kent, daughter of Samuel Kent's first marriage, 28
Constance Kent, daughter of Samuel Kent's first marriage, 16
William Kent, son of Samuel Kent's first marriage, 14
Mary Amelia Kent, daughter of Samuel Kent's second marriage, 5
Saville Kent, son of Samuel Kent's second marriage, 3
Eveline Kent, daughter of Samuel Kent's second marriage, 1
Elizabeth Gough, nursemaid, 22
Sarah Cox, housemaid, 22
Sarah Kerslake, cook, 23

LIVE-OUT SERVANTS

James Holcombe, gardener, groom and coachman, 49
John Alloway, odd-job boy, 18
Daniel Oliver, assistant gardener, 49
Emily Doel, assistant nursemaid, 14
Mary Holcombe, charwoman
Anna Silcox, retired monthly nurse, 76

OTHER VILLAGERS

The Reverend Edward Peacock, perpetual curate of Christ Church, 39
Hester Holley, washerwoman, 55
Martha Holley, daughter of Hester, 17
William Nutt, shoemaker, 36
Thomas Benger, farmer, 46
Stephen Millet, butcher, 55
Joe Moon, tilemaker, 39
James Fricker, plumber and glazier, 40
James Morgan, baker and parish constable, 56

THE POLICE

Superintendent John Foley, 64, of Trowbridge
Police Constable William Dallimore, 40, of Trowbridge
Eliza Dallimore, police 'searcher', 47, of Trowbridge
Police Constable Alfred Urch, 33, of Road
Police Constable Henry Heritage, of Southwick
Police Sergeant James Watts, of Frome
Captain Meredith, the Chief Constable of Wiltshire, 63, of Devizes
Superintendent Francis Wolfe, 48, of Devizes

THE DETECTIVES

Detective-Inspector Jonathan Whicher, 45
Detective-Sergeant Frederick Adolphus Williamson, 29
Detective-Sergeant Richard Tanner, 29
Ignatius Pollaky, private inquiry agent, 31

IN NEIGHBOURING TOWNS

George Sylvester, surgeon and county coroner, 71, of Trowbridge

Joshua Parsons, surgeon, 45, of Beckington

Joseph Stapleton, surgeon, 45, of Trowbridge

Benjamin Mallam, physician, of Frome

Rowland Rodway, solicitor, 46, of Trowbridge

William Dunn, solicitor, 30, of Frome

Henry Gaisford Gibbs Ludlow, landowner, magistrate for Wiltshire and Deputy Lieutenant for Somersetshire, 50, of Westbury

William Stancomb, wool manufacturer, magistrate for Wiltshire and Deputy Lieutenant for Wiltshire, 48, of Trowbridge

John Stancomb, wool manufacturer and magistrate for Wiltshire, 45, of Trowbridge

Peter Edlin, barrister, 40, of Bristol

Emma Moody, wool-worker's daughter, 15, of Warminster

Louisa Hatherill, farmer's daughter, 15, of Oldbury-on-the Hill, Gloucestershire

William Slack, solicitor, of Bath

Thomas Saunders, magistrate and former barrister, of Bradford-upon-Avon

A NOTE ON MONEY

In 1860, £1 had the purchasing power of £65 in today's money. A shilling (*s*) was worth a twentieth of £1 and had the purchasing power of about £3.25 today. A penny (*d*) was worth a twelfth of a shilling and had the purchasing power of about twenty-five modern pence. This measure – based on the retail price index – is useful for calculating the relative cost of everyday items, such as fares, food, drink.

When assessing salaries, a more meaningful calculation is that an income of £100 in 1860 is the equivalent of about £60,000 today.

Estimates based on the calculations of the American economics professors Lawrence H. Officer and Samuel H. Williamson, explained on their website measuringworth.com.

PROLOGUE

Paddington Railway Station,
15 July 1860

On Sunday, 15 July 1860, Detective-Inspector Jonathan Whicher of Scotland Yard paid two shillings for a hansom cab to take him from Millbank, just west of Westminster, to Paddington station, the London terminus of the Great Western Railway. There he bought two rail tickets: one to Chippenham, Wiltshire, ninety-four miles away, for 7*s*.10*d*., another from Chippenham to Trowbridge, about twenty miles on, for 1*s*.6*d*. The day was warm: for the first time that summer, the temperature in London had nudged into the seventies.

Paddington station was a shining vault of iron and glass, built by Isambard Kingdom Brunel six years earlier, its interior hot with smoke and sun. Jack Whicher knew the place well – the thieves of London thrived on the surging, anonymous crowds in the new railway stations, the swift comings and goings, the thrilling muddle of types and classes. This was the essence of the city that the detectives had been created to police. William Frith's *The Railway Station*, a panoramic painting of Paddington in 1860, shows a thief apprehended by two whiskered plain-clothes officers in black suits and top hats, quiet men able to steady the turmoil of the metropolis.

At this terminus in 1856 Whicher arrested the flashily dressed George Williams for stealing a purse containing £5 from the pocket of Lady Glamis – the detective told the magistrates' court that he had 'known the prisoner for years past as a member, and a first-rate one, of the swell mob'. At the same station in 1858 he apprehended a stout, blotchy woman of about forty in the second-class compartment of a Great Western train, with the words: 'Your name, I think, is Moutot.' Louisa Moutot was a notorious fraudster. She had used an alias – Constance Brown – to hire a brougham carriage, a page and a furnished house in Hyde Park. She then arranged for an assistant of the jewellers Messrs Hunt and Roskell to call round with bracelets and necklaces for the inspection of a Lady Campbell. Moutot asked to take the jewels upstairs to her mistress, who she claimed was sick in bed. The jeweller handed over a diamond bracelet, worth £325, with which Moutot left the room. After waiting for fifteen minutes he tried the door, to find he had been locked in.

When Whicher captured Moutot at Paddington station ten days later, he noticed that she was busying her arms beneath her cloak. He seized her wrists and turned up the stolen bracelet. Also on her person were a man's wig, a set of false whiskers and a false moustache. She was an up-to-the-minute urban criminal, a mistress of the twisty deceits that Whicher excelled in untangling.

Jack Whicher was one of the original eight Scotland Yard officers. In the eighteen years since the detective force had been formed, these men had become figures of mystery and glamour, the surreptitious, all-seeing little gods of London. Charles Dickens held them up as models of modernity. They were as magical and scientific as the other marvels of the 1840s and 1850s – the camera, the electric telegraph and the railway train. Like the telegraph and the train, a detective seemed able to jump time and place; like the camera, he seemed able to freeze them – Dickens reported that 'in a glance' a detective 'immediately takes an inventory of the furniture' in a room and makes 'an accurate sketch' of its inhabitants. A detective's investigations, wrote the novelist, were 'games of chess, played with live pieces' and 'chronicled nowhere'.

Whicher, at forty-five, was the doyen of the Metropolitan force – 'the prince of detectives', said a colleague. He was a stout, scuffed man with a delicate manner, 'shorter and thicker-set' than his fellow officers, Dickens observed, and possessed of 'a reserved and thoughtful air, as if he were engaged in deep arithmetical calculations'. His face was pitted with smallpox scars. William Henry Wills, Dickens' deputy at his magazine *Household Words*, saw Whicher in action in 1850. His account of what he witnessed was the first published description of Whicher, indeed of any English detective.

Wills was standing on the stairs of an Oxford hotel exchanging pleasantries with a Frenchman – he noted 'the jetty gloss of his boots, and the exceeding whiteness of his gloves' – when a stranger appeared in the hall below. 'On the mat at the stair-foot there stands a man. A plain, honest-looking fellow, with nothing formidable in his appearance, or dreadful in his countenance.' This 'apparition' had an extraordinary effect on the Frenchman, who 'raises himself on his toes, as if he had been suddenly overbalanced by a bullet; his cheek pales, and his lip quivers . . . He knows it is too late to turn back (he evidently would, if he could), for the man's eye is upon him.'

The stranger with a gaze like a gun mounted the stairs and instructed the Frenchman to leave Oxford, with the rest of his 'school', on the seven o'clock train. He then made for the hotel dining room, where he approached three men who were carousing over their supper. He put his knuckles on the table and leant forward, fixing the men with a stare, one by one. 'As if by magic', they froze and fell silent. The uncannily powerful stranger ordered the trio to pay their bill and catch the seven o'clock train to London. He followed them to Oxford railway station, and Wills followed him.

At the station, the reporter's curiosity overcame his fear of the man's 'evident omnipotence', and he asked him what was going on.

'The fact is,' the fellow told Wills, 'I am Sergeant Witchem, of the Detective police.'

Whicher was a 'man of mystery', in Wills' phrase, the prototype of the enigmatic, reserved investigator. He appeared from nowhere, and even his unmasking was masked with an alias. 'Witchem', the name given him by Wills, had suggestions of detection – 'which of 'em?' – and of magic – 'bewitch 'em'. He could turn a man to stone or strike him dumb. Many of the traits that Wills saw in Whicher became the stuff of the fictional detective hero: he was ordinary-looking, keen-sighted, sharp-witted, quiet. In accordance with his discretion, and his profession, no pictures of Whicher in this period seem to have survived. The only clues to what he looked like are the descriptions given by Dickens and Wills and the details on the police discharge papers: Whicher was five feet eight inches tall, his hair was brown, his skin was pale, his eyes were blue.

At railway station bookstalls, travellers could buy cheap, paperback detective 'memoirs' (actually collections of short stories) and magazines featuring mysteries by Dickens, Edgar Allan Poe and Wilkie Collins. That weekend's issue of Dickens' new journal *All the Year Round* ran the thirty-third instalment of Collins' *The Woman in White*, the first of the 'sensation' novels that were to dominate the 1860s. In the story so far, the villainous Sir Percival Glyde had imprisoned two women in a lunatic asylum in order to conceal a dark episode in his family's past. The instalment of 14 July had the dastardly Glyde burnt to death in the vestry of a church while trying to destroy evidence of his secret. The narrator watched as the church blazed: 'I heard nothing but the quickening crackle of the flames, and the sharp snap of the glass in the skylight above . . . We look for the body. The scorching heat on our faces drives us back: we see nothing – above, below, all through the room, we see nothing but a sheet of living fire.'

The death that Whicher was leaving London to investigate was a brutal, seemingly motiveless murder in a country house near Trowbridge in Wiltshire, which had confounded the local police and the national press. The victim's family, though outwardly respectable, was rumoured to harbour its own secrets, matters of adultery and madness.

A Great Western Railway telegraph had summoned Jack Whicher to Wiltshire, and one of the same company's trains bore him there. At 2 p.m. a huge six-wheeled steam engine pulled his carriage, liveried in chocolate and cream, out of Paddington station along a track that measured seven feet across. The Great Western was the smoothest, steadiest, fastest railway line in England. Even the penny-a-mile train, which Whicher took, seemed to skim across the flat country to Slough and glide over the broad arches of the railway bridge at Maidenhead. In J.M.W. Turner's painting *Rain, Steam, and Speed – the Great Western Railway* (1844) a locomotive hurtles over this bridge out of the east, a dark bullet casting off glittering sheets of silver, blue and gold.

Whicher's train reached Chippenham at 5.37 p.m., and eight minutes later the detective caught the connecting service to Trowbridge. He would be there in less than an hour. The story that awaited him – the sum of the facts gathered by the Wiltshire police, magistrates and newspaper reporters – began a fortnight earlier, on 29 June.

PART ONE

THE DEATH

'the secret may take air and fire, explode, and blow up '

From *Bleak House* (1853), by Charles Dickens

CHAPTER ONE

TO SEE WHAT WE HAVE GOT TO SEE

29–30 June

In the early hours of Friday, 29 June 1860 Samuel and Mary Kent were asleep on the first floor of their detached three-storey Georgian house above the village of Road, five miles from Trowbridge. They lay in a four-poster bed carved from Spanish mahogany in a bedroom decked out with crimson damask. He was fifty-nine; she was forty, and eight months pregnant. Their eldest daughter, the five-year-old Mary Amelia, shared their room. Through the door to the nursery, a few feet away, were Elizabeth Gough, twenty-two, the nursemaid, in a painted French bed, and her two youngest charges, Saville (three) and Eveline (one), in cane cots.

Two other live-in servants slept on the second floor of Road Hill House – Sarah Cox (twenty-two), the housemaid, and Sarah Kerslake (twenty-three), the cook – and so did Samuel's four children from his previous marriage: Mary Ann (twenty-nine), Elizabeth (twenty-eight), Constance (sixteen) and William (fourteen). Cox and Kerslake shared a bed in one room. Mary Ann and Elizabeth shared a bed in another. Constance and William had a room each.

The nursemaid, Elizabeth Gough, rose at 5.30 that morning to open the back door to a chimney sweep from Trowbridge. With his 'machine' of interlocking rods and brushes he cleaned the kitchen and nursery chimneys and the hotplate flue. At 7.30, the nursemaid paid him 4*s*.6*d*. and saw him out. Gough, a baker's daughter, was a well-mannered, good-looking young woman. She was thin, with fair skin, dark eyes, a long nose and a missing front tooth. When the sweep had gone she applied herself to cleaning the nursery of soot. Kerslake – the cook – sluiced down the kitchen. One other stranger called at the house that Friday, a knife-grinder, to whom Cox – the maid – answered the door.

In the grounds of Road Hill House, James Holcombe, the gardener, groom and coachman to the family, was cutting the lawn with a scythe – the Kents had a mowing machine, but a scythe was more effective when the grass was damp. That June had been the wettest and coldest on record in England, and it had again rained overnight. Having cut the grass, he hung the tool in a tree to dry.

Holcombe, who was forty-nine and crippled in one leg, had two helpers in the grounds that day: John Alloway, eighteen, 'a stupid-looking lad', according to one local newspaper, and Daniel Oliver, forty-nine. Both lived in the neighbouring village of Beckington. A week earlier Samuel Kent had turned down Alloway's request for a pay rise, and the young man had given his notice. On this, his penultimate afternoon in the Kents' employ, he was sent by the cook to see whether James Fricker, a plumber and glazier in the village, had finished fitting Mr Kent's square candle-lantern with a new pane of glass. Alloway had already called for it four times that week, but it had not been ready. This time he was successful: he brought the lamp back and put it on the kitchen dresser. A local girl of fourteen, Emily Doel, was also at work in the house. She helped Gough, the nursemaid, with the children from 7 a.m. to 7 p.m. each day.

Samuel Kent was in the library, drafting his report on a two-day tour of local wool mills from which he had returned the previous night. He had been employed as a government sub-inspector of factories for twenty-five years, and had recently applied for a full inspectorship, in support of which he had gathered signatures from two hundred West Country worthies – Members of Parliament, magistrates, clergymen. A wide-browed, scowling man, Kent was unpopular in the village, particularly with the inhabitants of the 'cottage corner', a slummy clutch of houses just across the lane from Road Hill House. He had banned the villagers from fishing the river near his house, and prosecuted one for taking apples from his orchard.

Saville, Samuel's three-year-old son, came into the library to play while the nursemaid cleaned the nursery. The child doodled on the government report – he made an 'S' -shaped pothook and a blot – and his father teased that he was a 'naughty boy'. At this Saville clambered onto Samuel's knee for a 'romp'. He was a strong, well-built child with pale yellow curls.

That Friday afternoon Saville also played with his half-sister, Constance. She and her other brother, William, had been home from their boarding schools for nearly a fortnight. Constance took after their father – muscular and plump, with squinty eyes in a broad face – while William resembled their mother, the first Mrs Kent, who had died eight years earlier: he had lively eyes and a delicate build. The boy was said to be timid, the girl sulky and wild.

The same afternoon Constance walked over to Beckington, a mile and a half away, to pay a bill. She met William there, and the two came home together.

In the early evening Hester Holley, a washerwoman who lived in the cottages next to the house, called to return the Kents' clothes and linen, which she had laundered each week since they moved to Road five years earlier. The older Misses Kent – Mary Ann and Elizabeth – took the clothes from the baskets and sorted them out for distribution to the bedrooms and cupboards.

At 7 p.m. the three gardeners and Emily Doel, the assistant nursemaid, left Road Hill House for their own homes. Holcombe locked the garden door from the outside as he went, and returned to his cottage across the lane. Samuel Kent locked the garden gate once all the live-out servants had gone. Twelve people were left in the house for the night.

Half an hour later Gough carried Eveline up to the nursery, and put her in the cot next to her own bed, opposite the door. Both the children's cots were made of thick cane backed with fabric, and set on wheels. Gough then went downstairs to give Saville a laxative, under Mrs Kent's supervision. The boy was recovering from a mild illness and the family doctor, Joshua Parsons, had sent a messenger to Road Hill House with an 'aperient' – the term was derived from the Latin for 'uncover' or 'open' – which took effect after six to ten hours. The pill 'consisted of one grain of blue pill and three grains of rhubarb', said Parsons, who had prepared it himself.

Saville was 'well and happy' that evening, said the nursemaid. At 8 p.m. she put him in his cot, in the right-hand corner of the nursery. The five-year-old Mary Amelia was put to bed in the room that she shared with her parents, across the landing. The doors to both bedrooms were left ajar, so that the nursemaid could hear if the older girl woke, and the mother could look in on her drowsing infants.

Once the children were asleep Gough tidied the nursery, restoring a stool to its place under her bed, returning stray objects to the dressing room. She lit a candle and sat down in the dressing room to eat her supper – that night she had only bread, butter and water. Then she joined the rest of the household downstairs for evening prayers, led by Samuel Kent. She also took a cup of tea with Kerslake in the kitchen. 'I don't usually have any tea at all,' Gough said afterwards, 'but I did that day take a cup from the general family teapot.'

When she went back up to the nursery, she said, Saville was lying 'as he usually did, with his face to the wall, with his arm under his head'. He was wearing a nightdress and a 'little flannel shirt'. He was 'a very heavy sleeper, and had not been to bed in the daytime that day, and so slept all the sounder'. She had been busy cleaning the room in the afternoon, when he usually had his nap. The nursery, as Gough described it, was a place of softness, hushed and muffled with fabric: 'The room is carpeted all over. The door opens very noiselessly, it is bound round with list to make it do so, that I might not wake the children.' Mrs Kent agreed that the door opened and closed quietly, if pushed and pulled with care, though the handle squeaked a little when turned. Later visitors to the house detected the rattle of a metal ring on the door, and the creak of the latch.

Mrs Kent came in to kiss Saville and Eveline goodnight, and then went upstairs to look out for the comet that was passing through the skies that week. In *The Times*, the newspaper her husband took, sightings were being reported each day. She called Gough to join her. When the nursemaid appeared Mrs Kent remarked on how sweetly Saville was sleeping. The mother and the nursemaid stood together at a window and watched the sky.

At 10 p.m. Mr Kent opened the yard door and unchained his black Newfoundland guard dog, a big, sweet-tempered creature that had been with the family for more than two years.

At about 10.30 William and Constance made their way up to bed, carrying their candles. Half an hour later Mary Ann and Elizabeth followed. Before going to sleep Elizabeth left her room to check that Constance and William had put out their lights. On seeing that their rooms were dark, she stopped at a window to watch for the comet. When she retired for the night her sister locked their bedroom door from within.

Two floors below, at about 10.45 p.m., Cox fastened the windows in the dining room, the hall, the drawing room and the library, and locked and bolted the front door and the doors to the library and the drawing room. The drawing-room shutters 'fasten with iron bars', she said later, 'and each has two brass bolts besides; that was all made secure'. The drawing-room door 'has a bolt and a lock, and I bolted it and turned the key of the lock'. Kerslake locked the kitchen, laundry and back doors. She and Cox went up to bed by the back stairs, a spiral staircase used mainly by the servants.

In the nursery at eleven, Gough tucked the bedclothes around Saville, lit a nightlight and then closed, barred and bolted the nursery windows before climbing into bed herself. She slept deeply that night, she said, exhausted by cleaning up after the sweep.

When Mrs Kent went to bed a little later, leaving her husband downstairs in the dining room, she pushed the nursery door gently shut.

Samuel Kent went out to the yard to feed the dog. By 11.30, he said, he had checked that every door and window on the ground floor was locked and bolted against intruders, as he did each evening. As usual, he left the key in the drawing-room door.

By midnight, everyone in the house was in bed, the knot of the new family on the first floor, the stepchildren and servants on the second.

Shortly before 1 a.m. on Saturday, 30 June, a man named Joe Moon, a tilemaker who lived alone on Road Common, was laying a net out to dry in a field near Road Hill House – he had probably been fishing by night to elude Samuel Kent – when he heard a dog bark. At the same time Alfred Urch, a police constable, was walking home after his shift when he heard the dog give about six yelps. He thought little of it, he said: the Kents' dog was known to bark at the slightest thing. James Holcombe heard nothing that night, even though there had been occasions in the past when he had been woken by the Newfoundland ('it kicked up a terrible noise') and had gone back to the courtyard to hush it. The heavily pregnant Mrs Kent was not disturbed by barking that night either, though she said she slept lightly: 'I awoke frequently.' She heard nothing out of the ordinary, she said, apart from 'a noise as of the drawing-room shutters opening' in the early morning, soon after dawn had broken – she imagined that the servants had started work downstairs.

The sun rose two or three minutes before 4 a.m. that Saturday. An hour later Holcombe let himself into the grounds of Road Hill House – 'I found the door safe as usual.' He chained up the Newfoundland and went to the stable.

At the same time Elizabeth Gough woke and saw that Eveline's bedclothes had slipped off. She raised herself on her knees to pull them back over the girl, whose cot was drawn up to the bed. She noticed, she said, that Saville was not in his cot across the room. 'The impression of the child was there as if he had been softly taken out,' Gough said. 'The clothes were smoothly put back as if his mother or myself had taken him out.' She assumed, she said, that Mrs Kent had heard her son crying and taken him to her own room across the hall.

Sarah Kerslake said she also woke briefly at 5 a.m., then went back to sleep. Just before six she woke again and roused Cox. The two rose, dressed and headed down to start work – Cox took the front stairs and Kerslake the back. When Cox went to unlock the drawing-room door, she was surprised to find it already open. 'I found the door a little way open, the shutters unfastened, and the window a little way up.' This was the middle of three floor-to-ceiling windows in the semi-circular bay at the back of the house. The bottom sash was raised by six inches or so. Cox said she supposed that someone had opened it to air the room. She closed it.

John Alloway walked over from his home in Beckington and at 6 a.m. found Holcombe in the Road Hill House stable, tending to the Kents' chestnut mare. Daniel Oliver arrived fifteen minutes later. Holcombe sent Alloway to water the plants in the greenhouse. The boy then fetched a basket of dirty knives – including two carving knives – from the kitchen, where Kerslake was at work, and two pairs of dirty boots from the passage. He took them to a shed in the yard known as the 'shoe-house' or the 'knife-house', turned the knives out onto a bench and started cleaning the boots – one pair belonged to Samuel Kent, one to William. 'There was nothing unusual about the boots that morning,' he said. Ordinarily he cleaned the knives as well, but today Holcombe took over the task so that the boy could be ready sooner: 'I want you in the garden,' he told him, 'to help me about some manure. I will clean the knives if you will clean the boots.' Holcombe used a knife-cleaning machine in the shed. As far as he could tell, he reported later, none of the knives was missing or bloodied. He took the clean cutlery to the kitchen at about 6.30. With Alloway, he then spread the mare's manure.

Soon after 6 a.m., Elizabeth Gough said, she rose, dressed, read a chapter of the Bible and said her prayers. The nightlight had burnt out, as usual, after six hours' use. Saville's cot was still empty. At 6.45 – she noticed the time on the clock that sat on the nursery mantelpiece – she tried Mr and Mrs Kent's room. 'I knocked twice at the door, but obtained no answer.' She claimed that she didn't persist because she was reluctant to wake Mrs Kent, whose pregnancy made it difficult for her to sleep. Gough returned to the nursery to dress Eveline. In the meantime Emily Doel had turned up for work. She entered the nursery carrying the children's bath shortly before 7 a.m., and took it to the adjoining dressing room. As she brought in buckets of hot and cold water with which to fill the tub she noticed Gough making her bed. They didn't say anything to one another.

Gough again knocked on Mr and Mrs Kent's bedroom door. This time it was opened – Mary Kent had got out of bed and put on her dressing gown, having just checked her husband's watch: it was 7.15. A confused conversation ensued, in which each woman seemed to assume Saville was with the other.

'Are the children awake?' Gough asked her mistress, as if she took for granted that Saville was in his parents' bedroom.

'What do you mean by children?' asked Mrs Kent. 'There is only one child.' She was referring to Mary Amelia, the five-year-old, who shared her parents' room.

'Master Saville!' said Gough. 'Isn't he with you?'

'With me!' returned Mrs Kent. 'Certainly not.'

'He is not in the nursery, ma'am.'

Mrs Kent went to the nursery to see for herself, and asked Gough if she had left a chair against the crib, by means of which Saville might have climbed out. The nursemaid said not. Mrs Kent asked when she had first noticed that he was gone. At five o'clock, Gough told her. Mrs Kent asked why she had not been roused immediately. Gough replied that she thought Mrs Kent must have heard the child crying in the night, and taken him to her room.

'How dare you say so?' said the mother. 'You know I could not do it.' The day before, she reminded Gough, she had mentioned that she could no longer carry Saville, he being a 'heavy, strong boy' of nearly four, and she being eight months pregnant.

Mrs Kent sent the nursemaid upstairs to ask her stepchildren if they knew where Saville was, then told her husband: 'Saville is missing.'

'You had better see where he is,' replied Samuel, who had, he said, been woken by Gough's knock. Mrs Kent left the room. When she returned with news that Saville had not been found, her husband got up, dressed, and headed downstairs.

Gough knocked on Mary Ann and Elizabeth's door at 7.20 or so and asked if Saville was with them. They said he wasn't, and asked whether Mrs Kent knew that he was missing. On hearing the commotion, Constance emerged from her room next door. She 'did not make any comment' on the news that her half-brother had disappeared, said Gough. Constance later said that she had been awake for forty-five minutes. 'I was dressing. I heard her knock at the door, and went to my own door to listen to hear what it was.' William, who said he woke at seven, was in a bedroom further along the landing, probably out of earshot.

Gough went two storeys down to the kitchen and asked Cox and Kerslake if they had seen the boy. Kerslake, who had lit a fire beneath the hotplate to scald milk for breakfast, said she hadn't. Cox said she had not either, but reported that she had found the drawing-room window open. The nursemaid told this to her mistress. By now Mr and Mrs Kent were scouring the house for their son. 'I was here, there and everywhere,' said Mrs Kent, 'looking for him. We were all in a state of bewilderment, going backwards and forwards from room to room.'

Samuel extended the search to the grounds. At about 7.30, said Holcombe, he told the gardeners that 'young Master Saville was lost, stolen, and carried away. That was all he said, and he ran round the garden . . . We went out directly in search of the child.'

'I desired the gardeners to search the premises to see if they could find any trace of the child,' explained Samuel. 'I mean to say traces of the child or any one having left the premises.' Gough helped search the gardens and the shrubbery.

Samuel asked the gardeners if there were any policemen nearby. 'There is Urch,' said Alloway. Alfred Urch was a police constable who had recently moved to Road with his wife and daughter; a month earlier he had been reprimanded for drinking at the George, a pub in Road, while on duty. It was Urch who had heard a dog bark at Road Hill House the previous night. Samuel sent Alloway to the village to fetch him. He also sent William to summon James Morgan, a baker and parish constable who lived in Upper Street. Urch was an officer of the Somersetshire county constabulary, set up in 1856, while Morgan was a member of the older policing system, still being phased out, in which villagers were appointed to serve as unpaid parish constables for a year at a time. The two were neighbours.

Morgan hurried Urch along. 'Let us make haste,' he urged. They headed for Road Hill House.

William, on his father's instructions, asked Holcombe to prepare the horse and carriage – Samuel had decided to ride to

Trowbridge to fetch John Foley, a police superintendent with whom he was acquainted. When Samuel took leave of his wife, she told him that the blanket was missing from Saville's bed. Gough had noticed its absence, she said. Mrs Kent 'seemed pleased with the idea' that he had been carried off in a blanket, said Samuel, 'as it would keep the child warm'.

Samuel put on a black overcoat and set out in his phaeton, a dashing, four-wheeled carriage with a skimpy body and high back wheels, pulled by the red mare. 'He went away in a great hurry,' said Holcombe. As Urch and Morgan approached the drive at about 8 a.m., they met him turning left onto the Trowbridge road. Morgan assured Samuel he need go only to Southwick, a mile or so away, from where a Wiltshire police officer could send a message on to the town. But Samuel wished to ride the full five miles to Trowbridge: 'I shall go on,' he said. He asked Urch and Morgan to join the search for his son.

At Southwick turnpike gate, Samuel pulled up his carriage and, as he was paying the toll (4½ *d.*), asked the keeper of the gate, Ann Hall, to direct him to the local policeman's house.

'I have had a child stolen and carried off in a blanket,' Samuel told her.

'When did you lose it?' asked Mrs Hall.

'This morning,' replied Samuel.

She pointed him towards Southwick Street, where Samuel gave a boy a halfpenny to show him the house of PC Henry Heritage. Ann Heritage answered the door and told Samuel that her husband was in bed.

'You must call him up,' said Samuel, without getting out of his carriage. 'I have had a child stolen out of my house tonight . . . a little boy aged three years and ten months . . . wrapped up in a blanket . . . I am going to Trowbridge to give information to Foley.'

Mrs Heritage asked him for his name and residence.

'Kent,' he replied. 'Road Hill House.'

* * *

When PC Urch and parish constable Morgan reached Road Hill House, they found Sarah Cox in the kitchen and asked her how the child had been taken away. She showed them the open window in the drawing room. Elizabeth Gough took them into the nursery and turned back the bedclothes in Saville's cot: Morgan noticed 'the mark where the little boy had lain on the bed, and on the pillow'. Gough told the constables that when she joined the Kent household, eight months earlier, the nurse she replaced had mentioned that the boy's mother sometimes fetched him to her room in the night. Morgan asked: 'Have you lost anything from the nursery besides the child?' She hesitated, he said, before replying that 'there was a blanket taken from the cot, or drawn from the cot'.

Urch and Morgan asked to see the cellar, but found it was locked. One of the elder Misses Kent held the key but the constables chose not to involve the family in their inquiries. They returned to the drawing room to look for 'foot-tracks', as Morgan referred to them – to Urch they were 'footmarks' or 'footprints'; the science of detection was young, and its vocabulary still unsettled. Soon afterwards Elizabeth Gough looked for footmarks there, and found the imprints of two large hobnailed boots on the white drugget, a coarse woollen rug that lay over the carpet by the window. It turned out that these had been made by PC Urch.

Mrs Kent sent her stepdaughter Constance to ask the Reverend Edward Peacock to come to Road Hill House. Peacock lived in a three-storey gothic parsonage next to Christ Church with his wife, their two daughters, two sons and five servants. He and Samuel were friends, and the parsonage was only a few minutes' walk from the Kents' house. The vicar agreed to help with the search.

William Nutt, a shoemaker with six children who lived in the tumbledown cottages by the house, was at work in his shop when he overheard Joseph Greenhill, an innkeeper, talking about Master Saville's disappearance. Nutt headed for Road Hill House: 'Having an affection like for the father, I said, "I must go and hear further about this."' Nutt was 'a strange-looking person', reported the *Western Daily Press*: 'sallow, thin, and bony, with prominent cheek bones, pointed nose, receding forehead, and a cast in one eye; while he is what is called "bumble-footed", and has a habit of placing his attenuated arms in front of his chest, with his hands drooping'. Just outside the gates, Nutt came across Thomas Benger, a farmer, driving his cows. Benger suggested to Nutt that they join the search. Nutt hesitated to go on the lawn without permission, and told Benger he 'did not like to go on a gentleman's premises'. Benger, who had heard Samuel Kent offer Urch and Morgan a £10 reward if they found his son, persuaded Nutt that no one could reprimand them for looking for a lost child.

As they searched the thick shrubbery to the left of the front drive, Nutt remarked that they would find a dead child if the living one was not found. He then struck off to the right, towards a servants' privy hidden in the bushes, and Benger followed. They came to the privy and looked in: a small pool of clotted blood lay on the floor.

'See, William,' said Benger, 'what we have got to see.'

'Oh, Benger,' said Nutt. 'It is as I predicted.'

'Get a light, William,' said Benger.

Nutt went to the back door of the house and along the passage to the scullery. There he found Mary Holcombe, the gardener's mother. She was employed by the Kents as a charwoman for two days or so each week. Nutt asked for a candle, and she looked at him.

'For God's sake, what's the matter, William?'

'Don't alarm yourself, Mary,' he said. 'I only want a candle for a minute to see what we can see.'

While Nutt was gone, Benger lifted the lavatory lid and peered in until his eyes adjusted to the darkness. 'By steadily looking down, I could see better, and saw a something like clothing below; I put my hand down and raised the blanket.' The blanket was soaked with blood. About two feet under the seat, on the wooden 'splashboard' that partly blocked the descent to the pit beneath, was the boy's body. Saville was lying on his side, one arm and one leg slightly drawn up.

'Look here,' said Benger as Nutt appeared with the candle. 'Oh, William, here it is.'

CHAPTER TWO

THE HORROR AND AMAZEMENT

30 June–1 July

As Thomas Benger lifted Saville's body from the privy, the boy's head tipped back to expose the clean cut through his neck.

'Its little head fell off almost,' said William Nutt, when he gave his account of the day's events in the Wiltshire magistrates' court.

'His throat was cut,' said Benger, 'and blood was splashed over his face . . . he was a little dark about the mouth and eyes, but he looked quite pleasant, and his little eyes were shut.' Pleasant, here, meant peaceful.

Nutt spread the blanket on the privy floor and Benger placed the body upon it. They wrapped the corpse together, Benger at the head, Nutt at the feet, and Benger, as the stronger of the two, took it in his arms and carried it to the house. Urch and Morgan watched him walk through the yard. The farmer bore the boy's body along the passage and into the kitchen.

Saville's corpse, already stiff, was laid on a table beneath the kitchen window; upstairs the shape of his sleeping self was still indented on the sheets and pillow of the cot. Mary Ann and Elizabeth Kent, the two older sisters, entered the kitchen, Elizabeth holding the one-year-old Eveline in her arms. 'I can't describe the horror and amazement they seemed to be in,' said Nutt. 'I thought they would fall and I took them both round the waist. I went through with them into the passage.'

The nursemaid was also in the kitchen. Nutt said to her 'that she must have slept very soundly to have admitted of any one taking the child from her room. She answered me, I thought rather harshly, by telling me I knew nothing of the matter.' Gough claimed that it was only now, when she saw the blanket wrapping Saville's corpse, that she realised it had been taken from his bed. Yet PC Urch, James Morgan and Mrs Kent all claimed that Gough had told them of the blanket's loss before Saville's body was found. The nursemaid's contradictory statements about the blanket were to make her a suspect.

Outside, the servants and a growing gaggle of villagers began to search for traces of the murderer and the weapon. Daniel Oliver, the jobbing gardener, showed Urch some footmarks on the lawn near the drawing-room windows: 'There's been someone here.' But Alloway said he had made the footprints the previous evening: 'I had been using the wheelbarrow.'

By the privy door Alloway found a piece of bloody newspaper, five or six inches square, folded and still moist. It looked as though a knife or razor might have been wiped upon it. The date of the newspaper was legible – 9 June – but not its title. Edward West, a farmer, advised Alloway: 'Don't destroy the paper; pick it up; take care of it – it will be the means of bringing about a discovery.' Alloway handed it to Stephen Millet, a butcher and parish constable, who was inspecting the privy. Millet estimated that there were two tablespoons of blood on the floor, and a pint and a half had soaked in to the blanket. West described the blood on the floor as 'about the size of a man's hand. I saw it in quite a coagulated state.'

Upstairs, Elizabeth Gough was arranging Mrs Kent's hair – her last position had been as a lady's maid, and in Road Hill House she tended to her mistress as well as to the children. Samuel had left orders that his wife be given no news of the boy, so Gough did not mention that Saville had now been found dead, but when Mrs Kent wondered aloud where her son could be, she said, 'Oh, ma'am, it's revenge.'

As soon as the Reverend Mr Peacock reached Road Hill House he was told that Saville had been found, and was shown the body in the kitchen. He went home, saddled his horse and set off after Samuel. He passed through Ann Hall's turnpike at Southwick.

'Sir,' she said to the vicar, 'this is a sad affair at Road.'

'But the child is found,' he replied.

'Where, sir?'

'In the garden.' Peacock did not explain that he was dead.

Peacock caught up with Kent. 'I am sorry to tell you I have had bad news for you,' he said. 'The little boy has been found murdered.'

Samuel Kent headed home: 'I was not long; I went as fast as I could.' When he passed the turnpike gate, Ann Hall asked after Saville.

'Then, sir, the child is found?'

'Yes, and murdered.' He did not stop.

Since his father was away it fell to William Kent to fetch Joshua Parsons, the family physician. The boy hurried down the narrow lane to the village of Beckington and found the doctor at his home in Goose Street. He told him that Saville had been discovered in the privy, his throat cut, and Parsons set off for Road Hill House, taking William with him in his carriage. When they arrived, the doctor recalled, 'I was taken round the back way by Master William, because he was not aware whether his mother knew what had occurred, so I went into the library.'

Samuel was now home. He greeted Parsons and gave him a key to the laundry room, opposite the kitchen, to which Saville's body had been moved. 'I went in by myself,' said Parsons. The corpse was entirely rigid, he noted, which indicated that the boy had been killed at least five hours earlier – that is, before three o'clock that morning. 'The blanket and the nightdress [were] stained with marks of blood and soil,' he reported – by 'soil', he meant excrement. 'The throat was cut to the bone by some sharp instrument, from left to right; it completely divided all the membranes, blood vessels, nerve vessels, and air tubes.' Parsons also noticed a stab to the chest, which had cut through the clothes and the cartilage of two ribs, but had produced little blood.

'The mouth of the child had a blackened appearance, with the tongue protruded between the teeth,' he said. 'My impression was that the blackened appearance had been produced by forcible pressure on it during life.'

Mrs Kent was sitting downstairs at the breakfast table when her husband came in to tell her that their son was dead.

'Someone in the house has done it,' she said.

Cox, the maid, overheard her. 'I have not done it,' Cox said. 'I have not done it.'

At nine, as usual, Kerslake put out the fire beneath the kitchen hotplate.

Superintendent John Foley reached Road Hill House from Trowbridge between 9 and 10 a.m. He was taken to the library and then the kitchen. Cox showed him the open window in the drawing room; Gough showed him the empty crib in the nursery. The nurse told him, he said, that 'she never missed the blanket till the child was brought in wrapped up in it'. Foley said that he asked Samuel Kent whether he had known that the blanket was missing before he set out for Trowbridge. 'Certainly not,' Samuel replied. Either Foley's recollection was at fault ('My memory is not as good as some persons',' he admitted), or Samuel was lying or seriously confused: his wife, the turnpike keeper and the wife of PC Heritage all testified that he knew of the blanket's loss before he left for Trowbridge, as did Samuel himself when asked about it by others.

Foley looked over the premises with the help of Parsons, who had finished his preliminary examination of the corpse. They inspected the household's clothing, including a nightgown on Constance's bed – 'It had not stains on it,' said Parsons. 'It was very clean.' The bedclothes on Saville's cot, he noted, were 'very neatly folded, as if by a practised hand'. In the kitchen the doctor examined the knives, and found no traces of blood. In any case, he said, he did not believe that any of those knives could have inflicted the injuries he had seen.

John Foley went to the laundry room to study Saville's body, taking with him Henry Heritage, the constable whom Kent had roused at Southwick and who had reached Road Hill House at ten. These two then examined the privy in which the body had been found. When Foley looked down into the vault beneath the privy seat, he thought he could see 'some linen substance' lying in the dirt. 'I sent for a crook, which I attached to a stick, and pulled up a piece of flannel.' The cloth was ten or twelve inches square, its edges neatly bound with narrow tape. At first Foley thought it a man's chest flannel, but it was then identified as a woman's 'breast or bosom flannel', a pad tied inside a corset to cushion the chest. The strings to this one seemed to have been cut off, and the flannel was sticky with thickening blood. 'There was blood upon it, which appeared to be recently there,' Foley said. 'It was still fluid . . . The blood had penetrated the flannel, but it appeared to have dropped so gently that it had congealed drop by drop as it fell.'

Late in the morning two professional men, acquaintances of Samuel Kent, arrived from Trowbridge to offer their services: Joseph Stapleton, a surgeon, and Rowland Rodway, a solicitor. Stapleton, who lived in the centre of Trowbridge with his wife and brother, was a certifying surgeon to several of the factories that Kent supervised. He assessed whether workers, particularly children, were fit enough to work in the mills, and reported on any injuries that befell them. (The following year Stapleton was to publish the first book about the murder at Road Hill House, which became the principal source for many accounts of the case.)

Rodway was a widower with a son of twenty-one. He said he found Samuel in a 'state of grief and horror . . . agitation and distress', insisting that he wanted to telegraph at once for a London detective, 'before any traces of the crime could disappear or be removed'. Superintendent Foley resisted the suggestion – it could cause difficulty and disappointment, he said – and instead sent to Trowbridge for a woman to search the female servants. He expressed 'some hesitation in intruding on the family privacy', according to Rodway, 'and in adopting those measures of surveillance which the case required'. Samuel told Rodway to tell Foley that he must 'not feel under the slightest restraint'.

Foley then put on his spectacles, got down on his hands and knees, and, he said, looked 'minutely at every step and every spot' between the nursery and the front and back doors. 'I viewed the posts, the sides of the stairs and passage, and even the grass minutely, the gravel and steps in front of the door, and the matting in the hall, and I could see nothing.'

In the afternoon Foley interviewed Gough in the dining room, in the presence of Stapleton and Rodway. She appeared tired, Stapleton said, but her answers were simple and consistent. She seemed 'a person of considerable intelligence'. Rodway, too, found that she answered questions 'frankly and fully, and without embarrassment'. When Foley asked her if she had any suspicions about who had killed Saville, she said she had not.

Samuel Kent asked Rodway whether he would represent him at the inquest. The solicitor replied that it might look bad, because it could suggest that Samuel was himself a suspect. Samuel later said he was prompted to ask for Rodway's help not on his own account, but to protect William, about whom rumours were circulating in the village: 'I did not know what might transpire there, as it was reported my son William had committed the murder.'

Benger and a group of other men emptied the ten-foot vault beneath the privy. When only six or eight inches of water remained they felt carefully with their hands all along the bottom, but found nothing. Fricker, the plumber and glazier, offered to examine the pipes, and went to the kitchen to fetch a candle. He met Elizabeth Gough, who asked him why he wanted a light. To check the cistern, he explained. She said she was sure he would find nothing there.

Several more police officers turned up at Road Hill House in the course of the day, as well as Eliza Dallimore, the 'searcher' employed by the police to examine the bodies and belongings of female suspects. Mrs Dallimore was married to William, one of the constables already on the premises. She took Gough to the nursery.

'What do you want with me?' Gough asked her.

'You must undress yourself,' Mrs Dallimore replied.

'I cannot,' said the nursemaid. Mrs Dallimore insisted that she must, and led her to the adjacent dressing room.

'Well, nurse,' said the searcher as Gough took off her clothes, 'this is a very shocking thing about the murder.'

'Yes, it is.'

'Can you give any account of it, do you think?'

Gough reiterated that at five in the morning she had woken and seen that Saville was missing. 'I thought he was with his mamma, because he generally goes in there of a morning.' According to Mrs Dallimore, she added: 'This is done through jealousy. The little boy goes into his mamma's room and tells everything.'

'No one would murder a child for doing such a thing as that,' said Mrs Dallimore. The nurse's characterisation of Saville as a tell-tale became, for many, the clue to the crime.

Eliza Dallimore and Elizabeth Gough went down to the kitchen. 'This is a shocking thing,' Mrs Dallimore told the servants, 'and I think the whole house is responsible for the child.'

When Fricker, the plumber, came in from the garden with his assistant, Gough asked, 'What have you been doing, Fricker?'

'I've been opening the water closet,' he said.

'And you haven't found anything?'

'No.'

'Then you won't.' Her remarks to the plumber, before and after his examination of the pipes, were later taken as indications that she knew more than she admitted about the crime.

Mrs Dallimore strip-searched the female servants but, on Foley's instructions, did not ask the women of the Kent family to disrobe. Instead, she examined their nightdresses. She found bloodstains on the nightdress of Mary Ann, the eldest daughter, so she passed it on to the police. They showed the garment to Parsons, who attributed the stains to 'natural causes'. Stapleton agreed that the blood was menstrual. The nightgown was none the less given to Mrs Dallimore for safekeeping.

At about four o'clock PC Urch asked two village women – Mary Holcombe and Anna Silcox – to wash and lay out the dead child. Mary Holcombe was the charwoman who had been cleaning the kitchen when Nutt and Benger found Saville's body. Silcox was a widow who used to work as a 'monthly nurse', tending a mother and her baby in the first weeks after a birth; she lived with her grandson, a carpenter, next to Road Hill House. Parsons told the women to 'do what was right to the poor boy'.

Parsons was talking to Samuel Kent in the library at about five o'clock when a messenger called at Road Hill House with instructions for the doctor to conduct a post-mortem examination of the body. The coroner, on being informed by the police of the child's murder, had scheduled an inquest for Monday. With Samuel's agreement, Parsons asked Stapleton to help him examine the corpse.

When he saw the body, Stapleton noted the 'expression of repose' on the child's face: 'Its upper lip, retracted slightly by the mortal spasm, had stiffened upon the upper teeth.' The doctors opened the boy's stomach and found the remains of his supper, which had included rice. To check whether he had been drugged, Parsons smelt for traces of laudanum or any other narcotic, but could detect none. The stab to his chest, a bit more than an inch wide, had pushed the heart out of place, punctured the diaphragm and grazed the outer edge of the stomach. 'It would have required very great force,' said Parsons, 'to inflict such a blow through the nightdress and to the depth to which it had penetrated.' This was a child of 'remarkably fine development', the doctor said. From the rips in the boy's clothes and his flesh, Parsons surmised that the weapon was shaped like a dagger. 'It could not have been done by a razor,' he said. 'It must have been, I think, a sharp-pointed, long, wide and strong knife.' He initially believed the cause of death was the cut to the throat.

The post-mortem examination uncovered two oddities. One was the 'blackened appearance round the mouth' that Parsons had noted earlier; the mouth was 'such as we do not usually see in dead bodies, as if something had been pressed tightly against it'. This something, he suggested, might have been 'the violent thrusting of a blanket into the mouth to prevent it crying, or it could have been done with a hand'.

The other mystery was the lack of blood. 'A sufficient quantity of blood . . . has not been accounted for,' reported Parsons, 'as would have flowed from the body, if the throat were cut in the closet, as blood from the arterial vessels would have produced a greater quantity of sparkles on the walls.' If the boy's throat had been cut while he was alive, 'the pulsations would have thrown out jets of blood'. Yet the blood was no longer in his body either: the internal organs, said Parsons, were completely drained.

The two doctors found Samuel Kent in tears when they returned to the library. Stapleton comforted him, assuring him that Saville had died swiftly. Parsons confirmed this: 'The child suffered much less than you will.'

Superintendent Foley watched over the body in the laundry. Towards evening, he reported, Elizabeth Gough came in and kissed her former charge on the hand. Before the superintendent went home he asked for something to eat or drink: 'I scarce wet my lips or ate a mouthful all day.' Samuel poured him a glass of port wine and water.

The life of the house went on. Holcombe cut the grass on the lawn with the mowing machine. Cox and Kerslake made the beds. As was her custom on a Saturday evening, Cox took a clean nightdress from Constance's room to air before the kitchen fire. Constance's linen was easily distinguished from that of her sisters, said Cox, because it was 'of a very coarse texture'. Her night-dresses had 'plain frills', while Mary Ann's had lace and Elizabeth's embroidery.

On Saturday night the older girls slept apart: Elizabeth went downstairs to share her stepmother's bed, 'as papa stayed up' till morning, and Constance joined Mary Ann, 'for the sake of company'. Elizabeth Gough, after helping Mrs Kent and Mary Amelia dress for bed, went upstairs to sleep in Cox and Kerslake's room. Eveline, presumably, was wheeled into her parents' bed-room, leaving the nursery empty; and only William went to bed alone.

Foley watched over Saville's corpse again the next day. All the Misses Kent came to kiss the boy's body, as did Elizabeth Gough. Afterwards the nursemaid told Mrs Kent that she had kissed 'the poor little child'. According to one report, Mrs Kent said that Gough 'appeared very sorry and cried because he was dead'; but according to another, she said that Gough 'frequently spoke of him with sorrow and affection, but I did not see her cry'. The female suspects in the case were constantly scrutinised for kisses and tears, the tokens of innocence.

On Sunday night Constance slept alone. William locked his door 'from fear'.

3

SHALL NOT GOD SEARCH THIS OUT?

2–14 July

On Monday, 2 July 1860, after months of wind and rain, the season turned: 'there is, after all, some chance of our having a taste of summer', reported the *Bristol Daily Post.* At 10 a.m. the coroner for Wiltshire, George Sylvester of Trowbridge, opened the inquiry into Saville Kent's death. As was customary, he convened the inquest in the village's main public house, the Red Lion inn. A long, low stone building with a wide doorway, the Red Lion sat at the dip in the centre of the village, where Upper Street and Lower Street converged. Both of these roads – lined with old cottages – led up towards Road Hill, the summit of which was half a mile from the pub.

Among the ten jurors were the innkeeper of the Red Lion, a butcher, two farmers, a shoemaker, a stonemason, a millwright and the registrar for local births and deaths. Most of them lived either in Upper Street or Lower Street. The Reverend Mr Peacock was foreman. Rowland Rodway, despite his misgivings, watched the proceedings on Samuel Kent's behalf.

The jury followed the coroner to Road Hill House to look at Saville's body in the laundry room. Superintendent Foley let them in. The corpse was that of a 'pretty little boy', reported the *Bath*

Chronicle, 'but it presented a horrible spectacle, from its hideous, gaping wounds which gave it a ghastly appearance; still, the child's face wore a placid, innocent expression'. The jurors also inspected the drawing room, the nursery, the master bedroom, the privy and the grounds. As they left to return to the Red Lion an hour and a half later, Foley asked the coroner which members of the household would be required as witnesses. Just the housemaid, who had fastened the windows, said the coroner, and the nursemaid, who had charge of the boy when he was abducted.

Sarah Cox and Elizabeth Gough headed down to the Red Lion together. Cox had sorted the week's washing into two large baskets, which she left in a lumber room for the laundress, Hester Holley. Before noon Mrs Holley and her youngest daughter, Martha, collected the baskets and carried them back to their cottage. They also took with them the laundry book, in which Mary Ann Kent had listed each item placed in the baskets. (Mary Ann's stained nightdress, which had been in the custody of Eliza Dallimore, the policeman's wife, was returned to her the same morning.)

As soon as Mrs Holley got home, within five minutes, she and all three of her daughters (one of them, Jane, the wife of William Nutt) opened the baskets and went through the clothes. 'It was not our custom to open the clothes so soon after receiving them,' said Mrs Holley later. Her reason for doing so was surprising: 'We heard a rumour that a nightdress was missing.' The Holley women discovered that Constance's nightdress, though listed in the book, was not in either of the baskets.

Down in the village the Red Lion had become so crowded with spectators that the coroner decided to move the inquest to the Temperance Hall, which lay a few minutes' walk up Lower Street towards Road Hill House. The hall was 'crammed to suffocation', reported the *Trowbridge and North Wilts Advertiser*. Foley produced Saville's nightclothes and his blanket, both matted with blood, and passed them to the jury.

Cox and Gough were first to give evidence. Cox described locking the house on Friday night, and finding the drawing-room window open the following morning. Gough gave a detailed account of putting Saville to bed on Friday night, and finding him missing in the morning. She described him as a cheerful, happy, good-tempered child.

The coroner next took evidence from Thomas Benger, who had discovered the body, and Stephen Millet, the butcher. Millet handed over the piece of bloodied newspaper found at the scene, and remarked on the quantity of blood in the privy: 'From my trade as a butcher I am acquainted with the loss of blood from animals when dying.' He estimated he had seen a pint and a half on the privy floor.

'My impression,' said Millet, 'is that the child was held with his legs upwards, and his head hanging down, and his throat cut in that position.' The spectators gasped.

No one could identify the piece of newspaper found by the privy. A reporter suggested that they were fragments of the *Morning Star*. Cox and Gough testified that Mr Kent did not take that paper: he subscribed to *The Times*, the *Frome Times* and the *Civil Service Gazette*. This suggested – faintly – that an outsider had been at the murder scene.

Joshua Parsons was the next witness. He reported his summons to the house and the conclusions of his post-mortem: Saville had been killed before three in the morning; his throat had been cut and his chest punctured, and he also showed signs of suffocation. Three pints of blood should have come out of the body 'at a gush', he said, but much less had been found.

After Parsons' evidence, the coroner tried to bring the inquest to a close, but the Reverend Mr Peacock, as foreman of the jury, said that his fellow jurors wanted to examine Constance and William Kent. Peacock himself dissented – he felt the family should be left alone – but he was obliged to report that the others were insistent. Some jurors were demanding to interview everyone in the Kent family: 'Try them all; show no respect to one more than to another,' 'Give us the whole.' The villagers, said Stapleton, suspected the coroner of protecting the Kents: 'One law for the rich and another for the poor.' Unwillingly, the coroner agreed that Constance and William be interviewed, but on condition that the examination take place at their home, so as not to 'expose those children to insult'. He was disturbed by the way the pair were 'spoken of loudly in terms of execration, as being the murderers'. The jury returned to the house.

The interviews, which took place in the kitchen, were brief – three or four minutes each.

'I knew nothing whatever of his death, until he was found,' said Constance. 'I know nothing whatever of the murder . . . Everyone was kind to the child.' When asked about Elizabeth Gough, she said, 'I have found the nursemaid generally quiet and attentive, and perform her duties in every respect as could be wished.' According to the *Somerset and Wilts Journal*, she 'gave evidence in a subdued and audible tone, without betraying any special emotion, her eyes fixed on the ground'.

William's evidence was virtually identical, but expressed with greater warmth: 'I know nothing nor heard anything of this circumstance till the morning – I wish I had. Saville was a great favourite with all. I have always found the nursemaid very kind and attentive. I know nothing whatever of the murder.' His manner was more engaging than that of his sister: 'he gave his evidence clearly and well, his eyes being fixed on the coroner throughout'. By comparison, Constance was muted, shuttered.

Back at the Temperance Hall, the coroner told the jurors that it was their job to find out how Saville had met his death, not who had killed him. With reluctance, they signed a sheet blaming a 'person or persons unknown' for the murder. 'It is unknown,' said one, 'but there is a very strong suspicion which don't at all settle on my stomach.' 'So with me,' said another man. 'The same here,' said another. A shoemaker stood up to say that most of his fellow jurors believed that the murderer was an inmate of Road Hill House. He accused Parsons, the Reverend Mr Peacock and the coroner of trying to hush the matter up.

The coroner ignored their disquiet. He comforted the jury with the thought that 'although the action was concealed from the eyes of men, yet it was seen and recorded by One above', and at 3.30 in the afternoon he declared the inquest closed. 'I say, gentlemen, it is the most extraordinary and mysterious murder that has ever been committed, to my knowledge.'

In Road Hill House after the inquest Foley handed the key to the laundry room to Mrs Silcox, who had laid Saville out. She finished arranging the body for burial. Elizabeth Gough and Sarah Cox then took it upstairs in a 'shell', the thin interior case of a coffin. Mrs Kent instructed Gough to 'screw down' the case.

Saville's mother was later asked if the nursemaid had kissed the corpse when she closed the coffin. 'It was then very much changed,' Mrs Kent said, 'and I do not think she could have kissed it at that time.'

On Monday night Constance asked Gough to share her bed.

At about eleven the next morning, Hester Holley returned the laundry book to Sarah Cox and collected her weekly payment of seven or eight shillings. She did not mention the missing nightdress. 'I never said anything to her about anything missing,' she later admitted. 'That's where my mistake was. I was in a hurry, like, but I knew it was missing.'

In the afternoon James Morgan, the parish constable, and four police constables called at Mrs Holley's cottage to question her about the breast flannel: they wanted to know if she had ever seen it among the clothes sent by the Kents. She said she had not, and when asked whether this week's laundry was all in order, said that 'the clothes were all right by the book'.

Straight afterwards she sent Martha to Road Hill House to tell the Kents that one of their nightdresses was missing, and that she had concealed this from the police. Mrs Kent called Sarah Cox and Mary Ann Kent to the library. They insisted they had packed three nightdresses, while Martha Holley swore that only two had been in the baskets.

Martha reported back to her mother, who at about six that evening went in person to the house: 'I saw Mrs Kent, the two Miss Kents, the housemaid, and cook; and Mr Kent spoke to me from his room door, and told me, not as a gentleman would speak, that if I did not produce the nightdress within eight and forty hours he would have me taken up by a special warrant . . . He spoke to me very gruff.'

On Friday, 6 July, Saville's remains were taken away for burial. The *Western Daily Press* reported that as the coffin was being carried across the grounds of Road Hill House, 'the list bands by which the bearers carried it snapped asunder, just after the group passed the water-closet [the privy], and before they reached the lawn gate, and the coffin fell down upon the gravel, where it remained until fresh bands were brought from the house'. A crowd of villagers watched as a coach bore away the coffin and the two family mourners, Samuel and William Kent. (Women did not usually attend funerals, though they adopted their mourning clothes on the burial day.)

Saville's funeral procession passed through Trowbridge at 9.30 a.m., reaching the village of East Coulston half an hour or so later. The boy's body was buried in the family vault alongside the remains of Samuel's first wife. The inscription on his gravestone closed with the words, 'SHALL NOT GOD SEARCH THIS OUT? FOR HE KNOWETH THE SECRETS OF THE HEART.' One newspaper report described the 'intense grief' displayed by both Samuel and William; another attributed 'intense emotion' only to Samuel. He had to be helped by a friend from the churchyard to his coach.

Four friends of the family – three doctors and a lawyer – attended the funeral: Benjamin Mallam, Saville's godfather, who practised as a surgeon in Frome; Joshua Parsons; Joseph Stapleton; and Rowland Rodway. They shared a coach back to Road, and discussed the murder. Parsons told the others that Mrs Kent had asked him to certify Constance as a lunatic.

Superintendent Foley continued to lead the investigation, though several other senior officers visited Road that week. The police looked in the spare rooms of Road Hill House and searched some uninhabited buildings at the bottom of the lawn. They tried to drag the river near the house, but found the water was too high – the Frome had flooded its banks only a few weeks earlier. They seemed to be getting no closer to clearing up the mystery, and even before the week was out the Wiltshire magistrates had applied to the Home Office to send a Scotland Yard detective. The request was refused. 'Now that the County Police is established,' pointed out the Permanent Under-Secretary, Horatio Waddington, 'the assistance of London officers is seldom resorted to.' The magistrates announced that they would open their own inquiry on Monday.

Since the dispute about the nightdress was unresolved, Mrs Holley refused to take in the family's washing on Monday, 9 July. That morning Foley sent Eliza Dallimore to Road Hill House with the breast flannel he had found in the privy. 'Mrs Dallimore,' said Foley, 'you must try this piece of flannel on them girls, and on the nurse.' Its stains were now washed away, the stench of blood and dirt having become overpowering.

Dallimore took Cox and Kerslake up to their room on the second floor and told them to undress. She asked them to try on the flannel, and found it was not wide enough for either. Next she told Elizabeth Gough to undress in the nursery. Gough complained: 'It's of no use. If the flannel fits me, that's no reason that I should have done the murder.' She took off her stays and tried on the flannel. It fitted.

'Well, it might fit a great many,' Mrs Dallimore conceded. 'It fits me. But there's no one in the house I have fitted it on to but you.' Foley had not instructed her to try the flannel on Mrs Kent or her three stepdaughters.

The same Monday, a week after the inquest, the five Wiltshire magistrates opened what the *Somerset and Wilts Journal* described as a 'profoundly secret' inquiry at the Temperance Hall, to which they summoned several of the inhabitants of Road Hill House. Mrs Kent told them that she believed the murderer was an inmate of the house, 'some one who knew the premises'. 'I have no reason to blame nurse,' she added. 'The only thing I blame her for is not telling me the instant she missed the child.'

The police working on the case suspected Elizabeth Gough. They thought it almost impossible that the child had been abducted from the nursery without the nursemaid's knowledge. The scenario that had shaped itself out in their minds was that Saville had woken up and seen a man in Gough's bed. To silence the boy, the lovers stopped his mouth and – by accident or design – suffocated him. Gough herself had depicted Saville as a tell-tale: 'The little boy goes into his mamma's room and tells everything.' The couple then mutilated the body to disguise the cause of death, the police surmised. If the lover was Samuel Kent, he could have disposed of the evidence when he rode off to Trowbridge. In the fuss and hurry, and because the pair had to be careful not to be seen conferring, their stories had clashed and changed: notably, their accounts of when they missed the blanket. This scenario also accounted for Gough's inadequate explanation of why she failed to rouse her mistress when she noticed that Saville was missing.

At eight o'clock in the evening of Tuesday, 10 July – William Kent's fifteenth birthday – the magistrates directed the police to apprehend Elizabeth Gough.

'Previous to being informed of the decision of the magistrates,' reported the *Bath Chronicle*, 'the girl was apparently in the highest spirits, at the house where the several witnesses stopped, and talked in a very off-handed manner of how she should have enjoyed herself at the haymaking, had not this "business" occurred. She said she was so conscious of her innocence in the matter, that she should not be afraid to go before a hundred judges and be examined.'

Her bravado swiftly fell away. 'On being told that she would be detained for the present, she fell senseless to the ground.' The *Somerset and Wilts Journal* described her as having succumbed to a 'fit of hysterics'. She was 'unconscious for a few minutes'. When she had regained her senses Foley took her in a trap, a two-wheeled pony cart, to the police station in Stallard Street, Trowbridge. The superintendent lived in the station house with his wife, his son (a lawyer's clerk) and a servant. The Dallimores – William, the constable, Eliza, the searcher, and their three children – also lived on the premises, and they were given custody of Gough. The nursemaid and the searcher shared a bed.

During her stay at the police station Gough told Foley and his wife that she was sure Constance was not the murderer.

'Was it you?' Foley asked.

'No,' she said.

She remarked to another policeman that she had decided 'never to love another child'. He asked her why. Because, she said, 'this is the second time that something has occurred to a child to which I was attached. In a former place where I lived two years there was a child I was very fond of, and it died.'

A rumour spread that she had confessed, naming Samuel as the murderer and herself as accessory. Several other rumours came into circulation during the week, all of them implicating Samuel: people said that Saville's life was insured, that the body of the first Mrs Kent was being exhumed for a post-mortem, that Samuel was seen in the grounds of his house at three o'clock on the morning of the murder.

On Friday Elizabeth Gough was taken back to Road to be examined. She waited at the house of Charles Stokes, a saddler who lived next to the Temperance Hall, while the magistrates went to Road Hill House. After a while the saddler's sister Ann, a maker of corsets and dresses, remarked on how long the magistrates had been gone: 'I suspect something has been found out,' she said. Gough 'manifested some alarm' and paced the room restlessly. 'I hope I shall not be called in today, for I feel I shall be as bad as I was on Tuesday,' she said, alluding to her bout of hysteria.

'Pressing her hands to her side,' reported Ann Stokes, 'she said she felt as if the blood had gone from one side to the other. She also said that she could not hold out much longer, and that she could not have held out so long but that Mrs Kent had begged of her to do so.' Gough claimed that Mrs Kent had urged her on: 'You must hold up a little longer, Elizabeth; do for my sake.' Afterwards, said Ann Stokes, Gough 'remarked that she had since the murder pulled some grey hairs from her head, which she had never done before, that no one knew how she suffered, and that if anything else occurred she thought she should die'.

In Road Hill House the magistrates interviewed Mrs Kent and Mary Ann Kent. Neither had been able to come to the Temperance Hall, the former because her pregnancy was so advanced, the latter because she was 'seized with violent hysterical fits, on hearing that her presence would be required'.

When the magistrates returned to the hall they summoned Gough. Eight reporters had turned up, but none was admitted – the proceedings were strictly private, they were told. A policeman stood outside to make sure no one got close enough to the doors to eavesdrop.

At about seven o'clock that evening, the magistrates adjourned the inquiry and told Gough she was free to spend the weekend with her father and cousin, who had arrived that afternoon from Isleworth, near London, as long as she returned to the Temperance Hall on Monday. She said she would remain at the police station in Trowbridge. The magistrates probably reassured her before releasing her, for when she reached the town she 'appeared quite cheerful', reported the *Bath Chronicle*, 'and jumped from the trap in a lively manner'.

On Tuesday, 10 July, an editorial in the *Morning Post*, an influential national newspaper, ridiculed the efforts of the Wiltshire police to discover Saville's killer. It criticised the rushed, peremptory way the coroner had conducted the inquest, and demanded that the investigation into the child's death be taken over by 'the most experienced of detectives'. The article argued that the security of all the homes of England rested on uncovering the secrets of Road Hill House. It acknowledged that this would mean violating a sacred space:

> *Every Englishman is accustomed to pride himself with more than usual complacency upon what is called the sanctity of an English home. No soldier, no policeman, no spy of the Government dare enter it . . . Unlike the tenant of a foreign domicile, the occupier of an English house, whether it be mansion or cottage, possesses an indisputable title against every kind of aggression upon his threshold. He defies everybody below the Home Secretary; and even he can only violate the traditional security of a man's house under extreme circumstances, and with the prospect of a Parliamentary indemnity. It is with this thoroughly innate feeling of security that every Englishman feels a strong sense of the inviolability of his own house. It is this that converts the moorside cottage into a castle. The moral sanctions of an English home are, in the nineteenth century, what the moat, and the keep, and the drawbridge were in the fourteenth. In the strength of these we lie down to sleep at night, and leave our homes in the day, feeling that a whole neighbourhood would be raised, nay, the whole country, were any attempt made to violate what so many traditions, and such long custom, have rendered sacred.*

These sentiments were felt deeply in Victorian England. On a visit to the country in the 1840s Dr Carus, physician to the King of Saxony, noted that the English house embodied 'the long-cherished principle of separation and retirement' that lay 'at the very foundation of the national character . . . it is this that gives the Englishman that proud feeling of personal independence, which is stereotyped in the phrase, "Every man's house is his castle."' The American poet Ralph Waldo Emerson observed that domesticity was the 'taproot' that enabled the British to 'branch wide and high. The motive and end of their trade and empire is to guard the independence and privacy of their homes.'

The *Morning Post* of 10 July 1860 held that 'in spite of all these proverbial sanctities, a crime has just been committed which for mystery, complication of probabilities, and hideous wickedness, is without parallel in our criminal records . . . the security of families, and the sacredness of English households demand that this matter should never be allowed to rest till the last shadow in its dark mystery shall have been chased away by the light of unquestionable truth'. The horror of this case was that the corruption lay inside the 'domestic sanctum', that the bolts, locks and fastenings of the house were hopelessly redundant. 'The secret lies with someone who was within . . . the household collectively must be responsible for this mysterious and dreadful event. Not one of them ought to be at large till the whole mystery is cleared up . . . one (or more) of the family is guilty.' The *Morning Post* article was reprinted in *The Times* the next day, and in newspapers throughout the country over the rest of the week. 'Let the best detective talent in the country be engaged,' demanded the *Somerset and Wilts Journal*.

On Thursday a Wiltshire magistrate renewed his plea to the Home Secretary to send a detective to Road, and this time the request was granted. On Saturday, 14 July, Sir George Cornewall Lewis, Lord Palmerston's Home Secretary, instructed Sir Richard Mayne, the Commissioner of the Metropolitan Police, to dispatch 'an intelligent officer' to Wiltshire as soon as possible. 'Inspector Whicher to go,' Mayne scribbled on the back of the Home Office directive.

The same day Detective-Inspector Jonathan Whicher received his orders to head for Road.

PART TWO
THE DETECTIVE

'I set forth to pave the way for discovery –
the dark and doubtful way'

From *The Woman in White* (1860), by Wilkie Collins

CHAPTER FOUR

A MAN OF MYSTERY

1 October 1814–15 July 1860

It was still light as Whicher's train rolled towards west Wiltshire on that Sunday in 1860. Usually by July the pastures were broken up with blocks of yellow – tawny wheat or bright gold corn – but this year the summer had come so late that the crops were green as grass.

At 6.20 p.m. the train pulled into Trowbridge – a forest of factory towers and chimneys – and Whicher stepped out onto the railway station's narrow platform. The first building he came to as he left the ticket hall was John Foley's police station on Stallard Street, a two-storey structure dating from 1854, when the local force was founded. This was where Elizabeth Gough was being detained, of her own volition, until her examination was resumed the next day.

Trowbridge had made money from cloth for centuries. The coming of the railway in 1848 had brought even more prosperity – now, with a population of eleven thousand, it was the biggest factory town in the south of England. Wool mills and dyeing houses spread out to the left and right of the station – about twenty of them, powered by more than thirty steam engines. These were the factories that Samuel Kent inspected. On a Sunday evening they lay idle, but in the morning the machines would start to pound and whirr, and the air would thicken with smoke, soot, the smells of urine (collected in tubs from public houses and used to scour wool) and of the vegetable dyes streaming into the river Biss.

Whicher hired a porter to carry his luggage to the Woolpack Inn, Market Place, half a mile from the station. The pair crossed the bridge over the Biss – a small, slow tributary of the Avon – and walked to the town centre. They passed the houses of the Parade, a terrace built by rich Georgian clothiers, and the side streets crammed with weavers' cottages. Trade had been poor that year. Many sheep had died over the harsh winter, so wool was scarcer than usual, and the competitive mill-owners of northern England were selling their muslin cheap.

When Whicher reached the Woolpack, on the corner of Red Hat Lane, he paid the porter sixpence and went in. The inn was a compact stone building, with an arch at its centre, which offered rooms at 1*s*.6*d*. a night. Wine, cider, spirits and home-brewed ale were sold at the bar. Whicher may have ordered a drink or two: when in a tight spot, he once told Dickens, 'I couldn't do better than have a drop of brandy-and-water to keep my courage up.'

Jonathan Whicher was born in Camberwell, three miles south of London, on 1 October 1814. His father was a gardener, probably one of the village's many market gardeners, who grew cherries, lettuces, roses and willow for sale in the city. He may have tended the lawns and flowerbeds of the richer residents of the district – Camberwell was studded with the stucco villas and ornamental cottages of merchants seeking an airy retreat from London.

On the day of Jonathan's baptism, 23 October, the curate of St Giles parish church also christened the child of another gardener, and the babies of a shoemaker, a cabinetmaker, two coachmen, a flutemaker and a labourer. In one of the many variants to which his surname was prey, Jonathan was recorded as the son of Richard and Rebecca Whitcher. He was known as Jack. He had an older sister, Eliza, and at least one older brother, James. Another sister, Sarah, was born in August 1819, when he was four. That summer was remembered for its abundance of Camberwell Beauties, the large, velvety, dark-claret butterflies first seen in the area in 1748.

In the mid-1830s Jack Whicher was still living in Camberwell, probably in Providence Row, a small terrace of cottages at the northern, poorer end of the village. The cottages lay on Wyndham Road, close to a mill and backing onto nursery gardens, but in a wretched neighbourhood – 'as proverbial for its depravity as for its ignorance', according to a report published by the local school. Wyndham Road was frequented by shifty types – hawkers, costermongers, chimney sweeps – and by outright villains.

When Jack Whicher applied to join the Metropolitan Police in the late summer of 1837 he was just old enough, at twenty-two, and just tall enough, at five feet eight inches, to meet the entrance requirements. He passed the tests for literacy and physical fitness, and two 'respectable householders' of his parish vouched for his good character. Like more than a third of the early recruits, he was working as a labourer when he submitted his application.

On 18 September, Whicher became a police constable. His weekly wage – about £1 – was only a slight improvement on his previous earnings, but his future was now a little more secure.

The Metropolitan Police, the first such force in the country, was eight years old. London had got so big, so fluid, so mysterious to itself that in 1829 its inhabitants had, reluctantly, accepted the need for a disciplined body of men to patrol the streets. The 3,500 policemen were known as 'bobbies' and 'peelers' (after their founder, Sir Robert Peel), as 'coppers' (they caught, or copped, villains), as 'crushers' (they crushed liberty), as 'Jenny Darbies' (from *gendarmes*), and as pigs (a term of abuse since the sixteenth century).

Whicher was issued with dark-blue trousers and a dark-blue long-tailed coat, its bright metal buttons imprinted with a crown and the word POLICE. His division and number – E47, the 'E' for Holborn – was boldly marked on a stiff, buckled collar; beneath this, a leather stock four inches deep encircled his neck as protection against 'garotters'. His coat was fitted with deep pockets in which to stash a truncheon and a wooden rattle. He wore a chimney-pot hat with a glazed leather crown and leather supports down the sides. A fellow officer detailed the costume: 'I had to put on a swallow-tail coat, and a rabbit-skin high-top-hat, covered with leather, weighing eighteen ounces, a pair of Wellington boots, the leather of which must have been at least a sixteenth of an inch thick, and a belt about four inches broad, with a great brass buckle six inches deep . . . I never felt so uncomfortable in all my life.' An officer had to wear his uniform even when he was not at work, so that he could never be accused of concealing his identity. He put a band around his wrist to show when he was on duty. Beards and moustaches were banned. Many men grew sideburns instead.

At a time when all clothes were a uniform of sorts, the police kit had its merits: the journalist Harriet Martineau noted that an ambitious young working-class man could 'pass along the street somewhat more proudly, and under more notice' in this get-up 'than the artisan in his apron and paper cap, or the labourer in his fustian, or bearing the porter's knot' – fustian was the rough fabric from which labourers' jackets were cut, the porter's knot a pad to protect the shoulders when carrying a heavy load.

The perfect policeman was defined by restraint, anonymity, an absence of emotion. 'A hot temper would never do,' said Martineau, 'nor any vanity which would lay a man open to arts of flirtation; nor too innocent good-nature; nor a hesitating temper or manner; nor any weakness for drink; nor any degree of stupidity.' Andrew Wynter, a physician and writer, described the ideal constable as 'stiff, calm, and inexorable, an *institution* rather than a man. We seem to have no more hold of his personality than we could possibly get of his coat buttoned up to the throttling-point . . . a machine, moving, thinking and speaking only as his instruction-book directs . . . He seems . . . to have neither hopes nor fears.'

Whicher shared a dormitory with about sixteen other men in the Hunter Place station house, in Hunter Street, just south of King's Cross. This was a substantial brick building that had recently been acquired by the force. The entrance was through a long, dark passage; as well as the dormitories upstairs, the station contained four cells, a library, a scullery, a mess room and a recreation room. All single men were expected to lodge in the station house, and to be in their quarters by midnight. When working the early shift, Whicher rose before six. He might wash in the dormitory, if he had his own tub and screen, and then breakfast on a chop, a potato and a cup of coffee. At six the men lined up in the yard. One of the division's four inspectors took the roll, then read out a paper from headquarters at Whitehall Place listing any punishments, rewards, dismissals and suspensions of individual officers. The inspector also informed the men of the latest crime reports, giving descriptions of suspects, missing persons and property. Having checked his men's uniforms and equipment, he gave the order to 'Close up!' A few of the constables were sent to the station house as a reserve force, while the rest were marched off to their beats by the sergeants.

In the daytime, a constable covered a seven-and-a-half-mile beat at two-and-a-half miles an hour for two four-hour stints: from 6 a.m. to 10 a.m., say, and from 2 p.m. to 6 p.m. He familiarised himself with every house on his beat, and strove to clear the roads of beggars, tramps, costermongers, drunks and prostitutes. He was subject to spot checks by a sergeant or an inspector, and the rules were strict: no leaning or sitting while on the beat, no swearing, no consorting with servant girls. The police were instructed to treat everyone with respect – the drivers of hansom cabs, for instance, were not to be referred to as 'cabbies' – and to avoid the use of force. These standards were to be observed off-duty, too. If found drunk at any time, a constable was issued with a warning, and if the offence was repeated he was dismissed from the force. In the early 1830s four out of five dismissals, of a total of three thousand, were for drunkenness.

At about eight in the evening Whicher ate supper in the station house – roast mutton, perhaps, with cabbage, potatoes and dumplings. When assigned the night shift, he took his place in the yard before nine, carrying a lantern, or 'bull's-eye', as well as a truncheon and a rattle. On this unbroken eight-hour stint he tested the locks on windows and doors, watched for fires, took the destitute into shelters, checked that public houses were closed on time. The circuit was much shorter at night – two miles – and Whicher was expected to pass each point on his beat every hour. If he needed help, he swung his rattle; a constable from a neighbouring beat should always be within earshot. Though this shift could be miserable in winter, it had its perks: tips for waking up market traders or labourers before dawn, and sometimes a 'toothful' of beer or brandy from each publican on the route.

Whicher patrolled Holborn in the years that the district was dominated by the great, eight-acre slum of St Giles. This dark complication of streets and alleys was laced with hidden passages through courtyards, attics, cellars. Hustlers and thieves spilled out to coax, hoax or steal cash from prosperous passers-by – around St Giles lay the law courts, the university, the British Museum, the fine squares of Bloomsbury and the posh shops of High Holborn. If spotted by the police, the criminals slipped back into their labyrinth.

Holborn teemed with tricksters, and the police of E division had to be expert in identifying them. A new vocabulary evolved to catalogue the various deceits. The police watched out for 'magsmen' (conmen, such as card sharps) who 'gammoned' (fooled) 'flats' (dupes) with the help of 'buttoners' or 'bonnets' (accomplices who drew people in by seeming to win money from the magsmen). A 'screever' (drafter of documents) might sell a 'fakement' to a vagrant 'on the blob' (telling hard-luck stories) – in 1837, fifty Londoners were arrested for producing such documents and eighty-six for bearing them. To 'work the kinchin lay' was to trick children out of their cash or clothing. To 'work the shallow' was to excite compassion by begging half-naked. To 'shake lurk' was to beg in the guise of a shipwrecked sailor. In November 1837 a magistrate noted that some thieves in the Holborn area were acting as decoys, feigning drunkenness in order to distract police constables while their friends burgled houses.

On occasion the officers of E division left their district. The entire police force was deployed to line the route from Buckingham Palace to Westminster Abbey when Victoria was crowned in June 1838. Already the police were familiar with lunatics who were fixated by the new queen. An inmate of a workhouse in St Giles, for instance, was taken before the magistrates because he had become convinced that Victoria was in love with him. He said they had 'exchanged looks' in Kensington Gardens. The magistrates recommended that he be committed to an asylum.

Jack Whicher's first reported arrest was in December 1840. In a brothel on the Gray's Inn Road, near King's Cross, he noticed a seventeen-year-old girl giddy with drink and flaunting a set of improbably fine clothes. A feather boa hung from her neck. Whicher remembered that a boa was among the items stolen from a house in Bloomsbury a fortnight earlier, and that a maid had absconded on the night of the burglary. He approached the girl with the boa and charged her with theft. Louisa Weller was convicted later that month of robbing Sarah Taylor of Gloucester Street. The story of her capture outlined in miniature Whicher's detective qualities: an excellent memory, an eye for the incongruous, psychological acuity, and confidence.

Straight afterwards, his name vanished from the newspapers for two years. This was probably because he had been recruited by the Metropolitan Police Commissioners – Colonel Charles Rowan, an army man, and Sir Richard Mayne, a lawyer – to a small band of plainclothes 'active officers', proto-detectives whose existence was a secret. The English public had a horror of surveillance. There had been outrage in the early 1830s when it came to light that a plainclothes policeman had infiltrated a political gathering. In this climate, the detectives had to be introduced by stealth.

Magistrates' court records indicate that Whicher was working undercover in April 1842, when he noticed a trio of crooks in Regent Street. He followed them until he saw one of them stand in the path of Sir Roger Palmer, an Anglo-Irish baronet who owned a house in Park Lane, while another gently lifted Sir Roger's coat tails and the last picked a purse from his pocket. Professional pickpockets such as these typically worked in teams of three or four, shielding and easing one another's work. Many were extraordinarily adroit, having been trained since childhood in the art of 'dipping' or 'diving'. Though one of the three escaped, Whicher spotted him in another part of town a fortnight later and hauled him into a police court, reporting that the fellow had compounded his offence by trying to buy him off with silver.

The Metropolitan Police files show that Whicher was again operating incognito later that month, when he took part in the hunt for Daniel Good, a Putney coachman who had killed and dismembered his lover. Whicher and his Holborn colleague Sergeant Stephen Thornton kept watch on the house of a female friend of Good's in Spitalfields, east London (Dickens later described Thornton, who was eleven years older than Whicher, as having 'a ruddy face and a high sunburnt forehead . . . He is famous for steadily pursuing the inductive process and, from small beginnings, working on from clue to clue until he bags his man'). Daniel Good was eventually caught in Kent, but by good luck rather than deft police work.

In June 1842 the commissioners asked the Home Office for permission to set up a small detective division: they argued that they needed a centralised, elite force to coordinate murder hunts – such as the search for Good – and other serious crimes that crossed different police districts. If these officers could wear plain clothes, they said, the force would be all the more efficient. The Home Office agreed. That August, Whicher, Thornton and the other six men picked as detectives formally abandoned their beats, shed their uniforms, became as anonymous and ubiquitous as the villains they sought. Jack Whicher and Charles Goff of L (Lambeth) division were the most junior, but both were made sergeants within weeks (Whicher was only a month short of having served five years as a constable, usually the minimum required for promotion). This brought the number of sergeants in the division to six, serving under two inspectors. Whicher was given a pay rise of almost 50 per cent, from about £50 to £73 a year – £10 more than a regular sergeant's salary. As before, his wages were supplemented with bonuses and rewards.

'Intelligent men have been recently selected to form a body called the "detective police",' reported *Chambers's Edinburgh Journal* in 1843. 'At times the detective policeman attires himself in the dress of ordinary individuals.' The public wariness persisted – a *Times* editorial of 1845 warned of the dangers of detective police, explaining that there 'always will be, something repugnant in the bare idea of espionage'.

The detectives' headquarters were a room alongside the commissioners' offices in Great Scotland Yard, by Trafalgar Square. The men technically became part of the A, or Whitehall, division. Whicher was designated A27. His job, now, was to disappear, to slip noiselessly between the classes – the detectives were to blend, eavesdrop, merge into 'flash-houses' (pubs frequented by criminals) and into crowds threaded with thieves. They were untethered. While an ordinary policeman circled his beat like the arm of a compass, passing each point every hour, the detectives crisscrossed the city and the country at will. In the London underworld they were known as 'Jacks', which captured their classless anonymity.

The first English detective story, by the journalist William Russell, writing as 'Waters', appeared in *Chambers's Edinburgh Journal* in July 1849. The next year Whicher and his colleagues were eulogised by Charles Dickens in several magazine articles: 'They are, one and all, respectable-looking men,' Dickens reported, 'of perfectly good deportment and unusual intelligence; with nothing lounging or slinking in their manners; with an air of keen observation and quick perception when addressed; and generally presenting in their faces, traces more or less marked of habitually leading lives of strong mental excitement. They have all good eyes; and they all can, and they all do, look full at whomsoever they speak to.' George Augustus Sala, a fellow journalist, found Dickens' enthusiasm cloying – he disliked the novelist's 'curious and almost morbid partiality for communing with and entertaining police officers . . . He seemed always at his ease with these personages, and never tired of questioning them.' The detectives, like Dickens, were working-class boys made good, thrilled to find themselves with the run of the city. In *Tom Fox; Or, the Revelations of a Detective*, a mock-memoir of 1860, John Bennett noted that the detective was socially superior to 'the common peeler', because he was better educated and 'of far higher intelligence'. He sought the secrets of the establishment and of the underworld alike, and since he had few precedents he made up his methods on the hoof.

These methods were sometimes criticised. In 1851 Whicher was accused of spying and entrapment when he caught two bank robbers in The Mall. While walking across Trafalgar Square in May that year, Whicher spotted 'an old acquaintance', an ex-convict who was back in town after a stint in the penal colonies of Australia. He saw him join another old lag on a bench in The Mall, opposite the London and Westminster Bank. Over the next few weeks Whicher and a colleague watched the pair size up the bank. The policemen lay in wait until, on 28 June, they caught the crooks red-handed, fleeing the bank with their loot. Correspondents to *The Times* censured the officers for letting the crime take place rather than nipping it in the bud. 'The credit for skill and ingenuity gained by the detectives is probably what greatly inclines them to detection rather than prevention,' complained one letter-writer, implying that they had become puffed up by the attentions of Dickens and the like.

Dickens recast his new heroes in the figure of Inspector Bucket in *Bleak House* (1853), the supreme fictional detective of the era. Mr Bucket was a 'sparkling stranger' who 'walks in an atmosphere of mysterious greatness'. The first police detective in an English novel, Bucket was a mythological figure for his age. He glided and floated into new zones, like a ghost or a cloud: 'Time and place cannot bind Mr Bucket.' He had 'adaptability to all grades'. He borrowed some of the dazzle of Edgar Allan Poe's amateur detective and intellectual magician Auguste Dupin, who preceded him by twelve years.

Bucket was broadly based on Whicher's friend and boss Charley Field – they shared a fat forefinger, an earthy charm, a relish for the 'beauty' of their work, a blithe assurance. Bucket was reminiscent of Jack Whicher, too. Like Whicher at the grand Oxford hotel, there was 'nothing remarkable about [Bucket] at first sight but his ghostly manner of appearing'. He was 'a stoutly-built, steady-looking, sharp-eyed man in black' who watched and listened with a face 'as unchanging as the great mourning ring on his little finger'.

Through the 1840s and 1850s Whicher worked on sleights of hand and of the mind. He dealt with criminals who slipped away into alternative identities, melted into the streets and alleys. He was set on the trail of men and women who counterfeited coin, signatures on cheques, money orders, who escaped from alias to alias, shuffling off names as snakes shuffle off skins. He was the specialist on the 'swell mob', conmen and pickpockets who dressed as gentlemen and could slit open a pocket with a concealed knife, whip out a tie pin under cover of a flourished handkerchief. They worked their dodges at theatres, shopping galleries, places of amusement such as Madame Tussaud's waxworks museum and the London Zoological Gardens. Their greatest harvests were reaped at big public occasions – race meetings, agricultural shows, political gatherings – to which they would travel by first-class train to insinuate themselves among the men and women they hoped to rob.

In 1850 Charley Field told Dickens of a trick that Whicher had pulled off at the Epsom Derby. Field, Whicher and a friend called Mr Tatt were drinking together at the bar – they were on their third or fourth sherry – when they were rushed by four swell mobsmen. The gangsters knocked them over, and a fierce scuffle broke out – 'There we are, all down together, heads and heels, knocking about on the floor of the bar – perhaps you never see such a scene of confusion!' When the villains tried to flee the bar, Whicher cut them off at the door. All four were taken to the local police station. Mr Tatt discovered that his diamond shirt-pin had been stolen during the fight, but there was no sign of it on any of the swell mobsmen. Field was feeling very 'blank' (dejected) about the thieves' victory, when Whicher opened his hand to reveal the pin in his palm. 'Why, in the name of wonder,' said Field, 'how did you come by that?' 'I'll tell you how I come by it,' said Whicher. 'I saw which of 'em took it; and when we were all down on the floor together, knocking about, I just gave him a little touch on the back of his hand, as I knew his pal would; and he thought it was his pal; and gave it me!'

'One of the most *beautiful* things that ever was done, perhaps,' said Field. 'Beautiful. Beau-ti-ful . . . It was a lovely idea!' The artistry of crime was a familiar conceit, most strikingly advanced in Thomas de Quincey's ironic essay 'On Murder Considered as One of the Fine Arts' (1827), but the artistry of the law enforcer was something new. In the early nineteenth century, the subject of a crime story was the daring, dashing crook; now he was more often the analytical detective.

Whicher, who was said to be Commissioner Mayne's favourite officer, was made an inspector in 1856, and his salary rose to more than £100. Charley Field had left the force to become a private investigator, and Whicher and Thornton were now in charge of the department. In 1858 Whicher caught the valet who had stolen Leonardo da Vinci's *Virgin and Child* from the Earl of Suffolk. In the same year he took part in the hunt for the Italian revolutionaries who had tried to assassinate Napoleon III in Paris – the terrorists had hatched their plot and built their bombs in London – and he led a reopened inquiry into the murder of a police constable in an Essex cornfield. In 1859 Whicher investigated whether the Reverend James Bonwell, rector of a church in east London, and his lover, a clergyman's daughter, had killed their illegitimate son. Bonwell had paid an undertaker eighteen shillings to bury the baby secretly by slipping him into someone else's coffin. The coroner's court cleared the couple of murder but censured them for their behaviour, and in July 1860 the Bishop of London sued Bonwell for misconduct.

A couple of months before he was dispatched to Road Hill, Whicher tracked down the perpetrators of a £12,000 jewellery heist near the Palais Royal, in Paris. The thieves, Emily Lawrence and James Pearce, used the trappings of gentility to work their cons in jewellers' shops, where Lawrence 'palmed' lockets and bracelets off the counters and into her handmuff (female thieves were well-equipped with places in which to stash their spoils – shawls, stoles, muffs, vast pockets in their crinolines). With his favourite sidekicks, Detective Sergeants 'Dolly' Williamson and 'Dick' Tanner, Whicher gained entry in April to the jewel thieves' house in Stoke Newington, just north of London. When he charged Emily Lawrence, he noticed her shuffle her hands, and asked to see what she was holding. A struggle ensued, during which her boyfriend threatened to smash Whicher's skull with a poker, and Lawrence let three diamond rings fall to the floor.

From his brief appearances in memoirs, newspapers and journals, Jack Whicher emerges as kind, laconic, alert to the comedy in his work. He was 'an excellent officer', said a fellow detective, 'quiet, shrewd and practical, never in a hurry, generally successful, and ready to take on any case'. He had a wry turn of phrase. If Whicher was certain of something, he was 'as sure as I'm alive'. 'That'll do!' he said when he found a clue. He was benevolent to his foes – he agreed to share a drink with one thief before taking him prisoner, and to spare him the handcuffs: 'I'm willing to behave as a man to you,' he said, 'if you are willing to behave as a man to me.' He was not above a practical joke: at Ascot in the late 1850s he and some fellow officers crept up on a sleeping inspector, who was known for the pride he took in his whiskers, and shaved the bushy black growth off his left cheek.

Yet Whicher was a reserved man, private about his past. At least one sadness attended him. On 15 April 1838 a woman who called herself Elizabeth Whicher, formerly Green, *née* Harding, had given birth in the borough of Lambeth to a boy named Jonathan Whicher. On the birth certificate she recorded the father's name as Jonathan Whicher, his occupation as police constable, their address as 4 Providence Row. She had been about four weeks pregnant when Jack Whicher applied to join the police force – it may have been the prospect of a child that prompted him to enlist.

Three years later, Whicher was living in the Hunter Place station house, Holborn, as a single man. Neither his son nor the child's mother seems to appear on a death register between 1838 and 1851, nor in any census taken that century. The certificate apart, there is no evidence that Jack Whicher ever had a child. Only the record of the boy's birth remains.

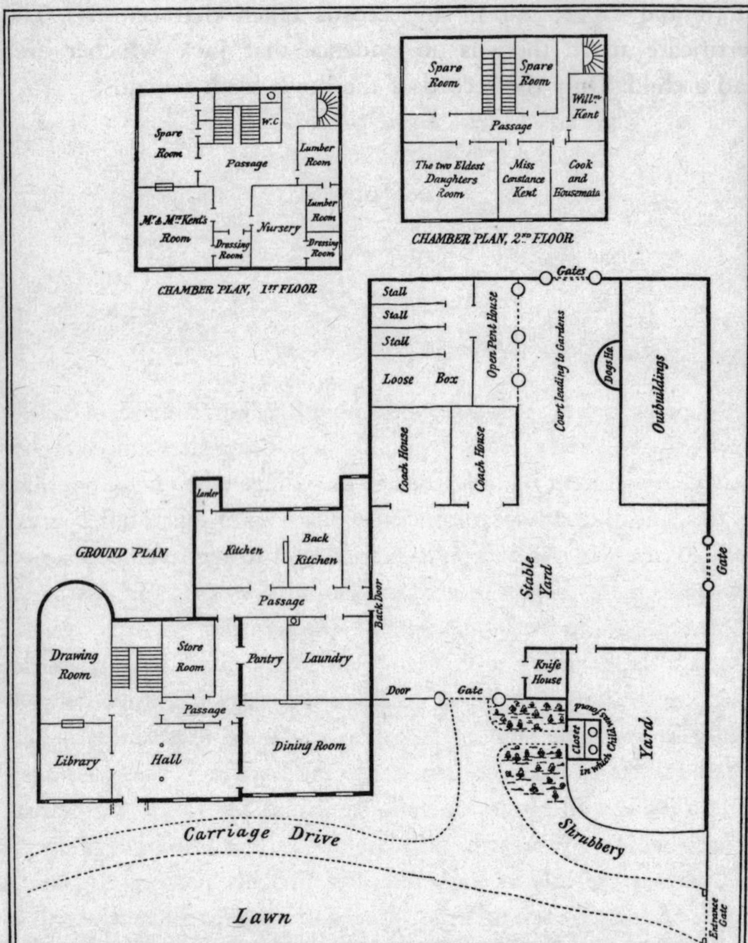

CHAMBER PLAN, 1ST FLOOR
Spare Room
W.C.
Passage
Lumber Room
Lumber Room
Mr. & Mrs. Kent's Room
Dressing Room
Nursery
Dressing Room
CHAMBER PLAN, 2ND FLOOR
Spare Room
Spare Room
Willm. Kent
Passage
The two Eldest Daughters Room
Miss Constance Kent
Cook and Housemaid
GROUND PLAN
Larder
Kitchen
Back Kitchen
Passage
Back Door
Drawing Room
Store Room
Pantry
Laundry
Passage
Library
Hall
Dining Room
Door
Gate
Stall
Stall
Stall
Loose Box
Open Pent House
Gates
Court leading to Gardens
Dogs Ho.
Outbuildings
Coach House
Coach House
Stable Yard
Gate
Knife House
Closet
in which Child was found
Yard
Shrubbery
Carriage Drive
Lawn
Entrance Gate

CHAPTER FIVE

EVERY CLUE SEEMS CUT OFF

16 July

On the morning of Monday, 16 July, Superintendent Foley drove Whicher to Road in a trap, taking the same lane by which Samuel Kent had returned to the village when he learnt that his son was dead. It was another dry day – no rain had fallen since Saville's murder. As the policemen rode further from the sooty town, the plains began to give way to hills, woods and pastures. There were sheep in the fields, dark birds in the trees: jackdaws, magpies, blackbirds, ravens and carrion crows. Smaller birds nested in the grass and gorse – olive chiffchaffs, chestnut-winged corncrakes – while swallows and swifts sailed overhead.

The village of Road sat smack on the border of two counties: though Road Hill House and the Reverend Mr Peacock's Christ Church were in Wiltshire, most of the several hundred villagers lived down the hill in Somersetshire. In this part of England, people addressed each other as 'thee' and 'thou', and spoke with a guttural burr – a farmer was a 'varmer', the sun was the 'zun', a thread was a 'dread'. The district had a distinctive vocabulary: someone marked with smallpox scars, like Whicher, was 'pock-fredden'; to 'skummer' a piece of cloth was to foul it with dirty liquid; to 'buddle' a creature was to suffocate it in mud.

Road was a picturesque village, its cottages built of limestone cobbles or flat blocks of sandstone punched through with square windows. There were at least four pubs (the Red Lion, the George, the Cross Keys, the Bell), a brewery, two Anglican churches, a Baptist chapel, a school, a post office, bakers, grocers, butchers, blacksmiths, shoemakers, tailors, dressmakers, saddlers and so on. Trowbridge lay five miles north-east, and Frome, a Somersetshire wool town, the same distance south-west. A few of the villagers wove on handlooms in their cottages. Most worked in the fields or at one of the several mills in the neighbourhood. Shawford Mill was a specialist wool-dyeing works, with a water-wheel driven by the river Frome – among the local dyes were dark green, from privet; brown, from yew; and indigo, from woad. Next to Road Bridge was a mill devoted to 'fulling', a process of hammering wet wool until the individual threads vanished and the cloth became dense, tight, impossible to unravel.

The village was alight with speculation about Saville's death. His murder had aroused 'a spirit' among the people, said Joseph Stapleton in his book about the case, 'which it might be difficult to govern or suppress'. In the words of the *Bath Chronicle*:

> *There is a very strong feeling amongst the lower class of inhabitants in the village against Mr Kent's family, as well as against himself, and none of them can scarcely walk in the village without being insulted. The poor little innocent, the victim of this dark assassination, is spoken of generally throughout the village in terms of much endearment. He is represented as having been a sturdy, handsome little fellow, with a merry, laughing face, and curly, flaxen hair. The women speak of him with tears in their eyes, and . . . call to remembrance his many little engaging ways and innocent prattling.*

The villagers remembered Saville as a sweet cherub, and reviled his family as fiends.

Samuel Kent was disliked in the district anyway. In part this was because of his job – he was responsible for enforcing the Factory Act of 1833, devised principally to protect children from overwork and injury, which was resented by mill-owners and workers alike. Factory inspectors, like police inspectors, were agents of surveillance. When Samuel moved into Road Hill House in 1855, reported the *Frome Times*, many locals said, 'We don't want him here; we want someone who will give us bread, and not someone who will take it from us.' He had recently turned more than twenty boys and girls under the age of thirteen out of a Trowbridge mill, depriving them of their earnings of three or four shillings a week.

Samuel did nothing to better relations with his neighbours. According to Stapleton, he built an 'impervious fence' 'against the oversight and intrusion' of the inhabitants of the cottages lining the lane next to Road Hill House. He put up 'No Trespassing' signs by the river in his grounds, where the cottagers had been accustomed to fish for trout. The villagers took their revenge on Samuel's servants and family. 'His children were called after,' wrote Stapleton, 'in their walks and on their way to church, by the cottagers' children.' Since Saville's death, Samuel had repeatedly voiced his suspicion that these cottagers had something to do with the murder.

At eleven o'clock Whicher and Foley joined the secret proceedings in the Temperance Hall. Whicher watched as the magistrates re-examined Samuel Kent, the Reverend Mr Peacock and then the local police's chief suspect, Elizabeth Gough. At one o'clock she was set free. The reporters who had gathered outside saw her emerge from the building. 'She appeared to have been suffering from severe mental anguish since she had been in custody,' wrote the man from the *Bath Chronicle*, 'as her face, which was bright and cheerful previously, now wore a very dejected and careworn appearance; in fact, we were astonished at the great change her features had undergone only during this slight detention.' The nursemaid told the reporters that she was returning to Road Hill House to help Mrs Kent during her confinement – the baby was due in a few weeks.

The reporters were then let into the hall, where they were addressed by one of the magistrates. He told them that the investigation was now in the hands of Detective-Inspector Whicher, and that there was a £200 reward for any person giving information that would lead to the conviction of Saville's murderer: £100 had been put up by the government and £100 by Samuel Kent. If an accomplice turned in the killer, he or she would be given a free pardon. The inquiry was adjourned until Friday.

Whicher was joining the murder investigation two weeks late. The victim's body had been boxed up and buried, the testimony of the witnesses had been rehearsed, the evidence had been collected, or destroyed. He would have to reopen the wounds, unseal the scene. Superintendents Foley and Wolfe, both of the Wiltshire constabulary, led him up the hill to the house.

Road Hill House sat hidden above the village, a smooth block of creamy Bath limestone shielded from the road by trees and walls. A cloth merchant, Thomas Ledyard, had built the property in about 1800, when he ran the Road Bridge fulling mill. It was one of the finest houses in the area. A driveway curved beneath the yews and elms to a shallow entrance porch, which nudged out like a sentry box from the building's flat face. Concealed in the shrubbery to the right of the front lawn was the privy in which Saville had been found – a lavatory in a shed built over a pit in the earth.

Through the front door of the house a large hall led to the main staircase. To the right of the hall was the dining room – an elegant rectangle that stretched out of the side of the building – and to the left was the snug square of the library, its tall arched windows overlooking the lawns. Behind the library was the drawing room, which ended in a crescent of bay windows leading on to the back gardens – it was one of these that had been found open by Sarah Cox on 30 June.

The stairs, laid with thick carpet, ran up to the first and second storeys. Between floors were landings with views across the grounds to the rear – a flower garden, a kitchen garden, an orchard, a greenhouse, and beyond them cows, sheep, a field of grass, a seam of trees along the river Frome.

On the first floor, behind the master bedroom and the nursery, were three spare rooms and a water closet. On the top floor, along with the four occupied bedrooms, were two spare rooms and a ladder to the attic. This floor was darker than those below, with lower ceilings and squatter windows. Most of the bedrooms in the house shared a view south over the drive and lawn and down to the village, though William's room looked east to the neighbouring cottages and the gothic twin turrets and spires of Christ Church.

Behind William's room the back stairs twisted steeply down to the first and ground floors. At their foot was the kitchen passage, busy with doors onto the scullery, kitchen, laundry, pantry, and the steps to the cellars. A door at the end of the passage led to a paved courtyard hemmed in by the carriage house, stable and outhouses. The privy lay just to the right, through a door by the knife-house. A ten-foot-high stone wall, with a gate for tradesmen, ran along the right-hand side of the property, by the cottage corner.

Stapleton gave a highly coloured sketch of this group of cottages, where the Holcombes, the Nutts and the Holleys had their homes: 'A beer-house obtrudes itself in the centre, flanked by a cottage kept from falling down only by the precarious support of wooden stakes stuck into the ground. The windows are crushed or thrust outwards by the tumbling walls, from the occupation of which the tenants had already fled. Several other cottages are grouped around, and some of them overlook Mr Kent's premises. It is indeed a "rookery" – a bit of St Giles's gone out of town to rusticate. It might be mistaken for a haunt of outcasts and a den of thieves.'

Since the murder, Road Hill House had become a puzzle, a riddle in three dimensions, its floor plans and furnishings an esoteric code. Whicher's task was to decipher the house – as a crime scene, and as a guide to the character of the family.

The walls and fences that Samuel had erected around his grounds indicated a liking for privacy. Within the house, though, children and adults, servants and employers were strangely entangled. Affluent mid-Victorians usually preferred to keep the servants apart from the family, and the children in their own quarters. Here, the nursemaid slept feet away from the master bedroom, and the five-year-old slept with her parents. The other servants and the stepchildren were thrown together on the top floor like so much lumber in an attic. The arrangement marked out the lower status of the children of the first Mrs Kent.

In his reports to Scotland Yard* Whicher noted that Constance and William were the only members of the household with rooms of their own. This was not indicative of status, only of the fact that neither had a sibling of the same sex and a similar age with whom they might share. Its significance was logistical: either child could have slipped out at night unnoticed.

In the nursery, Whicher was shown how the blanket had been drawn from between Saville's bedclothes on the night of his death, and the sheet and quilt 'folded neatly back' to the foot of the cot – which, he said, 'it can hardly be supposed a man would have done'. With Foley and Wolfe, he then conducted an experiment to

* Whicher's unfolding analysis of the murder was laid out in three reports to Sir Richard Mayne, the Metropolitan Police Commissioner: the first is missing; Whicher wrote the second on 22 July; and he started the third just over a week later. The surviving reports are in the Metropolitan Police file on the Road Hill murder at the National Archives – MEPO 3/61.

see whether it was possible to take a three-year-old child from the cot without waking it or anyone else in the room. The newspapers did not divulge which three-year-old was used in the experiment, nor how it was induced to fall asleep repeatedly, but they claimed that the police officers accomplished the task three times.

In the drawing room, Whicher saw that the window could have been unfastened only from the inside. 'This window which is about ten feet high, comes down within a few inches of the ground,' he reported to Sir Richard Mayne, 'and faces the lawn at the back of the house, and opens by lifting up the bottom sash, which was found up about six inches at the bottom. These shutters were fastened with a Bar inside, consequently no entry could be made from the outside.' Even if someone had broken into the house by this window, he pointed out, they could have got no further, since the drawing-room door was locked from the other side. 'Therefore it is quite certain,' he wrote, 'that no person came in by that window.' He was also sure that no one had fled the premises by that window, since Sarah Cox told him that the folding shutters were partly closed from within. This, he said, confirmed his conviction that an inmate of the house had killed the boy.

The only indication that an intruder might have been at the crime scene was the scrap of bloodied newspaper discovered next to the privy. Whicher found, though, that this had not been torn from the *Morning Star*, as suggested at the inquest, but from *The Times*, the paper Samuel Kent took every day.

Whicher explained in his reports that he thought that the murderer had not taken Saville out through the drawing-room window, but by another route altogether: down the back stairs, along the passage past the kitchen, out of the kitchen door to the courtyard, and through a further door from the yard to the privy in the shrubbery. The murderer would have had to unlock, unchain and unbolt the kitchen door and unbolt the yard door, then secure both doors again on returning to the house, but this was perfectly practicable, and worth the effort. The kitchen door was only twenty paces, or yards, from the privy, Whicher pointed out, whereas the distance from the drawing-room window to the privy was seventy-nine paces. To walk from the drawing room to the privy also meant passing round the front of the building, immediately under the windows where the rest of the family and servants had been sleeping. Anyone who lived in the house would have known that the kitchen passage offered a much more direct and discreet route – in Whicher's words, 'the shortest and most secret way'. It meant passing the guard dog, but then the dog might not have barked at a familiar face. 'The Dog,' wrote Whicher, 'is perfectly harmless.' Even when the detective, a perfect stranger, approached the animal in daylight, it did not bark or bite.*

'I therefore feel quite convinced,' Whicher concluded, 'that the window shutters were merely opened by one of the inmates, to lead to the supposition that the child had been stolen.'

Whicher was familiar with this kind of feint, the false trail laid in an attempt to fox the police. In 1850 he had described to a journalist the methods of the 'Dancing School' of London cat burglars. They would watch a house for days, and find out at what time its inhabitants dined; this was the ideal moment for a burglary, since dinner tied up servants and employers alike. At the appointed hour, a gang member crept noiselessly, or 'danced', into the garret and plundered the upper storeys of small valuables, typically jewels. Before he made off across the rooftops with his spoils, the burglar would 'sell' (frame) a maid by hiding one of the

* Thirty-two years later, in the Sherlock Holmes short story 'Silver Blaze' (1892), Arthur Conan Doyle referred to 'the curious incident of the dog in the night-time', the curious incident being that the dog did not bark when he encountered an intruder, and the solution to the riddle being that the intruder was known to the dog. But the Road Hill murder, being fact rather than fiction, had messier, more ambiguous clues: the dog did bark on the night of the murder, but not a lot.

jewels under her mattress. The planted jewel, like the open window in Road Hill House, was a 'blind', designed to point the detectives the wrong way.

Perhaps the killer did not only plan to mislead the police about how Saville had been removed, Whicher reasoned, but about where he had been taken – the open window faced the gardens and fields behind the house. The murderer might have hoped that the police would not find the body in the privy, which lay in the opposite direction. Whicher speculated that the killer's 'original intention was to have thrown the child down the privy . . . thinking it would sink into the soil out of sight'. The privy 'has a large cesspool about ten feet deep and seven feet square', he reported, 'and at the time contained several feet of water and soft soil'. Whicher believed that the assailant intended the child to drown or suffocate in the excrement, and then to disappear in it. If this plan had worked, there would have been no marks of blood to identify either the murder scene or the murderer. But the slanting splashboard, recently installed on the orders of Samuel Kent, left an opening of only a few inches between the lavatory seat and the wall, so that it blocked the body's descent into the vault. The killer, said Whicher, 'being thus foiled, resorted to the knife', snatching a weapon from the basket just inside the kitchen passage, and stabbing the boy in the throat and chest to make certain of his death. At least three of the knives in the basket, he said to the *Somerset and Wilts Journal*, would have served.

That afternoon Whicher searched Constance's bedroom. In her chest of drawers he found a list of the linen she had brought back from school, which included three nightdresses. He had already been told that one of these had vanished. He sent for Constance.

'Is this a list of your linen?'

'Yes.'

'In whose writing is it?'

'It is my own writing.'

He pointed to the list. ‘Here are three nightdresses; where are they?’

‘I have two; the other was lost at the wash the week after the murder.’

She showed him the two still in her possession – plain, roughly woven garments. Whicher noticed another nightdress and a nightcap lying on the bed. He asked Constance whose they were.

‘They are my sister’s,’ she replied. Since Mrs Holley was still refusing to take in the family’s laundry, Constance’s two nightdresses were now dirty, and she had borrowed a clean one on Saturday from Mary Ann or Elizabeth. Whicher told Constance he must confiscate her linen list and remaining nightclothes. The missing nightdress was his first clue.

The word ‘clue’ derives from ‘clew’, meaning a ball of thread or yarn. It had come to mean ‘that which points the way’ because of the Greek myth in which Theseus uses a ball of yarn, given to him by Ariadne, to find his way out of the Minotaur’s labyrinth. The writers of the mid-nineteenth century still had this image in mind when they used the word. ‘There is always a pleasure in unravelling a mystery, in catching at the gossamer clue which will guide to certainty,’ observed Elizabeth Gaskell in 1848. ‘I thought I saw the end of a good clew,’ said the narrator of Andrew Forrester’s *The Female Detective* (1864). William Wills, Dickens’ deputy, paid tribute in 1850 to Whicher’s brilliance by observing that the detective found the way even when ‘every clue seems cut off’. ‘I thought I had my hand on the clue,’ declared the narrator of *The Woman in White* in an instalment published in June 1860. ‘How little I knew, then, of the windings of the labyrinth which were still to mislead me!’ A plot was a knot, and a story ended in a ‘denouement’, an unknotting.

Then as now, many clues were literally made of cloth – criminals could be identified by pieces of fabric. One case that turned on such evidence was very close to home for Jack Whicher.

In 1837, a notorious murderer was traced to Wyndham Road, Whicher's own street in Camberwell. James Greenacre, a cabinet-maker who owned eight cottages in the road, killed and dismembered his fiancée, Hannah Brown, in his lodgings there in December 1836. He wrapped her head in a sack and carried it by omnibus to Stepney, east London, where he threw it in a canal. He dumped her torso on the Edgware Road, in the north-west of the city, and her legs in a ditch in Camberwell. The star of the police investigation was PC Pegler of the S (Hampstead) division, who found Hannah Brown's torso. He traced Greenacre through a piece of cloth – the sacking in which the body parts were wrapped – and secured his confession through another: a snippet of thick nankeen cotton found on the Edgware Road, which matched a patch on the frock of his girlfriend's baby. The unravelling of the crime was reported with fascination in the press. Greenacre was hanged in May 1837. Whicher joined the police force four months later.

In 1849 the London detectives, Whicher, Thornton and Field among them, found the Bermondsey murderess Maria Manning by way of a bloodstained dress she had stashed in a railway-station locker. Manning and her husband had murdered her former lover and buried him beneath their kitchen floor. The detectives tracked down the couple with the aid of telegraph messages, express trains and steamships. Whicher checked the hotels and railway stations in Paris, and then the ships sailing from Southampton and Plymouth. He used his experience in tracing banknotes to help shore up the evidence against the killers. Eventually, Manning was caught in Edinburgh, her husband in Jersey. Each accused the other of the crime, and both were sentenced to death. The executions drew tens of thousands of spectators, while the 'broadside' ballads about the case sold two and a half million copies. A series of woodcuts printed that year showed the investigators as dashing action heroes, and the Commissioner praised his men for the 'extraordinary skill and exertion' with which they had worked on the case. He awarded Whicher and Thornton a bonus of £10 each; Field, as an inspector, was given £15.

The next year Whicher told William Wills a more commonplace story of how clothes could help capture a criminal. A detective sergeant – probably Whicher himself – was called in by a smart London hotel to find a man who the previous night had ransacked a guest's portmanteau. On the carpet of the room in which the trunk had been looted, the detective noticed a button. He watched the hotel guests and staff all day, closely scanning their clothes – at the risk, said Whicher, of being 'set down for an eccentric critic of linen'. Eventually he spotted a man with a button missing from his shirt, the thread dangling; the remaining buttons matched the 'little tell-tale' that the detective had found.

The Road Hill case was dense with fabric. The setting of the murder happened to be clothmaking country, a land of sheep and wool mills. The family's dirty laundry lay at the heart of the investigation, their washerwoman was a key witness, and the investigation threw up three clues of cloth: a flannel, a blanket and a missing nightdress. Whicher closed in on the last of these, much as the narrator of Wilkie Collins' 'The Diary of Anne Rodway', a short story of 1856, closed in on a torn cravat: 'A kind of fever got possession of me – a vehement yearning to go on from this first discovery and find out more, no matter what the risk might be. The cravat now really became . . . the clue that I was resolved to follow.'

The thread that led Theseus out of the maze was true to another principle of Whicher's investigation: the progress of a detective was backwards. To find his way out of danger and confusion, Theseus had to retrace his steps, return to the origin. The solution to a crime was the beginning as well as the end of the story.

Through his interviews with the Kents and those who knew them, Whicher tracked the family back in time. Though there were gaps,

Samuel Kent, circa 1863

The second Mrs Kent, circa 1863

Sketch of Elizabeth Gough in 1860

Constance Kent, circa 1858

Edward Kent,
early 1850s

Mary Ann Windus
in 1828, a year
before she became
the first Mrs Kent

Road Hill House, front view

Road Hill House, back view, with the drawing-room windows to the right

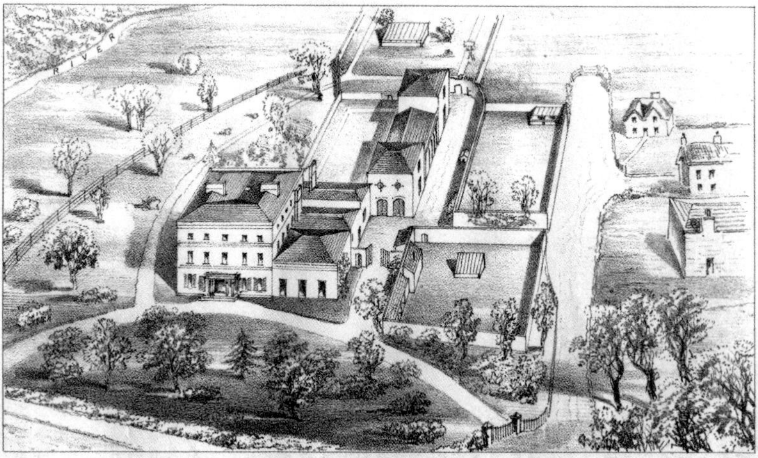

Engraving of Road Hill House in 1860, bird's-eye view

Engraving of Road Hill House in 1860, back view

Adolphus 'Dolly' Williamson, police detective, in the 1880s

Richard Mayne, Commissioner of the Metropolitan Police, in the 1840s

A view of Trowbridge, Wiltshire, in the mid-nineteenth century

The centre of Trowbridge in the late nineteenth century

Gravestone in East Coulston churchyard, Wiltshire

contradictions, indications of further secrets, he pieced together a narrative that he believed provided an explanation for murder. Much of it was chronicled in the book about the case that Joseph Stapleton published in 1861; the surgeon's account was heavily biased towards Samuel Kent, but it was scrupulous – and scurrilous – enough to hint at the many fissures in the family story.

In east London in 1829 Samuel Kent, the twenty-eight-year-old son of a carpetmaker from the north-eastern suburb of Clapton, married Mary Ann Windus, the twenty-one-year-old daughter of a prosperous coachmaker from the neighbouring district of Stamford Hill. In a miniature painted the year before the marriage, Mary Ann was shown with curly brown hair, dark eyes, bright, pursed lips in a pale face, and a wary, guarded cast to her features. Her father was a Fellow of the Royal Society of Antiquaries and an expert on the Portland Vase; the family home was crammed with paintings and curios.

The newlywed couple moved into a house near Finsbury Square, in the centre of London. Though their first child, Thomas, died of convulsions in 1831, they had a second – Mary Ann – before the year was out, and a third – Elizabeth – the year after that. Samuel worked as a partner in a firm of dry-salters, dealers in preserved meats and pickles, but in 1833 he resigned on account of an unspecified illness. 'The health of Mr Kent became so precarious,' said Stapleton, 'that he was compelled to relinquish his share of the business.' He took his family to Sidmouth on the Devonshire coast. There he secured a position as sub-inspector of factories for the west of England, the hub of the wool trade.

Mrs Kent first showed signs of madness in 1836, according to Samuel, a year after the birth of another son, Edward. She suffered from 'weakness and bewilderment of intellect' and 'various though harmless delusions'. Samuel later gave three examples of his wife's mental disturbance: she once got lost while out walking with her children near their home; on a Sunday, while he was at church, she tore the pictures out of one of his books and burnt them; and a knife was found hidden under her bed. Samuel consulted physicians about Mrs Kent's condition, and a Dr Blackall of Exeter confirmed that she was weak-minded. Her physical health was also poor.

Samuel continued nevertheless to impregnate her, and the couple saw four babies die in succession: Henry Saville in 1838, at fifteen months; Ellen in 1839, at three months; John Saville in 1841, at five months; and Julia in 1842, also at five months. ('Saville' – spelt sometimes with one 'l', sometimes without an 'e' – was the maiden name of Samuel's mother, who came from a well-to-do Essex family.) The cause of several of their deaths was given as 'atrophy', or wasting away. All were buried in the Sidmouth graveyard.

Constance Emily was born on 6 February 1844. Samuel gave the care of his new child to Mary Drewe Pratt, a twenty-three-year-old farmer's daughter who had joined the household the previous year as governess to the older girls. She was a short, attractive, self-assured young woman who had previously been employed as a live-out governess by the families of a solicitor and of a clergyman; she came recommended by a Sidmouth doctor. Miss Pratt was granted complete control of Constance, and she devoted herself to her charge. She fattened the frail baby into a sleek, powerful little girl. Constance was the first of the Kents' children to survive in nearly a decade.

The next year, on 10 July 1845, Mary Ann Kent gave birth to her last child, William Saville. During her confinements with Constance and William, Samuel said, her madness intensified. The management of the household was placed entirely in the hands of Miss Pratt.

In 1848 Samuel's boss, one of the four chief factory inspectors, urged him to move house in order to escape gossip about the family: the government inspector with the deranged wife and the favoured governess (the triangle echoed that in Charlotte Brontë's *Jane Eyre*, published the previous year). The Kents left their trellised, thatched cottage on the cliff and took up residence at Walton Manor in Walton-in-Gordano, a small Somersetshire village. In 1852 they again moved to avoid the scrutiny of their neighbours, this time to Baynton House in East Coulston, Wiltshire. At Baynton House on 5 May, while Miss Pratt was visiting her parents in Devonshire, Mary Ann Kent died aged forty-four of 'an obstruction of the bowel'.* She was buried in the neighbouring churchyard.

In August 1853, Samuel Kent married the governess. They travelled to Lewisham, just south of London, for the ceremony. Samuel's three daughters – Mary Ann, Elizabeth and Constance – were bridesmaids. Edward Kent, now a headstrong eighteen-year-old, had joined the merchant navy and was away at sea when his father and Miss Pratt were married. He was horrified upon his return to learn of the marriage, and argued bitterly with his father. A few months later – in 1854, the year Constance turned ten and William nine – the transport ship in which Edward was sailing went down on its way to Balaklava, and all its crew were thought to have drowned. As the Kents were setting out for Bath to buy mourning clothes, the postman arrived with a letter from Edward: he had survived the wreck. 'The father staggered back, almost fainting, into his house,' wrote Stapleton. 'We shall close the door upon the scene which ensued; upon that revulsion of feeling, under the shock of which his heart must have almost stood still with joy.'

That June, in another violent capsizing of emotions, Samuel's new wife was prematurely delivered of her first, and stillborn, child.

The second Mrs Kent was said to be an impatient woman who ran a strict household. Constance became troublesome at home,

---

* There are many possible causes for this condition, including tumours, hernias, the use of narcotics (such as opium), metabolic imbalance and kidney disease.

sometimes insolent. For punishment her former governess boxed her ears or, more usually, banished her from the parlour to the hall.

In 1855 Samuel's boss urged him to find another home, now that his first wife's death had removed the need to hide from the world. Baynton House was too secluded, said the chief inspector; Kent should be nearer to the mills that he supervised and to the railways by which he travelled round his region, an area that stretched hundreds of miles from Reading to Land's End. For the sake of his family – especially Mary Ann and Elizabeth, in their twenties and nowhere near married – he should be living closer to other people of his rank.

The move to Road Hill House, a slightly more modest residence, may also have eased some financial difficulties – Stapleton remarked that Baynton was beyond the means of a government employee with a family of four, being a house suited 'to the wants and pretensions of a country gentleman of considerable and independent fortune'.*

In June 1855 the second Mrs Kent gave birth to Mary Amelia Saville. In August the next year, she had her first son, Francis Saville, known as Saville. Her second daughter, Eveline, was born in October 1858. Mr and Mrs Kent were besotted with their new children. That year Edward, now twenty-two, sailed to the West Indies with the merchant navy, and in July died suddenly in Havana of yellow fever.

According to a rumour reported by Stapleton, Edward was the father of Saville, his supposed half-brother. If this were so,

---

* The press reported that Samuel Kent was paid £800 a year, a figure he did not correct; but the Home Office archives show that his salary was actually only £350 in 1860. He may also have had a small private income. In *The Book of Household Management* (1861) Mrs Beeton calculated that an income of £500 per annum was required to fund a three-servant household (the average wage for a cook, according to the same book, was £20, for a housemaid £12 and for a nursemaid £10).

Edward's anger about his own father's second marriage would have been prompted by sexual rivalry rather than disapproval. But Stapleton insisted that the new Mrs Kent and her stepson were not lovers – the evidence he gave for this, bizarrely, was the stillbirth of her first child. This event indicated that she had been made pregnant at least once by Samuel (Edward was at sea when the baby was conceived), although it suggested nothing about the paternity of her next two children, Mary Amelia and Saville.

The family story that Whicher pieced together at Road Hill House suggested that Saville's death was part of a mesh of deception and concealment. The detective stories that the case engendered, beginning with *The Moonstone* in 1868, took this lesson. All the suspects in a classic murder mystery have secrets, and to keep them they lie, dissemble, evade the interrogations of the investigator. Everyone seems guilty because everyone has something to hide. For most of them, though, the secret is not murder. This is the trick on which detective fiction turns.

The danger, in a real murder case, was that the detective might fail to solve the crime he had been sent to investigate. He might instead get lost in the tangle of the past, mired in the mess he had dug up.

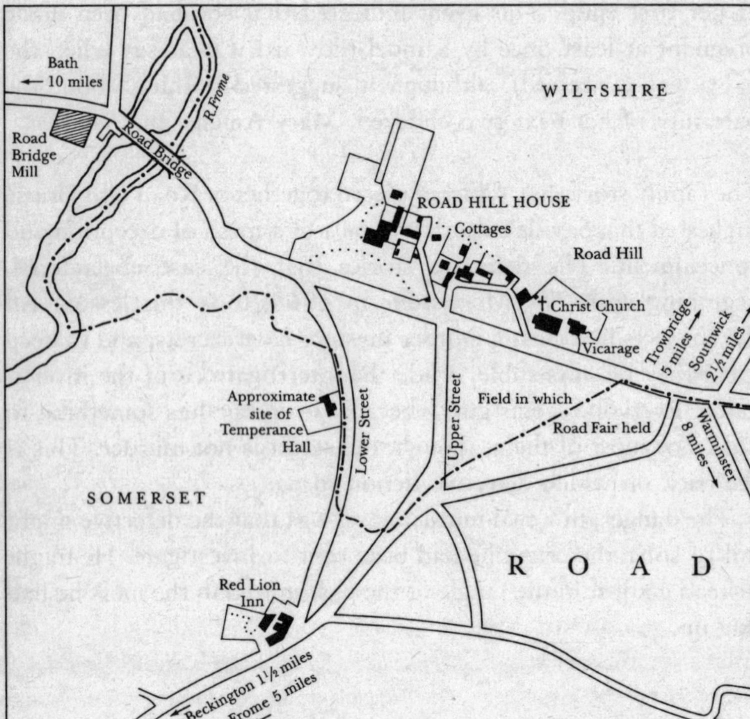

Bath
10 miles
WILTSHIRE
R.Frome
Road Bridge
Road
Bridge
Mill
ROAD HILL HOUSE
Cottages
Road Hill
Christ Church
Vicarage
Trowbridge
5 miles
Southwick
2½ miles
Approximate
site of
Temperance
Hall
Lower Street
Upper Street
Field in which
Road Fair held
Warminster
8 miles
SOMERSET
R O A D
Red Lion
Inn
Beckington 1½ miles
Frome 5 miles

CHAPTER SIX

SOMETHING IN HER DARK CHEEK

17 July

On Tuesday, 17 July, Jack Whicher started to make inquiries outside Road. Taking his lead from the missing nightdress, he began by visiting Constance's school in Beckington. He set off for the village, a mile and a half away, down a narrow road banked high with brambles, grasses and nettles, and flecked with white hogweed flowers. He was armed with the breast flannel found in the vault of the privy. The weather was fine, the haymaking almost done.

As a gardener's son, Whicher was at ease among fields and flowers. Sergeant Cuff, the detective in *The Moonstone*, had the same background. 'I haven't much time to be fond of anything,' says Cuff. 'But when I *have* a moment's fondness to bestow, most times . . . the roses get it. I began my life among them in my father's nursery garden, and I shall end my life among them, if I can. Yes. One of these days (please God) I shall retire from catching thieves, and try my hand at growing roses.'

'It seems an odd taste, sir,' his companion suggests, 'for a man in your line of life.'

'If you will look about you (which most people won't do),'

returns Cuff, 'you will see that the nature of a man's tastes is, most times, as opposite as possible to the nature of a man's business. Show me any two things more opposite one from the other than a rose and a thief; and I'll correct my tastes accordingly.' Cuff strokes the loose white blossoms on a musk rose, and speaks to it as tenderly as if it were a child: 'Pretty dear!' He does not like to pick the flowers, he says – 'It goes to my heart to break them off at the stem.'

When he reached the village Whicher called at Manor House, the school that Constance had been attending for the previous nine months, the last six as a boarder. The headmistress, Mary Williams, and her assistant Miss Scott had charge of thirty-five girls in term time, along with about four servants and two other teachers. Establishments such as this were, in effect, finishing schools that taught or perfected ladylike accomplishments: singing, piano-playing, needlework, dancing, deportment, the mastery of a little French and Italian. A girl of good family would typically attend for a year or two when in her teens, after being trained by a governess. The Misses Williams and Scott reported that Constance was doing well. The term before, she had been awarded the school's second prize for good conduct. Whicher showed the teachers the flannel with severed strings that Foley had found in the privy, asking if they recognised it. They said they did not. He requested the names and addresses of Constance's best friends, whom he would interview later in the week.

While in Beckington, Whicher also called on Joshua Parsons, the Kents' doctor, at the twin-gabled seventeenth-century house he shared with his wife, seven children and three servants. As a member of the new professional middle classes, Parsons was roughly Samuel Kent's social equal. One of his sons, Samuel, was just a few months older than Saville.

Joshua Parsons was born to Baptist parents at Laverton, a couple of miles north-west of Beckington, on 30 December 1814. The doctor was dark-haired, with full lips, a rounded nose and large brown eyes. In London, where he had trained as a general practitioner, he had been friends with Mark Lemon, later the editor of *Punch* and a friend of Dickens, and John Snow, the epidemiologist and anaesthetist who discovered the cause of cholera. Parsons and Whicher briefly lived in the same part of town: Whicher joined the police and moved to Holborn a month before Parsons left his lodgings near Soho Square to return to Somersetshire. In 1845 Parsons took up residence in Beckington with his wife Letitia, now thirty-six. He was a devoted gardener, particularly passionate about rock plants and hardy perennials.

Parsons explained to Whicher the conclusions he had drawn from the post-mortem. He had become convinced that Saville must have been partly or fully suffocated before he was attacked with a knife. This would account for the darkness around his lips, and the lack of blood on the privy walls: the boy's heart had been stilled before the wound was inflicted on his throat, so that his blood, instead of exploding in jets and sparkles, had leaked slowly away into the vault beneath the lavatory. The real murder weapon, Parsons believed, was not a knife but a length of cloth. Joseph Stapleton, with whom Parsons had performed the post-mortem, disagreed with the suffocation theory: Stapleton was sure that the throat-cutting was the cause of death, and that the blackening of Saville's lips was a result of his being left head-down in the privy. He suggested that most of the boy's blood had soaked into the blanket.

The difference in the doctors' views had important implications. If Saville was suffocated, and the stab wounds were made merely to disguise the cause of death, he might have been killed impulsively in order to secure his silence. The killers could have been his nursemaid and his father, surprised in bed. It was much harder to believe in this scenario if Saville was the victim of a furious knife attack.

Parsons didn't countenance the scenario anyway. He was sure that Constance was the killer. When he had examined the nightdress lying on her bed on the Saturday of the murder, he said, he found it not just clean but 'remarkably clean'. He thought it was a fresh nightgown, rather than one that had been six days in use. He had indicated as much to Foley, but the Superintendent had ignored the hint. Parsons told Whicher that Constance had a history of instability and spite. He was convinced, he said, that she was 'affected with homicidal madness', and he imagined that the cause lay in her blood.

Nineteenth-century physicians who specialised in mental illness, known as mad-doctors or alienists, believed that most madness was hereditary: the mother was the strongest source, and the daughter the most likely recipient. The first Mrs Kent was said to have undergone a bout of insanity while pregnant with Constance, and a child born in such circumstances was thought all the more liable to go mad herself: in 1881 George Henry Savage wrote that two babies he encountered at Bethlehem asylum 'were saturated with insanity while still in the womb . . . these infants seemed to be perfect little devils from birth'. Another theory – psychological rather than physiological – was that brooding on one's hereditary taint of madness could itself bring it on (this idea drove the plot of Wilkie Collins' 'Mad Monkton', a short story of 1852). The result was the same. Parsons told Whicher that he 'would not sleep in a house where Miss Constance was without having his door secured'.

There was a danger that Parsons' allegations about Constance would rebound on him. In the late 1850s several medical men were found to have consigned sane women to asylums – the ease of getting a doctor to testify to a woman's madness had become a national scandal. A parliamentary select committee investigated the phenomenon in 1858, and *The Woman in White* was dramatising it in 1860. The public was familiar, now, with the figure of the physician who falsely declared a woman insane.

Back in Road, Whicher put the breast flannel on display in the Temperance Hall and invited the villagers to identify it. This flannel, said the reporter for the *Somerset and Wilts Journal*, must have been used to administer chloroform to Saville or to stifle his screams; the only other explanation for its presence in the privy, he wrote, was that it was 'accidentally dropped from the murderer while bending over to accomplish the bloody work, which would appear to indicate a person in a state of comparative nudity'. From the fact of the flannel, the reporter conjured up the image of an almost naked woman stabbing the boy in the privy. He had become so infected with the search for significance that he had forgotten a fourth possibility: the flannel might have nothing to do with the murder at all.

Whicher pointed out in his report that the privy was used by all the servants of Road Hill House, and by visiting tradesmen and women. The flannel had not been found with the body, but on the 'soft soil' in the cesspool beneath it. The detective observed that 'it is quite possible it was down the privy before the murder, and if the person it belongs to has been shewn it since they may *from fear of being suspected* deny any knowledge of it'.* It took a cool head to accept that an apparently banal object was, sometimes, truly banal, and that people might lie not because they were guilty, but because they were scared. Whicher identified one further possibility: perhaps the murderer had

* In his reports to Mayne, Whicher underlined those phrases and sentences that he wished to emphasise. His underlined words are rendered here as italics.

dropped the flannel in the privy to trick the police: 'It may have been put there by design,' he noted, 'to throw suspicion on an innocent person.'

The breast flannel was one of several loose ends in the case that the investigators – police, reporters, newspaper readers – tried to endow with meaning, to turn into a clue. While a murder went unsolved, everything was potentially significant, packed with secrets. The observers, like paranoiacs, saw messages everywhere. Objects could regain their innocence only when the killer was caught.

Since Whicher was sure that the murderer was an inmate of the house, all his suspects were still at the scene. This was the original country-house murder mystery, a case in which the investigator had to find not a person but a person's hidden self. It was pure whodunnit, a contest of intelligence and nerve between the detective and the killer. Here were the twelve. One was the victim. Which was the traitor?

To get at the inner thoughts and feelings of the Kent household was more a matter of instinct than logic, what Charlotte Brontë described as 'sensitiveness – that peculiar, apprehensive, detective faculty'. A vocabulary was emerging to capture the elusive new detective methods. In 1849 the word 'hunch' was first used to mean a push or nudge towards a solution. In the 1850s 'lead' gained the meaning of a guiding indication or a clue.

Whicher observed the inhabitants of Road Hill House, their tics and intonations, the unconscious movements of their bodies and faces. He deduced their characters from their behaviour. In his own phrase, he 'reckoned 'em up'. An unnamed detective tried to explain this process to the journalist Andrew Wynter by describing how he caught a swell mobsman at a ceremony in Berkshire in 1856, when the Queen was laying the foundation stone of Wellington College, near Crowthorne. 'If you ask me to give my reason why I thought this person a thief the moment I saw him, I could not tell you,' said the detective. 'I did not even know myself. There was something about him, as about all swell mobsmen, that immediately attracted my attention, and led me to bend my eye upon them [sic]. He did not appear to notice my watching him, but passed into the thick of the crowd, but then he turned and looked towards the spot in which I was – this was enough for me, although I had never seen him before, and he had not to my knowledge attempted any pocket. I immediately made my way towards him, and tapping him on the shoulder, asked him abruptly, "What do you do here?" Without any hesitation, he said in an under tone, "I should not have come if I had known I should have seen any of you." I then asked him if he was working with any companions, and he said, "No, upon my word, I am alone;" upon this I took him off to the room which we had provided for the safe keeping of the swell mobsmen.' The detective's boldness, his instinct for a person being 'wrong', his familiarity with the swell mob and the plain, dramatic manner in which he told his story, suggest that Wynter's informant was Whicher. And there were telltale tics in his language: Whicher used the phrase 'That was enough for me' in a conversation recorded by Dickens.

It was hard to communicate in words the sorts of subtle movements on which a detective based his hunches: the momentary grimace, the fleeting gesture. The Edinburgh detective inspector James McLevy made a good go of it in the memoirs he published in 1861. As he watched a servant girl at a window, 'I could even notice the eye, nervous and snatchy, and the secret-like movement of withdrawing the head as she saw the man, and then protruding it a bit when she saw him busy.' The journalist William Russell, in one of the detective stories he published as 'Waters' in the 1850s, tried to capture the complexities of looking: 'her glare, for such it was, continuing fixed upon me – yet an introspective glare – searching the records of her own brain as well as the tablet of my face – considering, comparing both'. This formulation caught the way the accomplished detective worked: he looked keenly out at the world and, simultaneously, as sharply inwards, searching the records of his memory. The eyes of others were the books to be read, his own experience the dictionary that enabled him to read.

Whicher claimed he could see people's thoughts in their eyes. 'The eye,' he told William Wills, 'is the great detector. We can tell in a crowd what a swell-mobsman is about by the expression of his eye.' Whicher's experience 'guided him into tracks quite invisible to other eyes', wrote Wills. In faces, said McLevy, 'you can always find something readable . . . I am seldom *out* when I get my eyes on them.'

Whicher read bodies as well as faces – a twitch, a start, a rustle of hands beneath a cape, a sharp nod to an accomplice, a dart into an alley. He once arrested two well-dressed young men who had been loitering outside the Adelphi and Lyceum theatres because he 'suspected their movements' (when he searched them, he discovered that they did not have the money to pay for even the cheapest tickets in the pit, which confirmed his guess that they had been planning to pick pockets). His eye for the suspect movement had found him the diamonds stolen by Emily Lawrence and Louisa Moutot.

The seemingly supernatural sight of the early detective was crystallised by Dickens in Inspector Bucket, a 'mechanism of observation' with 'an unlimited number of eyes' who 'mounts a high tower in his mind and looks out far and wide'. The 'velocity and certainty' of Mr Bucket's interpretations was 'little short of miraculous'. The mid-Victorians were transfixed by the idea that faces and bodies could be 'read', that the inner life was imprinted on the shapes of the features and the flutter of the fingers. Perhaps the fascination stemmed from the premium placed on privacy: it was terrifying and thrilling that thoughts were visible, that the inner life, so jealously guarded, could be instantly exposed. People's bodies might betray them, like the heartbeats of the killer in Poe's 'The Tell-Tale Heart' (1843), which seemed to pound out his guilt. Later in the century, the unconscious give-aways of gesture and speech were to underpin the theories of Sigmund Freud.

The standard text on the art of face-reading was John Caspar Lavater's *Essays on Physiognomy* (1855). The physiognomist's 'eye, in particular, must be excellent, clear, acute, rapid and firm', wrote Lavater. 'Precision in observation is the very soul of physiognomy. The physiognomist must possess a most delicate, swift, certain, most extensive spirit of observation. To observe is to be selective.' As with detective work, the man with a good eye was the man who could discriminate, could see what mattered. 'The necessary knowledge is that of *what* to observe,' says Poe's Auguste Dupin. Detectives and physiognomists shared this excellence of the eye, which mirrored (perhaps even challenged) the Eye of Heaven that saw into the soul.

'There is nothing truer than physiognomy,' says the narrator of Dickens' short story 'Hunted Down' (1859), 'taken in connection with manner.' He explains how he formed his judgement of a man named Slinkton. 'I took his face to pieces in my mind, like a watch, and examined it in detail. I could not say much against any of his features separately; I could say even less against them when they were put together. "Then is it not monstrous," I asked myself, "that because a man happens to part his hair straight up the middle of his head, I should permit myself to suspect, and even to detest him?"' Yet he defends his violent dislike of Slinkton's centre parting: 'An observer of men who finds himself steadily repelled by some apparently trifling thing in a stranger is right to give it great weight. It may be the clue to the whole mystery. A hair or two will show where a lion is hidden. A very little key will open a very heavy door.' Faces and bodies held clues and keys; tiny things answered huge questions.

In his account of the Road Hill murder, Stapleton claimed that the secrets of the Kent family were written all over their faces. 'Nothing perhaps reveals more faithfully the history and secrets of a family than the countenances and expression of its children,' he wrote. 'Upon their countenances, in their behaviour and in their tempers, in their faults, and even in their very gestures and expression, there is written the history of their homes; as surely as upon the growing plant are found features correspondent to the nature of the soil in which it grew, to the storm that has torn its young tendrils and beat upon its tender shoots, to the care that pruned and watered it . . . Most truly may the physiognomy of children be regarded as the best index of the family weather.' Stapleton's rhetoric drew on the swirl of early Victorian ideas that had culminated in Darwin's *The Origin of Species*, published the year before – Darwin looked forward to a time 'when we regard every production of nature as one which has had a history; when we contemplate every complex structure as the summing up of many contrivances, each useful to the possessor'. People had become the sum of their pasts.

All the visitors to Road Hill House in the weeks after the murder scanned the inhabitants for clues. Most literally, the medical men examined Saville's corpse to read the story that it told. Others studied the faces and bodies of the living inmates of the house. Rowland Rodway said of Elizabeth Gough: 'I observed on her face traces of emotion and fatigue.' Albert Groser, a young reporter who sneaked into the house on the day of the murder, noticed Gough's 'agitated, troubled' demeanour. But where their suspicions were aroused by the nursemaid's frowns and fidgets, Whicher was to find his traces in absences, silences.

In his report to Sir Richard Mayne, Whicher outlined what he had noticed about the Kent family. Mr and Mrs Kent were 'doating' towards their younger children. William was 'very dejected'. Constance and William had a 'sympathy' and a 'close intimacy' ('close' in 1860 meant secretive). Whicher took account of how the family reacted to Saville's death. When Elizabeth Gough was 'telling the two elder Miss Kents that the child had been taken away during the night', he wrote, '*Miss Constance opened her door dressed, heard what was being said, but made no remark.*' Constance's composure, then and afterwards, might seem to betoken an easy conscience, a peaceful inner life, but a more sinister construction could be put on it. Coolness was a prerequisite for an artful crime.

The puzzle of the Road Hill case lay in the killer's peculiar combination of heat and cold, planning and passion. Whoever had murdered, mutilated and defiled Saville Kent must be horribly disturbed, possessed by unnaturally strong feelings; yet the same person, in remaining so far undiscovered, had shown startling powers of self-control. Whicher took Constance's cold quiet as a clue that she had killed her brother.

Whicher's confrontation with Constance over the nightdress may have been designed as an experiment on her nerves. If so, her unruffled blankness only confirmed his suspicions. As with the expressionless manner, so with the vanished nightdress: the clues lay in the gaps, in the hints of things hidden. What Whicher thought he saw in Constance was as slight as what Mr Bucket detected in the murderess Madame Hortense, 'her arms composedly crossed . . . [but] something in her dark cheek beating like a clock'. And Whicher's conviction of his suspect's guilt was as sure as Bucket's: 'By the living Lord it flashed upon me . . . that she had done it!' Or, in the words of Wilkie Collins' Sergeant Cuff, the fictional detective whom Whicher inspired: 'I don't suspect. I know.'

Even before Whicher's arrival, the Road Hill case had spawned would-be sleuths among the readers of English newspapers. They sent their tips to the police. 'I have had a dream which has given me a deal of uneasiness,' wrote a man from Stoke-on-Trent. 'I dreamed I saw 3 men making up the plot at a house near Finished Building, about half a mile from the sean of murder . . . I can give a minute description of the men I saw in my dream.' A newspaper vendor in Reading, Berkshire, suspected a man who had visited her shop on 4 July because he had asked 'in a tremulous way' whether there was anything about the murder in the previous day's *Daily Telegraph*.

On the day that Whicher reached Road another stranger had visited the village, introducing himself as a professor of phrenology. He offered to examine the heads of the murder suspects: by feeling the contours of their skulls, he claimed, he could determine who was guilty. A bump behind the ear indicated destructiveness; the part of the skull just above that was the seat of secretiveness. This was probably the same phrenologist who a week earlier had written from Warminster, five miles away, offering his services to the police. He practised a 'tried, disinterested science', he assured them: 'I find it as easy to detect the murderer's head, as it is to select a tiger from a sheep.' The police declined the offers – in 1860 phrenology was widely dismissed as quackery. But in some ways it was a close cousin of detective work. Much of the excitement about detection lay in its novelty, its mystery and its aura of science, the same qualities that had once attended phrenology. Poe wrote of his own detective stories: 'These tales of ratiocination owe most of their popularity to being something in a new key. I do not mean to say that they are not ingenious – but people think them more ingenious than they are – on account of their method and air of method.'

It was possible that Whicher's speculations were no better founded than those of any other observer of the crime. Detectives, like phrenologists, might be masters of mystification, men who cloaked common sense in complexity, dressed up guesses as science.

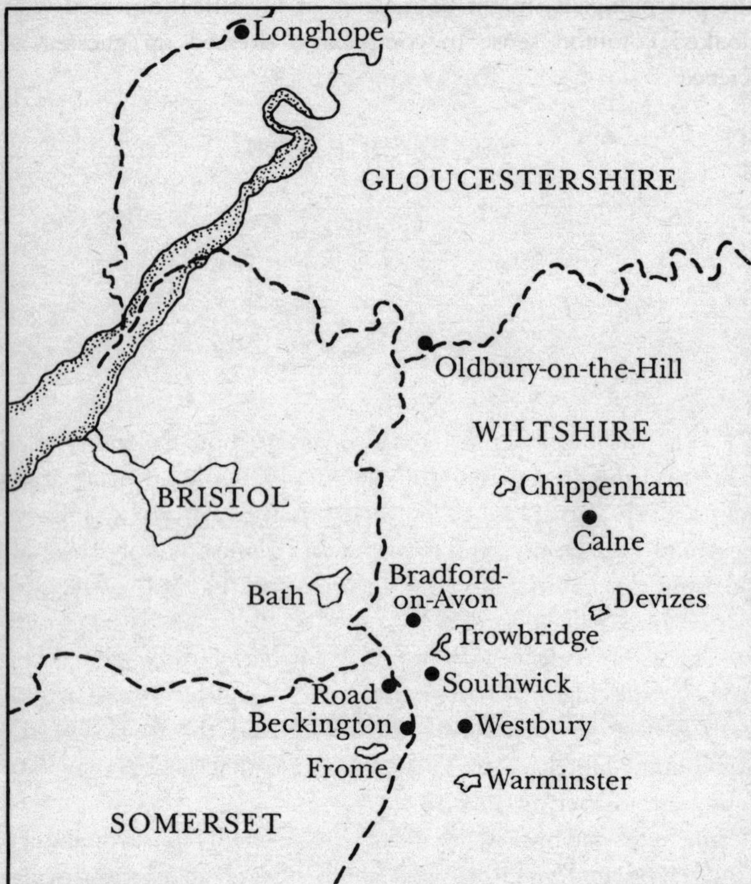
Longhope
GLOUCESTERSHIRE
Oldbury-on-the-Hill
WILTSHIRE
Chippenham
BRISTOL
Calne
Bradford-
on-Avon
Bath
Devizes
Trowbridge
Southwick
Road
Beckington
Westbury
Frome
Warminster
SOMERSET

CHAPTER SEVEN

SHAPE-SHIFTERS

18 July

The warm weather held on Wednesday, though clouds passed over the West Country in the afternoon, obscuring a partial eclipse of the sun. The local police maintained a strict surveillance on Road Hill House, and distributed a thousand handbills advertising the £200 reward for information that led to the conviction of Saville's murderer.

Whicher broadened his inquiries further. He took the train from Trowbridge to Bristol, and hired a cab for two hours in Bath. There he interviewed the police and the owner of the Greyhound Hotel about an odd episode that had taken place four years earlier, in July 1856.

The Kents had by then been living in Road Hill House for about a year. The second Mrs Kent was eight months pregnant with Saville. Constance and William, aged twelve and eleven, were both home from boarding school for the holidays, Constance apparently afflicted with weak ankles. A doctor advised that she wear laced stockings and avoid exercise. When the family visited Bath for the summer flower show she was pushed around in a wheeled chair.

One day Constance and William ran away. In the privy in the shrubbery on 17 July Constance changed into some of William's old clothes, which she had mended and hidden for this purpose. She then cut off her hair and threw it, with her discarded dress and petticoats, into the vault of the privy. She and William planned to go to sea as cabin boys, and were headed for Bristol. Like their older brother Edward, they hoped to flee the country. The two walked the ten miles to Bath by evening. When they tried to get a room for the night at the Greyhound Hotel, the innkeeper suspected that they were runaways, on account of their fine clothes and manners, and questioned them closely. Constance was 'very self-possessed, and even insolent, in her manner and language', Stapleton recounted, but 'William soon broke down, and burst into tears'. William was put to bed in the hotel, according to Stapleton, and Constance was handed over to the police. She spent the night at the station house, where she kept a 'determined silence'.

The reports of this incident in local papers differed from the account given by Stapleton, who may have emphasised William's sensitivity in order to play up Constance's dominant nature; the source for his account was almost certainly Samuel Kent. In one newspaper, which characterised the episode as 'an instance of extraordinary affection and adventurous daring', William did not break down in tears and Constance was not rude. They were both 'exceedingly polite' when interrogated by the landlord, simply repeating that they were going to sea. William was taken to the station. They kept their secret until the morning, when a servant from Road Hill House arrived in Bath and identified the children, complaining that he had worn out three horses searching for them.

William confessed to the police that he had run away from home, claiming that he had instigated the escapade: 'he desired to go to sea, he said, and his companion, his younger sister, had dressed herself in his clothes, and cut her hair short in order to accompany him to Bristol, where he hoped to be taken as cabin boy by some good-natured captain. All the money which they possessed was eighteenpence, but neither want of cash nor distance had been able to overcome the boy's determination or the sister's affection.' Another report also gave Constance the role of sidekick and William that of protector: 'the boy wanted to go to sea and entrusted his secret to his sister . . . whose ardent affection determined her to accompany him at all hazards'. She 'allowed him to cut her hair, which was then parted at the side'.

Stapleton and the Bath reporters agreed on Constance's unusual resolve, though they appraised it differently. According to one of the newspapers, 'The little girl, we are told, behaved like a little hero, acting the part of a boy to the admiration of all who saw her. We learn from Mr Inspector Norris . . . that Miss Kent manifested great shrewdness and resolution. The boy's clothes she wore were small for her, and she carried a small stick, which she used as if she had been accustomed to it. It was some time before he suspected that she was of the female sex, which he only discovered by a peculiarity in her mode of sitting.'

The servant took the children home. Samuel was away on a business trip, inspecting factories in Devonshire, but he returned to Road that afternoon. William 'at once expressed the greatest sorrow and contrition, and sobbed bitterly', according to Stapleton. But Constance refused to apologise to her father or her stepmother. She would say only that she had 'wished to be independent'.

It was, observed the *Bath Express*, 'a most strange circumstance in a delicately nurtured gentleman's family'.

When he had finished his inquiries in Bath on Wednesday, Whicher went by railway to Warminster, five miles east of Road, to speak to one of Constance's schoolfriends.

Emma Moody, fifteen, lived in a house in Gore Lane with her brother, sister and widowed mother, all wool-workers. Whicher showed Emma the breast flannel, which she said she had never seen before. He asked her if Constance had ever spoken about Saville.

'I have heard her say she disliked the child and pinched it, but it was done in fun,' said Emma. 'She was laughing at the time she said it.' When asked what made Constance tease the younger children, Emma said, 'I believe it was through jealousy, and because the parents showed great partiality.' She explained: 'I said upon one occasion, when we were talking about the holidays – we were going for a walk towards Road – I said, "Won't it be nice to go home so shortly?" She said, "Yes, perhaps it may be to your home, but mine is different" . . . She said that the second family were much better treated than herself and her brother William. She said this on several occasions. We were talking of dress at one time, and she said, Mamma will not let me have what I like. If I said I would have a brown dress she would let me have black, or just the contrary.' As Constance saw it, her stepmother felt such spite towards her that she was denied even the choice between black and brown. Like the coarse nightdress, the drab clothes cast Constance as a wronged and humiliated stepdaughter, a Cinderella shut out of the world of the other girls.

According to Whicher's reports to his superiors, Emma claimed to have often heard Constance express her aversion to Saville, on the grounds that he was so favoured by Mr and Mrs Kent. Once, Emma said, she remonstrated with Constance on this subject, 'telling her how wrong it was to dislike the child on that account as it was not his fault'. To this Constance replied, 'Well perhaps it is, but how would you like it if you was in my place?'

Whicher's job was not just to find things out, but to put them in order. The real business of detection was the invention of a plot. Whicher believed he understood Constance's motive: she killed Saville because of the 'jealousy or spite' she felt towards her stepmother's children, working upon a 'mind somewhat affected' by madness. The treatment of the first Mrs Kent could have stirred her youngest daughter into vengefulness. The second Mrs Kent, the woman who had brought Constance up as her own only to reject her once she bore children herself, might have been the object of the girl's rage.

The children's flight to Bath suggested to Whicher that Constance and William were peculiarly unhappy, and capable of acting on that unhappiness. It showed that they could make secret plans and see them through, that they were capable of disguise and deceit. Most significantly, it pointed to the privy as the children's hideway, the place in which Constance disposed of evidence and took on a new identity. In his reports, Whicher drew attention to 'the circumstance of the body being found in the same privy in which she cast her female apparel and hair before absconding from the home . . . disguised as a boy, previously having made a portion of the male attire herself, which she concealed in a hedge some distance from the house until the day of her departure'. The day she ran away could be construed as a step towards the murder of Saville.

Whicher worked alone that week. He 'has been actively and assiduously pursuing his inquiries', reported the *Somerset and Wilts Journal*, 'making no confidants, unless, indeed, Mr Foley be one. He has been plodding on, visiting for himself, and conversing with, all the persons engaged in this catastrophe, and following up, to its utmost, every gleam of light which might be seen to break in upon it.' The *Western Daily Press* described the detective's investigations as 'energetic' and 'ingenious'.

Whicher kept quiet about what the house-to-house interviews turned up. He put out word to the local press that he was 'in possession of a clue by which the mystery will shortly be unravelled', which was dutifully reported by the *Bath Chronicle*. This was an overstatement – what he had was a theory – but it stood a chance of rattling the culprit into a confession. The *Bristol Daily Post* was sceptical about the likelihood that Whicher would succeed: 'it is hoped, rather than expected, that his sagacity may unravel the mystery'.

'Sagacity' was a quality frequently attributed to detectives, in newspapers and in books. *The Times* referred to Jack Whicher's 'wonted sagacity'. Dickens praised Charley Field's 'horrible sharpness . . . knowledge and sagacity'. A detective story by Waters alluded to the hero's 'vulpine sagacity'. The word then denoted intuition rather than wisdom. In the seventeenth and eighteenth centuries a 'sagacious' beast had a keen sense of smell: the early detectives were being compared, in their quickness and sharpness, to wolves and dogs.

Charlotte Brontë described a detective as a 'sleuthhound', a dog that followed the scent of its quarry's 'sleuth' or trail.* In Waters' stories of the 1850s, the hero was an amalgam of huntsman and hound, closing on his prey: 'the chase was hot after him', 'I ran him to earth', 'I was upon the right track'. 'If any profession now-a-days can be enlivened by adventure,' wrote the celebrated Edinburgh detective James McLevy, 'it is that of a detective officer. With the enthusiasm of the sportsman, whose aim is merely to run down and destroy often innocent animals, he is impelled by the superior motive of benefiting mankind, by ridding society of pests.' Urban detectives hunted their prey through the city streets, deduced the identities of burglars and fraudsters by their signs and signatures, their unintended trails and traces. London was 'a vast Wood or Forest', wrote Henry Fielding a century earlier, 'in which a Thief may harbour with as great Security, as wild Beasts do in the Desarts of Africa or Arabia. For by wandering from one Part to another, and often shifting his quarters, he may almost avoid the Possibility of being discovered.' As Victorian explorers spanned out across the empire, charting new lands, the detectives moved inwards to the core of the cities, neighbourhoods that to the middle classes were as strange as Arabia. The detectives learnt to distinguish the different schools of prostitute, of pickpocket, of shoplifter and burglar, and to track them to their lairs.

---

* The abbreviation 'sleuth' was first used as a synonym for 'detective' in the 1870s.

Whicher was a specialist in the city's shape-shifters. Like the heroine of Andrew Forrester's *The Female Detective*, he 'had been much mixed up with people who wore masks'. In 1847, for instance, he caught Richard Martin, alias Aubrey, alias Beaufort Cooper, alias Captain Conyngham, who took delivery of orders of fancy shirts by impersonating a gentleman; and the next year he captured Frederick Herbert, a young man of 'fashionable exterior' who had conned a London saddler out of a gun case, an artist out of two enamel paintings, and an ornithologist out of eighteen hummingbird skins. Whicher's fictional double was Jack Hawkshaw, the detective in Tom Taylor's play *The Ticket-of-Leave Man* (1863), whose surname suggests a sure-sighted bird of prey. Hawkshaw is 'the 'cutest [acutest] detective on the force'. He pursues a master criminal who 'has as many outsides as he has aliases'. 'You may identify him for a felon today, and pull your hat off to him for a parson tomorrow,' says Hawkshaw. 'But I'll hunt him out of all his skins.'

Some of the local newspapers welcomed Whicher's presence in Wiltshire. 'The skill of a London detective, accustomed to the darker criminal atmosphere of a city, has been called in aid of our own able officers,' reported the *Bath Chronicle* that Wednesday. 'We cannot but believe the searchers are on the track.' Yet the crime in this pretty village took Whicher into murkier territory than he ever encountered in the city: this was not an investigation into aliases and false addresses, but into hidden fantasies, buried desires, secret selves.

CHAMBER FLOOR.

1. Nurse's bedroom.
2. Deceased's cot.
3. Nurse's bed.
4. Little girl's cot.
5. Lavatory.
7. Door of Mr. and Mrs. Kent's bedroom, which, it will be seen, faces the door of the nurse's room.
8. Mr. & Mrs. Kent's bedroom.
9. Door of Mr. Kent's dressing-room.
10. Dressing-room.

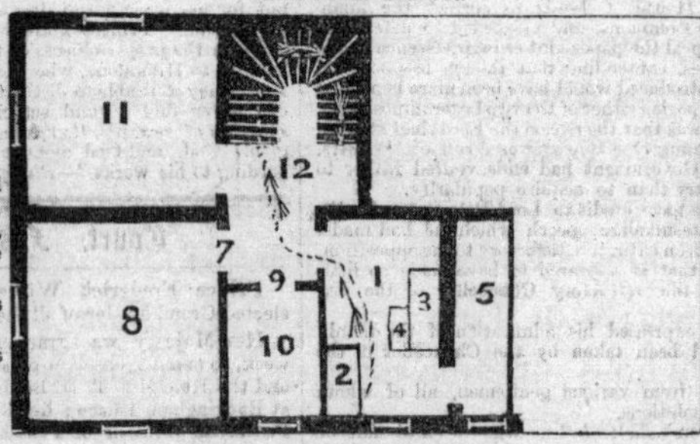

11. Young ladies' bedroom.
12. Landing & staircase.

In the vacant space near 5 are other rooms over kitchen and parlour.

The reader will now carry his eye to the letter A in the following out, which shows a continuation of the route.

GROUND FLOOR.

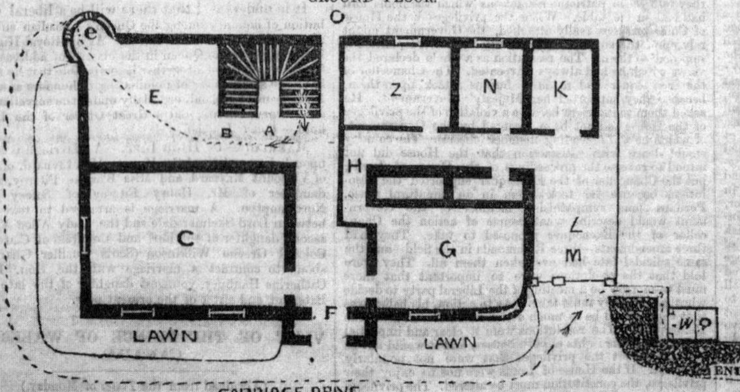

A. Bottom of staircase. B. Door of back drawing-room. E. Back drawing-room.
Small e. Window which was found open on the inside, and through which the murderer is supposed to have made his exit with the deceased, following the dotted line to W. O., the water-closet where the deed was committed.
M. Stable-yard door, where the watch-dog was loose inside. L. Stable-yard. K. Coach-house and stables.
N. Scullery. Z. Kitchen. O. Back door to kitchen garden. H. Passage to house from domestic offices.
C. Front drawing-room. G. Parlour. F. Front door. ENT. Entrance from turnpike road.

CHAPTER EIGHT

ALL TIGHT SHUT UP

19 July

On Thursday, 19 July, Whicher arranged for the waters of the Frome to be lowered so that the river could be dragged. The Frome lay at the edge of the Kents' grounds, down a steep bank and under a thick, feathery arch of trees. After almost three dry weeks, the river was not as swollen as it had been at the start of the month, but it was still full and restless. To lower its level, men blocked off the rush of water from the weir upstream, and then pushed out in their boats, scraping rakes or grappling hooks along the riverbed in the hope of pulling up a discarded weapon or garment.

The police rooted in the flowerbeds and gardens around the house. They combed the field beyond the lawns. Samuel Kent described the grounds behind his property: 'At the back of the house is a large garden, and a field in which was standing grass; that field is about seven acres in extent . . . The place is much exposed; the premises are large and very accessible.' His description of a home that was helplessly open, as if backing onto a plain, captured his feeling of defencelessness after Saville's death. The family's privacy was destroyed, its secrets uncovered, the house and grounds and the lives of everyone within exposed to all.

At first Samuel did his best to point the police away from the rooms of his family and servants. Like Elizabeth Gough, he insisted that a stranger had killed Saville. Perhaps the murderer was a disgruntled former servant, he suggested, taking revenge on the family. Before Whicher's arrival, Samuel showed Superintendent Wolfe the places in which an intruder could have hidden. 'Here is a room which is not often occupied,' he said, indicating a furnished spare room. Wolfe pointed out that a stranger could not have known that the room was rarely entered. Kent took him to a lumber room in which toys were stored. No one would hide here, Wolfe said, because they would have feared someone coming in to fetch a toy. As for the cockloft beneath the roof, said Wolfe, 'There was a considerable quantity of dust . . . and I think that if a person had been there I must have seen traces.'

A few newspapers speculated that a stranger had committed the crime. 'A intimate personal knowledge of every room in Road Hill House . . . convinces us that it would have been perfectly possible not only for one but for half-a-dozen persons to have been secreted on the premises, without risk of detection, on that night,' reported the *Somerset and Wilts Journal* later, in an astonishingly detailed exposure of the building's private places:

> *In no house of nineteen rooms that we know do we remember greater facilities for concealment. A cellar, divided into six large and small compartments, is entered by two several doorways and sets of steps. Midway up the back staircase is a large empty cupboard. A spare bedroom over the drawing-room contains a bedstead with valances, a dressing-table with a covering reaching to the ground, and two large and lofty closets, one of which are nearly always empty, and can be locked both inside and out. On this floor also are two small rooms, opening out of one another, each partly filled with lumber. On the floor above is a second spare bedroom, the bedstead having valances, a table, screen, and closets as in the room below . . . two small rooms,*

> *one almost empty, and the other containing Mr Kent's travelling apparatus; a large long closet, in which a dozen men might stand side by side; and a small room, without windows, containing two water tanks, and a ladder which communicates with the loft and the roof . . . All these we have ourselves seen.*

Any number of villagers were already familiar with the nooks and crannies of Road Hill House, said the *Journal*'s reporter, 'they having had the run of the house in a singular manner during the two years that it was void, previous to Mr Kent's occupation . . . this was so marked that, when the house was being prepared for him, six several times the stairs had to be painted, owing to the mischievous intrusion of village boys'. The building 'had almost been considered as public property', said the *Frome Times*, 'for those who chose to do so rambled over it without let or hindrance'.

The Kents kept indoors during Whicher's first week in Road, though the groom, Holcombe, took Mary Ann and Elizabeth by carriage to the shops in the town of Frome two or three times. In Frome, unlike Road or Trowbridge, members of the Kent family could usually pass an afternoon unmolested by hoots and hisses.

We have no physical descriptions of Elizabeth or of Mary Ann. They seem to move as one. Only in glimpses – Elizabeth standing alone as she scanned the night sky, or clutching the baby Eveline when Saville's corpse was brought into the kitchen – do they fleetingly acquire separate selves. They were intensely private young women. Mary Ann became hysterical when summoned to court. Elizabeth would not let the servants touch her clothes, either before or after they were washed: 'Miss Elizabeth makes up her own bundle herself,' said Cox, 'and I never meddle with it.' Since Mary Ann and Elizabeth were nearly thirty, neither was now likely to marry. The older sisters – like Constance and William – kept their own counsel, their bond with one another freeing them of the need to say much to anyone else.

By the end of the week Samuel had started to brief the police about Constance's insanity. Having denied the possibility of his daughter's guilt, he now seemed to be advancing it. 'Mr Kent,' said the *Devizes and Wilts Gazette* on 19 July, 'has not hesitated to intimate – and that in the plainest manner – that his *own daughter* committed the murder! and it has been alleged as a reason . . . that she has been guilty of freaks during childhood.' Was he incriminating her to protect himself? Was he shielding someone else in the family? Or was he trying to save Constance from the death penalty by advertising her instability? Dark rumours about Samuel were in circulation: some said that he and Mary Pratt had poisoned his first wife, even that he had killed the four Kent infants who died in Devonshire. Perhaps the first Mrs Kent had not been a raging lunatic, like the wife locked in Mr Rochester's attic in *Jane Eyre*, but an innocent, like the heroine of *The Woman in White*, sealed up in a wing of the house to seal her lips.

Publicly, Samuel still avoided any direct comment on his late wife's mental health: 'As to whether insanity had previously run in either branch of the family,' said the *Bath Chronicle* on Thursday, 'Mr Kent has been closely interrogated on that point; and he avers that he has never made an application to a medical man respecting anything of the kind.' This contradicted what he told Stapleton – that an Exeter doctor had diagnosed his late wife's madness – but it stopped short of denying that she had been insane. Parsons and Stapleton, both friends of Samuel, were on hand to insist on Constance's volatile nature: 'The two medical men . . . who have been privately examined, give it as their opinion that the young lady Constance possesses a temperament of mind likely to be influenced by sudden fits of passion.' To Whicher, Samuel openly stated that his former wife's family was riddled with madness: 'the Father . . . informed me that [Miss Constance's] Mother and Grandmother were of unsound mind', the detective wrote, 'and that her Uncle also on the Mother's side had been twice confined in a Lunatic Asylum'.

Whicher unearthed a peculiar incident that had taken place at Road Hill House in the spring of 1859, when Saville was two. One evening Saville's then nursemaid, Emma Sparks, put the boy to bed, as usual, in a pair of knitted socks. The next morning, wrote Whicher, the nursemaid found '*the clothes had been stripped from off the child, and both his socks taken off*'. The socks were discovered later: one on the nursery table, the other in Mrs Kent's bedroom. Whicher suspected that Constance was responsible, '*as she was the only grown up member of the family except Mrs Kent who was at home at the time*, Mr Kent being from home on business and the two elder sisters away on a visit'. He didn't mention the whereabouts of William – perhaps he was at boarding school. The incident, a piece of faintly malicious mischief, could in retrospect be understood as a rehearsal for a more savage interference. It echoed the terrible congruence of the tender and the stealthy in Saville's murder: the sleeping boy lifted gently from his bed, carried carefully downstairs, taken out of the house and killed. We don't know whether Whicher was tipped off about the matter of the missing socks by Emma Sparks or by Mr and Mrs Kent – he interviewed all three on the subject.

The bedsocks incident had no value at all as evidence: 'I can put no construction on this,' Whicher said of the story. Yet he took it as a psychological clue. In Waters' *Experiences of a Real Detective* (1862), Inspector 'F' explains: 'I contrived to elicit certain facts, which, though not worth twopence as legal evidence, were morally very suggestive.'

In 1906 Sigmund Freud was to compare detection to psychoanalysis:

> *In both we are concerned with a secret, with something hidden . . . In the case of the criminal it is a secret which he knows and hides from you, whereas in the case of the hysteric it is a secret which he himself does not know either, which is hidden even from himself . . . In this one respect, therefore, the difference*

between the criminal and the hysteric is fundamental. The task of the therapist, however, is the same as that of the examining magistrate. We have to uncover the hidden psychic material; and in order to do this we have invented a number of detective devices.

In effect, Whicher was gathering clues to Constance's inner life, her hidden psychic material, as well as the concealed facts of the crime. This murder was so dense with symbolism that it almost outdid interpretation. The child was thrust down a servants' lavatory, as if he were excrement. His attacker had tried to kill him, frantically or ritualistically, not once but four times: by suffocation, by slashing the throat, by stabbing the heart, by submersion in faeces.

Samuel informed Whicher of another morally suggestive fact – his daughter's fascination in the summer of 1857 with the Madeleine Smith murder trial.

Smith was a Glasgow architect's daughter of twenty-one who was charged with murdering her lover, a French clerk, by slipping arsenic into his hot chocolate. Her motive, allegedly, was to dispense with him in order to marry a richer suitor. After a sensational and widely reported court case, the jury declared the case against her 'not proven', a verdict available only in the Scottish courts. Smith was generally believed to be guilty, but the fact that she had outfaced the justice system with such breathtaking nerve only increased her allure. Henry James, for one, was an admirer – her crime was a 'rare work of art', he wrote. He hungered to have set eyes on her: 'I would give so much for a veracious portrait of her *then* face.'

Samuel told Whicher that the second Mrs Kent had taken the precaution of hiding from Constance the copies of *The Times* in which the trial was reported – this suggested that the girl was known to take an unusual interest in lurid crime, even at the age of thirteen. 'Owing to the peculiarity of the case the papers containing the account of the trial were studiously kept away from Miss Constance,' reported Whicher, 'and after her Trial they were concealed, locked up in a drawer by Mrs Kent.' When Mrs Kent checked the drawer a few days later she found the papers had vanished. 'Miss Constance was suspected and questioned but denied all knowledge of them, but on her bed room being searched they were found secreted between her bedstead and mattress.'

Perhaps reading the reports of Madeleine Smith's trial and acquittal had given Constance ideas about murder, as it had John Thomson, a man who in December 1857 said the case had inspired him to administer prussic acid to a woman who had spurned him. Though Saville was not killed with poison, his murder was well-plotted, silent, homespun: a blanket was a murder weapon as bland and comforting as a cup of chocolate. Madeleine Smith had shown that by being cunning and immovable a middle-class murderess could become a figure of glamour and mystery, a kind of heroine (Thomas Carlyle had used the phrase to describe the Bermondsey murderess Maria Manning). And if she kept her nerve she might never be caught.

There seemed to be a new breed of chilly female criminal whose concealed passions had twisted into violence. Usually the passions were sexual. Maria Manning and Madeleine Smith were apparently respectable women whose first sin was an illicit liaison, their second the murder of a former lover, a kind of violent extinction of their own lust. Madame Fosco in *The Woman in White* is sucked into crime by her passion for the dominating Count, and 'her present state of suppression may have sealed up something dangerous in her nature, which used to evaporate harmlessly in the freedom of her former life'. The murderess Madame Hortense in *Bleak House*, who was based on Maria Manning, was 'long accustomed to suppress emotion, and keep down reality'. She was 'schooled for her own purposes, in that destructive school which shuts up the natural feelings of the heart, like flies in amber'.

* * *

The dizzying expansion of the press in the 1850s prompted worries that readers might be corrupted, infected, inspired by the sex and violence in newspaper articles. The new journalists shared much with the detectives: they were seen alternately as crusaders for truth and as sleazy voyeurs. There were seven hundred newspaper titles published in Britain in 1855, and 1,100 by 1860 – of the papers printed closest to Road, the *Trowbridge and North Wilts Advertiser* was established in 1855, as was the *Somerset and Wilts Journal*, while the *Frome Times*, which the Kents took, was founded in 1859. There was a huge rise in crime reporting, aided by the speed with which news could be transmitted by the electric telegraph, and newspaper readers came across accounts of violent death every week. When Mr Wopsle in Dickens' *Great Expectations* (1861) reads the news, he becomes 'imbrued with blood to the eyebrows'.

At least three cut-throat domestic killings were reported in newspapers all over the country in the month before Saville Kent's death. In Shoreditch, east London, a pipemaker murdered his common-law wife: 'Her throat was cut so extensively that the head was nearly severed from the body,' according to the *Annual Register*. 'She must have died instantaneously without struggle or noise.' At Sandown Fort on the Isle of Wight, Sergeant William Whitworth of the Royal Artillery killed his wife and six children with a razor, leaving their throats 'gashed in so horrible a manner as to show the vertebrae of the neck'. Above a confectioner's shop in Oxford Street, London, a French tailor decapitated his wife with a saw, then went to Hyde Park and shot himself. 'His brother stated that he was in the habit of going to Dr Kahn's Museum, and studying the arteries about the neck and throat, and especially familiarising himself with the position of the jugular vein.' The tailor had educated himself in how to kill, and any newspaper reader could do the same.

* * *

In the middle of the week Whicher accompanied the magistrates to Road Hill House to conduct a further interview with Constance. In answer to their questions, she described her relations with some of the household: 'I was very fond of Saville . . . He used to be not very fond of me; he appeared fonder these holidays. The little boy was not fond of me because I teased him. I never struck him or pinched him . . . William is my favourite of my brothers and sisters. We write to each other when I am at school . . . The dog wouldn't fly at me if he recognised me. He would bite me if he didn't know me . . . I have a cat but I don't care anything for it . . . I like the cook best of the servants. I like the nurse very well.'

On being questioned about her own qualities, she replied: 'I am not considered very timid. I don't like being out in the dark . . . I could carry the deceased the length of this room easily. I was generally considered pretty strong at school.' She denied telling her schoolfriends that she didn't want to go home for the holidays. She was asked about the Madeleine Smith trial and agreed that she may have inadvertently taken a newspaper that reported it: 'I heard Madeleine Smith's friend was poisoned. I used to hear Papa talk about it.' She gave an account of her flight to Bath four years earlier: 'I once did cut off my hair and fling it down the same place where my little brother was found. I cut part of my hair and my brother cut the rest. I thought of the place to put it in. I and my brother William went to Bath by an indirect road . . . I went off because I was cross at being punished. I persuaded my brother William to go with me.'

As the week wore on, rumours began to emerge of the full extent of the county constabulary's incompetence, and of Samuel Kent's obstructions. In particular, a story took shape about what happened on the night after Saville's body was found.

In the evening of Saturday, 30 June, Superintendent Foley

directed PC Heritage, of the Wiltshire police, and PC Urch, of the Somersetshire police, to stay overnight at Road Hill House. 'Mr Kent will tell you what to do,' said Foley. 'Come quietly, because Mr Kent does not want the servants to know you are there.' Only Mrs Kent was told that the officers were on the premises. Already it was pretty clear that Saville had been killed by one of the inhabitants of Road Hill House but, astonishingly, Foley none the less handed over charge of the night's police operation to Samuel Kent.

At about eleven o'clock, when everyone but Samuel had gone to bed, Heritage and Urch knocked at a library window to be admitted to the house. Samuel let them in and led them to the kitchen, where he told them to remain. Their task, he informed them, was to watch out for anyone trying to destroy evidence in the kitchen fire. He gave the policemen bread, cheese and beer and then bolted the door after them. The two were ignorant of their imprisonment until, soon after two in the morning, Heritage tried to get out. On discovering that the door was locked, he knocked for Mr Kent. When he got no reply he rapped on the door with a stick.

'You are making enough noise to wake all the people in the house,' warned Urch.

'I am locked in and must get out,' replied Heritage.

When Samuel released him, about twenty minutes later, Heritage told him they hadn't known they were locked in. 'I have been walking about,' Samuel replied, ignoring the complaint. Urch stayed in the kitchen for the rest of the night, with the door bolted. Samuel looked in on him two or three times, and the constable left at five in the morning. 'I was in the library during a portion of the night,' Samuel said later, 'but left the house once or twice. I went out to see if the lights were out. I went out several times for the same object.' He circled the house, he claimed, to see if the candles were burning and if their wicks needed trimming.

Until now the police had kept quiet the fact that they had let themselves be locked in Samuel Kent's kitchen on the night after the murder. This 'extraordinary occurrence', in the words of the *Somerset and Wilts Journal*, had left anyone in the building free to destroy evidence. Samuel's actions smacked of contempt for the police, and a determination that his house escape their scrutiny. Or his behaviour could be seen as exemplary: the first duty of a father was to protect his family.

When asked by the police for floor plans of Road Hill House in the days and weeks after his son's murder, Samuel reacted as defensively as if someone were trying to take the roof off the place. He refused to supply a plan or to let anyone measure up the rooms. 'It is a sufficient explanation to say that Mr Kent simply resented an uncourteous intrusion,' said Rowland Rodway.

English family life had changed since the beginning of the century. The house, once a workplace as well as a home, had become a self-contained, private, exclusively domestic space. In the eighteenth century 'family' had meant 'kin', those related by blood; now its primary meaning was the inhabitants of a household, barring the servants – that is, the nuclear family. Though the 1850s had been christened with a great glasshouse – the Crystal Palace of the Great Exhibition of 1851 – the English home closed up and darkened over the decade, the cult of domesticity matched by a cult of privacy. 'Every Englishman . . . imagines a "home", with the woman of his choice, the pair of them alone with their children,' wrote the French scholar Hippolyte Taine after a visit to England in 1858. 'That is his own little universe, closed to the world.' Privacy had become the essential attribute of the middle-class Victorian family, and the bourgeoisie acquired an expertise in secrecy (the word 'secretive' was first recorded in 1853). They walled themselves in against strangers, the interiors of their homes almost invisible, except when opened by invitation to selected visitors for a staged show of family life – a dinner party, for instance, or a tea.

Yet this age of domesticity was also an age of information, of a prolific and ravenous press. On 7 July a reporter from the *Bath Chronicle* had sneaked into Road Hill House in the guise of a detective, and made notes on the layout. An inaccurate floor plan was published in the paper five days later. Whether Samuel Kent liked it or not, the house was dissected for all to see, carved up clumsily to expose each floor to scrutiny. The public seized on the information the diagrams provided. The landscape of the house took on emotional inflections: the locked cellar, the dusty attic, the lumber rooms furnished with unused beds and closets, the twisting back stairs. 'The whole moral interior of the house ought to be laid bare to the public gaze,' argued the *Bath Express*.

A murder like this could reveal what had been unfolding within the shuttered middle-class house. It seemed that the cloistered family, so honoured by Victorian society, might harbour a suppression of emotion that was noxious, toxic, a sexual and emotional miasma. Perhaps privacy was a source of sin, the condition that enabled the sweet domestic scene to rot from its core. The closer the house was kept, the more polluted its inner world might become.

Something had festered in Road Hill House, the emotional counterpart to the airborne infections that terrified the Victorians. A month before the murder, the *Devizes and Wiltshire Gazette* reported on a new edition of Florence Nightingale's *Notes on Nursing*, first published in 1859, quoting a passage about how disease and degeneration could be bred in sealed, respectable homes. Nightingale had known severe cases of 'pyaemia', or blood poisoning, in 'handsome private houses', she wrote, and the cause was 'foul air . . . it was that the uninhabited rooms were never sunned, or cleaned, or aired; – it was that the cupboards were always reservoirs of foul air; – it was that the windows were always tight shut up at night . . . you may often find a race thus degenerating and, still oftener, a family'.

On Thursday, 19 July, the *Bath Chronicle* published an editorial on the Road Hill murder:

> *No assassination within our recollection has caused so singular, and so painful a sensation in the homes of the country. It is not the mere mystery which at present enshrouds the deed that gives it this terrible interest . . . It is the strange character of the deed, and the helpless innocence of the victim that touch respectively the imagination and the heart . . . The mothers of England, thinking of their own little ones sleeping in peace and purity, shudder at the tale of a child, as gentle and innocent as their own, being dragged in the still morning from its slumbers, and cruelly sacrificed, and it is the mothers of England who write most earnestly, most indignantly, to the conductors of the journals, and almost clamour for the most unsparing search and the most untiring test . . . in many a home where intense affection is combined with much nervousness on the part of the most valuable member of the family, her peace will for many a day be broken, her dreams disturbed, by the recollection of the dreadful story from Road. Strange doubts, vague distrusts will arise in her mind . . . A deed that sends a shudder through every English home, acquires a social importance which justifies any amount of attention to the subject.*

Usually in an unsolved murder case the public feared that the killer might strike again. Here, though, the fear was that he or she could be duplicated in any home. The case undermined the very idea that a locked household was safe. Until it was solved, an English mother would sleep uneasily, haunted with the idea that her house harboured a child-killer – it could be her husband, her nanny, her daughter.

Though it would be an assault on the middle-class ideal if the master of the house, the protector, had destroyed his own son in order to disguise his depravity, the press and the public were surprisingly quick to believe in Samuel's guilt. Almost as horrible – and apparently equally believable – was the idea that the nursemaid had helped him to kill the boy she was hired to tend. The alternative was that this crime harked back to the original biblical murder, Cain's killing of Abel. On 19 July the *Devizes Gazette* implied that one of Saville's siblings was responsible for his death: 'The voice of the blood of one as innocent as Abel will be made to cry from the very ground in testimony against the murderer.'*

On the same day the *Bristol Daily Post* (founded that year) printed a letter from a man who believed that an examination of Saville's eyes might reveal the image of the killer. The correspondent based his suggestion on some inconclusive experiments conducted in the United States in 1857. 'The image of the last object seen in life remains printed, as it were, on the retina of the eye,' he explained, 'and can be traced after death.' According to this hypothesis, the eye was a kind of daguerreotype plate, registering impressions that could be exposed like a photograph in a darkroom – even the secrets locked up in a dead eye might be within the reach of the new technologies. This took to an extreme the way the eye had been turned into the symbol of detection: it was not only the 'great detector' but also the great giveaway, the telltale organ. The letter was reprinted in newspapers all over England. Few treated it with scepticism. The *Bath Chronicle*, though, dismissed its usefulness to the case on the grounds that Saville was asleep when the killer struck, so there could be no image of the murderer on his retina.

---

* The biblical text runs: 'And the Lord said unto Cain, Where is Abel thy brother? And he said, I know not: Am I my brother's keeper? And He said, What hast thou done? the voice of thy brother's blood crieth unto me from the ground.'

In the evening of 19 July a tremendous downpour over Somersetshire and Wiltshire brought the brief summer of 1860 to an end. The haystacks had not yet dried, and most were spoiled. The fields of corn and wheat, not having had time to ripen in the sun, were still green.

CHAPTER NINE

I KNOW YOU

20–22 July

At eleven on the morning of Friday, 20 July, Whicher reported to the magistrates at the Temperance Hall on his investigation so far. He told them that he suspected Constance Kent of the murder.

The magistrates conferred, and then told Whicher that they wished him to arrest Constance. He hesitated. 'I pointed out to them the unpleasant position such a course would place me in with the County Police,' he explained in his report to Mayne, 'especially as they held opinions opposed to mine, as to who was the guilty party, but they (the magistrates) declined to alter their determination, stating that they considered and wished the enquiries to be entirely in my hands.' The chairman of the magistrates was Henry Gaisford Gibbs Ludlow, commanding officer of the 13th Rifle Corps, Deputy Lieutenant of Somersetshire and a rich landowner who lived in Heywood House, Westbury, five miles east of Road, with his wife and eleven servants. Of the other magistrates, the most prominent were William and John Stancomb, mill-owners who had built themselves villas on opposite sides of the Hilperton Road, an exclusive new district of Trowbridge. It was William who had lobbied the Home Secretary for the services of a detective.

Shortly before three o'clock in the afternoon Whicher called at Road Hill House and sent for Constance. She came to him in the drawing room.

'I am a police officer,' he said, 'and I hold a warrant for your apprehension, charging you with the murder of your brother Francis Saville Kent, which I will read to you.'

Whicher read her the warrant and she began to cry.

'I am innocent,' she said. 'I am innocent.'

Constance said she wanted to collect a mourning bonnet and mantle from her bedroom. Whicher followed her and watched as she put them on. They rode to the Temperance Hall in a trap, in silence. 'She made no further remark to me,' said Whicher.

A large group of villagers had collected outside the Temperance Hall, having heard a rumour that an arrest was being made at Road Hill House. Most expected to see Samuel Kent brought before the magistrates.

Instead they watched as Elizabeth Gough and William Nutt approached the hall in the early afternoon – they had been called to give evidence – and then, at 3.20, they were startled to see the occupants of the trap that drew up before them: ''Tis Miss Constance!'

She came into the hall on Whicher's arm, with her head bent down, weeping. She was wearing deep mourning, with a veil closely drawn over her face. She 'walked with a firm step but was in tears', reported *The Times*. The crowd pressed in after her.

Constance sat facing the magistrates' table, Whicher on one side of her and Superintendent Wolfe on the other.

'Your name is Miss Constance Kent?' asked Ludlow, the chairman.

'Yes,' she whispered.

Despite the thick veil with which Constance had masked herself, and the pocket handkerchief that she pressed to her face, the reporters gave minute accounts of her features and manner, as if enough attention to these surfaces would yield her inner self.

'She looks to be about 18 years of age,' reported the *Bath Express*, 'though it is said that she is only 16. She is rather tall and stout, with a full face, which was very flushed, and a dimpled forehead, apparently somewhat contracted. Her eye is peculiar, being very small and deep set in her head, which perhaps leaves a somewhat unfavourable impression on the mind. In other respects there is nothing unprepossessing in her appearance, judging from her looks yesterday; at the same time, the fearful crime with which she stands charged doubtless modified in some degree the habitual expression of her countenance, the predominant characteristic of which is said to be sullenness. The young lady wore a black silk dress and mantle, trimmed with crape, and kept her veil down throughout the proceedings. She sat with her eyes fixed upon the ground, shedding tears, and never once looked up. Indeed, to judge from her demeanour, she seemed to feel her awful position most acutely, though she manifested no violent emotion from the time she was taken until she left, at the close of the inquiry.' The crêpe that trimmed the dresses worn during the initial period of deep mourning was a dull gauze made of tightly twisted silk threads, fixed with gum.

Constance was 'strongly formed', according to the *Western Daily Press*, 'with a round, chubby face, which does not convey at first either an impression of deep determination or of active intellect. She was collected in her manner, and preserved the same unmoved expression throughout the inquiry.'

The *Frome Times* reporter seemed to detect in her a disturbing quality: a stifled sexuality, or rage. She looked 'somewhat peculiar', he wrote. 'While she has a girlish look, her figure is remarkably developed for her age, which is only 16. Her features, which were very flushed, are rather pleasing, but have a heavy, almost sullen look, which we believe is a characteristic of the family.'*

* According to one implausible rumour, the Kents were illegitimate descendants of the royal family. Reporters occasionally remarked on Constance's resemblance to Queen Victoria.

Whicher made his statement to the court.

'I have been engaged since Sunday last in investigating all the circumstances connected with the murder of Francis Saville Kent, which took place on the night of Friday, June 29th last, at the house of his father, situate at Road, in the county of Wiltshire. In company with Captain Meredith, Superintendent Foley, and other members of the police force, I have made an examination of the premises, and I believe that the murder was committed by an inmate of the house. From many inquiries I have made, and from information which I have received, I sent for Constance Kent on Monday last, to her bedroom, having first previously examined her drawers, and found a list of her linen, which I now produce, on which are enumerated, among other articles of linen, three night-dresses as belonging to her.'

He read out Constance's answers to his questions about the nightdresses.

'I now pray the Bench for a remand of the prisoner, to enable me to collect evidence to show the animus which the prisoner entertained towards the deceased, and to search for the missing night-dress, which if in existence may possibly be found.'

The magistrates heard testimony about Saville's loss and discovery from Elizabeth Gough (who wept) and from William Nutt. Then they asked Whicher how much time he needed to gather his evidence against Constance. He asked for a remand until the next Wednesday or Thursday.

'Will Wednesday be time enough?' asked the Reverend Mr Crawley.

'Under ordinary circumstances,' said Whicher, 'a week is the time for a remand.'

The magistrates gave him a week, ordering that Constance be detained until 11 a.m. the following Friday. Ludlow then turned to her. 'I don't ask you to make a statement,' he said, 'but have you anything to say?' She did not reply.

Whicher and Wolfe escorted Constance out of the hall and took her by britzska – a long, soft-topped carriage – to the gaol at Devizes, about fifteen miles east of Road. They drove away under a dull sky, 'she during the journey remaining in a kind of sullen silence', wrote Whicher, 'and not displaying the slightest emotion'.

'The most blameless being on earth might have so demeaned herself under similar circumstances,' pointed out the *Bristol Daily Post*, 'and so (always supposing her to possess sufficient resolution) might the most offending.'

The crowd was quiet as the carriage departed, said the *Western Daily Press*. According to the *Trowbridge and North Wilts Advertiser*, Constance was seen off with 'repeated cheering'. Most of the villagers felt sure of her innocence, reported this newspaper. She was merely 'eccentric', they believed: the true murderer had stolen her nightdress in order to implicate her.

Once Whicher and Constance had left, the magistrates sent to Frome for Dr Mallam, Saville's godfather, and for 'a woman who had previously lived at Mr Kent's' – probably Emma Sparks, the former nursemaid. The likelihood was that Whicher had cited the testimony of both to the magistrates, who now wanted to hear it first-hand.

The magistrates ordered that Road Hill House be searched again for the nightdress. Samuel Kent let in the police, and in the late afternoon everything on the premises was 'turned over and emptied, from garret to cellar', said the *Frome Times*. The nightgown was not found.

Whicher must have hoped that the arrest would shock Constance into a confession. One of his favoured ruses was to bluff when he had no evidence, to accuse with confidence. This technique played a part in his first reported arrest – of the housemaid wearing a boa in a Holborn brothel – and in a story that he told Dickens about catching a horse-thief in a lonely country pub. 'It's no use,' Whicher said to the man he suspected but had never before met. 'I know you. I'm an officer from London and I take you into custody for felony.' He saw off the crook's two associates by pretending he had friends in tow: 'I'm not alone here, whatever you may think. You mind your own business, and keep yourselves to yourselves. It'll be better for you, for I know you both very well.' The horse-thief and his pals had given way. Constance had not. Whicher now had a week in which to find the evidence to justify her committal for trial.

From Trowbridge, Whicher sent a five-shilling telegraphic message to the day-and-night telegraph station on the Strand, near Scotland Yard, asking Sir Richard Mayne to send help. 'I have this day apprehended, on a warrant, Constance Kent the third daughter who is remanded for a week. The magistrates have left the case entirely in my hands to get up the evidence. I am awkwardly situated and want assistance. Pray send down Sgt Williamson or Tanner.' Williamson and Tanner were Whicher's most trusted sidekicks. When Mayne received the message later that day he wrote on the reverse: 'Let Sgt Williamson or Tanner go immediately.'

Detective-Sergeant Williamson was summoned urgently to Mayne's house in Chester Square, Belgravia, on Friday afternoon. The Commissioner gave him his instructions to go to Road, and Williamson took a cab on to the Strand telegraph office, from where he dispatched a message to Trowbridge telling Whicher he was coming.

Frederick Adolphus Williamson – 'Dolly' – was Whicher's protégé. They had worked together often, most recently on the capture of Emily Lawrence and James Pearce, the celebrated jewel thieves. Dolly was a clever, energetic man of twenty-nine, who studied French in his spare time. He had a round, soft face and kindly eyes. His father, a police superintendent, had set up the first police-station library. Dolly shared lodgings in 1 Palace Place,

Great Scotland Yard, with sixteen other single policemen. One of these, Tim Cavanagh, later gave an account of Dolly's relationship with a cat that had attached itself to the house. This animal, Tommas, had a habit of 'killing and eating the local cats', according to Cavanagh, and the officers' neighbours demanded that he be destroyed. 'Much to our regret, we had to put a stone around the poor old fellow's neck and drop him into the river. This was a great shock to "Dolly," who was much attached to "Tommas," and, if I may let a secret out now, actually trained the "warrior" for his midnight work. On more than one occasion did [Tommas] bring in a nice piece of venison, or a hare, or a rabbit from a near neighbour.' Williamson emerges from this as both ruthless and tender-hearted, a man who could train a cat to kill and then mourn its death. In time, he was to lead the detective department.

Whicher could not know whether the public would believe an adolescent girl capable of such a horrible, and well-organised, crime as the murder at Road Hill House. But he knew from his experience of the London 'rookeries', or slums, what dark mischief children could get up to. On 10 October 1837, during Whicher's first month in the force, a girl of eight was caught playing a sharp trick near the rookery of St Giles, Holborn. She stood in the street crying bitterly until she had gathered a crowd about her. Sobbing, she explained to her audience that she had lost two shillings and was afraid to go home for fear of punishment. Once she had been plied with halfpennies, she moved on, to repeat the ruse a few roads away. A constable of E division watched her do this three times before arresting her. In the magistrates' court, she again pleaded terror of her parents; it is hard to know whether she was justifying or replaying her scam. 'The prisoner, crying, said that her father and mother sent her out to sell combs,' reported *The Times*, 'and unless she took home 2*s*. or 3*s*. every night they beat her cruelly, and not having sold any during the day she acted in the way described to get the money required of her.' The next day, 11 October, a girl of ten was charged with having broken a pane of glass in a raid on a Holborn watchmaker's shop. A gang of fellow ten-year-olds accompanied her to the magistrates' court. 'They were attired in a flash style,' said *The Times*, 'and their appearance and manners indicated that they were thieves and prostitutes, although so young.' One of the boys said he had come to pay the girl's fine of three shillings and sixpence, the cost of replacing the window. He threw the money down scornfully.

Criminal children were nearly always ill-used children. In Whicher's first weeks in Holborn he saw many examples of the careless or vicious ways in which parents could treat their young. His colleague Stephen Thornton arrested a drunken crossing-sweeper, Mary Baldwin (alias Bryant), a member of the most notorious family in St Giles, who was seen trying to kill her three-year-old daughter. She put the child in a bag and dashed it violently against the pavement. When a passer-by heard the girl's cries and remonstrated with the mother, Mary Baldwin ran into the road to place the bag in the path of an omnibus. The child was rescued by some of the passengers.

Since those years, it had become apparent that middle-class children, too, could be damaged or corrupt; sometimes it was almost impossible to tell one from the other, the victim from the victimiser. In 1859 an eleven-year-old girl called Eugenia Plummer accused the Reverend Mr Hatch, her private tutor and the chaplain of Wandsworth gaol, of sexually molesting her and her eight-year-old sister while they were boarders at his house. The eight-year-old, Stephanie, confirmed the story. After a lurid trial, in which Hatch (as the defendant) was not allowed to testify,* he was sentenced to four years in prison, with hard

* A defendant was not allowed to give evidence at his or her own trial until 1898.

labour. But in May 1860, a few weeks before the Road Hill murder, Hatch successfully sued Eugenia for perjury. This time it was she who was the defendant, and therefore unable to give evidence. The jury decided that she had made it all up. They agreed with the clergyman's lawyer that her accusation was 'an entire fiction, the result of a prurient and depraved imagination'.

In its influential editorial on the Road Hill murder, the *Morning Post* alluded to this case: 'That it should be a child [who killed Saville] would be incredible if Eugenie Plummer had not taught us to what length the wicked precocity of some children will extend.' Eugenia's precocity was sexual, but it also rested in her cool deceit, her composure under pressure, the containment and channelling of her disturbance into bare lies. If newspaper readers had been horrified to find a clergyman convicted of sexually molesting a child in 1859, they must have been even more disturbed, a year later, to find the situation had been turned upside-down to reveal the child as the agent of evil, a creature who had undone a man's life with her lewd imaginings.* But even this was not certain. As *Blackwood's Edinburgh Magazine* pointed out in 1861, the only unassailable fact was that 'one jury or the other convicted an innocent person'.

On Saturday morning Whicher travelled to Bristol, twenty-five miles north-west of Trowbridge, where he visited Chief Superintendent John Handcock, who lived in the city with his wife, four sons and two servants. Handcock was an old colleague of Whicher, who had worked the streets of Holborn alongside him when both were police constables twenty years earlier. Whicher spent two hours making inquiries in and around Bristol by cab, and then took the train twenty miles north to Charbury,

---

* If Eugenia was lying, one wonders about the role played in her life by the family doctor, Mr Gay, to whom she was – at eleven – already betrothed. The surgeon referred to her as his 'little wife', and it was he who examined her body for signs of sexual molestation. Gay observed 'slight marks of violence', he said.

Gloucestershire. A carriage took him the remaining eighteen miles to Oldbury-on-the-Hill, the home of Louisa Hatherill, fifteen, another of Constance's schoolfriends.

'She has spoken to me of the younger children at home,' said Louisa, 'and said that there was a partiality shown to them by the parents. She spoke of her brother William being obliged to wheel the perambulator for the young children and said that he disliked doing it. She said she had heard her father, comparing the younger son with the older, say what a much finer man he would be . . . She never said anything particular about the deceased child.' From Louisa's account, it seemed that all the anger Constance felt was on William's behalf.

Louisa, like Emma Moody, confirmed to Whicher that her friend was a tough young woman. He observed in his report that Constance was a 'very stout, strong built girl, and her school fellows state that she was very fond of wrestling with them, and displaying her strength and wishing some times to play at Heenan and Sayers'. The heavyweight boxing match between the American John Heenan and the Briton Tom Sayers in April that year had been a national obsession, and turned out to be the last fought under the old, brutal, bare-knuckle rules. Heenan was six inches taller than Sayers, and forty-six pounds heavier. In an extremely bloody two-hour contest that ended in a draw, Sayers fractured his right arm blocking a punch, while Heenan broke his left hand and was almost blinded by the blows to his eyes. The girls told Whicher that Constance boasted of her strength, and a tussle with her 'was dreaded by all'.

That Saturday's piece in the *Somerset and Wilts Journal*, the newspaper most sympathetic to Whicher's views, gently hinted at William's complicity in the crime. It passed on to the readers Gough's observation that the boy was 'accustomed to use the back stairs because of his thicker boots'. This reinforced the sense that Mr and Mrs Kent demeaned William, and it associated him with the servants' staircase, by which Whicher believed the murderer had taken Saville from the house. The reporter suggested that the stabbing of Saville 'may have been done by the accomplice, if two were actually concerned, so that the two might be equally implicated'. While Constance was in gaol a rumour circulated that William, too, had been taken into custody.

In Bristol and back in Trowbridge, Whicher briefed reporters on his investigation, emphasising the unhappiness of Constance and the insanity in her mother's line. 'The question of probable insanity is one to which Mr Whicher's inquiries have been specially directed,' said the *Trowbridge and North Wilts Advertiser*. The reason for this, its reporter was told, was that 'there are few, if any, recorded instances of murder, the victims of which have been children of a few years old, in which the murderer has not been acting under the influence of a morbid condition of mind'. As for motive: 'The deceased child, we are told, was the pet of the family, and doated upon by his mother.' The reporter was informed that the servants and the children of the first family were treated harshly, the second Mrs Kent 'ruling, it is said, with a severe hand, all beneath her sway'.

Detective-Sergeant Williamson reached Trowbridge in the afternoon of 21 July. That day's issue of *All the Year Round* carried a piece by Wilkie Collins about a new biography of the French detective Eugène Vidocq. Collins praised Vidocq's 'impudent, ingenious, and daring' methods, his 'address and powers of endurance in tracking out and capturing his human game', his 'cleverness'. The Frenchman – a master criminal turned police chief – was the detective hero against whom his English counterparts were measured.

From his room in the Woolpack Inn on Sunday, 22 July, Whicher wrote his second report to Sir Richard Mayne, a five-page document that outlined the evidence against Constance. His case rested, he said, on the missing nightdress and on the testimony of Constance's schoolfellows. He listed the other suspicious circumstances: the murder took place soon after Constance and William came home from boarding school; she and William were the only people in the house who slept alone; the pair had used the privy as a hiding place before. She was powerful enough to have killed Saville, he assured Mayne, both physically and psychologically – 'she appears to possess a very strong mind'. Whicher thanked Mayne for sending him Williamson, and reminded him of his unhappy relations with the local police. 'I am very unpleasantly situated as regards acting with the County Police, in consequence of the natural jealousy entertained in this matter by them, they suspecting Mr Kent and the Nurse, and should it appear in the end that my opinions are correct, they would be considered at fault, but I have studiously endeavoured to act in concert with them as far as possible.' Whicher was careful to protect himself from charges of disrespect towards other policemen.

In his reports to Mayne, Whicher gave his reasons for rejecting the conjectures of the Wiltshire police. He defended Samuel Kent's behaviour in the immediate aftermath of the murder. Many were suspicious of Samuel's motives in leaving the house – if he had been involved with the murder, the flight to Trowbridge would have given him an opportunity to dispose of any incriminating evidence, as well as saving him from being present when the body was discovered. But there were innocent explanations for his behaviour: the desire to be sure that the alarm was raised, the restlessness aroused by anxiety. 'As regards the suspicion against Mr Kent,' wrote Whicher, 'in reference to his conduct after the murder was discovered in riding off four miles to Trowbridge to give notice to the Police that his child had been stolen, I think it perfectly consistent under the circumstances and the most natural course for him to have taken as it would in my opinion have been much more suspicious had he remained at home, a partial search of the premises having been made before and was being continued at the time of his departure.'

There were contradictory accounts of how long it took Samuel to make the trip to Trowbridge, and of whether Peacock caught up with him before or after he summoned Foley. The version in the *Somerset and Wilts Journal* of 7 July had it that Peacock overtook Kent before he reached Trowbridge, and that Kent returned instantly, while the clergyman rode on to the town to fetch Foley and his men. Since Kent was away for an hour, and Trowbridge was just four or five miles from Road, this left a lot of time unaccounted for. Could Kent have been using that time to dispose of a murder weapon or other evidence? A month later the *Journal* corrected its original story: Kent was on his way back to Road when Peacock accosted him, it reported, and he had already informed Foley of the loss of the child. This account – which concurred with the first published version of these events, in the *Bath Chronicle* of 5 July – made the timings more reasonable.

Some of the villagers spoke of Kent as an arrogant, bad-tempered master who was either rude or lascivious towards his servants, more than a hundred of whom were said to have passed through Road Hill House since he had moved in. But Whicher found him a decent, even sentimental man. 'As regards his moral character,' wrote Whicher, 'I cannot find that there is anything against him, and I am informed by the Servants now in the family, and by those who have left that he and Mrs Kent lived in perfect harmony, and one of them (the monthly nurse) stated that she considered him foolishly fond and indulgent towards her, and doatingly fond of the deceased child *which I fear led to his untimely death.*'

Another suspect was William Nutt, who had seemed to predict his own discovery of Saville's body. He had a grudge against Samuel, who had prosecuted a member of his family for stealing apples from the Road Hill orchard. Some named Nutt as Elizabeth Gough's imagined lover. 'I do not think there are grounds for the suspicion entertained relative to the witness

"Nutt" who found the child,' Whicher wrote, 'as it appears very natural that he would have made the remark of "looking for a dead child as well as a living one" as at that time he and Benger had searched other places and were then going to search the privy.' As for the suggestion 'that he was improperly connected with the Nursemaid, there is not the slightest grounds for that suspicion, as she in the first place was not acquainted with him and in the next place I do not suppose she hardly ever spoke to him nor would condescend to speak to him in any way much more as an admirer, as she is rather a superior girl for her station in looks and demeanour, while on the other hand "Nutt" is a slovenly dirty man, weakly, asthmatical, and lame'.

Whicher steadfastly defended Gough's innocence. He said he saw nothing in her conduct to make her a likely suspect. This ignored her strange contradictions about the time at which she became aware that Saville's blanket was missing: at first she said she had noticed before his body was found, then that she noticed only afterwards. But if this was a lie rather than a confusion, it seemed a pointless one. There was no need for Gough to conceal her knowledge that the blanket had been taken – it would have been natural for her to check the bedding carefully. By changing her story, she only drew suspicion to herself. A similar ambiguity hung over her account of why she did not raise the alarm when she noticed Saville was missing at 5 a.m.: her delay seemed odd; yet if she had been guilty, she would surely not have brought it up at all. Some thought it suspicious that Gough had not mentioned Saville's absence to Emily Doel, her assistant, just before seven on the morning of his disappearance; Whicher thought her silence 'seems to tell in her favour', because it indicated that she really did believe the boy's mother had taken him, and that there was no cause for alarm. He also pointed to the innocence implied by the words she used when she roused Mrs Kent at 7.15: 'Are the children awake?'

The police in Isleworth, Gough's home town, had been directed to make inquiries about her character, and the report they sent on 19 July accorded with Whicher's perceptions: she 'is well known to be respectable, quick, kind, good tempered and very fond of children'. As for her supposed lover, the detective could find no evidence 'that she was even acquainted with any male person, either at Road, or the Neighbourhood'.

Some people speculated that Mrs Holley had destroyed Constance's nightdress in order to incriminate the girl and protect William Nutt, who was married to one of her daughters – the fullest version of this theory identified five conspirators: Nutt, Holley, Benger (whom Samuel Kent had apparently once accused of overcharging him for coal), Emma Sparks (the nursemaid who testified about the bedsocks, and had been dismissed by Samuel the previous year) and an unnamed man whom Samuel had prosecuted for fishing in the river. There was little evidence against any of them, other than the mildly suspicious fact that Mrs Holley claimed to have heard a rumour before Monday, 2 July that a nightdress was missing. Whicher had an explanation for this: 'The rumour about the nightdress . . . must have related to Mary Ann's stained nightdress, which the police had confiscated and examined but which had that morning been returned to her.'

On Sunday, Samuel Kent was given permission to visit his daughter in prison. He was accompanied to Devizes, another Wiltshire wool town, by William Dunn, a widowed solicitor born in east London and living in Frome. (Rowland Rodway had resigned as Samuel's legal representative because he believed Constance was guilty; he later agreed to represent Mrs Kent, who must have shared his view.) This case was far outside Dunn's regular remit. In the county court the previous month he had represented a man who had been sold a faulty turnip-cutter, and another whose cow had developed a lump as fat as two fists after being 'pogged' (poked with a stick) by a rival dairy farmer.

When they reached the gaol – designed like a wheel, with the governor's office at the hub and a hundred cells radiating out from it – Samuel found himself unable to face his daughter and sent Dunn to her cell in his stead. His reasons were inscrutable. *The Times* said that 'the feelings of the father overcame him, and he was unable to undergo the interview', but did not make clear whether these were Samuel's feelings as a father to Constance or to Saville: he might have collapsed under the weight of his pity for Constance, or of his horror at her. The *Bath Chronicle* echoed the uncertainty: 'he could not bear the ordeal of an interview with his daughter, and, therefore, remained in an adjoining room, while the solicitor conferred with Miss Kent'. It could be that Samuel recoiled from any discussion of his son's death. In the weeks since the murder, his strategy had seemed to be silence. 'Mr Kent has never alluded to the murder to me from first to last,' Elizabeth Gough remarked later. 'The young ladies have, and so has Miss Constance, but not Mr Kent. Master William has frequently cried over it.'

When Dunn visited Constance in her cell, she repeatedly told him that she was innocent. The solicitor sent to a local hotel for a comfortable mattress, to make her week in gaol more pleasant, and arranged for her to be provided with special rations.

A prison officer afterwards briefed the waiting reporters. 'We are credibly informed that Miss Kent's demeanour in the prison was calm and quiet,' said the *Western Morning News*, 'and that she appeared to be conscious of her innocence and ashamed of being placed in such a position.'

'We understand she was perfectly calm and collected throughout the interview,' said the *Bath Chronicle*, 'as, indeed, she has continued to be since her incarceration, although the painfulness of her awfully critical position had, very naturally, wrought somewhat of a change in her features; still, her general demeanour has made such an impression upon the officials of the Gaol, that they do not hesitate to state that her appearance, at all events, bespeaks her innocence of this horrid transaction.'

CHAPTER TEN

TO LOOK AT A STAR BY GLANCES

23–26 July

At the time he was assigned the murder at Road, Whicher had twice before led an investigation into the mysterious death of a small boy. One was the case of the Reverend Mr Bonwell and his illegitimate son, which even now was being heard at the Court of Arches, the chief ecclesiastical court in London. The other took place a decade earlier, in December 1849, when a police superintendent from Nottinghamshire turned up at Scotland Yard and asked for the help of the London detectives in a suspected infanticide. Whicher was given the case.

A man in North Leverton, Nottinghamshire, had informed the police that he had received, by post, a box containing the corpse of a boy. The child was dressed in a frock, a straw hat, socks and boots, and wrapped in an apron marked 'S Drake'. The man told the police that his wife had a sister called Sarah Drake who worked as a cook and housekeeper in London.

Whicher and the Nottinghamshire superintendent went directly to the house in which Sarah Drake worked, 33 Upper Harley Street, and charged her with killing the child. 'How do you know that?' she asked. They told her about the apron marked with her name. She sat down and cried.

The same night at the police station Drake confessed to the 'searcher' employed to examine her clothes and belongings that she had killed the boy, whose name was Louis. He was her illegitimate son, Drake told the searcher, and for the first two years of his life she had managed to keep her job as a servant by paying another woman to look after him. When she had fallen behind with the payments, though, the foster mother angrily returned Louis to her. Terrified of losing her 'place' in Upper Harley Street, which paid about £50 a year, Sarah Drake had strangled her son with a handkerchief. She then packed him up in a box and sent him to her sister and brother-in-law in the country, hoping that they would bury him.

Whicher gathered the evidence to confirm Drake's confession. It was a pitifully easy task. In her bedroom he found three aprons identical to the one in the box, and a key that fitted the box's lock. He interviewed Mrs Johnston, the woman who had looked after Louis since he was three months old, for five shillings a week. She said that on 27 November she had returned Louis to his mother at Upper Harley Street. When Drake pleaded with her to keep him for another week, she refused. She was fond of the boy, she said, but his mother had too often defaulted on the payments and was now several months in arrears. Before leaving Louis at Upper Harley Street, Mrs Johnston urged Sarah Drake to take care of her son.

> *I told her that he was quite well, and had grown a hearty little fellow. I then told her she had better take his hat and pelisse [a fur-trimmed jacket] off, or he would take cold when he went out. She did so. There was a little handkerchief about his neck, and she said to me, 'This is yours, you had better take it.' I said, 'Yes, but keep it to put about him when he goes out to keep him warm.' I also told her he would soon want something to eat – to which she replied, 'Very well; will he eat anything?' I said, 'Yes', and left the house.*

As she was going, Drake called out to ask exactly how much she owed. Mrs Johnston replied that it was £9.10*s*., to which Drake said nothing.

Mrs Johnston told Whicher that when she called to see Louis the next Friday, Sarah Drake claimed that he was staying with a friend. 'I asked her to kiss the baby for me. She said, "Yes, I will."'

Whicher interviewed the staff at 33 Upper Harley Street. The kitchen maid recalled that on the evening of 27 November, Drake had asked her to carry a box from her bedroom to the butler's pantry: 'It was as much as I could lift.' The butler said that Drake asked him to address the box and to arrange for it to be taken the next morning to Euston Square station. The footman said that he took the box to the station, where it was weighed at thirty-eight pounds, and he paid eight shillings to send it to Nottinghamshire.

Mrs Johnston accompanied the police to North Leverton to identify the body. She confirmed that it was Louis. 'The handkerchief which I left on its neck, the pelisse, and the cape, were also there.' The surgeon who conducted the post-mortem said he was not sure that the handkerchief had been pulled tight enough to kill the boy; there was evidence that he had been beaten, and this was the more likely cause of death.

At her trial Sarah Drake stared at the ground and rocked her body to and fro, occasionally convulsing. She showed signs of great anguish. The judge told the jury that though she had no history of insanity, they might decide that the shock and terror of the child being suddenly left on her hands had unbalanced her reason. He warned that 'they must weigh well before they did so . . . it never could and never would be right or correct for juries to infer insanity merely from the atrocity of the crime'. The jurors found Sarah Drake not guilty, on the grounds of temporary insanity. She fainted.

Many illegitimate babies were killed by poor and desperate women in Victorian England: in 1860, child murders were reported in the newspapers almost daily. Usually the victims were newborns, and the assailants were their mothers. In the spring of 1860, in a weird reprisal of Sarah Drake's crime, Sarah Gough, a housekeeper and cook at Upper Seymour Street, a mile or so from Upper Harley Street, killed her illegitimate child, parcelled it up and sent it by train from Paddington to a convent near Windsor. She too was easily traced: in the package was a paper bearing the name of her employer.

Juries showed compassion to women such as Sarah Drake and Sarah Gough, preferring to find them deranged than depraved. They were helped in this by new legal and medical ideas. In the law courts the 'McNaghten rule' had since 1843 allowed 'temporary insanity' to be used as a defence. (In January 1843 a Scottish woodturner, Daniel McNaghten, had fatally shot Sir Robert Peel's secretary, mistaking him for the Prime Minister.) Alienists detailed the kinds of madness to which the apparently and usually sane could fall victim: a woman might suffer from puerperal mania just before or after giving birth; any woman might be overcome by hysteria; and anyone might be struck by monomania, a form of madness that left the intellect intact – the sufferer could be emotionally deranged yet show cold cunning. By these criteria, any unusually violent crime could be understood as evidence of insanity. *The Times* put the dilemma neatly in an editorial of 1853:

> *Nothing can be more slightly defined than the line of demarcation between sanity and insanity . . . Make the definition too narrow, it becomes meaningless; make it too wide, and the whole human race becomes involved in the dragnet. In strictness we are all mad when we give way to passion, to prejudice, to vice, to vanity; but if all the passionate, prejudiced and vain people were to be locked up as lunatics, who is to keep the key to the asylum?*

The suspicion that Constance Kent or Elizabeth Gough was mad kept surfacing in the press. It was even suggested that Mrs Kent had killed her son during a fit of puerperal mania. While Constance waited in prison, a Mr J.J. Bird wrote to the *Morning Star* to suggest that the murder of Saville was the act of a somnambulist. 'Most people know with what precision and care sleepwalkers act,' he said. 'The parties suspected should be watched by night for some time.' He cited a case in which a hallucinating somnambulist, his eyes open and fixed, had stabbed an empty bed three times. If sleepwalkers could commit unconscious violence, he said, it was possible that Saville's murderer was unaware of his or her own guilt. Perhaps the killer had a double consciousness. The idea that madness could take this form, that several selves could inhabit one body, fascinated mid-century alienists and newspaper readers. Bird's letter was reprinted over the next week in several provincial papers.

On Monday, 23 July, Whicher briefed Dolly Williamson on the investigation so far. He took him to Bath, to Beckington and to Road. On Tuesday, Whicher put a placard on the door of the Temperance Hall: '£5 reward – Missing from the residence of Mr Kent, a lady's nightdress, supposed to have been thrown in the river, burnt, or sold in the neighbourhood. The above reward will be paid to any person finding the same, and bringing it to the Police Station, Trowbridge.' That day he prepared the evidence he had gathered against Constance – Henry Clark, the magistrates' clerk, wrote up the findings on four foolscap pages. On Wednesday, Whicher went to Warminster to serve a subpoena on his key witness, Emma Moody, and sent Williamson to William's boarding school at Longhope, Gloucestershire, to see what he could glean about the boy.

As the rain came down, the two detectives searched the grounds of Road Hill House for the nightgown.

* * *

In that weekend's instalment of *The Woman in White* – the thirty-fourth – the hero had discovered the secret that Sir Percival Glyde had tried so desperately to hide, a shame that lay in his family's past. His knowledge, though, was not enough; to catch the villain, he had to find the proof. Whicher's predicament was similar. In the Sarah Drake case, he had elicited the confession he needed by presenting his suspect with her apron; if only he could find Constance's nightdress he might secure the same: the physical evidence and a confession in one.

Poe's Dupin observes: 'Experience has shown, and a true philosophy will always show, that a vast, perhaps the larger, portion of truth arises from the seemingly irrelevant.' Unremarkable events were inscribed with hidden stories, if you knew how to read them. 'I made a private inquiry last week,' remarks Sergeant Cuff in *The Moonstone*. 'At one end of the inquiry there was a murder, and at the other end there was a spot of ink on a tablecloth that nobody could account for. In all my experience along the dirtiest ways of this dirty little world, I have never met with such a thing as a trifle yet.'

Since he could not find the nightdress, Whicher returned to the moment at which it had vanished. He asked Sarah Cox, the maid, when she had sent it to be washed. The Monday after the murder, she told him, just before the inquest. At about ten o'clock on 2 July she had collected the family's dirty linen from their bedrooms. 'That of Miss Constance was generally thrown down either in the room or on the landing, some of it on Sunday, and some on Monday.' Constance's nightdress was on the landing, Cox remembered. It was not stained, she said, just lightly soiled as usual. 'It appeared to have been dirtied, as one would have been which had been worn nearly a week by Miss Constance.' Cox took the clothes to a lumber room on the first floor to sort out. Once she had done this, she asked Mary Ann and Elizabeth to enter the items in the laundry book while she packed them in the baskets for collection by Mrs Holley. She remembered packing three nightdresses – Mrs Kent's, Mary Ann's and Constance's – and she remembered Mary Ann noting them in the book. (Elizabeth wrapped her clothes in a separate bundle and listed them in a separate book.)

When Whicher questioned Cox more closely, she recalled that Constance had visited the lumber room while the laundry was being organised. The maid had already packed the clothes – 'I had it all in except the dusters' – and Mary Ann and Elizabeth had gone, leaving the laundry book. Constance 'stepped a step inside the room . . . She asked me if I would look in her slip pocket, and see if she had left her purse in it.' Cox searched the basket that contained the larger items until she found the slip. She pulled it out and checked the pocket. 'I told her the purse was not there. She then asked me if I would go down and get her a glass of water. I did so. She followed me to the top of the back stairs as I went out of the room. When I returned with the glass of water I found her where I had left her. I don't think I was gone a minute.' Constance drank the water, put the glass down and headed up to her room. Cox put the dusters in with the rest of the laundry and finished by laying a tablecloth over one basket, a dress belonging to Mrs Kent over the other.

At eleven o'clock, Cox and Elizabeth Gough set off to testify at the Red Lion, as the coroner had requested. Cox left the lumber room unlocked, she told Whicher, knowing that Mrs Holley would be arriving to collect the baskets within the hour.

Whicher put his mind to Cox's account. 'When I am deeply perplexed,' says the narrator of the fictional *Diary of an Ex-Detective* (1859), 'it is my practice to go to bed, and lie there till I have solved my doubts and perplexities. With my eyes closed, but wide awake, and nothing to disturb me, I can work out my problems.' From the start, a detective was imagined as a solitary thinker, who needed to withdraw from the sensory world to enter the free, fantastical world of his hypotheses. By piecing together the information he had gathered, Whicher compiled a story about the nightdress.

He reckoned that Constance asked Cox to look for the purse as a way of getting her to unpack the basket, so the girl could see where her nightdress had been placed. Then, when Cox was downstairs getting the water, Constance darted back into the room, snatched up her nightdress and hid it, perhaps beneath her skirts (the fashion for full skirts was at its peak in 1860*). Importantly, this was not the bloodied nightdress, which Whicher believed Constance had already destroyed, but a clean substitute that she had donned on Saturday. The reason for stealing it back from the basket was mathematical: if it seemed that an unstained nightdress had been lost by the laundress, the bloody one in which Constance had killed Saville would not be missed.

Whicher wrote:

> *I am of opinion that the night dress she wore when the murder was committed was afterwards burnt or concealed by her*, but still she would be apprehensive that the Police might ask her how many night dresses she had when she came from school *and to prepare for that contingency, she I believe, resorted to a very artful stratagem to make it appear that the one she was deficient of was lost by the washerwoman, the week after the murder, which I suspect she carried out in the following manner.*
>
> *The family soiled linen was collected as usual the Monday (two days) after the murder and amongst it was a night dress*

* That month, according to the *News of the World*, a worker at a crinoline steel factory in Sheffield was killed by her crinoline when it caught in the revolving shaft of a machine and pulled her to her death.

belonging to Miss Constance, the one I assume she put on after the murder. After the linen was collected it was taken into a spare room on the first floor where it was counted by the House Maid and entered into the Washing Book by the elder sister. It was then placed in two clothes baskets by the Housemaid but just before she quitted the room Miss Constance came in *and asked her to unpack the baskets . . . to see if she had left her purse in her slip pocket . . .* this I believe was part of her stratagem to ascertain *which basket her night dress was in*, as she immediately asked the Housemaid to go down stairs and fetch her a glass of water, *which she did, leaving her by the room door, where she found her on her return with the water*, and during this time I am of opinion she obtained possession of the night dress *which had then been entered in the washing book and took it again into use which at the end of the week when the washing came home she calculated it would be missed, and the Laundress blamed, and that would account for her* being one short if interrogated on that point.

To conceal the destruction of the evidence, Whicher believed, Constance engineered things so that an innocent nightdress was believed lost, by someone other than herself. Her sister and the housemaid would swear that the nightdress went in the basket; also that it was not bloodstained. She directed attention away from the stained nightdress, away from the house. It was a sidestep, a concealment of murder at one remove.

As Mr Bucket says in *Bleak House*, when struck by the cleverness of a murderer: 'It is a beautiful case – a beautiful case.' Then he corrects himself, remembering that he is addressing a respectable young lady. 'When I depict it as a beautiful case, you see, miss,' he goes on, 'I mean from my point of view.'

The detective's job was to reconstruct history from tiny indicators, clues, fossils. These traces were both pathways and remnants: trails back to the tangible event in the past – in this case a murder – and tiny scraps of that event, souvenirs. Like the natural historians and archaeologists of the mid-nineteenth century, Whicher tried to find a story to bind the fragments he had found. The nightdress was his missing link, an imagined object that made sense of his other discoveries, the equivalent of the skeleton that Charles Darwin needed in order to prove that men had evolved from apes.

Dickens compared the detectives to the astronomers Leverrier and Adams, who in 1846 simultaneously and separately discovered Neptune by observing deviations in the orbit of Uranus. These scientists, said Dickens, found a new planet as mysteriously as the detectives uncovered a new form of crime. In his book about Road Hill, Stapleton also likened astronomers to detectives. 'The detective instinct, brightened by genius,' he wrote, 'marked unerringly the place of that missing planet which no eye had seen, and whose only register was found in the calculations of astronomy.' Leverrier and Adams gathered their clues from observation, but they made their discovery by deduction, by guessing at the existence of one planet through its possible influence on another. It was a work of logic and imagination, like Darwin's theory of evolution and Whicher's theory about Constance's nightdress.

'To look at a star by glances, to view it in a sidelong way,' says Dupin in 'The Murders in the rue Morgue', 'is to behold the star distinctly.'

The Wiltshire police, meanwhile, were campaigning to discredit Whicher. His theory about the murderer was opposed to theirs, and he may have made it clear that he thought the investigation had been bungled in the fortnight before he was summoned from London. His manner – at best quiet and self-sufficient, at worst dismissive – may have riled them further. Things were only made worse by the arrival of his talented young colleague Dolly Williamson.

On Wednesday, 25 July, Superintendent Wolfe and Captain Meredith went to Constance's school in Beckington and interviewed the Misses Williams and Scott, as Whicher had done a week earlier. They then briefed the *Bath Chronicle* about their visit. The teachers 'spoke in the highest terms of Constance, saying that she was a well-conducted pupil in every respect . . . and that so assiduous was she to her studies, that she became a successful competitor at the half-yearly examination, and carried off the second prize. This fact, we certainly think, precludes the possibility of her having brooded over this fearful deed, as has been hinted at in some quarters, prior to coming home for the holidays.'

Wolfe told the *Bath Chronicle* and the *Trowbridge and North Wilts Advertiser* that he had traced Constance's life since childhood and discovered no evidence of insanity, 'her infancy having been most rational'. 'The unfounded rumour, which has been so industriously circulated, to the effect that the deceased child entertained a strong antipathy to Miss Constance, is as false as it is wicked,' said the *Chronicle*.

The *Frome Times* played down the importance of William and Constance's flight to Bath, and of the madness in their mother's line. Instead, it repeated information from 'an intimate friend of the family' that Constance and Saville were on very good terms, 'as may be proved by the fact that on the very day before his sad death he presented her with a bead ring, which he had made for her'. The *Bristol Post* repeated the theory that the true murderer was framing the 'frolicsome, mischievous' Constance.

Several newspapers voiced scepticism about the case against Constance. 'The new episode in the history of the case we regard as tentative only,' said the *Bath Chronicle* on Thursday, 'and upon a consideration of it, we are by no means inclined to declare the enquiry materially advanced'. There was 'not a tittle' of new evidence. The *Manchester Examiner* was similarly unconvinced: 'This step savours of a disposition on the part of a

London detective to incriminate somebody as a salve to public opinion'.

On Wednesday a Mr Knight Watson of Victoria Street, a new thoroughfare that cut through Pimlico, called at Scotland Yard and asked to speak to a detective. He knew a woman called Harriet, he said, who had previously worked for the Kents and who might be able to provide Whicher with useful information about the family. Detective-Sergeant Richard Tanner volunteered to interview the woman, now a housemaid in Gloucester Terrace, near Paddington. Dick Tanner had worked regularly with Whicher since joining the division in 1857. Commissioner Mayne gave him the go-ahead.

The next day Tanner wrote a report for Whicher on his meeting with Harriet Gollop. She had worked for the Kents as housemaid and parlourmaid for four months in 1850, he said, when they lived in Walton-in-Gordano, Somersetshire.

> *At that time the first 'Mrs Kent' was alive but during her service there 'Mrs Kent' never slept with 'Mr Kent' she always occupied separate sleeping apartments, and during the whole of her (Harriet Gollop's) time there, 'Mrs Kent' appeared very unhappy and miserable. At that time a 'Miss Pratt' was the governess in the family and her bedroom was close to that of 'Mr Kent' and also the servants in the establishment believed that an improper intimacy was going on between her and 'Mr Kent' and the wife thought so also. The Miss Pratt alluded to is now 'Mrs Kent' the mother of the child that has been murdered.*

Gollop claimed that Miss Pratt had 'the entire control of all the children and that "Mr Kent" gave directions to all the servants to consider "Miss Pratt" as their mistress'. The former housemaid had evidently disliked this arrangement. '"Harriet Gollop" says that the first "Mrs Kent" was a very ladylike person and she considered her perfectly sane.'

Whicher saw the letter on Friday morning. Gollop's evidence gave substance to the rumour that Samuel Kent and Mary Pratt were lovers while the first Mrs Kent was alive, and it painted a dark picture of life in the Kent household. But Whicher could make no use of it. The maid's recollections weakened the case against Constance – if the first Mrs Kent was sane, her daughter was less likely to be mad – and they might lend credence to the idea that Samuel, as a confirmed adulterer, had killed his son after being surprised in bed with Gough.

In the mid-Victorian home, servants were often feared as outsiders who might be spies or seducers, even aggressors. The Kent household, with its high turnover of domestic staff, had seen plenty of dangerous servants. There were Emma Sparks and Harriet Gollop, who acted as informants on the family's sex lives and peccadilloes. There were two that Samuel Kent summoned up as possible suspects: a cook whom he had got imprisoned, and a nursemaid he had sacked without pay because she had been in the habit of pinching the children. Both, it emerged, had been at least twenty miles from Road on the night of the murder.

Samuel claimed that a servant had left Road Hill House early in 1860 swearing revenge on Mrs Kent and her 'horrid children', particularly Saville. The boy had probably told on her: perhaps she was the pincher, or perhaps she was the nursemaid whom Samuel had banned from consorting with her sweetheart in the cottages next to the house. 'She had left in a dreadful rage,' said Samuel. 'She had been excessively insolent.' And deep in the family there was the former servant who had transformed herself into the mistress of the house, the governess who had ensnared the master, coaxed him into betraying his first wife and neglecting his first children.

Female servants could corrupt children as well as their parents. In *Governess Life: Its Trials, Duties, and Encouragements*, a manual of 1849, Mary Maurice warned that 'frightful instances have been discovered in which she, to whom the care of the young has been entrusted, instead of guarding their minds in innocence and purity, has become their corrupter – she has been the first to lead and to initiate into sin, to suggest and carry on intrigues, and finally to be the instrument of destroying the peace of families'. Forbes Benignus Winslow, an eminent alienist, in 1860 described such women as 'sources of moral contamination and mental deterioration from which the most vigilant parents are not always able to guard their children'.

The prevailing theory about Saville's murder also cast a servant as the serpent in the house. Elizabeth Gough, by this account, lured the father into a betrayal so complete that it ended in his killing his son. In the newspapers, the gap-toothed Gough became an object of sexual fantasy. The reporter for the *Western Daily Press* found her appearance 'decidedly pleasing, and altogether superior to her station in life'. The *Sherborne Journal* described her as an 'exceedingly good-looking' young woman, who at night 'lay . . . on a French bedstead without curtains, near the door of the bedroom'. She was dangerously embedded in the family, a step away from the master's quarters.

The detective was another member of the working classes whose pernicious imaginings could sully a middle-class home. Usually, as with the case of Sarah Drake and her dead boy, his investigations were confined to the servants' quarters. Occasionally, as at Road, he ventured upstairs. An article in *Household Words* in 1859 attributed the weaknesses in the police force to the origins of its officers: 'It is never a wise or safe proceeding to put arbitrary authority or power in the hands of the lower-classes.'

The second week of Whicher's investigation had yielded no new evidence at all – only a new idea: a thought about a nightdress.

CHAPTER ELEVEN

WHAT GAMES GOES ON

27–30 July

At eleven o'clock on the morning of Friday, 27 July the magistrates convened at the Temperance Hall for the examination of Constance Kent. Their task was to judge whether she should be sent for trial at a higher court. Twenty-four members of the press were waiting outside. Before the court rose, Whicher spoke in private to Samuel Kent. He told him that he believed him innocent, and was prepared to make a statement to that effect. Kent declined the offer – 'for prudential reasons', said his solicitor. The nuances of the relationships between father, daughter and detective were delicate; it might harm Samuel to seem in league with Constance's accuser.

There were other signs that Whicher was less than sure of succeeding in his case against Constance. That morning he paid a band of workmen to dismantle the water closet in which Saville had been found, and to scour the cesspool and drain. This was a last-ditch attempt to find the missing nightgown or the knife. The search was unsuccessful. Whicher gave the men *6s.6d.*, with an extra shilling for refreshments.

Constance arrived in Road at 11.30, escorted by the governor of Devizes gaol. After a brief delay to the start of the proceedings, during which she waited in the house of Charles Stokes, the saddler, she approached the hall. 'She was dressed as before,' reported *The Times*, 'in deep mourning, but wore a thick veil, which screened her countenance from the eager gaze of the majority of the spectators assembled outside.' The veil was understood as a sign of modesty and decorum. For a woman to hide herself, and her family's privacies, was not sinister but seemly. Yet it was also tantalising. In a novel of 1860, *A Skeleton in Every House*, Waters wrote of 'the dark secrets that palpitate and writhe beneath the flimsy veils'.

'On being brought into the hall,' continued *The Times*, 'Miss Constance Kent fell into her father's arms, and kissed him. She then took the seat which had been provided for her, and burst into tears.' The *Somerset and Wilts Journal* had her quivering into the courtroom: she entered 'walking with a faltering step, and going up to her father, gave him a trembling kiss'.

In contrast to her frailty, the crowd was strong and keen. The hall was 'instantly filled', said *The Times*. The spectators 'came in with a tremendous rush, occupying every available inch', said the *Journal*. Only half would fit; the rest thronged outside, awaiting news. Three rows of reporters stretched across the room. Their full, verbatim transcripts of the hearing were to be published all over England the next day.

The magistrates sat on their platform, alongside Detectives Whicher and Williamson, Captain Meredith, Superintendent Wolfe and Henry Clark, the magistrates' clerk. It would fall to Clark to examine Constance on behalf of the Bench.

At a table in front of the platform sat Samuel Kent and his solicitor, William Dunn of Frome, and in front of them the barrister hired to defend Constance: Peter Edlin, of Clifton, Bristol. He had a 'glaring eye, distinct utterance, and somewhat cadaverous expression of countenance', reported the *Somerset and Wilts Journal*.

Constance bent her head forward, and did not move or speak. She sat through the day frozen and bowed. 'The events of the past month had evidently told severely upon her,' said the *Somerset and Wilts Journal*, 'for in her thin pale face we should scarcely have recognised the robust, deeply complexioned girl of five weeks ago. The same singularly forbidding cast of countenance, however, characterised her features.'

Samuel rested his chin on his hand and stared ahead. He seemed 'much depressed', according to the *Bath Express*, 'his countenance bearing unmistakeable indications of deep grief . . . Next to the prisoner, himself and Mr Whicher divided the attention of the public.' Not one of these three had a formal part to play in the day's proceedings – they were there to watch and be watched. The law specifically excluded Constance, as the accused, from testifying.

Elizabeth Gough was called first, and the magistrates resumed their examination of the previous Friday. 'She appeared considerably emaciated,' according to the *Somerset and Wilts Journal*. This paper's reporter seemed to see the female suspects in the case diminishing before his eyes, as if slowly consumed by the public's hunger for the sight of them.

Clark asked Gough about the blanket. 'I did not miss the blanket from the little boy's cot until it was brought in with the body,' she said.

Edlin asked the nursemaid about the relationship between his client and her young half-brother. 'I have never heard Constance say anything unkind to Saville,' Gough said. 'I have never seen her conduct herself otherwise than kindly towards him.' She was unable to confirm that Saville had given Constance a bead ring on the day he died, or that Constance had given Saville a picture.

William Nutt was recalled. Edlin asked him about his 'prediction' that Saville would be found dead, and Nutt repeated the evidence he had given at the inquest: he had only meant that he feared the worst.

Constance's schoolfriend Emma Moody was then examined.

'Have you ever heard the prisoner make use of any expression of ill-feeling towards the deceased?' asked Henry Clark.

'She disliked it through jealousy,' said Emma.

At this Edlin jumped in: 'That is not an answer to the question. What did the prisoner say?'

Emma repeated some of what she had told Whicher: that Constance admitted to teasing and pinching Saville and Eveline, that she was not looking forward to going home for the holidays, that she felt her parents favoured the younger children.

Clark asked if she remembered Constance saying anything else about Saville. Though Emma had told Whicher that she had once reproved Constance for claiming that she hated her half-brother, the girl made no reference to it now. 'I do not remember any other conversation with her about the deceased child. I have only heard her slightly refer to him.'

'Have you ever heard her say anything more with regard to her deceased brother?' urged Clark, but Edlin intervened.

'I submit that this is wrong; the examination is most unusual and improper . . . It seems to me to be a most unusual and unprecedented line of examination.'

'I have only endeavoured to elicit facts,' Clark protested.

'I give you credit for a sincere desire to do your duty,' replied Edlin, 'but in your desire to discharge it, you have unintentionally very far exceeded it.'

Now Henry Ludlow interrupted to defend his clerk. 'Perhaps you will say in what way. That is rather a strong expression.'

'I most courteously express it,' said Edlin. 'I think Mr Clark has exceeded his duty; he seems to have misconceived it. He has a school-fellow of the prisoner's before him, and instead of confining himself to questions, and being satisfied with the answers, he has pursued the examination rather after the method of a cross-examination, and not in the manner examinations in chief are generally conducted, still less in a case of this important nature.' Applause broke out in the hall, which Ludlow angrily hushed.

'If another demonstration of that kind is made,' he warned, 'the magistrates will order the court to be cleared.' He turned to Edlin. 'Perhaps you will make some specific objection, Mr Edlin, instead of advancing those of a general nature.'

Clark added: 'If we get a witness that does not understand what you ask, I do not know how you are to get at the evidence, unless you ask the question again.'

'But after you have got an answer,' said Edlin, 'you must not repeat the question after the manner of a cross-examination.'

'I have been putting questions according to the rule of evidence,' said Clark, 'and if I do not get an answer, I must put the question again.'

'Then you have asked it again and again, and therefore your business is at an end.'

Clark addressed Emma. 'Have you heard the prisoner say anything with regard to her deceased brother?'

'This question has been put again and again,' said Edlin, 'and it has been answered in the negative, so there is an end of it.' Edlin was doing just what he accused Clark of doing: using repetition as a means of intimidation.

Ludlow took over from the clerk. 'We wish you to state what actually took place,' he told Emma, 'any conversation between you and the prisoner – not hearsay evidence. We do not wish to bring out anything not strictly legal and right. Perhaps you were never in a court of justice before, certainly never on so solemn an occasion; now I ask you if ever any conversation took place between you and the prisoner at the school with regard to her feelings towards the deceased.'

'I do not remember anything more.'

In his cross-examination, Edlin asked detailed questions about Whicher's visits to Warminster. 'He called once at our house,' said Emma, 'and another time at Mr Baily's, a private gentleman; he is a married gentleman. I know him; he lives exactly opposite. Mrs Baily, seeing me in my mother's garden, sent for me, and I went and saw Mr Whicher, I was not surprised at seeing him there because Mrs Baily had taken an interest in the matter, and asked me about it.' She testified that Whicher had shown her a breast flannel.

Edlin's line of questioning cast Whicher as sneaky and insinuating – to elicit evidence from Emma Moody, he implied, Whicher stalked her, sent a decoy from a house across the road to reel her in, showed her a piece of female underwear, coaxed her to work up her recollections into a damnation of her schoolfriend.

In the course of this, Whicher interrupted to address Emma directly: 'And I impressed upon you the importance of telling the truth and nothing but the truth.' He hoped, with this prompt, to encourage her to give the testimony he wanted.

Edlin tried to defuse the appeal. 'We take it for granted,' he said to Whicher.

'I would rather have it from the prisoner,' said Whicher. (Emma was not a prisoner but a witness – Whicher's slip reflected his frustration with the girl.)

Emma agreed that Whicher had admonished her to tell the truth.

Ludlow once more asked her if she recalled any other conversation with Constance about Saville. She said not.

'The question has been asked again and again,' said Edlin, again.

'Have you remonstrated with the prisoner respecting any conversation you have had with her?' asked Ludlow.

'Yes, sir,' said Emma, at last approaching the conversation she had reported to Whicher. But Edlin instantly objected. The Bench should not be putting such questions, he said; in the interests of humanity he appealed to them to let Emma go.

After a private consultation with Edlin, the magistrates agreed to dismiss Emma Moody.

Joshua Parsons gave his evidence about the post-mortem, which followed what he had reported at the inquest. 'I knew the poor little fellow that was killed, very well,' he added. The doctor testified that he had seen a very clean nightdress on Constance's bed on the morning of the murder. In reply to Edlin, he acknowledged that 'it *might* have been worn a week or nearly so', and that 'very great force' would have been needed to inflict the stab at Saville's heart. He was not asked for his views on whether Constance was a maniac.

When Henry Clark questioned Louisa Hatherill, Constance's other schoolfriend, she repeated what Constance had told her about the partiality shown to the new family and the slights to William.

Sarah Cox gave evidence about the missing nightdress: she described how Constance had visited the room in which she was packing the laundry on the Monday after the murder, and the furore in the household when the nightdress was found to be missing. Yet Clark failed to bring out Whicher's theory about how Constance had stolen back an innocent nightdress in order to conceal the destruction of the guilty one.

Cox showed no hostility or suspicion towards Constance. 'I observed nothing unusual in the prisoner's manner or behaviour after the murder, except ordinary grief,' she testified. 'I have never seen or heard from her anything unkind or unsisterly in her conduct to the deceased.'

Mrs Holley was the last witness. She was questioned about the missing nightdress. In the five years that she had been washing the Kents' clothes, she said, only two things had gone missing before: 'one an old duster, the other an old towel'.

Edlin began his closing speech by asking the magistrates instantly to liberate Constance Kent. 'There is not one tittle of evidence against this young lady.' With extraordinary nerve, he equated the investigation of the crime with the crime itself: 'I say that an atrocious murder has been committed, but I am afraid that it has been followed by a judicial murder of a scarcely less atrocious character.'

'It will never, never be forgotten,' he continued, 'that this young lady has been dragged from her home and sent like a common felon – a common vagrant – to Devizes gaol. I say, therefore, that this step ought to have been taken only after the most mature consideration and after something like tangible evidence, and not upon the fact that a paltry bedgown was missing – as to which Inspector Whicher knew that it was in the house, and that Mr Foley examined it with the medical man the day after the murder, together with the young lady's drawers.' Edlin was drawing attention to the many men who had rummaged in Constance's underwear. Deliberately or not, he misunderstood Whicher's theory about how the nightgown's destruction had been disguised. If the nightgown was unstained, Edlin asked, what object could there be in removing it? He insisted that the fact of the missing nightgown 'had been cleared up to the satisfaction of everyone who had heard the evidence that day, and no doubt could remain that this little peg, upon which this fearful charge had been grounded, had fallen to the ground'.

'I say that to drag this young lady from her home in such a way and at such a time, when her heart was already harrowed by the death of her dear little brother, is quite sufficient to excite in her favour the sympathy of every man in the county, and not only that, but every man in this land of unbiased mind, who has heard – and there are few who have not heard – of this horrible murder.'

At this point both Samuel and Constance Kent succumbed to tears, and hid their faces in their hands. Edlin continued:

'The steps you have taken will be such as to ruin her for life – every hope is gone with regard to this young girl . . . And where is the evidence? The one fact – and I am ashamed in this land of liberty and justice to refer to it – is the *suspicion* of Mr Whicher, a man eager in the pursuit of the murderer, and anxious for the reward that has been offered . . . I do not mean to find fault with Mr Whicher unnecessarily; but I think in the present instance, his professional eagerness in the pursuit of the criminal has led him to take a most unprecedented course to prove a motive; and I cannot help alluding to the meanness – I say the indelible meanness, I may say the discredit, and I was about to say the disgrace, but I do not wish to say anything that shall leave an unfavourable impression hereafter; – but I will say the ineffable discredit with which he has hunted up two school-fellows and brought them here to give the evidence we had heard. Let the responsibility and disgrace of such a proceeding rest upon those who have brought the witnesses here! . . . It seems to me that he has allowed himself to be strangely led away in this matter. He was baffled, and annoyed by not finding a clue, and he has caught at that which was no clue at all.'

The barrister concluded: 'A more unjust, a more improper, a more improbable case, having regard to the facts elicited in evidence, was never brought before any court of justice in any place, as far as I know, upon a charge of this serious nature, and seeking, as it does, to fix that charge upon a young lady in the position of life of Miss Constance Kent.'

Edlin's speech was much interrupted by applause from the audience. He ended shortly before 7 p.m. The magistrates conferred, and when the spectators were let back into the hall Ludlow announced that Constance was free to go, on condition that her father put up £200, as a guarantee that she would appear in court again if required.

Constance left the Temperance Hall, escorted by William Dunn. The crowd outside fell back to let them pass.

When Constance reached Road Hill House, reported the *Western Daily Press*, 'her sisters and parents clasped her in the most passionate and exciting manner, embracing her most tenderly, and the sobbing and weeping and embraces were continued for a considerable time. At length, however, it subsided, and since then the young lady has presented a very subdued and contemplative demeanour.' She resumed her silence.

By any standards, Whicher's case had been weak. There were several practical reasons for his failure: he was called to the murder scene late, was thwarted by incompetent and defensive local police officers, was hurried into making an arrest, and was poorly represented in court – as he stressed in his report to Mayne, '*there was no professional man to conduct the case for the prosecution*'. Samuel Kent, who in normal circumstances would have been expected to arrange the prosecution of the suspected murderer of his son, was hardly going to fund an attack on his daughter. Whicher felt sure that a professional lawyer could have better explained the theory of the missing nightdress, and persuaded Emma Moody to repeat what she had told him about Constance's dislike of Saville; these two things might have made all the difference. The magistrates did not need to decide on Constance's guilt, after all, but only whether there was enough evidence to justify sending her for trial.

What finally swung things against Whicher that day was Edlin's speech, his depiction of the detective as vulgar, greedy, rapacious in his destruction of a young woman's life. There was a sexual undertone, a suggestion that the policeman was a clumsy, lower-class despoiler of a virginal innocent. The public were drawn to Edlin's analysis. Though the villagers of Road had been ready to believe that Samuel Kent's strange, unhappy adolescent children had killed their little brother, most Englishmen and women dismissed the idea as grotesque. It was almost inconceivable that a respectable girl could be possessed of enough fury and emotion to kill, and enough cool to cover it. The public preferred to believe in the detective's villainy, to attribute the moral pollution to him.

Jack Whicher's investigation had let light into the closed-up house, thrown the windows open to the air; but in doing so it had exposed the family to the prurient imaginings of the outside world. There was a necessary grubbiness to the police procedures: breasts were measured, nightclothes examined for marks of sweat and blood, indelicate questions asked of nice young ladies. In *Bleak House*, Dickens imagines the feelings of Sir Leicester Dedlock when his house is searched: 'the noble house, the pictures of his forefathers, strangers defacing them, officers of police coarsely handling his most precious heirlooms, thousands of fingers pointing at him, thousands of faces sneering at him'. While the crime fiction of the 1830s and 1840s had inhabited the rookeries of London, sensational crime in the 1850s had begun to invade the middle-class home, in fiction and in fact. 'Very strange things comes to our knowledge in families,' says Bucket. 'Aye, and even in gen-teel families, in high families, in great families . . . you have no idea . . . what games goes on.'

During Whicher's inquiries the *Frome Times* made 'an indignant protest against the conduct of some of the representatives of the press. We have been informed on reliable authority that one person penetrated into the house in the guise of a detective, – while another had the audacity to force himself into the presence of Mr Kent, and to ask of him the particulars of the murder of his son! In our opinion, this person's audacity and hard-heartedness can scarcely be equalled by the villain who perpetrated the dreadful crime.' This rhetoric, also deployed by Edlin, was made possible by the mid-Victorian sensitivity to 'exposure', to scandal and loss of privacy. The inquiries into a middle-class home, by the press and above all by the detectives, were felt as a series of assaults. Exposure could destroy, as murder made clear – when the lungs, airways, arteries, heart were suddenly opened to the air, they collapsed. Stapleton described Saville's death in these terms: the inhabitant of the 'house of life' had been 'rudely driven out by an unauthorised and violent intruder'.

The word 'detect' stemmed from the Latin '*de-tegere*' or 'unroof', and the original figure of the detective was the lame devil

Asmodeus, 'the prince of demons', who took the roofs off houses to spy on the lives inside. 'The Devil Asmodeus is the Devil of Observation', explained the French novelist Jules Janin. In his book about the Road Hill murder, Stapleton used the figure of Asmodeus, 'peering into the privacies' of the Kent family house, to embody the public fascination with the case.

'If every room of a house were seen into by a secret watcher,' wrote the Scottish detective McLevy in 1861, 'it would be a show-box even more wonderful than a travelling exhibition.' A plain-clothes police officer was just such a secret watcher, a man licensed to pry. The detective hero might at any moment turn to reveal his grinning double, the voyeur.

'Angel and devil by turns, eh?' remarks Mr Bucket.

After Constance was bailed, Whicher told Ludlow that he saw no point in remaining in Wiltshire. 'I did not see any hope of getting further evidence by prolonging my stay,' he said in his report, 'as the only piece of further evidence would be to find the night dress which I feared was destroyed.' Ludlow agreed that he should go. He assured Whicher that he was convinced of Constance's guilt, and would send letters to that effect to Sir George Cornewall Lewis, the Home Secretary, and to Mayne. Henry Clark composed the letters at once: 'We are requested by the magistrates . . . to convey to you their thanks for the services of Mr Inspector Whicher and Mr Sgt Williamson. Although the evidence failed in establishing the guilt of the person arrested yet the magistrates are fully impressed with the idea that Miss Constance Kent is the guilty party and hope that evidence may yet be forthcoming to bring the perpetrator of the crime to justice. They are thoroughly satisfied with the exertions made by the officers above mentioned.'

Whicher and Williamson returned to London the next day. Whicher took with him the relics of his investigation: Constance's two remaining nightdresses, her list of linen, the bloodied piece of newspaper. In the new edition of *All the Year Round*, the hero of *The Woman in White* also finished his inquiries in the country. The episode ended: 'Half an hour later I was speeding back to London by the express train.'

That weekend there were severe thunderstorms around Road. Lightning lit the fields, the river Frome rose almost three feet, and hail thrashed down the corn.

During the proceedings in the Temperance Hall, Mrs Kent had gone into labour. 'The agitation and suspense of awaiting the result of the re-examination proved too great for her,' reported the *Bath Chronicle*, 'and the consequence was, premature labour set in.' It was rumoured that the baby was stillborn, but this proved false. Mrs Kent gave birth to a boy on Monday, 30 July, a month after her first son's murder, and named him Acland Saville Kent.

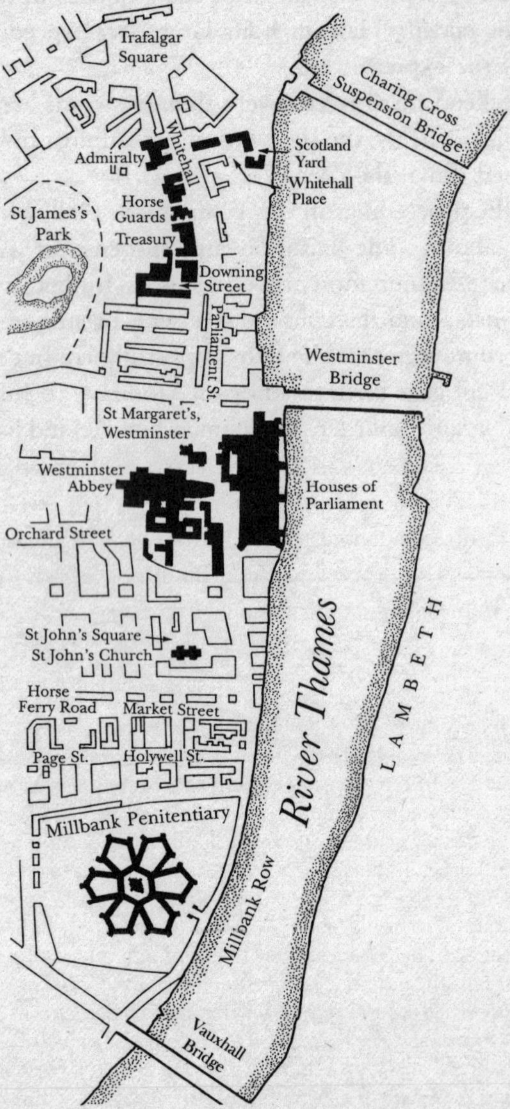
Trafalgar Square
Charing Cross Suspension Bridge
Whitehall
Admiralty
Scotland Yard
Whitehall Place
Horse Guards
St James's Park
Treasury
Downing Street
Parliament St.
Westminster Bridge
St Margaret's, Westminster
Westminster Abbey
Houses of Parliament
Orchard Street
St John's Square
St John's Church
Horse Ferry Road
Market Street
Page St.
Holywell St.
River Thames
LAMBETH
Millbank Penitentiary
Millbank Row
Vauxhall Bridge

CHAPTER TWELVE

DETECTIVE-FEVER

London, July–August 1860

Whicher reached Paddington station in the afternoon of Saturday, 28 July, and hailed a cab to take him and his luggage to Pimlico – probably to 31 Holywell Street, off Millbank Row. This was the house in which his niece, Sarah Whicher, an unmarried housekeeper of thirty, rented a room, and it was the address he gave as his own three years later.* In the 1850s, his

* Though his name did not appear on the census of 1861, there are indications that Whicher was living in this house by 1860. In a police circular of 1858 he asked fellow officers to inform him, at Scotland Yard, if they saw a twenty-four-year-old gentleman who had gone missing, 'mind supposed affected'; two weeks afterwards a private advertisement appeared in *The Times* requesting news of this same young man, with his 'rather pale full face', and offering a £10 reward – it was presumably placed by Whicher, but it asked that information be passed to 'Mr Wilson' of 31 Holywell Street. The pseudonym concealed the fact that the police were looking for the wan gentleman. 'The tricks of detective police officers are infinite,' observes the narrator of *The Female Detective*. 'I am afraid many a kindly-disposed advertisement hides the hoof of detection.' A year later, in 1859, the Commissioner's office put out a request for information about a white, wolf-breed dog that had gone missing from 31 Holywell Street. A lost dog was not usually a matter for Scotland Yard – maybe the white wolfhound belonged to Whicher's landlady (Charlotte Piper, a widow of forty-eight with a private income) or to the detective himself.

friend and colleague Charley Field lived at number 27, with his wife and mother-in-law, while Whicher's niece Mary Ann worked as a servant to a family of upholsterers at number 40.

The district was changing swiftly. To the west, Victoria railway station was almost complete, and to the north Sir Charles Barry's gothic Palace of Westminster was also nearly finished – the 'Big Ben' clock had been put in place a year before, though as yet it had only one hand and no chime. On the new Westminster bridge thirteen limelight lamps had been installed that summer: these were powered by a series of tiny explosions of oxygen and hydrogen that made the sticks of lime so hot that they burnt white, giving off a brilliant incandescence. Dickens visited Millbank one warm day in January 1861, and headed west along the river: 'I walked straight on *for three miles* on a splendid broad esplanade overhanging the Thames, with immense factories, railway work, and what not, erected on it, and with the strangest beginnings and ends of wealthy streets pushing themselves into the very Thames. When I was a rower on that river it was all broken ground and ditch, with here and there a public house or two, an old mill, and a tall chimney. I had never seen it in any state of transition, though I suppose myself to know this rather large city as well as anyone in it.'

The part of Millbank in which Whicher lived was a noisy, industrial riverside neighbourhood of mean yellow terraces, dominated by the great six-pronged flower of Millbank prison. The novelist Anthony Trollope described the area as 'extremely dull, and one might almost say, ugly'. Holywell Street was separated from the prison's boundary wall only by gasometers, a sawmill and a marble works. Number 31 backed onto these, and faced a huge brewery and a burial ground. Broadwood's piano factory lay a block north, and Seager's gin distillery a block south. Just beyond the distillery, coal barges were moored at the wharfs, while on the far side of the river lay the vast potteries and putrid bone-grinding factories of Lambeth. Paddle steamers carried

Londoners to and from work, churning up the sewage poured into the Thames – the air was thick with the stench rising off the river.

On Monday, 30 July, Jack Whicher went to his office at Scotland Yard, just over a mile north of Holywell Street, along the Thames past the noxious slums of the 'Devil's Acre' and then the high buildings of Westminster and Whitehall. The public entrance to the police headquarters was in Great Scotland Yard, though its address was 4 Whitehall Place. There was a large clock on the wall that looked over the yard, a weathervane on the roof, and fifty rooms within. These had housed the Metropolitan Police administration since 1829, and the detective force (in three small chambers) since its formation in 1842. The boarding house that Dolly Williamson shared with other single officers stood in a corner of Great Scotland Yard, behind Groves the fishmongers. In another corner was a public house, outside which a drunken old woman sold pigs' trotters on Saturday nights. To the north of the yard was Trafalgar Square, and to the south the river.

Sir Richard Mayne, whose office was also in Scotland Yard, rated Whicher above all other policemen: in the late 1850s 'every important case was placed in his hands by Sir Richard', reported Tim Cavanagh in his memoirs. Commissioner Mayne, now sixty-six, 'was about five feet eight inches, spare, but well-built', wrote Cavanagh; he had a 'thin face, a very hard compressed mouth, grey hair and whiskers, an eye like that of a hawk, and a slightly limping gait, due, I believe, to rheumatic affection of the hip-joint'. He was 'respected but feared by all in the service'. When Whicher and Williamson got back to work, Mayne duly signed their expenses, including claims for extra pay for being out of town (eleven shillings a day for an inspector, six shillings for a sergeant). The Commissioner passed Whicher a slew of letters from members of the public proposing solutions to the Road Hill case. The letters, addressed to Mayne or the Home Secretary, kept coming throughout the month.

'I beg to offer you an idea which suggested itself to me and which might tend to unravel the mystery,' wrote a Mr Farrer. 'I send it to you in perfect confidence, and hope you will keep my name as its author, a strict secret . . . That Eliz Gough the Nurse may have had William Nutt passing the night with her, and the child (FS Kent) waking up, and fearing he might alarm his parents by crying out, they strangled him, and whilst Nutt conveyed the body to the closet she remade the bed.' Mr Farrer added a postscript: 'As Willm Nutt is connected by marriage with the Laundress' family he may have been enabled to abstract the night dress so as to throw suspicion on another party.'

The theory that Nutt and Gough had killed the boy was, overwhelmingly, the most popular. A writer who thought Constance 'most cruelly used and made a scapegoat' argued that the medical evidence indicated a knife with a '*skew*point' had been used in the murder – 'very likely a shoemakers knife *very much used*'. Nutt was a shoemaker. '*The throat was cut from one ear to the other dividing it all down to the spine*, this is more indicative of the power and determination of a man than a nervous girl of 16,' and, 'Shoemakers often have *two* knives and *one* might be *down the Closet*.' A correspondent from Mile End took a similar view, as did the chaplain of the Bath Union Workhouse, Bath, the master of the workhouse in Axbridge, Somersetshire, Mr Minot of Southwark and a Mr Dalton, writing from a hotel in Manchester. A tailor from Cheshire wanted Gough 'put under strickt servilance'.

A curate from Lancashire, himself a magistrate, gave the fullest account of the theory:

> *Though the suspicions I am about to mention have frequently from the commencement of the enquiry been broached in my own family, yet I should have thought it unfair to give them wider range had not the public press (the* Morning Post*) hinted at the individual named – I mean in the matter of the Kent murder.*

Is it not possible that the nursemaid may have had a paramour either in the house or so well acquainted with the premises that he could gain ready access in the night . . . Of course, from what we have heard one's thoughts fall at once on Nutt . . . If he be an admirer of the girl, should not medical examination establish whether she was likely to have received nightly visits or not? He had all means at command – knives &c – he had the night to work in. He is a connection of the laundress and if the laundress knew of anything going on between these two a suspicion flashed for a moment upon her mind, especially as he had found the body so easily – may she not have been the one to conceal the night-dress and so immediately changed the direction of anything which might then exist in the form of suspicion and fasten it upon that eccentric Miss Kent who sometime ago had run away in man's attire. All these are of course mere suspicions – but when all seems so wide of the mark so far – it leads one to think that the persons employed have gone to work with an a priori view of the case, and rejected or at any rate neglected what did not tell in favour of their own suspicions . . . having had a little experience on the Bench in rather a wild district I have learned to study people's possible motives more than I should otherwise have done.

In early August Sir George Cornewall Lewis, the Home Secretary, received two letters identifying Elizabeth Gough and a lover as the murderers. One was from a Guildford barrister, who wrote patronisingly of Whicher's efforts: 'A policeman may be a good hand at discovering a *criminal*: but it requires intellect and a mind enlarged by observation to detect a *crime* and unravel a mystery.' The other letter was from Sir John Eardley Wilmot of Bath, a baronet and former barrister, who took such a passionate interest in the case that he persuaded Samuel Kent to let him visit Road Hill House and interview a few of the inmates. Horatio Waddington, the formidable Permanent Under-Secretary of State at the Home Office, forwarded the letters to Mayne. 'This is now the favourite theory,' Waddington wrote on one of the envelopes, in a spiky hand. 'I should like to hear Inspector Whicher's remarks upon these two letters, surely if the girl had a lover, somebody must have known or at least suspected it.' Once Whicher had complied, with a report outlining his counter-arguments ('I fear that Sir John has not gone sufficiently into the facts . . .'), Waddington agreed: 'I rather incline to the opinion of the police man.'

When Eardley Wilmot sent another letter, this time suggesting that Gough had a soldier boyfriend, Waddington wrote on the envelope: 'I never heard of this *soldier* before. I don't know where he picked him up.' The Permanent Under-Secretary scratched his comments on the ensuing stream of letters from the baronet: 'A strange infatuation as it seems to me'; 'This Gentleman has a monomania on the subject'; and 'Does he wish to be employed as a Detective, or what?'

The letter-writers suggested a few other suspects. George Larkin of Wapping confided:

> *Sir, For three successive weeks I have had the Frome Murder in my Mind every time I wake and cannot get rid of the thought of it. That Mr Kent is the Murderer has appeared to me in the following manner and that his offering a* reward *is all a delusion (Bosh) my impression is that Mr Kent has gone to the* Nurse Maids Room *for* some Purpose, *that the child has woke and recognised its Father that the Father through Fear of an Exposure in the Family strangled it in the Room after the Nurse Maid had gone to sleep that he there carried it to the Closet and cut the Throat.*

A resident of Blandford, Dorset, wrote, '*I* firmly believe that *Mrs Kent* killed the child at Road,' while Sarah Cunningham of west London claimed that 'step by step I can trace the murderer in *the brother* of William Nutt and the son-in-law of Mrs Holly the Laundress'.

Lieutenant-Colonel Maugham wrote from Hanover Square, London,

> *With grace allow me to suggest . . . that inquiries be made as to whether chloroform was kept in the house where the child was murdered . . . if not, whether any had been purchased in the neighbourhood, or at the towns, or villages, where the children of Mr Kent's family had been at school . . . I would further suggest whether any weapon was taken from or purchased in* the neighbourhood of the schools.

In a note to Mayne, Whicher observed that Joshua Parsons had not detected any trace of chloroform in Saville's body. 'As regards the suggestion that a weapon might have been purchased in the Neighbourhood or brought from School by Miss Kent, inquiry has been made on that point already.'

On most of the letters from the public Whicher scrawled 'There is nothing in this to assist the enquiry'; occasionally he expanded, impatiently, 'all the points having been duly considered previously by me', or 'I saw all the persons alluded to while I was on the spot and am satisfied they are not connected with the murder.'

The only letter to offer information, rather than speculation, was from William Gee, of Bath: 'As to Mr Kent himself I learn from the widow of a schoolmaster a friend of mine that 4 years ago he was so straitened as not to be able to pay the Bills of the Son £15 or £20 half-yearly. I cannot reconcile his occupying so handsome a mansion (second to few in the neighborhood) with the way in which he [illegible] a poor Teacher.' Samuel's failure to pay his son's school bills suggested he was as cash-strapped as Joseph Stapleton implied; it also indicated a carelessness about William's welfare.

The letters to Scotland Yard were the fruit of a new English obsession with detection. The public was fascinated by murder, especially when it was domestic and mysterious, and was becoming engrossed by the investigation of murder, too. 'I like a good murder that can't be found out,' says Mrs Hopkinson in Emily Eden's novel *The Semi-Detached House* (1859). 'That is, of course, it is very shocking, but I like to hear about it.' The Road Hill case took the national enthusiasm for baffling crimes to a new level. In *The Moonstone*, Wilkie Collins dubbed this mania 'a detective-fever'.

While the press and the public condemned Whicher's prurient, impertinent speculations, they freely made their own. The first detective in English literature, like them, was an armchair detective: Poe's Auguste Dupin solved crimes not by searching for clues at the scene but by picking them out of newspaper reports. The time of the professional police detective had barely begun; the era of the amateur was already in full flower.

In an anonymous penny pamphlet printed in Manchester – the sixteen-page *Who Committed the Road Murder? Or, The Track of Blood Followed* – 'a Disciple of Edgar Allan Poe' poured scorn on Whicher's investigation. 'Hitherto the brilliant "Detective's" effort has been to associate that nightdress with Miss Constance Kent; to prove that her guilt is wrapped up in it! and to find out where it is. All wrong! I perceive her purity in its loss; and, in its loss, another's guilt. The thief purloined that dress to shield *herself*, by casting suspicion on *one of her own sex*.' The pamphleteer had already absorbed one tenet of detective fiction: the solution must always be labyrinthine, indirect, paradoxical. The lost nightdress must mean just the opposite of what it seemed to mean: 'I perceive her purity in its loss'.

The author wondered if the village had been searched thoroughly for bloodstained clothing, if the Road Hill House chimneys had been examined for scraps of burnt evidence, if the records of local knife-sellers had been checked. He or she used an unsettling piece of imaginative reconstruction to argue that, since Saville's throat was cut from left to right, the murderer must be left-handed: 'Draw an imaginary line on the body of a chubby child . . . An ordinary person, committing such a crime, would (in an ordinary way) place his left hand on the child's breast and cut towards him with his right hand.'

The newspapers too made their conjectures. The *Globe* blamed William Nutt, the *Frome Times* pointed at Elizabeth Gough, the *Bath Express* hinted at William Kent's guilt. The *Bath Chronicle* – in an article that provoked a libel suit – fixed on Samuel:

> *If the hypothesis that a girl had an illicit intrigue, and that the other party to that intrigue preferred murder to exposure, be well founded, we must unhappily endeavour to find some one to whom such exposure would have been ruin, or at all events would have produced a state of things so terrible to himself that in a moment of wild terror he seized the most dreadful means of avoiding it. Who is there to whom such terms would at all apply? . . . at that strange, pale hour of morning when we have all the power of thought, almost painfully vivid, but are without the same will and wise resolution which come when we arise and buckle ourselves to the duties of the day . . . A weak, bad, terrified, violent man sees a child between him and ruin – and the fearful deed is madly done.*

So far, the identity of the 'violent man' was at least partly ambiguous, but in the closing sentences of the piece the author all but named Samuel Kent:

> *A child is lost from its bed-room, not an exposed one, but upstairs, and in the penetralia of the mansion, at an hour when no visitor from outside can have approached the room, and a man, to whom that child should have been most dear, a man who should be most intense and practical in his researches after*

it, adopts the frivolous, novel-reader's idea that the child has been stolen by gipsies! Had he said that it had been flown away with by angels, the suggestion under the circumstances could not have been more ridiculous.

There was a consensus that sex was the motive for the murder – more particularly, that the catastrophe sprang from the fact that a child had witnessed a sexual transgression. In Whicher's view, Constance avenged the sexual affair between her father and her former governess by destroying the offspring of that liaison. In the popular view, it was Saville who witnessed a sexual encounter, and was killed for what he saw.

The dominant theme in the press was bewilderment. So much was known and yet so little could be concluded: the columns of coverage only amplified the mystery. 'Here our knowledge ends,' ran an editorial in the *Daily Telegraph*. 'Here our inquiries are baffled. We stumble on the threshold, and the vast vista of the crime lies all undiscovered beyond.' The story behind the murder was momentous, but hidden from view. Road Hill House may have been searched from cellar to cockloft but, symbolically, its door was shut fast.

In the absence of a solution, Saville's death became a pretext for unfettered speculation; it let loose a kind of wild imagining. There was no knowing what hidden identities might emerge at 'that strange, pale hour of morning'. The characters in the case had come to have double selves: Constance Kent and Elizabeth Gough were angels in the house, or she-devils; Samuel was the loving father, overwhelmed with grief and insult, or a ruthless, sex-crazed tyrant; Whicher was a visionary, or a vulgar fool.

An editorial in the *Morning Post* showed how suspicion still fell on just about everyone in the house, and several beyond it. Samuel or William might have killed Saville, the piece argued, or Mrs Kent might have done it, 'under one of those delusions to which women in her condition [that is, pregnancy] are sometimes liable'.

Saville could have been murdered by 'one or more of the juveniles in the family, in a passion of jealousy; or, by anyone who wished to wound the parents in the tenderest point'. The writer wondered about the antecedents of Sarah Kerslake, the knives of William Nutt, the lies of Hester Holley. His imagination took him into the dips and hollows of Road Hill House, its tenderest points. 'Have the wells been searched, the ponds, the drains, the chimnies, the trunks of trees, the soft earth in the garden?'

'Dark as the mystery is,' he wrote, 'we are persuaded it turns on the nightgown and the knife.'

Within days of reaching London, Jack Whicher and Dolly Williamson were set to work on a fresh murder case, another domestic horror show that featured nightgowns and a knife. 'No sooner do we hear of one atrocious and cruel murder being committed,' observed the *News of the World*, 'and that it is not likely to be discovered, than we are startled at finding that the impunity is causing its usual result, and murder upon murder springs up in different directions, as though it were some fearful epidemic suddenly bursting forth.' An unsolved murder seemed to be infectious. By failing to catch one killer, a detective might unleash a host of them.

On Tuesday, 31 July, the police were called to a house in Walworth, a district of south London between Camberwell and the river. The landlord and a lodger had heard a scream and a thump soon after dawn. When the local police officers reached the house, they found a short, very pale young man in a nightshirt standing over the dead bodies of his mother, his two brothers (aged eleven and six) and a woman of twenty-seven. All were dressed for bed. 'This is my mother's doing,' said the man. 'She came to the bedside where my brother and I were sleeping. She killed him with a knife and made a stab at me. In my own defence I wrenched the knife from her hand and killed her, if she is dead.' The survivor of the massacre was

William Youngman. When he was arrested on suspicion of murder, he said: 'Very well.'

Whicher and Williamson were assigned to assist Inspector Dann of the Lambeth division. Unlike Foley, Dann was an able officer, and he remained in charge of the investigation. The police soon established that Youngman had been engaged to marry the young woman, Mary Streeter, and had taken out a £100 insurance policy on her life six days before she died. Whicher found that the banns to the couple's marriage had already been published at the parish church. It emerged that Youngman had purchased the murder weapon two weeks before the killings – he claimed he had bought it to cut his bread and cheese.

There were similarities between the murders at Road and at Walworth: the composure of the chief suspects, the extreme violence towards members of the immediate family, the intimations of madness. But *The Times* found the differences were greater. The London killing had a 'repulsive literality and distinctness', it argued, appearing to accept that Youngman's motive for slaughtering his family was purely financial. 'The public mind is neither harrowed by suspense nor excited by uncertainty.' The solution was too obvious, and the crime meant nothing beyond its own ugly horror. There was nothing missing. The Road case, by contrast, posed a tantalising riddle, and its solution seemed of urgent, personal concern to many middle-class families.

The *News of the World* concurred that there was something about the Road Hill murder that 'seems to set it altogether apart, in a class by itself'. Yet the newspaper saw a disturbing connection between the various vicious murders of 1860 – all were virtually motiveless: 'you are astonished, at once, by the brutality of the crime and the smallness of the motive'. Both the Road and the Walworth killers seemed almost, but not quite, insane: their ferocity seemed disproportionate to any possible gain, and yet they had carefully planned to commit and then conceal their crimes. The newspaper remarked of the Walworth murders,

'Either, then, this crime is an outbreak of insanity, or else it is the most horrible and appalling murder that has ever been committed by human hands.'

Just over a fortnight after the investigation began, Youngman was tried at the Old Bailey. He 'appeared perfectly unconcerned', reported *The Times*, 'exhibited the most extraordinary coolness and self-possession, and . . . did not evince the least emotion'. When the jury convicted him of murder, he said, 'I am not guilty,' turned around and 'walked with a firm step out of the dock'. The suggestions that he was insane were rejected, and he was sentenced to death. As soon as Youngman reached his cell he demanded supper. He ate it with gusto. While he waited in prison for his execution a lady sent him a religious tract, on which she had underlined the passages she thought applicable to his case. 'I wish she had sent me something to eat instead,' he remarked, 'as I could do a fowl and a piece of pickled pork.'

Whicher's part in the Walworth case went almost unnoted in the press, which continued to publish indignant criticisms of his investigation at Road Hill. As he scribbled his ripostes on the letters that arrived at Scotland Yard, he had to stay silent on the public discussion of his conduct.

On 15 August, the day before Youngman's trial, Whicher was denounced in Parliament. Sir George Bowyer, the leading Roman Catholic spokesman in the Commons, complained about the quality of Britain's police inspectors, using Whicher as his example. 'The recent investigation with regard to the Road murder afforded striking proof of the unfitness of some of the present officers,' he said. 'An inspector named Whicher was sent down to inquire into the matter. Upon the slightest possible grounds, merely because one of her nightgowns happened to be missing, that officer arrested a young lady who lived in the house where the murder was committed, and assured the magistrates that he would be prepared in a few days to produce evidence which would bring home the murder to her.' He accused Whicher of acting 'in a most objectionable manner. After all his boasting of the evidence he could produce, the young lady was discharged by the magistrates.' Sir George Cornewall Lewis, the Home Secretary, mildly defended the detective, arguing that 'the officer was justified in the course he adopted'.

The national mood, though, was with Bowyer. 'We can unhesitatingly state the public feeling,' claimed the *Frome Times*. 'An officer who can play at hap-hazard with such an awful charge as that of wilful murder, and can promise that which he must have known he could not perform, cannot expect to be looked on otherwise than with distrust.' 'The Whicher theory has failed to throw any light whatever upon the thick darkness of this horrible mystery,' said the *Newcastle Daily Chronicle*. 'A new clue must be discovered before justice can thread the mazes of the labyrinth of Road.' The *Morning Star* was dismissive of the 'frivolous, gossiping, and utterly vapid school-girl testimony' upon which Whicher had relied.

The *Bath Chronicle* criticised 'the slender speculations which were loosely strung together and adduced as evidence . . . the experiment made, has been a fearfully cruel one'. In an essay in the *Cornhill Magazine*, the distinguished lawyer Sir James Fitzjames Stephen argued that the cost of trying to solve a murder – the damage wrought by the exposure, the police intrusion – was sometimes too high: 'The circumstances of the Road murder are extremely curious, because they happen to afford an illustration of the amount of this price so exact that had it been committed on purpose it could hardly have been better arranged.' Since no other culprit could be found, Whicher was blamed for the muddle and mystery of Road. The 'Disciple of Edgar Allan Poe' played on the sinister associations of his name when he noted in his pamphlet that 'Constance is recognised as innocent, though metropolitan *witchery* once jeopardised her.'

One of the most damaging charges laid against Jack Whicher was that he was driven by greed. The early detectives were often presented as glamorous rogues, only a step away from the villains they sought. The French felon-turned-detective Eugène Vidocq, whose heavily fictionalised memoirs were translated into English in 1828 and dramatised for the London stage in 1852, had breezily swapped villainy for police work when it served his financial interests.

The rewards that detectives could earn were descendants of the eighteenth-century 'blood money' paid to thief-takers or informants. In August 1860 the *Western Daily Press* scornfully alluded to Whicher's 'zeal sharpened by the offer of a handsome reward'. A letter from 'Justice' in the *Devizes and Wiltshire Gazette* compared Whicher to Jack Ketch, a notoriously clumsy seventeenth-century hangman who inflicted great suffering on his victims: Whicher was 'utterly irresponsible', wrote 'Justice', 'tempted with the vision of £200 reward, getting a young lady of 15 incarcerated in a common gaol for a week'. Like many correspondents, 'Justice' showed distaste for the working-class fellow who had meddled in middle-class affairs. The detectives were greedy and inept because they were not gentlemen. Perhaps Whicher was so vehemently condemned because he was doing in fact what the legions of new newspaper readers were doing in the mind's eye – peeping and prying, goggling and wondering at the sins and sufferings of others. The Victorians saw in the detective a picture of themselves, and in collective self-revulsion they cast him out.

A few voices were raised in Whicher's defence. The ever-loyal *Somerset and Wilts Journal* criticised Edlin's 'ingenious bamboozling', and the 'cunning trick' whereby he had distorted the theory about the nightgown. The *Daily Telegraph* agreed: 'We cannot concur with Mr Edlin in his fervid denunciations of the cruelty of arresting this young lady . . . To believe the *ad captandum* reasoning of this young lady's advocate, the important point of her garment not being forthcoming has been satisfactorily cleared up; but the contrary would seem to be the case. Where is the nightgown? . . . *Far different would it have been if a bedgown stained with blood had been discovered.* Some of our readers may remember the awful circumstance of the gory sheet in the story of Beatrice Cenci. That one link would complete a chain of evidence that would speedily change into a halter of hemp.' Beatrice Cenci was a sixteenth-century Roman noblewoman executed for killing her father; in the nineteenth century she had become something of a romantic heroine, the beautiful avenger of a violent, incestuous bully. A bloody bedsheet provided proof of her guilt. Shelley cast Beatrice as an impassioned rebel in his verse drama *The Cenci* (1819). A character in Nathaniel Hawthorne's *The Marble Faun* (1860) describes her as 'a fallen angel, fallen and yet sinless'.

The *Northern Daily Express* remarked that 'The nightdress of Constance Kent, with plain frills – the wearer not having reached the years of maturity and lace – bids fair to become as famous as the ruffs of Queen Elizabeth and Shakespere, the snuff-coloured suit of Dr Johnson, Cowper's nightcap as painted by Romney, or the striped waistcoat of Burns.'

Henry Ludlow, the chairman of the Wiltshire magistrates, continued to lend Whicher his support. 'Mr Inspector Whicher's conduct in regard to the Road Murder has been much blamed,' he wrote in a letter to Mayne. 'Mr Ludlow feels much pleasure in bearing testimony to his good judgment and ability in the case. I fully agree with Mr Whicher as to the perpetrator of that most mysterious murder . . . he was perfectly justified in acting as he did.' Perhaps Ludlow felt guilty for the part he had played in encouraging Whicher to arrest Constance. All the blame for the case had attached to the detective.

'I beg further to report,' began Whicher on Monday, 30 July, 'for the information of Sir R. Mayne in reference to the murder of "Francis Saville Kent" at Road Wilts on the night of the 29th June that the re-examination of "Constance Kent" took place at the Temperance Hall Road on Friday Last . . .'

Over sixteen pages, in a forward-thrusting hand, Whicher argued his case. He irritably discounted the various rival theories advanced by the letter-writers and the journalists. He expressed his frustrations with the local police investigation: the evidence against Constance 'would have been far more conclusive', he said, 'if the Police had ascertained as soon as they arrived, *how many night gowns she ought to have* had in her possession'. If Foley had only 'taken *the hint given*' by Parsons as to the nightdress on Constance's bed appearing very clean, and had 'interrogated her at once *as to how many* she had in her possession I believe the blood stained bed gown would have been *missed at once and possibly found*'. Constance's lawyer, Whicher complained, had 'said that the mystery respecting the missing night dress *had been cleared up*, but such is not the case, as one of her three which she brought home from school *is still missing* and I have possession for the present of the remaining two'. He suspected that a confession would come soon but 'would no doubt be made to some of the family, and then possibly not made known'.

Whicher signed but did not send the document. Shortly afterwards he scratched out his signature and continued: 'I beg further to report . . .' and wrote two more pages, expanding and clarifying his findings. And nine days after that, still unable to let the matter rest, he resumed: 'I beg to add the following remarks and explanations . . .' The report that he submitted to Mayne on 8 August – twenty-three pages in total – was strewn with inky underlinings, corrections, adjustments, insertions, asterisks, double asterisks and crossings-out.

CHAPTER THIRTEEN

A GENERAL PUTTING OF THIS AND THAT TOGETHER BY THE WRONG END

August–October 1860

In early August, with the Home Secretary's permission, the Wiltshire police exhumed Saville Kent's body. They said they hoped to find his sister's nightdress hidden inside the coffin. It was as if the police, in their frustration, could do no more than return to where they began. The officers dug up and unscrewed the box, but were faced only with Saville's corpse in its death robes. The foul gases that emanated from the coffin were so powerful that Superintendent Wolfe fell ill, and did not recover for several days.

The constables watched Road Hill House around the clock. They yet again examined the sewer that ran from the house to the river. Their chiefs briefed the local press on their tireless efforts: 'The assertion that the local police did not render Mr Whicher that assistance they should have done in investigating the circumstances of this mysterious case, is totally unfounded,' reported the *Bath Chronicle*, 'they having furnished him with all the information they had previously obtained, in addition to accompanying him on every occasion when necessary. There is no doubt that the late hasty steps taken by Inspector Whicher have, in a very great measure, impeded, if not increased, the difficulty which the County Police have to contend with in pursuing their enquiries.'

The police continued to receive letters from the public. A man in Queenstown, Ireland, informed them that Constance Kent had committed the murder; if they would send him the fare, he added, he would bring the missing nightdress to them. They turned down the offer.

At Wolverton railway station, Buckinghamshire, on Friday, 10 August – the day after Saville Kent would have turned four – a stumpy man with a round, red face approached Sergeant Roper of the North-Western Railway Police and confessed to the murder: 'It was I did it.' The man claimed to be a London bricklayer who had been promised a sovereign (about £1) if he killed the boy. He refused to identify the person who had hired him, or to give his own name – he said he did not want his mother to know where he was. He had given himself up, he said, because he could picture the murdered child walking before him wherever he went. He had been about to lay his head on the track and let a train pass over him, but he had decided to surrender himself instead.

The next morning the police took him by train to Trowbridge. The news of his arrest was sent on by telegraph, and hundreds of people lined the track from Wolverton, via Oxford and Chippenham. At one stop a man put his head into the carriage and asked which was the murderer. The bricklayer shook his clenched, handcuffed fists and confided to the policeman next to him: 'I've a good mind to give him a rattle in the guts.' When they reached Trowbridge police station the magistrates remanded the prisoner until Monday. He had 'a florid complexion', said the *Somerset and Wilts Journal*, 'and a large head, singularly flat at the crown. He complained of headache greatly, and refused any food.'

By Monday the bricklayer was protesting his innocence. He supplied an alibi for the night of 29 June – he had been at an inn in Portsmouth, he said, having a boil on his back bathed in sugar-water – and he wrote down his name for the magistrates: John

Edmund Gagg. When he was asked what had driven him to confess to a murder he had not committed, he said, 'I confessed because I was hard up, and thought it better if I could be hung. I am sick and tired of my life.' He had a history of falls, carbuncles, fits, 'an overflow of blood to the head', but was apparently sane. The strain of an unsolved murder could tell on a fragile man already under pressure. Like many, Gagg was haunted by the crime. His decision to confess took the ambition of the amateur detective to an extreme: he solved the murder by claiming it as his own.

The magistrates sent a message to Jack Whicher at Scotland Yard, asking him to track down Gagg's wife in London. Whicher notified them that she was 'a most respectable woman living by her own industry, with her mother and children'. Gagg's alibis in Portsmouth proved solid. On Wednesday, 22 August he was discharged, and the magistrates paid his train fare to Paddington.

That week Elizabeth Gough told the Kents that she wished to leave their employ. The *Somerset and Wilts Journal* explained that she had 'been subject to a most disagreeable surveillance by the household'. It was later reported by the Frome journalist Albert Groser in a letter to *The Times* that after Saville's murder the Kents had not let their little girls, Mary Amelia and Eveline, sleep in Gough's room. On Monday, 27 August she left Road Hill House with her father and returned with him to Isleworth, to join her mother, her two younger sisters and two younger brothers in the family bakery.

On 29 August the case of the Reverend Mr Bonwell, which Whicher had investigated in 1859, reached its conclusion: the Church of England defrocked Bonwell as punishment for his scandalous affair and his attempt to conceal the birth and death of his child. A week afterwards, on 5 September, more than twenty thousand Londoners gathered to see William Youngman, the Walworth murderer, executed outside Horsemonger Lane gaol. This was the largest gallows crowd since Frederick and

Maria Manning had been hanged on the same spot in 1849. On the day of his death Youngman breakfasted on cocoa, bread and butter. Outside, boys played leapfrog beneath the gallows, and the public house facing the 'drop' did a roaring trade. When Youngman fell through the trapdoor, 'quivering and twisting in the air', reported the *News of the World*, 'several persons of both sexes, who had been tippling all morning, burst out into unrestrained crying'. Just over a month had passed since the quadruple murder of Youngman's mother, brothers and sweetheart. In the final instalment of *The Woman in White*, on 25 August, Count Fosco's description of England as 'the land of domestic happiness' was unmistakably ironic.

The last of the wheat and corn was harvested with scythes in the fields around Road in September. At the beginning of the month two petitions were sent to the Home Secretary – one organised by the *Bath Express*, one by the *Somerset and Wilts Journal* – asking for a special commission to investigate the Road murder. Sir George Cornewall Lewis, the Home Secretary, turned down these pleas, but at the suggestion of the Wiltshire magistrates he quietly appointed E.F. Slack, a Bath solicitor, to conduct an investigation. The source of Slack's authority was at first unclear, and William Dunn, acting for the Kents, expressed the family's reluctance to cooperate: 'for aught we know you *may* be acting under the instructions of the detective officer whose former proceedings in this case have been condemned by the almost universal voice of the country'. Eventually, Slack divulged that he was working for the government. The *Bath Express*, among others, was disparaging about the way Lord Palmerston's Liberal administration was handling the inquiry – the paper described Cornewall Lewis as timid, terrified of criticism, and absurdly secretive.

Slack talked to everyone involved with the case. He conducted private interviews over three weeks, in his office in Bath, in a pub in Beckington and in the drawing room of Road Hill House. At one point he learnt that a small plot of land in the grounds was known as 'Miss Constance's garden', and ordered that it be dug up. Nothing of significance was found. He tried to interview the five-year-old Mary Amelia Kent, but was thwarted by Dunn, who argued that his client's daughter was too young to be examined. Dunn later described how it had been established that she was unfit to testify: when asked how old she was, she incorrectly gave her age as four; she claimed her family went to church daily, though Christ Church was not open every day; and she could not spell her murdered brother Saville's name: 'Please, sir, I have not been taught that.'

On Monday, 24 September, Slack closed his inquiry, letting it be known that he believed Constance Kent quite innocent. Her purse, he said, had been discovered behind her chest of drawers, which supported her claim to have been searching for it when she asked Sarah Cox to look through the laundry baskets on the day of the inquest. At Slack's behest, Superintendent Wolfe arrested Elizabeth Gough in Isleworth.

On Monday, 1 October, Gough was brought before the magistrates at the Trowbridge police court. The Kent family arrived in a fly, 'and were fortunate to get in unobserved', said the *Bristol Daily Post*, 'and therefore without any unpleasant demonstration from those congregated in the locality'.

In court, Gough sat with her hands drawn up to her throat, as if in prayer or protection. She was even 'thinner and more pale and careworn', according to the *Bristol Daily Post*, and watched the proceedings of the next four days with 'feverish anxiety'.

Gough's prosecutor argued that no one could have abducted and killed Saville alone, and that if two people had done it, one was surely the nurse. He questioned the credibility of Gough's statements so far. Why would she assume Saville's mother had taken him that morning, since she was too pregnant to lift him? Why did she change her story about the time at which she noticed the loss of the blanket? How could she see whether Saville was in his cot without getting out of her bed?

When Samuel Kent took the stand he was asked why he had been reluctant to let anyone draw up a plan of his house, why he had ridden to Trowbridge on the morning his son disappeared, and why he had locked the two policemen in the kitchen that night. He expressed confusion about the events of the day of Saville's death: 'my mind is so disturbed that there are many things I am not so clear about as I could wish'. On the question of the constables' incarceration in the kitchen, he said, 'I bolted the door that the house might appear as usual, and that no one might know there was a policeman in the house.' Foley was asked about the incident. 'I did not desire him to lock them up,' said the Superintendent. 'I was very much surprised when I heard of it.' He tried to make light of his part in the botched job with a weak, but pointed joke: 'They were, I understood, to have the whole range of the house, but they only had the kitchen range.' Samuel wept when he recounted the moment at which Peacock had told him of his son's murder.

The testimony of the rest of the Kent family was distinguished by its blandness. Mary Kent reluctantly lifted her thick black mourning veil to give her evidence; she was barely audible, and was repeatedly requested to speak up. She said of Gough: 'This girl, to the best of my belief, was particularly kind to the child, and seemed very fond of him; he was very fond of her; I can't tell whether she was much distressed that morning; I was too much occupied with my own and my husband's feelings . . . The boy was a nice little, playful, good-tempered, chatty boy, and a general favourite; I don't know of any one who entertained revengeful feelings against my family or little boy.'

Mary Ann Kent said, 'The poor little one who was murdered was my brother.' Elizabeth said, 'I am . . . the sister of the poor little fellow who was murdered.' They divulged little else beyond the times at which they had gone to bed and awoken on the night of his death.

Constance, with a veil pulled over her face, testified that Saville 'was a merry, good-tempered lad, fond of romping. I was accustomed to play with him often. I had played with him that day. He appeared to be fond of me, and I was fond of him.' William, who had been summoned from his boarding school near Gloucester, answered the questions put to him with 'Yes, sir' and 'No, sir' – 'not a strong-looking youth', remarked the *Bristol Daily Post*. Elizabeth brought the five-year-old Mary Amelia into the courtroom to testify, but an argument broke out about whether she was fit to do so: did she know her catechism or understand an oath? Eventually she was removed from the court without being examined.

The servants of Road Hill House made ingenious – and touching – attempts to help Gough by showing that a stranger might have taken Saville. On Tuesday, Sarah Kerslake, the cook, told the court that she and Sarah Cox, the maid, had experimented on the drawing-room window that very morning. They wanted to establish whether someone standing outside the house could have pulled it down to within six inches of the ground, the condition in which it had been found on the day Saville died. 'People said it could not be done from the outside, and Cox and I were determined to see whether it could or not; we found that it could be done from the outside quite easy.' The chairman of the magistrates pointed out that, even if they were right, it remained impossible that the window had been opened from the outside in the first place.

When Sarah Cox was called the next day, she told the court that she had followed up this experiment by trying to adjust the shutters of the drawing-room window from outside the house, but had been unsuccessful because the wind had been too strong. Superintendent Wolfe took issue with her: he had witnessed the exercise, he said, and the wind had nothing to do with its failure. He added that he had conducted his own experiment that morning, and it had confirmed his theory that Gough could not have detected the child's loss as she described. In Wolfe's experiment Mrs Kent took Eveline, now twenty-three months old, into the nursery, and Elizabeth Kent tucked her into Saville's crib. PC Dallimore's wife Eliza, who was a similar size to Gough, then knelt on the nursemaid's bed to test whether she could see the child. She reported that she could see only a small portion of pillow.

It was Eliza Dallimore's amateur detective work that excited the strongest disapproval in court. When she took the stand she gave detailed accounts of conversations between herself and Gough while the nursemaid was lodged at the police station in early July.

On one occasion, said Eliza Dallimore, Gough asked: 'Mrs Dallimore, do you know there's a nightdress missing?'

'No – whose was it?'

'Miss Constance Kent's,' said Gough. 'You may depend upon it that nightdress will lead to the discovery of the murderer.'

On another occasion Mrs Dallimore asked her whether Constance might be the killer. 'I don't think Miss Constance Kent would do it,' said Gough. Asked if William could have helped the girl commit the crime, Gough exclaimed, 'Oh, Master William is more fit for a girl than a boy.' As for Mr Kent: 'No, I could not think for a moment that he committed the murder. He's too fond of his children.'

One evening Mrs Dallimore asked Gough, again: 'What do you think of Miss Constance doing the murder?'

'I can't say anything about that,' the nursemaid replied, 'but I saw the nightgown put into the basket.'

William Dallimore came in and, having overheard the end of the conversation, asked, 'Then you saw the nightgown put into the basket, nurse, as well as Cox?'

'No,' said Gough. 'I have nothing to say about that. I have enough of my own to contend with.' With this, said Eliza Dallimore, she went to bed.

Mrs Dallimore also reported other remarks Gough had made to her, some of them seemingly suspicious – for instance, her prediction that the plumber would not find any evidence in the privy, and her description of Saville as a teller of tales.

Gough's counsel, Mr Ribton, tried to discredit Mrs Dallimore's evidence by making sarcastic allusions to her 'marvellous memory', and by mocking her. Mrs Dallimore mentioned that breast flannels were worn by young women as well as the elderly and ill: 'I wear one myself.' This provoked whoops of laughter, which were renewed when Ribton retorted, 'I shall not take the liberty of asking you your age, ma'am.'

Mrs Dallimore was dismayed by the levity of the courtroom. 'I don't think so serious a matter should be turned to ridicule,' she said. 'It gives me the horrors to think about it.'

'You are very irritable, are you not?' asked Ribton.

'Yes, sir. Perhaps you are too.'

'Then don't give us the horrors,' said Ribton. 'How about the breast flannel? It fits you nicely?'

'Yes, sir.'

'Very nicely indeed?'

'Yes, sir.'

'Perhaps you have been wearing it?' This was greeted with more laughter.

'It's a very serious thing, sir, who done the murder.'

Mrs Dallimore was a real-life version of a nineteenth-century fictional heroine: the amateur female detective, as featured in W.S. Hayward's *The Experiences of a Lady Detective* (1861) and Andrew Forrester's *The Female Detective* (1864). Her investigations, like those of Mrs Bucket in *Bleak House*, were as spirited and probing as the inquiries made by her policeman husband and his fellow officers. Inspector Bucket, though, refers to his wife, respectfully, as 'a lady of natural detective genius', while Mrs Dallimore was treated as a gossip and a fool. In theory, detection was understood as a distinctly feminine talent – women had the opportunities for 'intimate watching', said Forrester, and an instinct for deciphering what they saw. In practice, a woman who indulged in detection was perceived as a sister to Mrs Snagsby in *Bleak House*, whose jealous curiosity drives her 'to nocturnal examinations of Mr Snagsby's pockets; to secret perusals of Mr Snagsby's letters . . . to watching at windows, listenings behind doors, and a general putting of this and that together by the wrong end'.

In his summing-up on Thursday, Ribton said he had 'seldom seen anything so disgraceful in a witness as the evidence of the woman Dallimore, or more calculated to send a thrill of horror through everybody, and make them fear for their lives, their liberties, their characters'. Mrs Dallimore had taken Whicher's place as the spy incarnate. Ribton dealt with Gough's contradictions about the blanket by suggesting that she had noticed its loss early in the day and then, in the confusion and distress of the morning, had forgotten she had done so. He dismissed the fact that the flannel fitted her, arguing that it might in any case have no connection to the crime.

The magistrates released the nursemaid, to wild applause, on condition that her family put up a £100 bond to ensure that she would return for further examination if necessary. This was paid by one of Gough's two uncles, who had come to take her home. The party caught the last train to Paddington, via Chippenham, which left Trowbridge at 7.50 p.m. At every stop along the route people were gathered on the station platforms to peer in through the carriage windows.

'If the late Edgar Poe had sat down to invent a tale of mystery,' observed *The Times* two days after Elizabeth Gough's release, 'he could not have imagined anything more strange and perplexing . . . The matter – remains still as dark as ever. If three or four persons meet they are nearly sure to have so many different theories . . . People are unquiet . . . There has been an uncontrollable desire to get at the bottom of the Road child-murder.'

The unrest and disorder were in evidence in Road the next day. On Sunday, 7 October, six well-dressed, moustachioed men rode into the grounds of Road Hill House laughing, smoking and joking. One sandy-haired fellow rode a black horse and wore a black suit and a Scotch cap; another, on a grey horse, had light frizzy hair. They saw a girl at a window and shouted, 'There is Constance!' When confronted by Samuel Kent they took off.

As Mr and Mrs Kent made their way to Christ Church the same day a large party yelled and hooted at them: 'Who murdered his boy?' 'Who killed the child?' At this, Mrs Kent almost collapsed in distress. When police surveillance of Road Hill House was lifted the next week, the *Somerset and Wilts Journal* reported, 'inquisitive gentlefolk' took to driving through the Kents' grounds. According to the *Western Daily Press*, two policemen continued to accompany Samuel to Christ Church each Sunday.

The *Manchester Examiner*, identifying another species of thrill-seeker, claimed that Constance Kent had received several offers of marriage. The *Somerset and Wilts Journal* denied this: 'She has had unnumbered invitations from strangers to visit them, however, some being from the aristocracy.' This newspaper, despite hinting at Constance's guilt, repeated the idea that Whicher's accusation of her might prove a crime much worse than murder: 'If Mr Whicher's opinion was wrong, then beyond all question a crime infinitely exceeding in enormity the murder of Francis Saville Kent has been since committed, from which, Constance, poor girl, will suffer till her dying day.'

The local police continued to hound Elizabeth Gough. At the end of October Superintendent Wolfe passed on to Scotland Yard a rumour that she had once been dismissed from service in Knightsbridge for 'harbouring soldiers'. Whicher tersely reported back that Wolfe's information 'appears incorrect' – there was no evidence of the nursemaid ever having been employed in that part of London. A few weeks later it emerged that a servant called Elizabeth Gough, with a missing front tooth, had once been dismissed for 'misconduct' from a household in Eton, Berkshire. The Eton employer went to the Gough family bakery in Isleworth to identify her, Whicher reported, but discovered that she was not his former maid.

When Gough was accused in the Wiltshire magistrates' court, Samuel Kent was indirectly accused too: 'If Mr Kent has not yet been put formally upon his trial,' noted Joseph Stapleton, 'he has not the less been subjected to its infamy by the convenient proxy of Elizabeth Gough.' After the nursemaid's release, both Joshua Parsons and Mrs Kent – sensing that the feeling against Samuel was running higher than ever – made statements to the press in his defence. Mrs Kent said that Samuel had not left her side on the night of Saville's death; she could be sure of this because her advanced pregnancy made her sleep very lightly. Parsons said that Samuel's 'mind was so affected by intense excitement, and by the persecution he had undergone, that no amount of reliance ought to be placed in any statements which under such circumstances he might make'. He thought his mental state 'very precarious'. Stapleton made similar excuses for his friend: Samuel was 'stupefied and confused' by his son's death, the surgeon argued, so that 'his mind seemed to wander irregularly, discursively, and unsteadily over a large field'.

Dickens thought that Gough and her employer were the killers. The novelist had lost faith in the detectives' powers of deduction. In a letter to Wilkie Collins on 24 October he sketched his theory: 'Mr Kent, intriguing with the nursemaid, poor little child wakes in Crib, and sits up, contemplating blissful proceedings. Nursemaid strangles him then and there. Mr Kent gashes body, to mystify discoverers, and disposes of same.'

The press was disillusioned with detection. The *Saturday Review* in September dismissed even Poe's stories as 'delusions' of cleverness, 'playing chess with the right hand against the left'. As for live detectives, 'they are very ordinary people, who are worth nothing when they are taken beyond their routine'. The consensus in Road, according to the *Western Daily Press*, was that only a confession would put an end to the uncertainty, and the confession might be a long time coming: 'Ay,' the villagers predicted, 'this'll be a deathbed job.'

The idea took hold that England had become prey to outbreaks of weird violence. Some blamed the weather. 'How is it that the daily newspapers are stuffed so full of horrors just now?' asked the magazine *Once a Week*. The broadsheets, it estimated, were devoting sixteen to twenty columns a day to murder. 'People . . . have said . . . that the long continuance of bad weather – the eternal gloom – the perennial rain of the last twelvemonth, has inspired a certain degree of moroseness and acrimony into the minds of our countrymen.'

A freak storm had hit Wiltshire as the year dawned. On 30 December 1859 a hurricane descended on Calne, twenty miles or so north-east of Road, and stripped a six-mile swathe of land in five minutes: the tornado ripped trees out of the earth and snapped them like matchsticks, upending their trunks and ramming the limbs into the ground; it tore the roofs off cottages and hurled them aside; it threw a wagon over a hedge. Giant hailstones fell from the sky and slashed the hands of those who tried to catch them; the chunks of ice were shaped like crosses, cogs and spears, according to a local woman, and one took the form of a small child. In January tourists came to look on the scene of the storm, as they came towards the close of the year to look at the place in which Saville Kent had died.

CHAPTER FOURTEEN

WOMEN! HOLD YOUR TONGUES!

November–December 1860

In the first, cold days of November, the strangest inquiry yet opened at the Temperance Hall. Thomas Saunders, a barrister and magistrate of Bradford-upon-Avon, Wiltshire, had become convinced that the villagers of Road were in possession of important information about the murder, and he took it upon himself to elicit it from them. Though he was acting entirely on his own initiative, his status as a Wiltshire magistrate gave him an apparent authority, and no one at first challenged his right to investigate the case.

From 3 November onwards, Saunders summoned an array of local people to offer their thoughts and observations, some of it illuminating about the life of the village and of Road Hill House, but nearly all of it utterly irrelevant to the murder. This was the stuff that Whicher had sifted through during his fortnight in Road, the huge bank of rumour and peripheral detail that a police investigation threw up, and that usually never reached the public. Saunders aired these bits and bobs in a distinctly haphazard fashion: 'evidence, if evidence it may be called, was adduced in a most singular and undignified manner', said the *Bristol Daily Post*. 'On several occasions those present were at no pains to conceal the laughter which the proceedings were calculated to give rise to, and all throughout they seemed to consider that the whole affair was got up for their special amusement, rather than for the elucidation of a mysterious and terrible crime.'

The next two weeks in Road resembled a comic interlude in a tragic play, with Saunders as the buffoon who stumbled onstage to mangle and misunderstand all that had preceded him. He opened and closed the proceedings at whim, forgot the witnesses' names and puffed himself up with mysterious allusions to 'the secrets within my breast', while wandering in and out of the Temperance Hall with a bottle of liquid that according to the *Bristol Daily Post* 'had very much the appearance of brandy'. Saunders said it was medicine to treat a cold he had caught from a window draught on the premises (he castigated the hall's caretaker, Charles Stokes, for the poor insulation). The magistrate gulped at his potion during the proceedings, and nibbled on biscuits. He frequently interrupted his witnesses by issuing demands that squalling babies be removed from the hall or women silenced: 'Women! Hold your tongues!'

A typical witness was Mrs Quance, an old lady who lived in the cottages by Road Hill House. On Tuesday Saunders examined her about a rumour that she had said that her husband, who worked in the mill at Tellisford, saw Samuel Kent in a field at 5 a.m. on 30 June. She flatly denied it, complaining that the police had already questioned her on the matter.

'I think it is done too clever to be found out,' she added, 'except one of the party "peaches" [informs on another].'

'What has been too cleverly done?' asked Saunders.

'The child-murder.' Then Mrs Quance abruptly rose, shuffled about, said, 'Oh, Lord, I can't stay yer, my boiler's a-goin all the while,' and scampered out, to appreciative hoots from the onlookers.

James Fricker, the plumber and glazier, testified to having been pestered to fix Samuel Kent's lantern in the last week of June: 'It did not strike me at first that there was anything singular in this particular hurry for the lamp in the summer time, but it has since.'

Before Saunders opened his inquiry he had snooped around Road for a few days, and he now reported his observations to the court. One evening, he said, he and a police officer saw a young lady dressed in black, with a white petticoat, heading for Road Hill House. She paused at the gate, walked past it a little way, turned back and went in. A few minutes later Saunders saw a young lady, possibly the same one, combing her hair at an upstairs window. His account of this unremarkable incident drew complaints from the Kent family, and later in the week he apologised, acknowledging that the 'slight trepidation' the lady had shown may have been prompted by her awareness of the 'two strange persons who were watching her movements'. Someone in the audience called out that the young woman was Mary Ann.

The last witness examined by Saunders was Charles Lansdowne, a labourer, 'the pith of whose statement', observed the *Frome Times*, drily, 'was that he had seen nothing, had heard nothing, and knew nothing, about what had been done at Road Hill House, on the night of 29th June'.

The newspapermen who had been covering the case since July were flabbergasted by Saunders' inquiry. The reporter from the *Morning Star*, astounded at the 'absurd proceedings' of the 'crack-brained boggler', said he was caught between 'wonder at [Saunders'] audacity and contempt for his folly'. The *Bristol Mercury* described the magistrate as 'monomaniacal'. Saunders was an unintentional satirist, a caricature of the amateur detective who saw meaning in every banality, every trivial circumstance, who believed that he alone could unravel a mystery that had foxed the professionals. He felt a right to spy, a duty to speculate. He had a keen 'sense of the profound importance of immaterial statements', noticed the *Somerset and Wilts Journal*, and paid great respect to the letters he received from the public: 'each contains hints of great importance'. He read out several of these letters in court, including one from a fellow barrister who observed: 'You are an ill-conditioned meddling vain old idiot.'

Yet this inquiry uncovered one significant fact. A letter from James Watts, a police sergeant of Frome, prompted Saunders to examine several officers about a discovery the police had made at Road Hill House on the day of the murder, and then concealed. In the Temperance Hall on Thursday, 8 November, he questioned PC Alfred Urch on the matter, and on Friday he took evidence from Sergeant James Watts and Superintendent Foley.

At about five p.m. on 30 June, the audience heard, Watts had found a woman's shift, wrapped in newspaper, in the kitchen boiler hole, the fire-hole beneath the hotplate. Urch and PC Dallimore saw it too: 'It was dry, sir,' said Urch to Saunders, 'but very dirty . . . as if it had been worn a long time . . . It had some blood about it . . . I did not touch it myself. Sergeant Watts unfolded it, looked at it, and carried it to the coach house.' Was it coarse or fine, Saunders asked. 'I should think, sir, it was one of the servants' . . . We remarked, two or three of us who were there, that it was a small one.'

A shift was a linen garment worn under a dress in the day, or by itself at night. It could fall to the knee, the shin or the ankle; its sleeves were usually short, and its style plain. A nightdress was typically a fuller garment that reached to the floor, with sleeves to the wrists, strips of lace or embroidery at the collar, cuffs or hem. There was a borderland, where a shift and a simple nightdress might be confused. It was at least possible that the item in the boiler hole was the missing nightdress.

'Was it a night-shift or a day-shift?' Saunders asked Urch, to laughter from the audience.

'Well, sir, it was a shift.'

'Have you a sufficient knowledge of shifts?' At this the onlookers howled with merriment. 'Silence!' cried Saunders. 'Silence!'

Watts examined the shift in the coach house. It was 'very bloody', he said. 'It was dry then, but I should not think the stains had been on it a long time . . . Some of the blood was on the front and some on the back. I wrapped up the shift again, and as I was coming out I saw Mr Kent just outside the stable-door in the yard. He asked me what I had found, and said he must have it seen, and that Dr Parsons must see it. I did not let Mr Kent see it, but handed it over to Mr Foley.'

Foley immediately set to concealing the discovery of the shift. He 'shuddered', he explained to the court, 'to think the man who found it was so foolish as to expose it'. He was sure that the stains were innocent, and that the shift had been hidden, in shame, by a servant. A medical man – Stapleton – had confirmed his own view that the stains had 'natural causes' (that is, they were marks of menstrual blood).

Saunders asked Foley: 'Did he [Stapleton] look at it with a microscope?'

Foley replied indignantly: 'No, I should think he did not!'

The Superintendent had then given the garment to PC Dallimore, who took it back to the Stallard Street police station.

In September Watts had run into Dallimore at the Road Hill cheese and cattle fair, and asked what had become of the shift. Dallimore told him that he had returned the 'shimmy' (an Anglicisation of 'chemise') to the kitchen on Monday, the day of the inquest. He planned to put it back in the boiler hole but was surprised by the cook entering the scullery, and so thrust it down the side of the boiler. Straight afterwards the nursemaid, just back from walking the two little girls, suggested he search the roof above the kitchen, and he did so – he had to clamber through a window overgrown with ivy. When he returned to the kitchen half an hour later the shift had vanished, presumably retrieved by its owner.

If the distinction between types of shift was bewildering territory for the police officers, so were the distinctions between types of blood. The ways of identifying menstrual blood and female underwear were hazy, all the more so when the items to be examined were whisked away so quickly. Much of the confusion about the underclothes and their stains was caused by embarrassment.

On the Thursday that the boiler-hole story came out, by strange chance, the private investigator Ignatius Pollaky arrived in Road to sit in on Saunders' proceedings. Pollaky, a Hungarian, was 'superintendent' of an inquiry office run by Charley Field, friend to Charles Dickens and Jack Whicher, who had retired from the Metropolitan Police in 1852. Private inquiry agents, as they were known, were a new breed, some of them retired detective officers such as Field. (Field briefly had his police pension withdrawn in the 1850s for improperly continuing to use his former title, Detective-Inspector, in his private practice.) The agents' main business was the sleazy stuff of the divorce court – divorce had been legalised in 1858, but proof of adultery was required if a man was to rid himself of his wife; a woman needed to prove cruelty to end a marriage.

'The mysterious Mr Pollaky', as *The Times* described him, at first refused to speak to Saunders or to the police. Over the weekend he was seen in Bath and Bradford. The next week he visited Frome, Westbury and Warminster, made a trip back to London (probably to report his findings and take further instructions) and then returned to Road. 'There is good reason for believing that his direct object is not the detection of the murderer,' said the *Bristol Daily Post*; rather, this paper's reporter gathered, the agent was there to keep an eye on Saunders. Other newspapers confirmed this: his job was to intimidate rather than to investigate. Perhaps Field sent Pollaky down to Road as a favour to Whicher, whose findings Saunders was tending to undermine. Pollaky took notes whenever Saunders made particularly eccentric statements, and he succeeded in unnerving the magistrate. The *Frome Times* reported that 'we were informed that Mr Saunders had an interview with that gentleman . . . and asked if it were true that his mission was to collect evidence for a *lunatico inquirendo* against him. We understand that Mr Pollaky declined to reply.' Now even the investigators of the Road Hill murder feared accusations of insanity. Saunders' inquiry was suspended on 15 November.

Inadvertently, Saunders had furthered Whicher's case. When a report about the bloody shift appeared in *The Times*, Whicher sent Sir Richard Mayne a memorandum drawing his attention to the news item. 'Seen,' Mayne wrote on the memo the next day.

There was a danger that the investigations into the murder were now doing more to conceal than to reveal the solution. 'The consciences of those who may be privy to the secret are not likely to have become more sensitive or their invention less fertile in the course of the numerous proceedings which have already taken place,' observed *The Times*. 'Every futile investigation is a gain to the guilty party; it shows him what gaps should be stopped and what contradictions avoided.' The writer worried about the lack of method in detective work – its reliance on imagination, intuition, guesswork – and yearned for a more dispassionate procedure: 'it is well known that detectives begin by assuming the guilt of some one, and then try how far their hypothesis will fit the circumstances. There is still room for the application of a more scientific process, and it may be that the facts, more calmly and impartially interrogated, will tell their own story.' The *Saturday Review* echoed this, calling for a 'more severe Baconian process' of deduction from empirical facts: rather than start with a theory, the detective should simply make 'a rigid, impartial, and unimpassioned registration of phenomena'. The perfect detective, it seemed, was not so much a scientist as a machine.

The persistent feeling against Samuel Kent, which underpinned Saunders' inquiry, was evident in a sixpenny pamphlet by the anonymous 'A Barrister-at-Law'. The author identified himself with the 'amateur detectives, keen-witted, forensic readers of the newspapers, local quidnuncs and sharp-eyed idlers', and listed fifteen questions about the behaviour of Samuel Kent on the day of the murder (for instance, 'Why did he order his carriage and seek a policeman at a distance, when one lived nearer?'), as well as nine about Elizabeth Gough ('Could she, from her own bed, have seen the child in the cot?') and one about Constance ('What became of the night-dress?').

Rowland Rodway, the Trowbridge solicitor, came to Samuel's defence, protesting in a letter to the *Morning Post* that 'the press, with few exceptions, seems to point at Mr Kent as the murderer of his child, and is gathering about him a storm of public indignation which has destroyed the social position of his family, and now threatens his own personal safety'. There was no chance now that Samuel would be granted the full inspectorship for which he had applied.

His colleagues had to conduct his factory inspections. 'It would be quite impossible for Kent at present to visit factories at Trowbridge,' wrote one of them, 'such is the feeling of the lower orders against him . . . Mr Stapleton . . . took a gentleman with him to Brown & Palmer's factory, who the people in the weaving shed mistook for Kent and an immediate yell was set up which continued until they were undeceived.' This inspector added that the hostility to Kent was most prevalent among the working classes: 'I do not think well informed and respectable people in Trowbridge think him guilty.' Another inspector wrote to the Home Secretary arguing that the ill-will against the 'most unjustly accused' Kent was so acute 'not only in his own neighbourhood, but everywhere else' that even a transfer would be useless. What was more, it was 'scarcely possible that Mr Kent will be able to leave home and be absent during the night for some time to come'. This line gives an indication of how the Kent family was passing that winter: in a state of such anxiety, perhaps even of mutual fear, that the father felt unable to leave them alone after dark. Cornewall Lewis scribbled his response on the envelope: 'I do not myself believe Kent to be guilty, but whether he is or not, he is too much an object of public suspicion to be able to perform his duties – could he be suspended for a time?' Two weeks later, on 24

November, Samuel was given six months' leave of absence.

In the last days of November Jack Whicher wrote to his former colleague John Handcock of the Bristol police, reiterating his theory of the missing nightdress.

> *After all that has been said in reference to this case, and the different theories that have been advanced, there is in my humble judgment but one solution to it; and if you had made the personal investigations I did I am certain you would have come to the same conclusion. But possibly you, like others, have entirely been led by what you have heard, especially as regards the theory of Mr Kent and the nurse being concerned in the murder, simply upon the vague suspicion that he might have been in her room, &c. Now, in my opinion if there ever was one man more to be pitied, or who has been more calumniated than another, that unfortunate man is Mr Kent. It was bad enough to have his darling child cruelly murdered; but to be branded as the murderer is far worse; and, according to the present state of public opinion he will be so branded to the day of his death unless a confession is made by the person who I firmly believe committed the deed. I have little doubt but that that confession would have been made if Miss Constance had been remanded for another week. Now, my opinion is . . . that the fact of there being two families . . . was the primal cause of the murder; and that the motive was jealousy towards the children by the second marriage. The deceased was the favourite child, and spite towards the parents, the mother in particular, I believe to have been the actuating motive of Constance Kent . . . Miss Constance possesses an extraordinary mind.*

Whicher's anger about Samuel's treatment may have been sharpened by the fact that he also stood forever to be stigmatised by the case. Both men were government inspectors who had become the objects of highly critical inspection.

In his letter, Whicher mentioned that one of the Wiltshire magistrates had been to visit him, to discuss the shift that the 'bungling' police had lost. Whicher suspected that the police had returned it to the boiler hole as bait, to lure back its owner and catch her red-handed – this might account for why the constables were posted to the kitchen on the night of 30 June. 'Foley never would explain that to me . . . Mr Kent said in his evidence that Foley told him it was to see if anyone got up to destroy anything.' When the dress vanished, Whicher concluded, the police entered 'a compact of secrecy'.

After the revelations at Saunders' inquiry, the Wiltshire magistrates investigated the affair of the shift in the boiler hole. On 1 December they convened a public hearing, at which both Cox and Kerslake denied that the shift was theirs. Watts described finding the garment: 'It was in . . . as if to light the fire . . . pushed back as far as possible.' This meant that the shift must have been hidden after 9 a.m., when Kerslake put out the fire. Watts said the shift was flimsy, with 'a flap to tie down before, and another behind', and was nearly worn out – there were holes beneath the arms. The blood 'nearly covered the fore and hind parts. There were no marks of blood above the waist; the blood extended about 16 inches from the bottom. I should think, from the appearance, the blood had been caused from the inside.'

Eliza Dallimore said she thought the shift was Kerslake's because it was 'very dirty and very short . . . it would not come to my knees'. The cook had told her that her 'under linen was very dirty, because she had so much work to do'. Dallimore observed that neither Kerslake nor Cox was wearing a clean shift on the Saturday of Saville's death – she had seen their underclothes when they tried on the breast flannel.

Mrs Dallimore's enthusiastic detailing of the servants' underwear stood in strong contrast to Foley's distaste for the subject. The Superintendent said he had not discussed the discovery of the shift with the magistrates because he was too 'ashamed'. 'I did not keep it in my possession a minute. I did not like to touch it . . . I said, "You see, it is a nasty dirty chemise, so put it away" . . . I considered it would be an indecent and improper thing to expose it publicly. I have seen a great many stained garments. I don't suppose any man has seen more. One Sunday morning I searched fifty-two beds in Bath, and you may think I saw some scenes there . . . but I never saw a filthier garment than this.' He said he had wished to 'screen' the shift's owner.

The magistrates castigated Foley but forgave him, describing him as a 'shrewd, clever' officer whose error had been prompted by feelings of decency and delicacy.

On Henry Ludlow's instructions, the clerk read out a letter from Whicher: the shift hidden in the scullery, the detective said, 'was never mentioned to me by any member of the police during the fortnight I was engaged with them at Road assisting in the inquiry, and in daily communication with Supt Foley and his assistants . . . If, therefore, the magistrates feel annoyed at the matter being kept secret from them, I beg to state that I was no party to it . . . I wish them to know that I am in no way to blame.'

Joseph Stapleton's book about the murder quoted a further letter from Whicher, which argued that the shift and the missing nightdress were one and the same. 'When the finding of the blood-stained garment in the flue, and the "direful secresy" that had been previously kept respecting it, oozed out,' he wrote, 'I felt quite satisfied that it was the actual nightdress in which the deed was committed . . . I have no doubt it was placed there as a temporary hiding-place, and that the police afterwards, by some negligence, let it slip through their fingers. Hence the necessity for secrecy before, as well as after, it oozed out.' Whicher's repetition of the phrase 'oozed out' is striking. He seems to have a vivid, visceral apprehension of the blood he had nearly got his hands on, echoed in his image of a dress slipping, like liquid, through the constables' fingers.

PART THREE

THE UNRAVELLING

'I seemed to float not into clearness, but into a darker obscure, and within a minute there had come to me out of my very pity the appalling alarm of his being perhaps innocent. It was for the instant confounding and bottomless, for if he *were* innocent, what then on earth was *I*? Paralysed, while it lasted, by the mere brush of the question, I let him go a little . . .'

From *The Turn of the Screw* (1898), by Henry James

CHAPTER FIFTEEN

LIKE A CRAVE

1861–1864

The inquiries into the Road Hill murder petered out. At the beginning of 1861 the Lord Chief Justice turned down a proposal to open a new inquest into Saville Kent's death, dismissing the allegations that the coroner had acted improperly in failing to examine Samuel. The Bath police collected a few more clues, or rumours of clues, which found their way into the newspapers in January but were taken no further: a pair of India-rubber galoshes had been seen at the foot of the back stairs soon after the murder; a pair of stockings had gone missing. Joseph Stapleton claimed that some damp and dirty socks were found in a cupboard under the back stairs. The *Frome Times* said that Constance Kent, when at Miss Ducker's school in Bath many years earlier, 'in retaliation for a supposed slight, destroyed and then threw down a water-closet some property belonging to her governess'. At this school, it was reported elsewhere, she had tried to cause an explosion by turning on the gas.

In a letter to a Swiss friend on 1 February, Charles Dickens expanded on his theory about the culprits. 'You talk of the Road Murder, I suppose, even at Lausanne? Not all the Detective Police in existence shall ever persuade me out of the hypothesis that the circumstances have gradually shaped out to my mind. The father was in bed with the nurse: The child was discovered by them, sitting up in his little bed, staring, and evidently going to "tell Ma". The nurse leaped out of bed and instantly suffocated him in the father's presence. The father cut the child about, to distract suspicion (which was effectually done), and took the body out where it was found. Either when he was going for the Police, or when he locked the police up in his house, or at both times, he got rid of the knife and so forth. It is likely enough that the truth may be never discovered now.'

It might be as Poe suggested in 'The Man of the Crowd' (1840): 'There are some secrets which do not permit themselves to be told . . . mysteries which will not *suffer themselves* to be revealed. Now and then, alas, the conscience of man takes up a burthen so heavy in horror that it can be thrown down only into the grave.'

Joseph Stapleton was gathering material for his book in defence of Samuel. In February he wrote to William Hughes, the Chief Superintendent of the Bath police, asking him formally to refute the rumours that Mr Kent 'led a life of habitual debauchery' with his female servants. On 4 March Hughes replied, confirming that he had examined more than twenty people on this matter: 'they all most emphatically assert that there is not the slightest foundation for any such rumour. From all I could glean on the subject, I feel convinced that his conduct towards his female servants was the very *reverse of familiar*, and that at all times he has treated them rather with undue haughtiness than familiarity.'

Later that month, Samuel applied to the Home Secretary to take early retirement from the civil service – he was by now more than halfway through his six months' leave. He asked to be granted a pension of £350, his full salary. 'In June 1860 I was overtaken by that great calamity, the murder of my child,' he explained, 'a calamity which has not only embittered the rest of my life, but has overwhelmed me with popular prejudice and calumny through the confounded representations of the public press . . . My family is large my income limited and I cannot without much deprivation resign upon my official pension.' In response, Cornewall Lewis observed that this was 'a strange proposal as ever I heard of – inform him that his request cannot be acceded to'. The newspapers reported a rumour that Constance had in March confessed to a relative that she had killed Saville, but the detectives who had worked on the case found it 'unadvisable' to reopen the investigation.

On Thursday, 18 April 1861 the Kents left Road. Constance was sent to a finishing school in Dinan, a walled medieval town in northern France, and William returned to his school in Longhope, where he boarded with about twenty-five other boys aged between seven and sixteen. The rest of the family moved to Camden Villa in Weston-super-Mare, a resort on the north coast of Somersetshire. Mrs Kent was again pregnant.

The Kents instructed a Trowbridge auctioneer to dispose of their belongings. Two days after their departure he opened Road Hill House to the public for viewing. He had already had so many enquiries that he had taken the unprecedented step of selling the catalogues, at a shilling apiece, and limiting them to one per person – seven hundred were purchased. At 11 a.m. on Saturday, the crowds swarmed over the building. In the drawing room the visitors took turns at lifting the central bay window to test its weight, and in the nursery they made their own appraisals about whether Elizabeth Gough could have seen into Saville's cot from her bed (the consensus was that she could). They minutely examined the staircases and doors. Superintendent John Foley, who had been enlisted to keep order, was besieged by requests from young ladies to see the privy, where spots of blood were still visible on the floor. The visitors took less interest in the furniture up for sale. In his opening address the auctioneer conceded that the contents of the house were 'not of a very elegant character', but argued that they were well-made, 'and I would observe that the effects have not only an artificial, but an historical value attached to them. They have been witnesses to a crime which has astonished, terrified, and paralysed the civilised world.'

The sums achieved on the paintings were disappointing – an oil of Mary Queen of Scots by Federico Zuccari, for which Samuel Kent claimed to have been offered £100, went for £14. But Mr and Mrs Kent's splendid Spanish four-poster fetched an impressive £7.15*s*., and the washstand and ware from their bedroom £7. The auctioneer also sold 250 ounces of silver plate, more than five hundred books, several cases of wine, including golden and pale sherries, a lucernal microscope (when used with a gaslight, this could project enlarged images onto a wall), two telescopes, some pieces of iron garden furniture and a fine yearling. Samuel's 1820 port (an exceptionally rich, sweet vintage) went for eleven shillings a bottle, his mare for £11.15*s*., his carriage for £6 and his pure-bred Alderney (a small, fawn cow that yielded creamy milk) for £19. The Kents' chamber organ was acquired for the Methodist chapel in Beckington. A Mr Pearman of Frome paid about £1 each for Constance's bed, Elizabeth Gough's bed and Eveline's cot, which Saville had used as a baby, bringing the total raised by the sale to £1,000. The cot from which Saville had been abducted was not put up for auction, in case it found its way to the 'Chamber of Horrors' in Madame Tussaud's waxworks museum.

During the sale a pickpocket stole a purse containing £4 from a woman in the crowd. Though Foley's men locked the doors to Road Hill House, conducted a search and arrested a suspect, the culprit was not found.*

---

* In the next decade Road Hill House was renamed Langham House (after the neighbouring farm). By 1871 the head of the household was Sarah Ann Turberwell, a widow of sixty-six, who employed six staff: a butler, a lady's maid, a housekeeper, a housemaid, a kitchen maid and a footman. In the twentieth century the county boundaries were altered, so that the house now falls within Somerset, like the rest of the village, and the name of the village itself was changed, from Road to Rode.

Samuel and Mary Kent's last child, Florence Saville Kent, was born in their new home on the Somersetshire coast on 19 July 1861. Over the summer the factory commissioners discussed where they could send Samuel. Posts came up in Yorkshire and Ireland, but they feared that he would be unable to exercise his authority in these areas, where the hostility towards him was great. In October, though, a job fell vacant for a sub-inspector of factories in north Wales, and the Kent family moved to Llangollen in the Dee valley.

An Englishwoman who lived in Dinan in 1861 later wrote to the *Devizes Gazette* about Constance Kent: 'I never saw her, but everyone I know did, and all describe her as a flat-faced, reddish-haired ugly girl, neither stupid nor clever, lively nor morose, and only remarkable for one particular trait, viz, her extreme tenderness and kindness to very young children . . . In the whole school in which she was a pupil she was the one who would probably be the least remarked if all were seen together.' Constance did her best to become invisible, and was known at the school by her second name, Emily, but the other girls were aware of her identity. She was the object of gossip and bullying. By the end of the year Samuel had removed her to the care of the nuns of the Convent de la Sagesse, on a cliff above the town.

For several months Whicher withdrew from the public eye, working only on cases unlikely to attract attention. Just one was covered in any depth by the newspapers – his capture of a clergyman who had obtained £6,000 by forging his uncle's will. Whicher's young colleague Timothy Cavanagh, then a clerk in the Commissioner's office, claimed that the Road Hill murder had undone 'the best man the Detective Department ever possessed'. The case 'almost broke the heart of poor Whicher' – he 'returned to head-quarters thoroughly chapfallen. This was a great blow to him . . . the commissioner and others losing faith in him for the first time.' According to Cavanagh, the Road Hill case changed Dolly Williamson as well. When Williamson came back from

Wiltshire, he put away his playfulness, his penchant for practical jokes and dangerous games. He became subdued, detached.

In the summer of 1861 Whicher was given charge of a murder investigation for the first time since Road Hill. It was an apparently straightforward case. On 10 June a fifty-five-year-old woman called Mary Halliday was found dead in a rectory at Kingswood, near Reigate, Surrey, where she had been keeping house while the vicar was away. Mrs Halliday seemed to have been the victim of a botched burglary – a sock stuffed into her mouth, probably to silence her, had suffocated her. The intruder or intruders had left clues: a beech cudgel, some lengths of unusual hemp cord tied around the victim's wrists and ankles, and a packet of papers. These papers included a letter from a famous German opera singer, a begging letter signed 'Adolphe Krohn', and identification documents in the name of Johann Karl Franz of Saxony.

The police had descriptions of two foreigners who had been in the area that day, one short and dark, the other taller and fairer; they had been seen in a pub, in fields near the rectory and in a Reigate shop, where they had bought the same kind of cord as that found at the murder scene. The descriptions of the taller of the two matched the details on the identification papers. A £200 reward was offered for the capture of the pair, presumed to be Krohn and Franz.

Whicher sent Detective-Sergeant Robinson to interview Mademoiselle Thérèse Tietjens, the celebrated opera singer whose letter had been found in the rectory, at her house in St John's Wood, near Paddington. She said that a young, tallish German with light-brown hair had turned up on her doorstep a week earlier, pleading poverty and asking for her help in returning to Hamburg. She had promised to pay his expenses, and had given him a letter to this effect. Whicher asked Dolly Williamson to check the sailings to Hamburg and to make enquiries at the Austrian, Prussian and Hanseatic embassies and consulates.

Extra constables were sent to the sugar-baking district of Whitechapel, in the East End, where many itinerant Germans took lodgings. Several German tramps were taken in for questioning. One by one, Whicher ruled them out. 'Altho' he somewhat answers the description of one of the men concerned in the murder of Mrs Halliday,' he reported of a suspect on 18 June, 'I do not think he is one of them.'

The next week, though, Whicher told Mayne he had found Johann Franz: a twenty-four-year-old German vagrant picked up in Whitechapel who claimed his name was Auguste Salzmann. At first, Whicher could find no eyewitnesses to confirm that this was one of the Kingswood Germans. On the contrary: 'He has been seen by three persons from Reigate and Kingswood who saw two foreigners in the neighbourhood the day before and on the day of the murder, but they are unable to identify him as one of them,' Whicher wrote to Mayne on 25 June. 'He has also been seen by PC Peck, P Division, who met the two men at Sutton on the morning of the murder, but he cannot recognise him. Altho' these persons have failed to identify him, I have no doubt but he is "Johann Carl Franz" the owner of the book left behind, and as there are other persons who saw the two foreigners in the neighbourhood, I beg to suggest that Serjeant Robinson should fetch them to London to see the prisoner.' Whicher's self-assurance – or his fixation – paid off. On 26 June witnesses from the pub and the string shop in Reigate agreed that this was the taller and fairer of the two Germans who had visited the town. Whicher declared himself 'thoroughly confident' of securing a conviction.

He sent photographs of the identification papers to officials in Saxony, who confirmed their authenticity, adding that their owner had a prison record. Whicher also discovered that two days after the murder the suspect had given his landlord a blue checked shirt for safekeeping. The shirt exactly matched the description of that worn by one of the men seen at Kingswood, and wrapped around it was a piece of cord just like that which had bound the murder victim's body. The detectives traced the maker of the cord, who confirmed that he had spun the string which was found round the shirt and round Mrs Halliday's ankles: 'They are all off the same ball. I am quite sure of it.' More eyewitnesses agreed that they had seen the prisoner in Surrey. Even PC Peck said he now believed the suspect was one of the men he met at Sutton. Whicher had put together a strong chain of circumstantial evidence. On 8 July the prisoner admitted he was Franz. He was committed for trial.

The story the German gave in his defence sounded trumped-up from beginning to end. After disembarking from a steamer at Hull in April, he said, he had fallen in with two other German vagrants, Wilhelm Gerstenberg and Adolphe Krohn. Gerstenberg, who in build and colouring resembled Franz, pestered him to hand over some of his identification papers. Franz refused. One night in May, while Franz was asleep behind a haystack near Leeds, his two companions robbed him, taking not only the papers but also his pack and his spare clothes, which were cut from the same cloth as those he was wearing. This explained the similarity between his shirt and that seen near Kingswood, while his resemblance to Gerstenberg explained why some of the eyewitnesses thought they had seen Franz in Surrey. The destitute Franz made his way to London alone. When he reached the city he heard that a German called Franz was wanted for murder, so he quickly adopted a new name. As for the cord in his room, he said he had found it on the pavement outside a tobacconist's shop near his lodgings. His defence, then, was that he had been robbed of his clothes and papers by a German tramp who looked very like him, had changed his name for fear he would be mistaken for a murderer, and had happened to pick up a piece of cord on a London street that exactly matched the distinctive twine at the murder scene.

All this seemed the invention of a desperate and guilty man. But in the days leading up to the trial various facts emerged that seemed to corroborate Franz's account. A vagrant in Northamptonshire presented the police with some stray papers from the packet that Franz claimed had been stolen from him – he said he had found them on a heap of straw in a roadside hovel. This suggested that at least some of

Franz's papers had gone astray, as he claimed. When Mademoiselle Tietjens came to see the prisoner she swore that he was not the light-haired man who had asked for her help in early June. This raised the possibility that there was indeed another light-haired German who had been associated with the darker Krohn. And it came to light that the London supplier of the hemp twine sold in Reigate, and found on Mary Halliday's body, was based in Whitechapel, just a few doors away from the stretch of pavement where Franz said he picked up the piece with which he tied his shirt.

The inquiry was slipping away from Whicher. He searched desperately for Krohn, whose capture he was convinced would make the case against Franz. He was so keen to find the missing German that he more than once expressed a conviction that he almost had him: 'I have little doubt but that the man described as Adolphe Krohn is a young Polish Jew named Marks Cohen,' he wrote to Mayne. He was proved wrong. Soon afterwards he was 'strongly impressed' that another man was Krohn, and again was mistaken. Whicher did not find him.

At the trial for Mary Halliday's murder on 8 August, Franz's counsel argued, in a passionate four-hour speech, that the circumstantial evidence in the case needed not only to be consistent with guilt but also to be inconsistent with innocence. It was said that ten of the twelve jurors went into the jury room convinced that Franz was the murderer, but when they came out they declared him not guilty. The Saxon Embassy paid his fare home.

The Times the next day, clearly convinced that Franz had killed Mrs Halliday, pointed out that circumstantial evidence was always – theoretically – consistent with innocence. Such evidence was never proof of anything: 'it is only an hypothesis binding together certain facts, though it is at the same time an hypothesis which, by a law of nature, we cannot in certain cases help believing to be the right one'.

The Kingswood investigation had unfolded like a nasty joke, a mockery of a detective's skills. It was a reminder that detective work relied on good fortune as well as acuity. 'If I was not the cleverest, of which I had grave doubts, I was certainly the luckiest of detectives,' says Inspector 'F', the narrator of Waters' *Experiences of a Real Detective* (1862). 'I had but held my mouth open, and fat things had dropped in of their own accord.' Whicher's luck seemed to have run out. He had probably been right about the identity of the Kingswood murderer, but once Franz was acquitted the detective's confidence started to look like something else – arrogance, perhaps, or delusion, or obsession. This was the last murder he investigated.

In the nineteenth century the idea was gaining ground that human witness (confession or eyewitness evidence) was too subjective to be trusted. Jeremy Bentham's *A Treatise on Judicial Evidence* (1825), for instance, argued that testimony needed to be backed up by material proof. Only *things* would do: the button, the boa, the nightgown, the knife. As Waters' Inspector 'F' puts it: 'I believe that a chain of circumstantial evidence in which there shall be no material break . . . [is] the most reliable testimony upon which human judgment can be based – since a circumstance cannot be perjured, or bear corrupt testimony.' The same preference could be discerned in the fiction of Edgar Allan Poe: 'he ushers in the scientific and analytical literature in which things play a more important part than people', observed the French writers Edmond and Jules de Goncourt in 1856. Objects were incorruptible in their silence. They were mute witnesses to history, fragments – like Darwin's fossils – that could freeze the past.

Yet the Kingswood case and the Road Hill case showed up the slipperiness of things, made it clear that objects as well as memories were endlessly open to interpretation. Darwin had to decipher his fossils. Whicher had to read his murder scenes. A chain of evidence was constructed, not unearthed. Forrester's lady detective puts it simply: 'The value of the detective lies not so much in discovering facts, as in putting them together, and finding out what they mean.' The mutilated body at Road Hill might be evidence of rage, or of the impersonation of rage. The open window could indicate an escape route, or the cunning of a killer still ensconced in the house. At Kingswood, Whicher found the most definitive kind of clue: a piece of paper bearing a name and a physical description. Even this, it turned out, could point to the opposite of what it seemed – the theft of an identity rather than identity itself.

A new mood was taking hold in England. By contrast with the vigorous, buoyant 1850s, the next decade was to be characterised by unease, self-doubt. Queen Victoria's mother died in March 1861 and her adored husband, Prince Albert, in December. The Queen went into mourning, and spent the rest of her life in black.

In the early 1860s the emotions aroused by the Road Hill murder went underground, leaving the pages of the press to reappear, disguised and intensified, in the pages of fiction. On 6 July 1861, almost exactly a year after the murder, the first instalment of Mary Elizabeth Braddon's *Lady Audley's Secret* appeared in *Robin Goodfellow* magazine. This novel, a huge bestseller when it was published in full in 1862, featured a wicked stepmother (a governess who married a gentleman), a brutal, mysterious murder at an elegant country house, a body thrust into a well; its characters were fascinated with madness and with detective work, and terrified of exposure. Braddon's story gave expression to the disquiet and excitement that Saville Kent's murder had awakened.

Constance Kent was refracted into every woman in the book: the sweet-faced, possibly insane murderess Lady Audley; the tomboyish, spirited daughter of the house, Alicia Audley; the impassive lady's maid Phoebe Marks ('Silent and self-contained, she seemed to hold herself within herself, and take no colour from the outer world . . . that is a woman who can keep a secret'); and the lonely, passionate Clara Talboys, sister to the murdered man:

'I have grown up in an atmosphere of suppression. . . . I have stifled and dwarfed the natural feelings of my heart, until they have become unnatural in their intensity; I have been allowed neither friends nor lovers. My mother died when I was very young . . . I have had no one but my brother.'

Jack Whicher surfaces in the figure of the tormented amateur detective Robert Audley, who conducts a 'backward investigation', a journey into his suspect's past. Where Inspector Bucket in *Bleak House* is suave, twinkling with secret knowledge, Robert Audley is racked with a guilty fear that he is insane. Who is the monomaniac, he wonders: is it the childlike woman he suspects of madness and murder, or by fixing on her is he merely proving himself in the grip of an obsessive delusion?

> *Was it a monition or a monomania? What if I am wrong after all? What if this chain of evidence which I have constructed link by link is constructed out of my own folly? What if this edifice of horror and suspicion is a mere collection of crotchets – the nervous fancies of a hypochondriacal bachelor? . . . Oh, my God, if it should be in myself all this time that the misery lies.*

Whicher's chain of evidence at Road could be proof of his suspect's guilt or of his own delusions, just as his chain of evidence at Kingswood had proved. The uncertainty was torture: 'Am I never to get any nearer the truth,' asks Robert Audley, 'but am I to be tormented all my life by vague doubts, and wretched suspicions, which may grow upon me till I become a monomaniac?' Yet if he succeeds in solving the mystery it might only magnify the horror: 'why should I try to unravel the tangled skein, to fit the pieces of the terrible puzzle, and gather together the stray fragments which when collected may make such a hideous whole?'

Lady Audley's Secret was one of the earliest and best of the 'sensation' or 'enigma' novels that dominated the 1860s literary scene, labyrinthine tales of domestic misery, deception, madness, intrigue. They dealt in what Henry James called 'those most mysterious of mysteries, the mysteries that are at our own doors . . . the terrors of the cheerful country house, or the busy London lodgings'. Their secrets were exotic, but their settings immediate – they took place in England, now, a land of telegrams, trains, policemen. The characters in these novels were at the mercy of their feelings, which pressed out, unmediated, onto their flesh: emotion compelled them to blanch, flush, darken, tremble, start, convulse, their eyes to burn and flash and dim. The books, it was feared, worked on their readers in the same way.

In 1863 the philosopher Henry Mansel described such novels as 'indications of a widespread corruption, of which they are in part both the effect and the cause: called into existence to satisfy the cravings of a diseased appetite, and contributing themselves to foster the disease, and to stimulate the want they supply'. Mansel expressed himself with unusual force, but his views were widespread. Many feared that sensation novels were a 'virus' that might create the corruption they described, forming a circle of excitement – sexual and violent – that coursed through every stratum of society. These books, the original psychological thrillers, were seen as agents of social collapse, even in the way they were consumed – they were read in the scullery and the drawing room, by servants and mistresses alike. They alluded to real crimes, such as the Road Hill case, to add a frisson of authenticity. 'There is something unspeakably disgusting in this ravenous appetite for carrion,' wrote Mansel, 'this vulture-like instinct which smells out the newest mass of social corruption, and hurries to devour the loathsome dainty before the scent has evaporated.' Sensation novels called forth their readers' brutish sensations, their animal appetites; they threatened religious belief and social order in a similar way to Darwinism. Mansel noted that the typical jacket illustration to one of these novels was of 'a pale young lady in a white dress, with a dagger in her hand' – the scene Whicher had conjured at Road.

Joseph Stapleton's book about the killing, *The Great Crime of 1860*, was published in May 1861, with an endorsement from Rowland Rodway. Stapleton was fantastically well-informed: he knew the suspects in the case and he had heard the local gossip. Henry Clark, the magistrates' clerk, had supplied him with information about the magistrates' inquiries and the police investigations, and Samuel Kent had briefed him on the family's history. Stapleton hinted heavily at Constance's guilt. Yet his book's tone was often frenzied and bizarre – the dark suggestions he threw out were not only about the identity of the murderer but about the decay and collapse of English society, a racial catastrophe.

In prose as heated as that of the sensation novelists, Stapleton urged his readers to 'think of the human hearts that pulsate' in the homes of the new middle classes, 'of the human passions that riot there . . . of family wrongs, of family conflicts, of family disgraces, covered over only by the miserable tinsel of gentility; flashing out here and there, fitfully, into a sudden, devouring, and inextinguishable flame'. He likened such families to volcanoes: 'in many an English household, the amenities of social life are found to clothe with grace a rugged and a shallow crust. The tempest . . . gathers strength in those deep recesses where the crater is instinct with fire; and . . . it bursts out, in its full fury, to hurl parents, children, servants, into one common, inevitable, and promiscuous destruction.'

The public had been corrupted by the Road Hill murder, Stapleton suggested. 'As the mystery attached to the crime has been deepened and prolonged, suspicion has become a passion.' He gave a lurid account of the spectators at Saville's inquest, comparing them to the women at a Spanish bullfight. 'Women had crowded into the room to hear how a throat had been cut,' he wrote, 'and they held young children in their arms to gaze upon the bloody relic.' It was as if the domestic angel of Victorian fantasy momentarily gave way to a bloodthirsty ghoul: 'Her sympathies for suffering are suspended till her instincts have been indulged; and, when curiosity and the love of the horrible have been satiated, the Englishwoman recovers from her eclipse and comes forth among us in the brightness of her better attributes again.' In Stapleton's eyes, the observers of a murder investigation were themselves transformed, briefly mutated by the vision of violence. Though he was eager to assign all the appetite for gore to the working-class women of the village, and to liken them to foreigners for good measure, the greedy curiosity about this case extended to all the English social classes, and both sexes. He was himself hungry for the matter of the murder, as his book made clear.

Stapleton suggested that the murder was evidence of 'a national decay': 'An imputed degradation of race has become amongst ourselves a national reproach,' he wrote, 'just because we recognise in it the natural consequences and expression of a long ancestral series of debasing pleasures, grovelling occupations, and corrupting sins.' He was subscribing here to the theory of racial degeneration: if human beings could evolve, as Darwin argued, they could surely regress as well. A family's decadent past could tell on its children, dragging the race backwards. Mansel, too, cited the Road Hill murder as evidence of degeneration, along with the spread of alcoholism, consumerism, hysteria, pollution, prostitution and adultery. Stapleton, though eager to absolve Samuel of the murder, implied that his former colleague's corruptions and pretensions had undone his family. Dipsomania could mark a man's offspring, said the doctor, as could other kinds of intemperance, such as greed for money or an excess of sexual desire.

The unsolved murder at Road played out the sensation novelist's vision of Britain. The case didn't deliver meaning; only a jolt, like electricity. Its influence was evident in Charlotte Yonge's *The Trial* (1863), about a middle-class adolescent boy accused of murder, and in the anonymous *Such Things Are* (1862), about smart young ladies with horrifying criminal histories: 'Time was . . . when the English girl was looked upon, both abroad and at home, as the type of all that was pure and innocent, but things are altered now.' The reverberations of the case could be discerned in the books that depicted a crude police officer defiling a refined domestic scene – Grimstone of the Yard, for instance, with his 'greasy little memorandum book' and 'stumpy pencil' in Mary Elizabeth Braddon's *Aurora Floyd* (1863).

The novelist Margaret Oliphant blamed it all on the detectives. Sensation fiction, she said, was 'a literary institutionalisation of the habits of mind of the new police force'. The 'literary Detective', she wrote in 1862, 'is not a *collaborateur* whom we welcome with any pleasure into the republic of letters. His appearance is neither favourable to taste or morals.' A year later she complained of 'detectivism', the 'police-court aspect of modern fiction'.

In the wake of the Road Hill murder, detectives were, in Robert Audley's words, 'stained with vile associations, and unfit company for honest gentlemen'. Audley was disgusted at the detective persona he himself had adopted: 'His generous nature revolted at the office into which he had found himself drawn – the office of spy, the collector of damning facts that led on to horrible deductions . . . onward upon the loathsome path – the crooked by-way of watchfulness and suspicion.'

In the feverish figure of Robert Audley, compelled to seek what he fears, 'sensation' and 'detectivism' were fused. The detective could be understood as a sensation-addict himself, hungry for the shudder and thrill of crime. James McLevy, the Edinburgh detective whose two volumes of memoirs were bestsellers in 1861, confessed to the unsettling excitement of his work. He depicted his desire to retrieve stolen goods as an animal urge, like the thief's desire to steal: 'It is scarcely possible to imagine a detective's feelings on pulling out of a mysterious bag the very things he wants. Even the robber, when his fingers are all of a quiver in the rapid clutch of a diamond necklace, feels no greater delight than we do when we retract that watch from the same fingers now closed with a nervous grasp.' McLevy said that he was drawn to danger, to mystery, to 'places where secret things have been done'. The yearning he felt for a 'wanted' man was physical: 'every look . . . seemed to send a back energy down through my arm, imparting something like a crave in the fingers to lay hold of him'. With a creepy eroticism, McLevy compared capturing a villain to seizing a lover: 'what a glorious grip that was I got of him . . . I would not have exchanged it for the touch of a bride's hand, with the marriage ring upon her finger . . . such was my weakness, that when I saw Thomson struggling ineffectually in the grasp of the officer, one whom I had so often sighed for in secret, and eyed in openness . . . I absolutely burned to embrace the dauntless leader of the gang.' McLevy portrayed himself as a solitary man whose energies were diverted and his emotions warped by his obsession with the cases he worked on, the crooks he craved. Like Jack Whicher, and most fictional detectives since, he was unmarried, his solitude the price of his excellence.

The press stepped up its assaults on Whicher and his colleagues. 'The modern detective is generally at fault,' stated the *Dublin Review* – the Road Hill case had 'justly shaken' public confidence in his 'sagacity and long-headed-ness . . . The detective system in this country is essentially low and mean.' The word 'clueless' was first recorded in 1862. *Reynolds* magazine compared the Metropolitan Police to 'a cowardly and clumsy giant, who . . . wreaks all the meanness and malignity of his nature on every feeble and helpless creature who comes in his way'. There were echoes here of the 'meanness' Whicher showed in arresting the helpless Constance Kent. A parody in *Punch* in 1863 referred to 'Inspector Watcher' of the 'Defective Police'. In the *Saturday Review*, James Fitzjames Stephen attacked the romantic presentation of police in fiction – 'this detective worship' – arguing that in reality they were useless at solving middle-class crimes.

In the summer of 1863 Samuel and William Kent visited Constance in Dinan, and on 10 August she returned to England to become a paying boarder at St Mary's Home in Brighton. This establishment, founded by the Reverend Arthur Douglas Wagner in 1855, was one of the first convents in the Church of England. A band of novice nuns, led by a Lady Superior, ran a lying-in hospital for unmarried mothers, assisted by about thirty penitents. Wagner was a disciple of Edward Pusey, a leader of the nineteenth-century Tractarian or Oxford Movement that advocated a revival of vestments, incense, candles and sacramental confession in the Anglican Church. By joining Wagner's Community of St Mary the Virgin, Constance was replacing her natural family with a religious family, freeing herself of the ties of blood. Having adopted the French spelling of her middle name, she was known as Emilie Kent.

In London, Jack Whicher's life had emptied out. There was little sign of the former 'prince of detectives' in the newspapers. His friend Detective-Inspector Stephen Thornton dropped dead of apoplexy at his house in Lambeth in September 1861, aged fifty-eight, leaving the way clear for Dolly Williamson to be promoted Inspector in October. Williamson was put in charge of the department.

After Kingswood, Whicher only once appears in the Metropolitan Police files on important cases. In September 1862 he and a colleague, Superintendent Walker, were sent to Warsaw at the request of the Russian rulers of the city to give advice on how to set up a detective service. The Russians were worried about the Polish nationalist insurgents, who had made assassination attempts on the Tsar's family. 'Everything seems very quiet,' the English officers reported from the Hotel Europe on 8 September, 'and no further attempts at assassination have been made, altho' . . . the government seems to be in constant apprehension. Our mission here is being kept entirely secret . . . as our personal safety might be endangered by a wrong construction being placed on the object of our visit.' Afterwards the Russians were polite about their guests – 'the two Officers . . . have entirely satisfied his

Highness's expectations by the justice and sagacity of their remarks' – but did not take up their suggestions. In March 1863, when Russian soldiers were shooting insurgents in Warsaw, questions were asked in the House of Commons about the ethics of the detectives' secret mission.

On 18 March 1864 Jack Whicher left the Metropolitan Police, aged forty-nine, with an annual pension of £133.*6s.8d.* He returned to his rooms in Holywell Street, Pimlico. On his discharge papers he described his marital state as single and his next of kin as William Wort, a Wiltshire coach proprietor who in 1860 had married one of the detective's nieces, Mary Ann. The discharge papers gave the reason for Whicher's early retirement as 'congestion of the brain'. This diagnosis was applied to all sorts of conditions, such as epilepsy, anxiety, vascular dementia. An essay of 1866 described the symptoms as throbbing headaches, a flushed, swollen face and bloodshot eyes, and argued that its cause was 'protracted mental tension'. It was as if Whicher's thoughts had run too obsessively on the conundrum of the Road Hill murder and his mind had become as 'over-heated' as Robert Audley's. Perhaps congestion of the brain was what happened when the detective instinct went unanswered, when the hunger for resolution was not satisfied, when the truth could not be disentangled from the seeming.

'Nothing in the world is hidden for ever,' wrote Wilkie Collins in *No Name* (1862). 'Sand turns traitor, and betrays the footstep that has passed over it; water gives back to the tell-tale surface the body that has been drowned . . . Hate breaks its prison-secrecy in the thoughts, through the doorway of the eyes . . . Look where we will, the inevitable law of revelation is one of the laws of nature: the lasting preservation of a secret is a miracle which the world has never yet seen.'

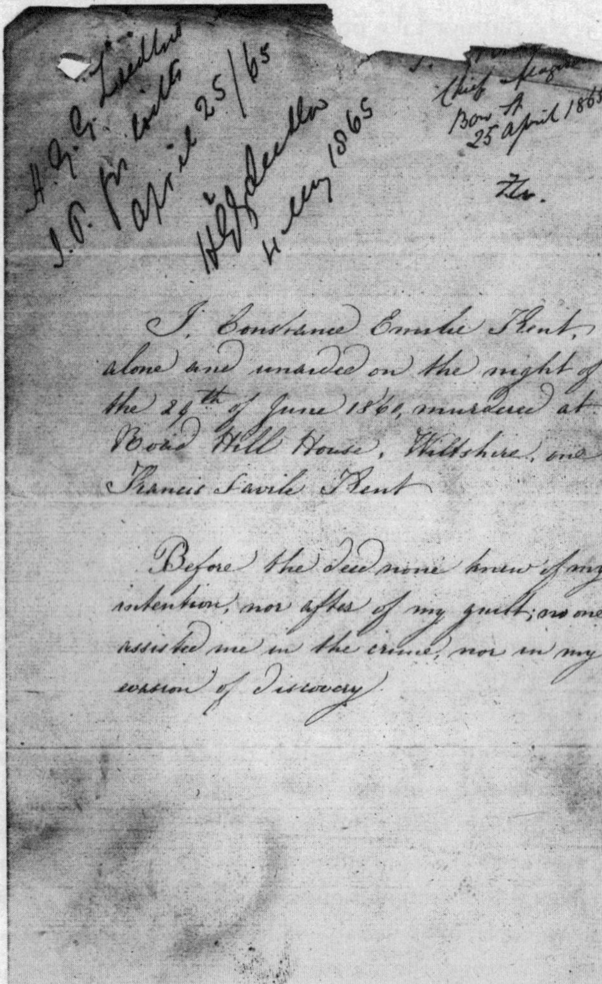
H. G. Liddon
April 25/65
H. G. Liddon
4 May 1865
Bow St
25 April 1865

I, Constance Emilie Kent, alone and unaided on the night of the 29th of June 1860, murdered at Road Hill House, Wiltshire, one Francis Savile Kent.

Before the deed none knew of my intention, nor after of my guilt; no one assisted me in the crime, nor in my evasion of discovery.

CHAPTER SIXTEEN

BETTER SHE BE MAD

April–June 1865

On Tuesday, 25 April 1865 Constance Kent, now twenty-one, took the train from Brighton to Victoria station, under a fierce sun, and then a cab to Bow Street magistrates' court, Covent Garden. She was accompanied by the Reverend Mr Wagner, in his vicar's garb, and by Katharine Gream, the Lady Superior of St Mary's, in full regalia (a long black cloak with a high white frill). Constance wore a loose veil. She appeared 'pale and sorrowful', said the *Daily Telegraph*, 'but perfectly composed'. When she reached the court shortly before four o'clock, she told the officials inside that she had come to confess to a murder.

The Bow Street office, the first and most famous of the London magistrates' courts, occupied two stucco-fronted terrace houses in the disreputable district around Covent Garden market and the opera house. A policeman stood guard outside, under a gaslamp and a carving of the royal arms. Constance and her companions were shown down a narrow passage to a single-storey courtroom behind the main building. The room was criss-crossed with metal railings and wooden platforms; the sun shone through a skylight in the ceiling; a clock and several oil paintings hung on the discoloured walls. Sir Thomas Henry, the chief magistrate of

Bow Street, was sitting at the Bench. Constance handed him the letter that she had brought with her. She took a seat. The room, on an April day as hot as midsummer, was close and airless.

Henry read the letter, written on silky notepaper in a confident, flowery hand:

I, Constance Emilie Kent, alone and unaided on the night of the 29th of June 1860, murdered at Road Hill House, Wiltshire, one Francis Savile Kent. Before the deed none knew of my intention, nor after of my guilt; no one assisted me in the crime, nor in my evasion of discovery.

The magistrate looked at Constance. 'Am I to understand, Miss Kent,' he asked, 'that you have given yourself up of your own free act and will on this charge?'

'Yes, sir.' Constance spoke 'firmly, though sadly', said *The Times*.

'Anything you may say here will be written down, and may be used against you. Do you quite understand that?'

'Yes, sir.'

'Is this paper, now produced before me, in your own handwriting, and written of your own free will?'

'It is, sir.'

'Then let the charge be entered in her own words.' The magistrates' clerk wrote down the murder charge on a blue form, asking Constance only whether she spelt her middle name 'Emily' or 'Emilie'.

'It is quite indifferent,' she replied. 'I sometimes spell it one way, and sometimes the other.'

'I observe that on this paper, which you say is your own handwriting, it is spelt "Emilie".'

'Yes, sir.'

Henry asked her if she would sign her confession. 'I must again remind you,' he added, 'that it is the most serious crime that can be committed, and that your statement will be used against you at your trial. I have had the words written copied upon this charge sheet, but I do not wish you to sign it unless you desire to do so.'

'I will do so if necessary,' said Constance.

'It is not absolutely necessary,' Henry told her. 'There is no occasion for you to sign the charge unless you wish it. I will have your statement attached to the depositions, and I will again ask you if you have made it by your own desire, and without any inducement from any quarter whatever to give yourself up.'

'Yes.'

Henry turned his attention to the Reverend Mr Wagner, and asked him to identify himself. Wagner was a well-known figure, an Eton- and Oxford-educated curate who used his inherited riches to build five churches in Brighton, for which he commissioned ornate windows and altar-pieces from artists such as Edward Burne-Jones, Augustus Pugin and William Morris. He established the seaside town as a centre of the Anglo-Catholic movement. Some considered him a papist, and a danger to the English Church.

'I am a clerk in holy orders and perpetual curate of St Paul's Church, Brighton,' said Wagner. The vicar had a handsome, fleshy face, inset with small, appraising eyes. 'I have known Constance Kent nearly two years – since the summer of 1863.'

Constance interrupted: 'In August.'

'About twenty-one months?' asked Henry.

'Yes,' said Wagner. 'As far as I can remember an English family wrote to me, asking for her admission to St Mary's . . . in consequence of her having no home, or of some difficulty respecting her. The "home", or rather "hospital", as it is now called, is a house for religious ladies, and is attached to St Mary's Church. She came about that time as a visitor, and has been there up to the present day.'

'Now, Mr Wagner,' said Henry, 'it is my duty to ask you if any inducement has been made to the prisoner in any way to make this confession.'

'None whatever has been made by me. The confession is entirely her own voluntary act, to the best of my belief. It was about a fortnight ago, as far as I can recollect, that the circumstance first came to my knowledge. It was entirely her own proposition that she should be taken before a London magistrate. She herself proposed to come to London for the purpose. The nature of the confession she made to me was the same, in substance, as the statement produced in her own writing, and copied upon the charge sheet.'

Wagner added that when he spoke of Constance's confession he was referring to her public statement, not to anything that she had told him in private.

'I will not go into that point here,' replied Henry. 'It may be gone into at the trial, perhaps very fully.' He turned to Constance again, clearly uneasy about the priest's role in her surrender. 'I hope you understand that whatever you say must be entirely your own free and voluntary statement, and that no inducement that may have been held out to you is to have any effect upon your mind.'

'No inducement ever has, sir.'

'I am anxious you should most seriously consider that.'

Wagner spoke up: 'I wish to mention that many are in the habit of coming to confess to me as a religious exercise, but I never held out any inducement to her to make a public confession.'

'Yes,' said Henry, a little sternly, 'I think you ought to mention that. Did you in the first instance induce her to make the confession to you?'

'No, sir. I did not seek her out or in any way ask her to come to confession. She herself wished to do so.'

'If you think that the confession she now makes has been

induced in consequence of anything which she has said to you, or which you have said to her, you ought to say so.'

'I never even recommended it,' insisted Wagner. 'I have been simply passive. I thought she was doing right, and I did not dissuade her.'

'But do you say that you did not persuade her?'

'I do say so.'

Henry lifted up Constance's letter of confession. 'This is the paper you wish to hand in as your statement, is it?' he asked. 'It is not too late even now . . . You are not bound to make any statement unless you desire to do so.'

The chief clerk asked her if the document was in her own handwriting.

'Yes,' she said, 'it is.'

Henry asked Wagner if he knew Miss Kent's handwriting but he said he did not, having never seen her write.

The clerk read Constance's confession back to her and she confirmed its accuracy. She signed it, using the original spelling of her middle name: Emily. When Henry explained that he would be committing her for trial she sighed, as if in relief, and sat back in her chair.

In the course of this examination Superintendent Durkin and Inspector Williamson had entered the chamber, having been summoned from Scotland Yard.

'The offence was committed in Wiltshire,' observed Henry, 'and the trial must be in that county. It will therefore be necessary to send her to be examined before the magistrates in that county. Inspector Williamson was present at the former inquiry, and knows what took place and who were the magistrates.'

'Yes, Sir Thomas,' said Dolly Williamson. 'I do.'

'And the residences of the magistrates?'

'One of them resides at Trowbridge.'

'One justice of the peace can hear the case in the first instance,' said Henry. He asked where Detective-Inspector Whicher was, and Williamson told him that he had retired.

Williamson took Constance Kent and Miss Gream to Paddington railway station, where, with Detective-Sergeant Robinson, who had worked on the Kingswood case, they caught the 8.10 p.m. train to Chippenham. During the journey Constance was silent, even when the Inspector tried to prompt her with friendly questions. This was the first time she had been back to Wiltshire since 1861. She seemed, Williamson said, 'in a state of deep dejection'. The party reached Chippenham just before midnight and then took a post-chaise – a closed, four-wheeled carriage – on to Trowbridge, about fifteen miles away. Again Williamson tried to interest Constance in conversation, asking her if she knew how far they were from the town, but met with silence. The driver of the chaise got so lost on the country lanes that they did not reach Trowbridge until 2 a.m. At the police station, Constance was looked after by a Mrs Harris, the wife of the new Superintendent (John Foley had died the previous September, aged sixty-nine).

The press greeted Constance's confession with astonishment. Several newspapers were reluctant to accept the validity of her statement. After all, some disturbed people committed crimes; others, like the troubled bricklayer who had claimed to have killed Saville Kent, pretended to have done so, perhaps in the hope that confession to a crime might bring relief from a morbid, unfocused sense of guilt and misery. Maybe Constance was 'mad instead of guilty', suggested the *Daily Telegraph*; the past five years of 'slow agony' could have deprived her of her senses, incited her to a false confession. 'Better a hundred times that she should prove a maniac than a murderess.' Yet the lucidity and 'terrible courage' of her words, the newspaper admitted, 'do not look at all like insanity'. The *Morning Star* suggested that Constance had murdered her half-brother out of 'passionate fondness' for William. Quasi-romantic friendships between brothers and sisters were familiar to a Victorian audience – in the cloistered, chaperoned middle-class family, a sibling might be a young man or woman's only close acquaintance of the opposite sex. The *London Standard* thought there was something fishy about Constance's statement, which she had supposedly penned herself: 'There is an attorney's stamp upon it.' The *London Review*, hinting that sinister papist forces were at work, found 'in the language of the document palpable indications of a foreign hand and a strange influence'.

The Times, though, took Constance at her word, and offered an explanation for the crime that assigned feelings of violent hatred to half of the English population. 'From twelve or fourteen to eighteen or twenty is that period of life in which the tide of natural affection runs the lowest, leaving the body and the intellect unfettered and unweakened in the work of development, and leaving the heart itself open for the strong passions and overwhelming preferences that will then seize it . . . sad to say, it is the softer sex especially which is said to go through a period of almost utter heartlessness.' Girls were 'harder and more selfish' than boys; in preparation for the sexual passion to come, their hearts were emptied of all tenderness. And when a girl happened also to have a 'peculiar brooding, imaginative, inventive tendency . . . the dream seems to grow and become an inner life, unchecked by social feeling and by outward occupation, till a mere idea, equally causeless and wicked, fills the soul'. The newspaper, in defiance of the idea of the middle-class Victorian woman as an 'angel in the house', was suggesting that most adolescent girls were given to murderous desires: 'Constance Kent, it is said, only did what myriads of her age and sex only wish should come to pass by other agency than their own.'

Some newspapers reported that Constance had already written to her father in Wales, to spare him the shock of first hearing of her confession through the pages of the press. But an anecdote recounted in the *Somerset and Wilts Journal* contradicted this. An acquaintance of Samuel Kent noticed that he was in good spirits when he visited the Welsh town of Oswestry, near his home in Llangollen, on the morning of Wednesday, 26 April. At about 2 p.m., he was seen buying a newspaper at the railway station. While reading the newspaper, which carried an account of his daughter's confession at Bow Street the previous afternoon, he became 'temporarily paralysed' before rushing up the main street to a hotel, from which he ordered a carriage and immediately started for home. He failed to keep an appointment he had made in Oswestry that afternoon.

Williamson, who had been given sole charge of the case, gathered several magistrates at the Trowbridge police court at eleven on Wednesday morning. The chairman, as before, was Henry Ludlow. The magistrates' clerk, Henry Clark, was also present, as were Captain Meredith, the Chief Constable of the Wiltshire police, Superintendent Harris, Joseph Stapleton and the two solicitors who had been employed by Samuel Kent in 1860, Rowland Rodway and William Dunn. The proceedings were delayed by the late arrival of a key witness, the Reverend Mr Wagner. Hundreds of people who had not gained entry waited outside in the sun.

Wagner reached Trowbridge railway station at twelve o'clock, accompanied by Detective-Sergeant Thomas, and went straight into the court. The room was packed. He sat down, his eyes half-closed, his plump hands resting on top of his umbrella and his chin on his hands.

Constance walked 'calmly and firmly' into the courtroom, reported the *Daily Telegraph*. She was a stout girl of average height, according to this paper's reporter, and looked to be 'in robust health . . . her cheeks had a ruddy look which did not at all impress upon the spectators the idea that she had been a prey to an accusing conscience. For the first few minutes she looked like a person who felt herself placed in some unpleasant situation.' Miss Gream, who sat next to her, appeared rigid with nerves.

The clerk began by reading out Wagner's statement and then Ludlow, the chairman, asked Wagner: 'Is that true?' 'Yes,' he replied. Ludlow turned to Constance: 'Have you any question to ask this witness?' 'No, sir. I have not.' The magistrate turned back to Wagner: 'You may retire.'

Williamson took the stand and the clerk read out his deposition. As the confession was read to the court, Constance's composure gave way. At the word 'murdered' she burst into tears and half-fell to her knees, leaning against Miss Gream and sobbing bitterly. The Lady Superior wept alongside her. Though Constance was offered a vinaigrette – a box of smelling salts – by one woman sitting nearby and a glass of water by another, she was too agitated to accept either. When the Inspector stepped down, Ludlow told Constance that she was remanded for a week. She was taken to Devizes gaol that day.

Williamson posted a letter to Sir Richard Mayne, asking him to authorise a detective to find Elizabeth Gough, and the next day sent a telegraphic message direct to Dick Tanner, asking him to track the nursemaid down. Detective-Inspector Tanner, who had interviewed the Kents' former servant Harriet Gollop for Whicher in 1860, had become fêted for solving the North London Railway case of 1864, the first murder in England to take place on a train (he traced the killer, Franz Muller, by means of a hat found in the carriage, and chased him to New York by steamship). Though the press reported a rumour that Gough had married an Australian sheep farmer, Tanner found that she was at the family home in Isleworth, twelve miles from London. Jack Whicher, still living in Pimlico, was invited by Mayne to go with Tanner to interview the woman he had defended so fiercely, and fruitlessly, in 1860. The two discovered that she was earning a scant living as a dressmaker, occasionally employed to do needlework in gentlemen's houses for a week at a time.

Williamson, meanwhile, made inquiries in Road and in Frome, where he interviewed William Dunn and Joshua Parsons – the doctor had moved there from Beckington in 1862, and now ran a busy general practice. The Inspector returned to London on Saturday, and on Sunday visited Gough himself, taking Whicher with him.

The ex-detective and his one-time protégé worked together that week. Afterwards the younger man applied for his former boss to be refunded £5.7*s*.6*d*. for 'travelling and other expenses'. It was just over a year since Whicher had retired from the department, humiliated and disowned. A few newspapers referred to how unjustly he had been maligned. *The Times* published a letter from Lord Folkestone: 'Will you allow me to state, in justice to Detective Whicher . . . that the last words he said to a friend of mine at the time were, "Mark my words, Sir, nothing now will be known about the murder till Miss Constance Kent confesses."' The *Somerset and Wilts Journal* reminded its readers of the 'merciless and almost universal . . . censure' to which this 'able and experienced' officer had been subjected. But the fact that Constance had confessed was not taken as a sign that the detective had triumphed; as the words on Saville's tombstone had promised, God had triumphed where man – and science, and detection – had failed.

On Monday, 1 May, Samuel Kent visited his daughter in Devizes gaol, accompanied by Rowland Rodway. Constance was sitting at a desk, writing. She stood up to greet Rodway, but on seeing her father she broke down in tears, recoiled and staggered backwards towards her bed. Samuel caught her in his arms. As the men left, Constance told her father that 'the course she had adopted was due to him and her God'.

The *Standard* reported that Samuel was 'completely stunned' by the meeting with his daughter: 'He walks and talks, as it were, mechanically.' He visited Constance every day that week, and arranged for the staff of the Bear Hotel in Devizes to supply her with dinners. To pass the time in prison, she read, wrote and sewed.

On Thursday Constance returned to the Trowbridge police court. The chief magistrate was Henry Ludlow and his task, as in 1860, was to establish whether there was enough evidence to send Constance for trial at a higher court. At 11 a.m. about thirty reporters rushed in through the narrow passage to the stifling courtroom and scrambled for seats. The crude bench erected for the press at the first Road murder hearings was still in place, but was not large enough for all of them; some grabbed the seats reserved for the lawyers, which prompted angry reprimands from the policemen trying to keep order. There was standing room for only a fraction of the huge crowd that had gathered outside.

Though Constance at first seemed calm, once she had taken her place in the dock 'her heaving bosom told of the tumult raging within', said the *Somerset and Wilts Journal*. The witnesses came and went, as they had five years earlier, repeating the little they knew: Gough, Benger, Parsons, Cox (now Sarah Rogers, having married a farmer from the Wiltshire village of Steeple Ashton), Mrs Holley, her daughter Martha (now Martha Nutt, having married one of the Nutts of Road Hill), Police Sergeant James Watts. To some, the images of the murder were still vivid – Benger recalled that when he lifted Saville's body from the privy 'blood was catched on the folds of his little night dress'. Parsons, slightly altering his conclusions of 1860, said that he thought the immediate cause of Saville's death was the incision in his throat, but that he might have been partly suffocated before it was inflicted. He repeated that it was impossible that a razor caused the wound to the chest, which could 'only have been inflicted by a long, strong, sharp-pointed knife . . . there was a notch on one side as though the knife had been withdrawn in a different direction to that which it was forced in'. He said that when he examined the nightdress on Constance's bed on 30 June 1860, he noticed that the cuffs were still stiff with starch.

After each witness had testified, Constance was asked if she had any questions to put. 'No,' she breathed. She kept her face veiled and her eyes cast down throughout the proceedings, lifting her head only to glance at a new witness or to motion an answer to a question from the chairman.

Whicher took the stand. As he gave his evidence he produced his relics: the two nightdresses he had confiscated from Constance's room five years earlier, Constance's handwritten list of linen, and the warrant issued for her arrest – he must have been waiting for this day. ('You ought to have been a detective police officer,' Lady Audley tells Robert Audley, her pursuer. He replies: 'I sometimes think I should have been a good one.' 'Why?' 'Because I am patient.') Whicher's account of his investigation at Road Hill in 1860 rehearsed, almost word for word, what he had told the magistrates then. It was as if the story had become an incantation. He expressed no emotion at the turn events had taken – no rancour, no triumph, no relief. Ludlow gave him the opportunity to make clear that the local police had concealed from him their discovery of a bloodstained shift in the boiler hole.

'Did you ever hear of any bloody garment having been found?' asked the magistrate.

'No such communication was ever made to me by any member of the police force,' said Whicher. 'I never heard a word of it until some three months after, when I read an account of it in the newspapers.'

Katharine Gream took the stand next, and the drama in the courtroom escalated. She began by asking the court to respect the confidences Constance had made to her, as they would the confidences between a mother and her child: 'from the first she came to me as a daughter'. Then she explained that Wagner had told her in Holy Week, which ran that year from 9 to 16 April, that Constance had confessed to the killing, and wished to make her confession public. Miss Gream had raised the subject with the girl, never mentioning the word 'murder'. She asked her if she 'fully realised what it involved' to give herself up. Constance said that she did. The next week, Constance told

Miss Gream that she had carried Saville downstairs while he was sleeping, that she had left the house through the drawing-room window, and that she had used a razor, taken from her father's dressing case 'for the purpose'. She said that 'it' was done 'not from any dislike to the child, but that it was revenge on her stepmother'. Later, she told Miss Gream that she had stolen a nightdress back from the laundry basket, as Whicher had surmised.

Ludlow, who was seeking to establish whether any pressure had been exerted on the girl to confess, asked Katharine Gream what had prompted Constance to give these extra details about the murder. 'I think I asked her if the child cried to her for mercy,' said Miss Gream. Ludlow asked what conversation preceded this. 'I was trying to point out the greatness of the sin in God's sight, and I was pointing out to her the things that would aggravate the sin in God's sight.'

'After all the conversation between you,' asked Ludlow, 'did you at any time offer her any inducement to give herself up?'

'Never,' said Miss Gream. 'Never.'

When Wagner took the witness box he folded his arms across his chest and asked ('in a whining tone', said the *Somerset and Wilts Journal*) to read a brief statement he had written. Ludlow said he could not do so until he had given his evidence. None the less, as soon as the examination began Wagner stated: 'All the communication I have had with Miss Constance Kent was made to me under the seal of confession, and therefore I must decline to answer any question that would involve a breach of that secrecy.'

This was strong stuff. The Roman Catholic Church might hold the confessional to be sacred, but the Anglican Church was subject to the laws of the state. The spectators hissed their disapproval.

Ludlow warned him: 'You have sworn, Mr Wagner, before God, that you will tell the truth, the whole truth and nothing but the truth in this inquiry.'

'My duty to God,' returned Wagner, 'forbids me to divulge anything received in confession.' Again the courtroom was filled with hissing.

All that he could disclose, Wagner said, was that three or four weeks earlier Constance had asked him to communicate to Sir George Grey, who had replaced Cornewall Lewis as Home Secretary in 1861, that she was guilty of the Road murder. He insisted that he had on no occasion induced her to confess. Ludlow did not pursue Wagner's defiance over the confessional – that could wait for the trial.

Shortly before six o'clock the last witness was dismissed and Constance was asked if she had anything to say. She lightly shook her head. Ludlow committed her for trial, and she quietly left the dock. At seven o'clock she was sent back to Devizes gaol.

Almost three months passed before Constance was tried for murder. In the interim Williamson continued to round up witnesses and evidence in case she changed her plea. In late May Dr Mallam, Saville's godfather, wrote to Scotland Yard from Holloway, north London, offering to talk to the detectives. When Williamson interviewed him, Mallam said he had witnessed the way in which the children of Samuel Kent's first wife were slighted by their father and their stepmother. If the police wanted corroboration, he suggested they ask Mary Ann. He also described the conversation between himself, Parsons, Stapleton and Rodway after Saville's funeral, in which they had all agreed that Constance was guilty. 'Dr Mallam also informed me,' wrote Williamson, 'that he had heard that a man named Stephens now residing in Frome and who was formerly gardener in Mr Kent's family, had stated that Miss Constance on an occasion about 18 months before the murder asked him how she could get a razor out of her father's dressing case.' This implausible rumour may have had some substance, since a man named William Stevens was among the few new witnesses listed to appear at Constance's trial in July.

Williamson went to Dublin on 29 June to subpoena Emma Moody. He went to Oldbury-on-the-Hill, Gloucestershire, two weeks later to summon Louisa Long, formerly Hatherill, the other schoolfriend Whicher had interviewed in 1860.

The Reverend Mr Wagner, far from being thanked for helping to solve the crime, became a scapegoat for the press and the public. He was excoriated in the English newspapers, in the House of Commons and in the House of Lords (Lord Ebury said the 'scandal' of his involvement with Constance Kent revealed how the Church of England was being 'undermined and destroyed'). By presenting himself as the keeper of Constance's secrets, Wagner drove some into a frenzy of frustration. Gangs in Brighton tore down confessional notices at St Paul's, where Wagner preached, assaulted him in the street and threw objects at the windows of St Mary's Home. On 6 May an anonymous correspondent to the *Standard* asked what had become of the £1,000 bequest that Constance had received on her twenty-first birthday, in February. Wagner's solicitor replied that Constance had tried to hand over £800 of the inheritance to St Mary's, but the clergyman had refused it. On the night before they set off for Bow Street, she stuffed the money into a collection box at St Paul's. Wagner found it there the next day, and notified the Home Secretary. This story was confirmed by Rowland Rodway, who wrote to the newspapers to say that Wagner had given the money to Samuel Kent to use on his daughter's behalf.

The Road Hill case had become a battleground for the great religious controversy of the century, the fight between the High and Low elements in the Anglican Church. The Reverend James Davies argued in a pamphlet that Constance Kent's confession proved the value of monastic, Anglo-Catholic institutions. St Mary's, he said, had inspired the girl to confess: 'the devoted lives, the self-denying discipline which she saw around her, and the very atmosphere which she breathed within the holy retreat, subdued, and melted, and moulded her, as a preparation. Then when the heart is *softened*, it must be *opened*.' The semi-erotic tones in which Davies described the girl's surrender to God recalled the raptures of the female Catholic saints rather than the sober piety of a Protestant heroine.

In reply, the congregational minister Edwin Paxton Hood published a pamphlet that cast doubt on the substitute religious families to which a young woman might 'submit herself' without her natural family's assent – High Church practices could undermine the authority of the Victorian home. Paxton Hood was impatient with the romance that had come to surround Constance Kent: 'There is nothing at all wonderful about her or her crime, or her five years' silence, or her confession, except that she was very cruel, very close, and very callous. And much as she was she probably is. Her confession does not exalt her; and we decline to accept her either as a model penitent or, as has been attempted, as a heroine. She is simply a very wicked young woman.'

Some said that Wagner had encouraged Constance to confess because he wanted to publicise his views about the sanctity of the confessional. Some suspected that his High Church fervour had stirred the girl into a false confession. James Redding Ware reprinted his pamphlet of 1862, in which he had implied that a somnambulant Elizabeth Gough had committed the crime, with 'further remarks' that cast doubt on Constance's admission of guilt. He argued that the 'Romanish' Church cultivated the idea of self-sacrifice: 'If Miss Constance Kent's confession shows one "style" more than other, it is that of emphatically gathering to herself all the odium attached to the death of her brother.'

A Wiltshire rector who visited Constance in prison in May tried to ascertain the state of her soul. When he entered her cell he found her writing at a table strewn with open books. She was 'very plain and stout', he told the *Salisbury and Winchester Journal*, 'and her cheeks very full'. Her manner was 'perfectly self-possessed, hard and cold'. He asked her if she believed that God had forgiven her. She answered: 'I do not feel sure that my sin is forgiven, for no one on this side of the grave can feel sure of that.' She showed no self-pity, he said, nor any regret.

From her cell Constance wrote to her solicitor, Rodway:

It has been stated that my feelings of revenge were excited in consequence of cruel treatment. This is entirely false. I have received the greatest kindness from both the persons accused of subjecting me to it. I have never had any ill will towards either of them on account of their behaviour to me, which has been very kind. I shall feel obliged if you will make use of this statement in order that the public may be undeceived on this point.

This seemed straightforward enough, but it left the matter of Constance's motive more mysterious than ever. The newspapers continued to hope that she was crazy. If mad, she could be excused, pitied, accommodated. 'The insane theory is the one that resolves all difficulties,' observed the *Saturday Review* on 20 May.

Women accused of murder often pleaded insanity in the hope that the courts would treat them with leniency, and it would have been easy for Constance or her representatives to argue that she had been afflicted by homicidal monomania when she killed her brother.* Her apparent sanity was no bar to such a plea – as Mary Braddon wrote in *Lady Audley's Secret*, 'remember how many minds must tremble upon the narrow boundary between reason

* To demonstrate the weird logic of homicidal monomania, Stapleton recounted a horrible story about a mild-mannered young man who was so obsessed with windmills that he would gaze at them for days on end. In 1843 friends tried to distract him from his fixation by moving him to an area with no mills. There the windmill man lured a boy into a wood, then killed and mutilated him. His motive, he explained, was the hope that as punishment he would be taken to a place where there just might be a mill.

and unreason, mad to-day and sane to-morrow, mad yesterday and sane to-day'. Inherited insanity, argued the alienist James Prichard, could lie dormant until startled into life by circumstances, and could as quickly subside. Women were thought to be prone to insanity, whether as a result of suppressed menstruation, a surplus of sexual energy, or the upheavals of puberty. In an article of 1860 the physician James Crichton-Browne argued that monomania was most common in childhood. 'Impressions, created by the ever fertile imagination of a child . . . are soon believed in as realities, and become a part of the child's psychical existence. They become, in fact, actual delusions.' Children, he wrote elsewhere, were 'diamond editions of remote ancestors, full of savage whims and impulses'. Many doctors emphasised the madness, disorder, even devilishness that could flourish in young breasts – not all Victorians were set on sweetening or sanctifying the figure of the child.

Yet when the eminent alienist Charles Bucknill examined Constance in gaol, she insisted that she was sane, then and now. The doctor interrogated her about her motive for killing Saville, asking why she had not attacked the real object of her anger, her stepmother. Constance replied that this would have been 'too short'. Bucknill understood her to mean that by killing Saville she intended to inflict a prolonged torture on the woman she hated, rather than a quick extinction. Later, Bucknill told the Home Secretary that he thought Constance 'had inherited a strong tendency to insanity', but that she had 'refused to let him' state his belief in public, because she wished to protect the interests of her father and brother. Rodway explained Constance's rationale in similar terms: 'A plea of insanity at the time of the deed might, it is believed, have been set up with success,' he told the Home Secretary, 'but she, fearing that such a plea might affect prejudicially her brother's chances in life, earnestly entreated that it should not be urged on her behalf.' She was determined to protect William from the taint of madness.

After meeting Constance, Bucknill fell in with her wishes and declared her sane, but he gave the newspapers a hint of his unease. Like Whicher, he found the clue to Constance's disturbance in her stillness. The sensationalism of the murder sat strangely with the blankness of the girl. 'The only peculiarity which at all struck Bucknill,' reported the *Salisbury and Winchester Journal*, 'was her extreme calmness – the utter absence of any symptom of emotion.'

Miss Constance Emily Kent

CHAPTER SEVENTEEN

MY LOVE TURNED

July–August 1865

On the evening of Tuesday, 18 July Constance was transferred to the county gaol at Salisbury. Usually prisoners were moved between towns by train, but the governor of Devizes prison took Constance by post-chaise across Salisbury Plain, a journey of forty miles. She joined about forty-five men and five women at Fisherton gaol, on the outskirts of the city. That Wednesday – two days before the trial – Rowland Rodway visited her to tell her that her lawyers believed that, despite her confession, she would be acquitted if she pleaded not guilty. He urged her to make her peace with God in private: her spiritual atonement, he argued, did not depend on a public confession and conviction. Constance reiterated her intention to plead guilty; it was 'her plain duty', she told the lawyer, 'the only course which would satisfy her conscience', and the only one that would lift suspicion from others.

Salisbury was filling with visitors. Samuel, Mary, Mary Ann and William Kent had rooms at the White Hart, a handsome Georgian hotel opposite the cathedral. Williamson was in town, as was Whicher, who may have stayed with his niece Mary Ann and her husband, William Wort, at their house in New Street. More than thirty witnesses for the prosecution were on hand in case they were required. These included Constance's schoolfriend Louisa, though Emma Moody had fallen ill and was unable to make the journey from Ireland.

John Duke Coleridge QC, one of the most successful barristers of his generation, had been appointed to represent Constance. On Thursday he met Mary Ann and William Kent to discuss their sister's case, 'and then', he wrote in his diary, 'sat up till near three, getting up my speech'. He composed a letter to his client: 'If you plead Not Guilty then whatever I can do shall be done for your acquittal. If you plead Guilty anything I can say to set others right shall be said. But I advise you against any intermediate course.' Constance replied early in the morning of Friday, 21 July, the day of the trial: 'I am persuaded that nothing will tend to clear the innocent so completely as my conviction.'

The Wiltshire constabulary had erected barriers outside the courthouse and drafted in constables from all over the county. About thirty reporters had turned up, and they were furious to discover that no provision had been made for them – the city authorities had failed to build the press balcony they had promised. Only fourteen places were allocated to the reporters; the others had to take their chances with the rest of the mob when the doors were opened at nine.

The judge was Sir James Willes, a tall man with luxuriant dark hair, eyebrows and whiskers, a prominent nose and a melancholy, harsh stare. He was reserved and courteous in manner, and his voice had an Irish lilt – he was born in Cork, to Protestant parents, in 1814. Once he and the twenty-four magistrates of the Grand Jury had taken their seats, Constance was brought in. She wore a black worsted veil, a plain black cloak, a black bonnet adorned with glass beads, a pair of black gauntlet gloves. She spoke briefly to Rodway, at the back of the dock, then lifted her veil and came to the front. Her face, judged the *Daily Telegraph* reporter, was 'broad, full, uninteresting', with an 'expression of stupid dulness'. 'She has full eyes, in which at times there is a look as if she was suspicious of those surrounding her, and which may be best described as the glance of a person who is afraid of something.' The *News of the World* described her as 'dull and heavy, her forehead low, her eyes small and her figure tending to plumpness, and there being an entire absence of anything like vivacity in her air or countenance'.

The clerk of the court read out the charge and asked, 'How say you, Constance Emilie Kent, are you guilty or not guilty?'

'Guilty,' she said, in a low tone.

Willes turned to her. 'Are you aware that you are charged with having wilfully, intentionally and with malice killed your brother?'

'Yes.'

The judge paused. 'And you plead guilty to that?' Constance was silent.

After a few moments Willes pressed her: 'What is your answer?' Again she said nothing. Despite her determination to plead guilty, silence and secrecy seemed still to exert a pull on her.

'You are charged with having wilfully, intentionally and with malice killed your brother,' repeated Willes. 'Are you guilty or not guilty?'

Finally she replied: 'Guilty.'

'The plea must be recorded,' said Willes. The room was perfectly quiet as the clerk wrote it down.

Coleridge rose and addressed the court on Constance's behalf. 'I desire to say two things before the sentence of the court is passed.' He was a lean man with a long face, sharp, sympathetic eyes, and a melodious voice. 'In the first place the prisoner solemnly, in the presence of Almighty God, and as a person who values her own soul, desires me to say that the guilt is hers alone, and that her father and others, who have so long suffered most unjust and cruel suspicions, are wholly and absolutely innocent. Next she desires me to say that she was not driven to act, as has been asserted, by any unkind treatment in her home. She met nothing there but tender and forbearing love, and I hope I may add not improperly that it gives me a melancholy pleasure to be made the organ of these statements, because on my honour I believe them to be true.'

Coleridge sat down. The clerk of the court asked Constance if she could give any reason why a sentence of death should not be passed upon her. She said nothing.

Mr Justice Willes put on his black cap, in preparation for delivering the death sentence, and addressed Constance. 'I can entertain no doubt, after having read the evidence, and considering it in connexion with your three confessions of crime, that your plea is the plea of a guilty person. You appear to have allowed feelings of jealousy –' 'Not jealousy!' Constance burst out. The judge continued '– and anger to have worked in your breast until at last they assumed over you the influence and power of the evil one.'

At this point Willes' voice broke. As he paused, unable to speak, Constance glanced up at him, and on seeing his distress was herself overcome. She turned away from the judge, trying to hold back her tears. Willes was now openly weeping. He went on with difficulty. 'Whether Her Majesty, with whom the prerogative of mercy rests, may be advised to exercise that prerogative in your case on account of the fact of your youth at the time when the murder was committed, the fact that you are convicted on your own confession, and the fact that that confession removes suspicion from others, is a question which it would be presumptuous in me to answer. It now well behoves you to live what is left to you of life as one about to die, and to seek a more enduring mercy by sincere and deep contrition, and by a reliance on the holy redemption.' He passed the death sentence, finishing with the words, 'And may God have mercy on your soul.'

Constance stood utterly still for a moment, then pulled down her veil. She was led out of the courtroom by a female prison warder, whose face was wet with tears. The trial had lasted twenty minutes.

Constance's cry 'Not jealousy!' was the only spontaneous statement she made in public over the months of her confession and trial. She would admit to anger, she would admit to murder, but she refused to agree that she had experienced envy. Perhaps she protested too much: if she had killed Saville out of anger, she could imagine herself as a heroic avenger of her natural mother and of William; but if out of jealousy, she was self-centred, childish, vulnerable. If she was jealous, she did not merely rage against her stepmother and her father; she wanted their love.

As soon as the death sentence was passed, 'broadside' ballads about the Road Hill murder were produced. These were formulaic, single-sheet accounts of crimes, published quickly and cheaply in large quantities, then sung and sold by street vendors. Their role had been largely usurped by the newspapers, which now reported crime just as cheaply and more fully, to an increasingly literate population. Most broadside ballads were written in the first person, in the form of a confession and lament:

His little throat I cut from ear to ear,
Wrapped him in a blanket and away did steer
To the water-closet, which soon I found,
In the dirty soil then I pushed him down.

For all Constance's denials, the balladeers were clear about her motive:

My father married a second wife,
Which filled my bosom with spleen & strife.

In the words of another, she was 'jealous of her mother-in-law'. More than one balladeer described Constance as haunted by Saville's ghost: 'Not night nor day no rest I get, in my dreams my brother see.' Some conveyed a lascivious excitement at the surrender that she was expected to make on the gallows:

I see the hangman before me stand,
Ready to seize me by the law's command . . .
Oh, what a sight it will be to see,
A maiden die on the fatal tree.

But the broadside publishers were jumping the gun – the public was clamouring for Constance Kent to be spared the death sentence. A Devonshire magistrate came forward to testify to the madness of the first Mrs Kent, claiming that he and other neighbours of the Kents had witnessed her outbreaks of lunacy in the 1840s. On the Sunday after Constance's conviction, the Reverend Charles Spurgeon, the most popular preacher of his time, delivered a sermon to more than four thousand people at the Metropolitan Tabernacle, Elephant & Castle, which compared Constance Kent's crime to that of Dr Edward Pritchard of Glasgow, another murderer convicted that month. Pritchard was arrested when traces of poison were found in the bodies of his wife and her mother, who had both died soon after discovering his liaison with a fifteen-year-old servant girl. He did not confess. Even when he was found guilty of murder, he tried to blame the killings on others: 'I feel now as though I had been living in a species of madness since my connection with Mary McLeod.' Constance, by contrast, had made a voluntary admission of guilt in order to lift suspicion from those close to her. The Reverend Mr Spurgeon argued that she should be shown mercy. Rowland Rodway, Dr Bucknill, and the Reverend Mr Wagner joined in pleading with the Home Secretary not to execute her, as did Mr Justice Willes.* The newspapers were in overwhelming agreement. For a

* James Willes separated from his wife in 1865 and moved to a house on the banks of the Colne, in Essex. Over the next few years, according to the *Dictionary of National Biography*, he walked his three dogs by the river and fed the trout. Though he had been a keen fisherman in his youth, he developed such a fondness for the fish that he banned the sport in his waters. In 1872, on becoming sleepless, forgetful and depressed, he shot himself in the heart with a revolver.

cold-blooded child-murderer, Constance had aroused an extraordinary level of sympathy. Within days Sir George Grey recommended to the Queen that her sentence be commuted to one of penal servitude for life, which was usually a twenty-year term.

On the morning of Thursday, 27 July, Victoria agreed to spare the young woman. The governor of Fisherton gaol hurried to Constance's cell to give her the news, which she received with her customary calm: 'She did not show the slightest emotion.'

That week, Joseph Stapleton wrote a letter to *The Times*, inviting the newspaper's readers to contribute to a fund he had set up for Elizabeth Gough at the North Wilts Bank, Trowbridge. For 'five long years', he said, she 'has been shut out from profitable domestic employment' because of the suspicions that attached to her at Road. He attested to 'the uniform modesty and purity of her character, her fidelity to her master and his family, her unwavering courage and simple truthfulness in her time of trial and peril'. Stapleton also drew attention to the plight of William Kent. 'This young man, now nearly 21 years of age, is a good son, a devoted brother, amiable and talented beyond the ordinary endowment of such qualities; but the thick dark cloud of this enduring family sorrow rests on him and bars his entrance into life. Will no one bring William Kent under the notice of the Government? Would the Government resist an appeal on his behalf for employment suitable to his education and habits?'

Because Constance pleaded guilty, Wagner's refusal to disclose all that she had told him was never challenged in court (in fact, Willes had decided that he would defend Wagner's right to silence on this issue – he told Coleridge afterwards that he had satisfied himself that there was 'a legal privilege in a priest to withhold what had passed in confession'). The clergyman remained loyal to Constance. He and Katharine Gream paid her regular visits in prison.

In August, an effigy of Constance Kent was modelled by the waxworkers of Madame Tussaud's to put on display in the museum's Chamber of Horrors, alongside newly made figures of two other murderers – Dr Pritchard, the poisoner, and John

Wilkes Booth. Wilkes Booth had assassinated Abraham Lincoln in the week that Constance made her confession to Wagner; on the day that she was imprisoned at Devizes he was hunted down and shot dead in a barn in Virginia.*

On 4 August the Wiltshire magistrates wrote to Sir Richard Mayne to suggest that Whicher and Williamson be given the £100 reward that the government had offered in 1860 for evidence that led to the conviction of the Road Hill murderer. This would serve, they wrote, as 'a slight acknowledgement of the great skill and sagacity displayed by them in their difficult task'. The suggestion was ignored.

Just before she left Brighton for Bow Street magistrates' court in April, Constance had written a letter to Sir John Eardley Wilmot, the baronet who in 1860 had taken such an interest in helping the Kents to clear their names. A part of this letter, in which she gave her fullest account of what drove her to murder, was forwarded in July to Peter Edlin, who helped prepare the case for the defence. Since no defence was presented, the letter remained private. The surviving section ran as follows:

> *The murder I committed to avenge my mother whose place had been usurped by my stepmother. The latter had been living in the family ever since my birth. She treated me with all the kindness and affection of a mother (for my own mother never loved or cared for me) and I loved her as though she had been.*
>
> *When no more than three years old I began to observe that my mother held quite a secondary place both as a wife and as mistress of the house. She it was who really ruled. Many conversations on the subject, which I was considered too young*

* In the event, Madame Tussaud's did not put the Constance Kent waxwork on show until after Samuel Kent's death – perhaps out of respect for his feelings. According to the museum catalogues, it was displayed from 1873 to 1877.

to understand, I heard and remembered in after years. At that time I always took part against my mother, whom being spoken of with contempt I too despised. As I grew older and understood that my father loved her *and treated my mother with indifference my opinion began to alter. I felt a secret dislike to* her *when she spoke scornfully or disparagingly of my mother.*

Mamma died. From that time my love turned to the most bitter hatred. Even after her death she *continued to speak of her with scorn. At such times my hate grew so intense that I could not remain in the room. I vowed a deadly vengeance, renounced all belief in religion and devoted myself body and soul to the Evil Spirit, invoking his aid in my scheme of revenge. At first I thought of murdering* her *but that seemed to me too short a pang. I would have her feel my revenge. She had robbed my mother of the affection which was her due, so I would rob* her *of what she most loved. From that time I became a demon always seeking to do evil and to lead others into it, ever trying to find an occasion to accomplish my evil design. I found it.*

Nearly five years have since passed away during which time I have either been in a wild feverish state of mind only happy in doing evil, or else so very wretched that I often could have put an end to myself had means been near at the moment. I felt hatred towards everyone, and a wish to make them as wretched as myself.

At last a change came. My conscience tormented me with remorse. Miserable, wretched, suspicious, I felt as though Hell were in me. Then I resolved to confess.

I am now ready to make what restitution is in my power. A life for a life is all that I can give, as the Evil done can never be repaired.

I had no mercy, let none ask it for me, though indeed all must regard me with too much horror.

Forgiveness from those I have so deeply injured I dared not ask. I hated, so is their hatred my just retribution.

It was a beautifully composed atonement. Constance's explanation of why she killed Saville – that she wished to inflict on her bad mother the exact pain that had been inflicted on her good one – was breathtaking, at once crazy and logical, just as the killing itself had been both methodical and impassioned. There was an uncanny control to the narrative: her furious attack on a child was rendered as an abstraction; she sought an opportunity to do evil, and 'I found it.'

After the trial Dolly Williamson filed a report to Sir Richard Mayne, in a clear, curving hand. He had been told, he said, that Constance claimed she twice intended to kill her stepmother, 'but was prevented by circumstances and then the thought struck her that before she killed her she would kill the children, as that would cause her additional agony, that it was with such feelings in her heart she returned home from school in June 1860'. His informant was probably Dr Bucknill, who had discussed the murder with Constance at some length. It was not until the end of August that the alienist, in a letter to the newspapers, divulged the girl's account of how she killed Saville:

> *A few days before the murder she obtained possession of a razor from a green case in her father's wardrobe, and secreted it. This was the sole instrument which she used. She also secreted a candle with matches, by placing them in the corner of the closet in the garden, where the murder was committed. On the night of the murder she undressed herself and went to bed, because she expected that her sisters would visit her room. She lay awake watching until she thought that the household were all asleep, and soon after midnight she left her bedroom and went downstairs and opened the drawing-room door and window shutters. She then went up into the nursery, withdrew the blanket from between the sheet and the counterpane, and placed it on the side of the cot. She then took the child from his bed and carried him downstairs through the drawing-room. She had on her nightdress, and in the drawing-room she put on her*

goloshes. Having the child in one arm, she raised the drawing-room window with the other hand, went round the house and into the closet, lighted the candle and placed it on the seat of the closet, the child being wrapped in the blanket and still sleeping, and while the child was in this position she inflicted the wound in the throat. She says that she thought the blood would never come, and that the child was not killed, so she thrust the razor into its left side, and put the body, with the blanket round it, into the vault. The light burnt out. The piece of flannel which she had with her was torn from an old flannel garment placed in the waste bag, and which she had taken some time before and sewn it to use in washing herself. She went back into her bedroom, examined her dress, and found only two spots of blood on it. These she washed out in the basin, and threw the water, which was but little discoloured, into the footpan in which she had washed her feet over night. She took another of her nightdresses and got into bed. In the morning her nightdress had become dry where it had been washed. She folded it up and put it into the drawer. Her three nightdresses were examined by Mr Foley, and she believes also by Mr Parsons, the medical attendant of the family. She thought the blood stains had been effectually washed out, but on holding the dress up to the light a day or two afterwards she found the stains were still visible. She secreted the dress, moving it from place to place, and she eventually burnt it in her own bedroom, and put the ashes or tinder into the kitchen grate. It was about five or six days after the child's death that she burnt the nightdress. On the Saturday morning, having cleaned the razor, she took an opportunity of replacing it unobserved in the case in the wardrobe. She abstracted her nightdress from the clothes basket when the housemaid went to fetch a glass of water. The stained garment found in the boiler-hole had no connexion whatever with the deed. As regards the motive of her crime it seems that, although she entertained at one time a great regard for the present Mrs Kent, yet if any remark was at any time made which in her opinion was disparaging to any member of the first family she treasured it up and determined to revenge it. She had no ill-will against the little boy, except as one of the children of her stepmother . . .

She told me that when the nursemaid was accused she had fully made up her mind to confess if the nurse had been convicted, and that she had also made up her mind to commit suicide if she was herself convicted. She said that she had felt herself under the influence of the devil before she committed the murder, but that she did not believe, and had not believed, that the devil had more to do with her crime than he had with any wicked action. She had not said her prayers for a year before the murder, and not afterwards till she came to reside at Brighton. She said that the circumstance which revived religious feelings in her mind was thinking about receiving sacrament when confirmed.

Bucknill finished his letter by observing that, though Constance was not in his opinion insane, even as a child she had 'a peculiar disposition' and 'great determination of character', which indicated that 'for good or evil, her future life would be remarkable'. If placed in solitary confinement, he warned, she could succumb to insanity.

Emotionally, the explanation that Constance gave Bucknill had the eerie detachment that this crime must have required. The methodology of the murder supplanted any feeling about it. At the moment of Saville's death, her focus switched from the failing body to the sputtering candle on the toilet seat: 'The light burnt out.'

Despite its air of cold precision, though, the account was strangely imprecise. Constance's story of the murder didn't add up – as the press was quick to point out. How did she fold back and smooth the bedclothes in the cot while she was holding in one arm a large, sleeping boy of nearly four? How did she, still holding the boy, bend to the ground to lift up the drawing-room window? How did she manage to then crawl under it, still without waking him, and light a candle in the water closet to which she carried him? Why did she take the facecloth to the privy, and why had no one noticed it in her room before? How was it that she had splashed only a couple of spots of blood onto her nightdress while stabbing repeatedly at the boy? How had those who searched the house after the murder missed the stains on her nightdress, and the loss of Samuel Kent's razor? And how had she managed to make those deep stabs with a razor, a feat the doctors had declared impossible? Yet some of the details, if only because they complicated the picture, were persuasive: for instance, Constance's panic when it seemed that the 'blood would never come' seemed too particular and grisly to be invented.

The Times observed, with dismay, that the crime 'seems not to diminish in perplexity and strangeness as it is unravelled step by step. It is evident that we have not yet obtained a complete account of all the circumstances.' Even now, after a confession of murder, it seemed that there were secrets still. 'We are but little enlightened,' said *the News of the World* – Constance's explanation merely added 'a new pang of horror'.

Forty years later, Freud made a gloriously confident assertion about how helplessly human beings betrayed themselves, how surely their thoughts could be read. 'He that has eyes to see and ears to hear may convince himself that no mortal can keep a secret. If his lips are silent, he chatters with his finger-tips; betrayal oozes out of him at every pore.' Like a sensation novelist or a super-detective, Freud fancied that people's secrets would flood up to the surface, in blushes and blanches, or work their way out to the world in the fingers' twitches. Perhaps somewhere in Constance's confessions and evasions the suppressed story of the crime and its motive lay in hiding, waiting to tell itself.

CHAPTER EIGHTEEN

SURELY OUR REAL DETECTIVE LIVETH

1865–1885

In October 1865, Constance was transferred from Salisbury to Millbank, a thousand-cell holding prison on the Thames – 'a big, dark building with towers', wrote Henry James in *The Princess Casamassima*, 'lying there and sprawling over the whole neighbourhood, with brown, bare, windowless walls, ugly, truncated pinnacles, and a character unspeakably sad and stern . . . there were walls within walls and galleries on top of galleries; even the daylight lost its colour, and you couldn't imagine what o'clock it was'. The female prisoners occupied a wing known as the Third Pentagon. A visitor to the gaol would see them 'erect themselves, suddenly and spectrally, with dowdy untied bonnets, in uncanny corners and recesses of the draughty labyrinth'. The *Penny Illustrated Paper* sent a reporter to see in what conditions Constance was confined. He found Millbank 'a geometrical puzzle', 'an eccentric maze' with three miles of airless, seemingly subterranean 'twisting passages', 'dark nooks or "doublings" in the zigzag corridors', 'double-locked doors, opening at all sorts of queer angles, and leading sometimes into blind entries, and frequently to the stone staircases which . . . seem as though they had been *cut out* of the solid brickwork'.

Constance was assigned a cell equipped with a gaslight, a washing tub, a slop pan, a shelf, tin mugs, a salt cellar, a plate, a wooden spoon, a Bible, a slate, a pencil, a hammock, bedding, a comb, a towel, a broom and a grated peephole. Like the other inmates, she wore a brown serge dress. Her breakfast was a pint of cocoa and molasses; lunch was beef, potatoes and bread; supper bread and a pint of gruel. For the first few months of her sentence she was forbidden from speaking to other inmates and from receiving visitors – the Reverend Mr Wagner and Miss Gream applied for special permission to see her, but were turned down. Each day she cleaned her cell and went to chapel. Usually she was then set to work, perhaps making clothes, stockings or brushes for fellow prisoners. She had a bath a week, and a library book if she chose. For exercise she walked in single file, six feet behind the preceding convict, around the enclosed marshy waste ground that ringed the prison buildings. She could see Westminster Abbey to the north, smell the river to the east. Jack Whicher's home was a block away, invisible behind Millbank's high walls.

Whicher, meanwhile, took up his life again. In 1866 he married his landlady, Charlotte Piper, a widow three years his senior. If he had ever been legally married to Elizabeth Green, the mother of his lost son, she must have been dead now. The service took place on 21 August at St Margaret's, an exquisite sixteenth-century church in the grounds of Westminister Abbey, where sheep grazed on the green.

Elizabeth Gough had also married that year. At the church of St Mary Newington, Southwark, on 24 April 1866, almost a year to the day after Constance Kent's confession, she became the wife of John Cockburn, a wine merchant.

By the beginning of the next year Whicher was working as a private investigator. He didn't need the money – his pension was adequate, and the new Mrs Whicher had a private income. But now that he had been vindicated, his brain was cleared of congestion and his appetite for detection had returned.

Private inquiry agents, such as Charley Field and Ignatius Pollaky, were thought to embody the most sinister aspects of detection. Sir Cresswell Cresswell, the judge who presided over the divorce court, fulminated in 1858 against 'such a person as Field': 'of all the people in the world the people of England have the greatest objection to anything like a spy system. To have men running after them wherever they go and making notes of all their actions is what they hold in utter abhorrence. Everything of the kind is held in the greatest detestation in this country.' In Wilkie Collins' *Armadale*, published in 1866, the private detective is a 'vile creature whom the viler need of Society has fashioned for its own use. There he sat – the Confidential Spy of modern times, whose business is steadily enlarging, whose Private Inquiry Offices are steadily on the increase. There he sat – the necessary Detective . . . a man professionally ready on the merest suspicion (if the merest suspicion paid him) to get under our beds, and to look through gimlet-holes in our doors; a man who . . . would have deservedly forfeited his situation, if, under any circumstances whatever, he had been personally accessible to a sense of pity or a sense of shame.' The work was well-paid, if uncertain: in 1854 Field received fifteen shillings a day, plus expenses, to spy on a Mrs Evans, and an extra six shillings a day if he obtained the evidence of adultery that her husband required in order to divorce her.

In his new role Whicher took part in the longest and most famous court battle of the late nineteenth century: the case of the Tichborne Claimant. At the end of 1866 a plump, jowly fellow turned up in London declaring himself to be Sir Roger Tichborne, a Roman Catholic baronet and heir to his family's fortune. Sir Roger had been lost in a shipwreck in 1854, his body never found; the Claimant said that he had been rescued and taken to Chile, from where he made his way to Australia. He had been living in Wagga Wagga, New South Wales, under the assumed name Thomas Castro until he learnt that the Dowager Lady Tichborne, an eccentric Frenchwoman who persisted in believing her son was alive, had placed in the Australian press a plea for news of his whereabouts.

The Dowager Lady Tichborne greeted the Claimant as her son; friends, acquaintances, former servants also signed documents testifying to his identity. Even the family doctor insisted that this was the man he had attended since boyhood, right down to his peculiar genitals (when flaccid, the penis withdrew into the body, like that of a horse). Yet many others who had known Sir Roger derided the Claimant as an inept impostor. In some respects his knowledge was remarkable – he noticed that a painting at the Tichborne estate had been cleaned during his absence, for instance – but he made elementary errors, too, and had somehow forgotten every word of his first language, French.

One of the sceptics, Lord Arundell of Wardour, who was related to the Tichbornes, hired Whicher to unmask the Claimant. The detective was told that he would be paid handsomely if he gave the matter his unceasing attention. Over the next seven years the case claimed not only Whicher's unceasing attention but the attention of the whole country. It was a puzzle so confounding that it brought on a kind of national paralysis. 'It has weighed upon the public mind like an incubus,' wrote a barrister in 1872; 'no subject whatever occupied so large a space of the human mind', reported the *Observer* in 1874.

Whicher had two decades of experience in this kind of investigative work: shadowing, tailing, rustling up witnesses, fathoming lies and half-truths, coaxing information out of unwilling participants, using photographs to secure identifications, appraising personalities. Acting on a tip-off from an Australian detective, he began by making inquiries in Wapping, a poor district by the east London docks. He discovered that on Christmas Day 1866, within hours of reaching England, the Claimant had visited the Globe public house on Wapping High Street, ordered a sherry and a cigar, and asked after the Orton family. He claimed to be enquiring on behalf of an Arthur Orton, a butcher he had known in Australia. Whicher suspected that the Claimant was the Wapping butcher himself.

For months Whicher prowled the streets of Wapping. He invited a stream of locals who had known Orton – victuallers, confectioners, sailmakers and so on – to accompany him to the Claimant's lodgings in Croydon, south of London. One by one they met the detective at London Bridge station, took the train to Croydon and waited outside the Claimant's house until he emerged, or could be glimpsed through a window. Most, but not all, said they recognised the Claimant as Arthur Orton. Whicher would hide if the Claimant stepped out of the house. According to one witness, 'He said it would not do for him to be seen there – it would raise suspicion probably, and stop him coming out.' Whicher tracked down Orton's former girlfriend, Mary Ann Loder, who swore that the Claimant was the man who had deserted her in 1852 to seek his fortune overseas. She proved an important witness – amazingly, she even testified that Arthur Orton had a regressive penis.

Whicher's brief was wide. He not only sought evidence against the Claimant, but also tried to persuade his supporters to defect. In October 1868 he visited a Mr Rous, the landlord of the Swan in Alresford, Hampshire, and one of the Claimant's chief advisers. After ordering a glass of grog (rum and water) and a cigar, the detective asked him: 'You believe in him being the man?'

'Most certainly,' said Rous. 'I have no doubt he is the right man but foolish.'

'Mr Rous, don't you believe anything of the kind. You may depend upon it, he is no such person. What I shall tell you will make you very uncomfortable.' Whicher proceeded to unpick the Claimant's story.

The Claimant – who weighed twenty stone when he reached England – was growing fatter and fatter. His working-class supporters hailed him as a hero who was being punished by the aristocracy and the Catholic Church for the vulgarities he had adopted in the Australian bush. Once again Whicher was working for the establishment, and against the class from which he came – he was the turncoat, the archetypal policeman.

When the Claimant sued for control of the family estates in 1871, the Tichbornes hired Sir John Duke Coleridge, who had defended Constance, to represent their interests. In the course of the trial, as at Road Hill, the other side sought to discredit Whicher and his discoveries. The Claimant's lawyers complained that their client had been 'haunted' by detectives, and by one in particular. 'I believe that the story of Arthur Orton has emanated from the brain of one of them,' said his barrister, 'and I think we shall yet learn how it has been concocted. I am not fond of people of this description. They are totally irresponsible, they belong to no known body, they are not called upon to account for their conduct. They don't belong to the recognised police, they are amateurs, and many of them superannuated officers who gain an honest livelihood by private enquiries. Without imputing to the honourable body that they invent evidence, I may say there is such a thing as torturing evidence so as to make it look uncommonly different from what it is.'

In 1872 the Claimant lost his case, and the Crown promptly sued him for perjury. Again the Claimant's lawyers – by then led by the Irish barrister Edward Kenealy – tried to demean Whicher, with accusations that he had bribed and coached his witnesses. Kenealy made snide comments to the prosecution witnesses when they took the stand: 'I suppose you and Whicher have had many a little drop of drink over this case?'

Since Road Hill, Whicher had learnt to shrug at vilification, to take a longer view. He had regained his old assurance. In 1873 he wrote in a letter to a friend: 'I daresay you hear me frequently abused in reference to the Tichborne case, but whether I shall live (as in the Road murder case) to outlive the innuendoes and slanders of – Kenealy I know not, but that the Claimant is

Arthur Orton is as certain as that I am – Your Old Friend, Jack Whicher'.

In 1874, the Claimant was found guilty, and sentenced to fourteen years of penal servitude. He was sent to Millbank. Though the Tichbornes' solicitor urged the family to pay Whicher a bonus of a hundred guineas for his outstanding work on the case, there is no record of whether they did so.

Jack Whicher was still living with Charlotte at 63 Page Street, off Millbank Row – formerly 31 Holywell Street, but now renamed and renumbered. His niece Sarah had moved out in 1862, when she married Charlotte's nephew, James Holliwell, who had been awarded one of the first Victoria Crosses for his part in the Indian Mutiny of 1857: while under siege in a house in Lucknow, according to the citation, he had behaved 'in a most admirable manner, encouraging the other nine men, who were in low spirits, to keep going . . . His cheerful persuasion prevailed and they made a successful defence in a burning house with the enemy firing through four windows.' James and Sarah now lived in Whitechapel, east London, with their three sons. Jack and Charlotte, though childless, looked after children too – Amy Gray, born in Camberwell in about 1856, was a regular visitor from the age of five, and Emma Sangways, born in Camberwell in about 1863, was recorded as the Whichers' ward in 1871. The nature of the couple's connection with these girls is a mystery, but the bonds between them lasted until death.

In January 1868, while Whicher was hunting down witnesses in Wapping, the first instalment of Wilkie Collins' *The Moonstone* appeared in *All the Year Round*. It was an immediate bestseller. 'It is a very curious story,' observed Dickens, 'wild and yet domestic.' *The Moonstone*, a founding fable of detective fiction, adopted many of the characteristics of the real investigation at Road: the country-house crime in which the criminal must be one of the inmates of the house; the secret lives led behind a veneer of propriety; the bumbling, pompous local policeman; the behaviour that seems to point to one thing yet turns out to point to another; the way that the innocent and the guilty alike act suspiciously, because all have something to hide; the scattering of 'real clues and pseudo clues', as a reviewer described them (the term 'red herring' – something that puts bloodhounds off the scent – was not used to mean 'pseudo clue' until 1884). In *The Moonstone*, as at Road Hill, the original source of the crime was a wrong done in a previous generation: the sins of the father were visited on the children, like a curse. These ideas were taken up by many of the detective novelists who succeeded Collins, as was the novel's air of uncertainty, what one of its characters calls 'the atmosphere of mystery and suspicion in which we are all living now'.

The story diluted the horror of Road Hill: instead of a child-murder, there was a jewel theft; instead of bloodstains, splashes of paint. Yet the plot borrowed many specifics from the Road case: the stained and missing nightdress; the laundry book that proves its loss; the renowned detective policeman summoned to the countryside from London; a household that shudders at his invasion; the indelicacy of a lower-class man accusing a middle-class girl. Most significantly, it translated Whicher into the prototypical detective hero, 'the celebrated Cuff'. ('To cuff', in contemporary slang, was to handcuff.) The seventeen-year-old Robert Louis Stevenson, when he read the novel that year, wrote to his mother: 'Isn't the detective prime?'

Physically, Sergeant Cuff is a papery, hawkish old thing, quite unlike Whicher. In character, though, they are akin. Cuff is melancholy, sharp-witted, enigmatic, oblique – he has 'round-about' and 'underground' ways of working, by which he lures his sources into disclosing more than they intend. His eyes 'had a very disconcerting trick, when they encountered your eyes, of looking as if they expected something more from you than you were aware of yourself'. Cuff is after unconscious secrets as well as facts that are deliberately withheld. He acts as a foil to the novel's sensation, a thinking machine to interpret the palpitations and pulsings of the other characters. By identifying with Cuff, readers could shield themselves from the thrills they sought – the story's untrammelled emotion, the tremble of danger. The fever of feeling was transmuted into the 'detective-fever' that burnt in the novel's characters and its readers, a compulsion to solve the riddle. In this way the detective novel tamed the sensation novel, caging the emotional wildness in an elegant, formulaic structure. There was madness, but it was mastered by method. It was Detective Sergeant Cuff who made *The Moonstone* a new kind of book.

Yet Cuff, unlike the detectives he inspired, gets the solution wrong: 'I own that I made a mess of it,' he says. He is mistaken in believing that the criminal is the daughter of the house – the secretive, 'devilish self-willed', 'odd and wild' Miss Rachel. She turns out to be more noble than his policeman's nature can understand. In so far as it reflected the events at Road Hill, the novel ignored the official solution – Constance Kent's guilt – and instead gave voice to the unease that still surrounded the story. It aired the notions of somnambulism, unconscious deeds, double selves that the Road case had aroused, the dizzying whirl of perspectives that had been brought to bear upon the investigation. The solution Collins gave to the mystery of the moonstone was that the odd and wild Miss Rachel had drawn suspicion to herself in order to protect someone else.

In 1927 T.S. Eliot compared *The Moonstone*, favourably, to the fiction of Edgar Allan Poe and Arthur Conan Doyle:

> *The detective story, as created by Poe, is something as specialised and as intellectual as a chess problem, whereas the best English detective fiction has relied less on the beauty of the mathematical problem and much more on the intangible human element . . . the best heroes of English detective fiction have been, like Sergeant Cuff, fallible.*

In his lifetime, Collins was often dismissed as a master of plot with little aptitude for depicting his characters' interior lives. By comparison with novelists such as George Eliot, he built his stories from the outside rather than from within. Henry James characterised them as 'monuments of mosaic art', then amended this: 'They are not so much works of art,' he said, 'as works of science.'

In May 1866 Samuel Kent renewed his plea to the Home Office to retire on his full salary, which had risen to £500 when he completed thirty years' service that April. Since Saville's death, he explained in his letter, the family had experienced 'indescribable pain and anguish greatly aggravated by the disclosures which the penitence of his daughter Constance ultimately constrained her to make'. His attempts to find the murderer and shield his family, he said, had left him in debt. The health of his second wife was 'entirely shattered' – Mrs Kent was losing her sight and had fallen prey to a 'hopeless and helpless paralysis', so he had to nurse her and tend to their four young children.

In August, to his dismay, the Home Office granted Samuel a pension of £250, half of what he had requested but the maximum the rules allowed. He desperately backtracked, begging to withdraw his resignation – he would continue working, he said; he had not intended to resign, only to enquire into the possibility; he could not manage on so little money. The Home Office questioned whether he was fit to discharge his duties. Yes, he replied at the end of August: he no longer needed to nurse his wife – Mary Kent, *née* Pratt, had died earlier in the month aged forty-six, of congestion of the lungs.

The Home Office allowed Samuel to continue as a sub-inspector. That summer he was awarded £350 damages by the Edinburgh *Daily News* for an article that had portrayed his second wife as common and cruel. With the four surviving children of his second marriage – Mary Amelia, Eveline, Acland,

Florence – Samuel went north to the small Welsh town of Denbigh, where he employed an Australian governess and two other servants. His eldest daughters, Mary Ann and Elizabeth, moved to London together. William also headed for the capital city, with the £1,000 inheritance he had secured on his twenty-first birthday in July.

Through the winter of 1867, William took evening classes at King's College, where he studied the 'new science' being forged by Darwin and others. William's passion was microscopy, and by the end of the year he had been elected a Fellow of the Microscopical Society. The biologist Thomas Huxley, one of the most influential scientists of his time, became William's sponsor. He encouraged the young man to investigate infusoria, single-celled water bacteria visible only through a magnifying lens.

Huxley was known as 'Darwin's bulldog' for his ardent advocacy of the natural historian's ideas. He gave the name 'retrospective prophecy' to the process of imagining the past by observing the present. A natural historian sought to see into the past as a prophet saw into the future – 'Would that there were such a word as "backteller"!' said Huxley. In a lecture to working men in 1868, he took the piece of chalk he was holding as the starting point for an account of the geological history of the earth. 'A small beginning,' he concluded, 'has led us to a great ending.' From the tiny, a world could unfold.

William Kent had a furious curiosity about little things, a conviction that they held the big secrets. Over the next five years he pursued his calling at the Cambridge Zoological Museum, then at the invertebrate collection of the Royal College of Surgeons, and then at the zoology department of the British Museum, where his salary rose above £300. Here he fell for corals – he declared himself 'smitten with them'. Corals are small, soft marine animals whose limestone skeletons create reefs in tropical seas. Through their 'agency', in William's words, 'new islands and countries are made to rise from the bed of the trackless ocean' – they connected zoology and geology, the quick and the dead.

Charles Dickens died in 1870, leaving an unfinished work, *The Mystery of Edwin Drood*. By dint of its author's death, this novel became the purest kind of murder story, the kind whose tension was never dissolved. 'Alone, perhaps, among detective-story writers, he never lived to destroy his mystery,' wrote G.K. Chesterton. 'Edwin Drood may or may not have really died; but surely Dickens did not really die. Surely our real detective liveth and shall appear in the latter days of the earth. For a finished tale may give a man immortality in the light and literary sense; but an unfinished tale suggests another immortality, more essential and more strange.'

In 1865 Dickens, like many others, had been forced to question his belief that Samuel Kent and Elizabeth Gough had committed the Road Hill murder. As if revisiting the case, his last novel featured a brother and sister who recall Constance and William Kent. The orphaned and exotic Helena and Neville Landless frequently ran away from their unhappy home. 'Nothing in our misery ever subdued her,' Neville says of his sister, 'though it often cowed me. When we ran away . . . the flight was always of her planning and leading. Each time she dressed as a boy, and showed the daring of a man. I take it we were seven years old when we first decamped; but I remember, when I lost the pocket-knife with which she was to have cut her hair short, how desperately she tried to tear it out, or bite it off.' Helena may have been the leader, but Neville admits to having a 'misshapen young mind' and murderous desires. He matches his sister in loathing and in cunning: 'I have had, sir, from my earliest remembrance, to suppress a deadly and bitter hatred. This has made me secret and revengeful.'

Dickens depicted the two as dark, foreign creatures, the embodiment of suspense. They are 'slender, supple, quick of eye and limb; half shy, half defiant; fierce of look; an indefinable kind of pause coming and going on their whole expression, both of face and form, which might be equally likened to the pause before a crouch or a bound'.

In January 1872 Samuel Kent fell seriously ill with liver disease and William took the train up to Wales. From his father's bedside he wrote a letter to his supervisor at the British Museum, who had lent him £5 for the trip: 'You can imagine how thankful I am to have the opportunity to stay with him for a few days there being so many little things I can do to contribute to his comfort.' On 5 February he wrote in another letter: 'All is *over*! In the sorrow in which we are all plunged you will I am sure excuse my absence for a few more days.' Samuel was buried next to his second wife at Llangollen. He left his money to the children of his second marriage, to be held in trust until they reached the age of twenty-one. William and the proprietor of the *Manchester Guardian* – presumably a friend of the family – were joint executors.

Four months after his father's death, William married Elizabeth Bennett, a barrister's daughter of twenty-two, and moved to Stoke Newington. At William's request, his new father-in-law petitioned the government for Constance's release, but without success. In 1873 William was appointed resident biologist at the Brighton Aquarium, which had opened the previous year, a spectacular gothic arcade sunk into the promenade by the pier. He and Elizabeth took up residence at Upper Rock Gardens, a Regency terrace near the seafront.

The public craze for aquaria provided scientists with unprecedented opportunities for studying live sea creatures, but William claimed that the commercial backers of the Brighton venture thought a resident naturalist 'an unnecessary extravagance', and were hostile towards him. He fell out with his colleagues as well. He accused one of his juniors of undermining him, and then was himself accused of ungentlemanly conduct by a fellow researcher. The pair had witnessed the aquarium's two octopuses copulating, and agreed to write a joint paper on the subject. When some of William's observations appeared in a letter to *The Times*, the colleague accused him of duplicity. William indignantly resigned his post. He had a high-handed, insensitive streak, a side-effect of the sometimes maniacal passion with which he approached his work.

The next year William was appointed curator and naturalist at the new Manchester Aquarium. He rebuilt the tanks, fitted blinds to block out glare, installed a system to circulate the water and solved the problem of how to keep large seaweeds alive in artificial conditions. His official guidebook to the creatures in his care, published in 1875, conjured up an underwater world of great range and drama, in which he observed the victims and the predators alike with unflinching yet tender fascination. He wrote of the 'brilliant expressive eyes' of the smooth blenny in tank 13, a 'brave little knight' who protected his blenny 'wives'; of the 'remarkably pugnacious' spider crab in tank 6, who tore the limbs off his brother crabs; and of the spotted dogfish in tank 10, whose second eyelid during the day remained 'entirely closed over the true eye. When darkness has fully set in, this diaphragm is completely retracted, leaving the eyeball free and gleaming.'

At the Manchester Aquarium, William discovered that sea-horses used sound to communicate:

> *The knowledge of this remarkable circumstance was arrived at in the following manner. Early last May, the majority of the specimens of the fine collection of these singular little fish were brought to England from the Mediterranean . . . Among them were several examples remarkable at the time, for the brightness of their colours, some being bright red, others pale pink, yellow, almost pure white . . . A few of these were kept by the writer for some days in a private room, to permit the opportunity of a hurried coloured sketch. An ordinary inverted bell-*

glass was devoted to their reception, while the individuals 'sitting for their likeness' were for a short time isolated in a still smaller glass receptacle. During one of these occasions a sharp little snapping noise was heard at short and even intervals, to proceed from the larger vase on a side table, and which was immediately afterwards responded to in a similar manner from the smaller one close at hand. Surprise and admiration was intense on discovering that it proceeded from the mouth of the usually regarded dumb little fish, and closer inspection elicited that the sound was produced by a complex muscular contraction and sudden expansion of the lower jaw.

In 1875 William's wife, Elizabeth, died suddenly aged twenty-five, of an obstruction of the bowel. Within a year he married again – his second wife was Mary Ann Livesey, a handsome, square-faced woman of thirty – and moved to London to become curator and naturalist of the new Royal Aquarium, a magnificent construction opposite the Palace of Westminster. Over the next few years William won a reputation as an expert in marine biology. In 1882 he published the third and last volume of his nine-hundred-page *A Manual of the Infusoria*, with fifty of his own illustrations of the microscopic water creatures. At 87 St Stephen's Avenue, Shepherd's Bush, his wife was delivered that May of a stillborn boy.

Jack and Charlotte Whicher moved south of the river in about 1880, to a small terrace on the brow of Lavender Hill, Battersea. This district, a mile from Westminster, was known for its market gardens, like the village in which Whicher was raised, but the flowerbeds and nurseries were disappearing under rows of suburban houses. The Whichers' house, 1 Cumberland Villas, had a substantial garden to the rear – the biggest in the block – with views down to the railway. From January 1881, horse-drawn trams rattled along the road in front of the house. Directly opposite, a Mr Merryweather ran a nursery garden, the last to survive on a hill that only a few years earlier had been famous for its fields of lavender.

In the summer of 1881 Whicher fell ill with gastritis and a stomach ulcer, and on 29 June, after his stomach wall was perforated, he died, aged sixty-six. His ward Amy Gray, now a twenty-five-year-old milliner, was at the deathbed; on the death certificate she was registered as his niece. Whicher left Amy £150 in his will, and a gold Swiss watch. He left £100 to Emma Sangways, the other girl whom he and Charlotte had looked after, and £300 to his niece Sarah Holliwell. He bequeathed £150, a gold watch and chain and a signet ring to a friend called John Potter, a surveyor's clerk who worked in Whitehall Place, and £100 to his friend and protégé Dolly Williamson, now Chief Superintendent of Scotland Yard. These two were appointed executors of the will. The remainder of his estate – about £700 – went to his wife.

A three-sentence obituary of Jonathan Whicher appeared in the *Police Gazette*. He had been almost forgotten. For all the brilliance with which he investigated the Road Hill murder, Whicher had been powerless to give the public the certainty that they craved or to deliver them from the evils that he saw. He was punished for his failure. From now on, the detective heroes of England would be found only in the realm of fiction.*

After Jack's death, Charlotte moved to the house of John Potter in Saunders Road, Notting Hill. Amy Gray and Emma Sangways went with her. Charlotte died in January 1883, at the age of sixty-nine, leaving the bulk of her assets to Amy and Emma. She appointed Dolly Williamson the sole executor of her will.

---

* Six years later, in 1887, Arthur Conan Doyle created the first of his hugely successful Sherlock Holmes mysteries. Unlike Jack Whicher, Conan Doyle's fantasy detective is an amateur and a gentleman, and he is always right – 'the most perfect reasoning and observing machine the world has seen', says his sidekick Dr Watson in 'A Scandal in Bohemia'.

Williamson was 'a quiet, unpretending, middle-aged man', recalled the police historian and prison governor Major Arthur Griffiths, 'who walked leisurely along Whitehall, balancing a hat that was a little large for him loosely on his head, and often with a sprig of a leaf or flower between his lips. He was by nature very reticent; no outsider could win from him any details of the many big things he had "put through". His talk, for choice, was about gardening, for which he had a perfect passion; and his blooms were famous in the neighbourhood where he spent his unofficial hours.'

The Chief Superintendent was known as 'the Philosopher' for his abstracted, intellectual manner, and was said to direct operations from his desk as if playing a game of chess. A colleague described him as 'A Scot, from the crown of his head to the sole of his foot, loyal, hardworking, persevering, phlegmatic, obstinate, unenthusiastic, courageous, always having his own opinion, never afraid to express it, slow to grasp a new idea, doubtful of its efficacy, seeing its disadvantages rather than its advantages, but withal so clear-headed, and so honest, and kind-hearted to a fault, he was a most upright and valuable public servant.' Williamson was the antithesis of Whicher's early partner Charley Field, who revelled in his proximity to a criminal underworld. These two men bracketed Whicher, defined the range of what a Victorian detective could be. Field – who by the 1870s was reduced almost to poverty – recalled the daredevil thief-takers of the eighteenth century, while Williamson gestured forward to the careful commanders of the twentieth.

In a notorious trial of 1877, several of Williamson's men were found guilty of corruption, confirming the public suspicion that professional detectives were greedy and duplicitous. Williamson was said to be heartbroken by the betrayal. He took charge of the Criminal Investigation Department when it was founded the next year. Though he led the department during the investigations into the 'Jack the Ripper' murders of Whitechapel prostitutes in 1888, he was too unwell to take an active part. According to a police commissioner, he was 'worn out before his time by the constant strain of very harassing work'. He died in 1889, aged fifty-eight, leaving a wife and five children. Williamson's coffin was covered with flowers and carried to St John's Church, opposite his house in Smith Square, Westminster, by six detective inspectors.

'Most of the prominent detectives of to-day learnt their work under Williamson,' wrote Griffiths in 1904. 'Butcher, the chief inspector . . . is as fond of flowers as was his master, and may be known by the fine rose in his buttonhole.' This love of flowers had originated with Jack Whicher's father, the Camberwell gardener, and seemed now to have been passed on through the first sixty years of the detective force, from man to man.

Constance Kent was shuffled between gaols – from Millbank to Parkhurst, on the Isle of Wight, to Woking in Surrey, and back to Millbank. At Parkhurst she made mosaics, geometrical puzzles pieced together on boards and dispatched to be laid on the floors of churches in southern England: St Katharine's in Merstham, Surrey; St Peter's in Portland, Dorset; St Swithun's in East Grinstead, Sussex. She was a gifted mosaicist. While at Woking she worked on the floor for the crypt of St Paul's Cathedral in London. Like her brother William, she was drawn to the tiny, to fragments that told stories. Among the images on the floor of the St Paul's crypt is the fat-cheeked face of an infant boy, his eyes wide as if startled, wings sprouting from the sides of his head.

At Millbank, Constance worked variously in the kitchens, the laundry and the infirmary – a set of 'naked and grated chambers', wrote Henry James, washed in 'a sallow light'. Major Arthur Griffiths, then the deputy governor of the gaol, praised her work in the sickroom: 'nothing could exceed the devoted attention she gave the sick under her charge as a nurse'. He recalled her in his memoirs as

THE PENNY ILLUSTRATED PAPER

WITH THE NEWS OF THE WEEK.

REGISTERED AT THE GENERAL POST OFFICE FOR TRANSMISSION ABROAD

No. 189. LONDON, SATURDAY, MAY 13, 1865. VOL. VIII.

THE HIDDEN MILLION; or, THE NABOB'S REVENGE, a novel and exciting Serial Tale, will shortly be commenced in a new and improved Series of this Journal, printed on better paper, with the first number of which will be issued a COLOURED SUPPLEMENT, GRATIS.

MISS GREAM GIVING HER EVIDENCE.

Katharine Gream testifying at the Trowbridge magistrates' court, April 1865

Two nineteenth-century photographs of Road Hill House.
The origin of these pictures is discussed in the postscript on page 307

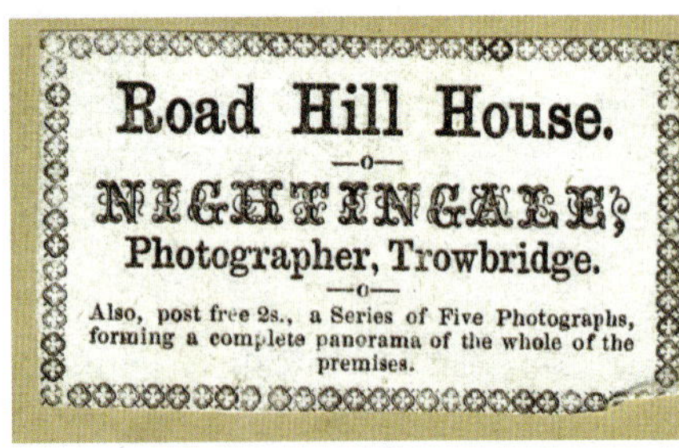

Road Hill House.

—o—

NIGHTINGALE,

Photographer, Trowbridge.

—o—

Also, post free 2s., a Series of Five Photographs, forming a complete panorama of the whole of the premises.

Label pasted to the back of the images above

Detail of drawing-room window
in the left-hand picture

Constance Kent in 1874

William Saville-Kent in the 1880s

William Saville-Kent photographing the fish and corals of the Great Barrier Reef, circa 1890

Some of William Saville-Kent's photographs of fish, published in his book *The Naturalist in Australia* (1897)

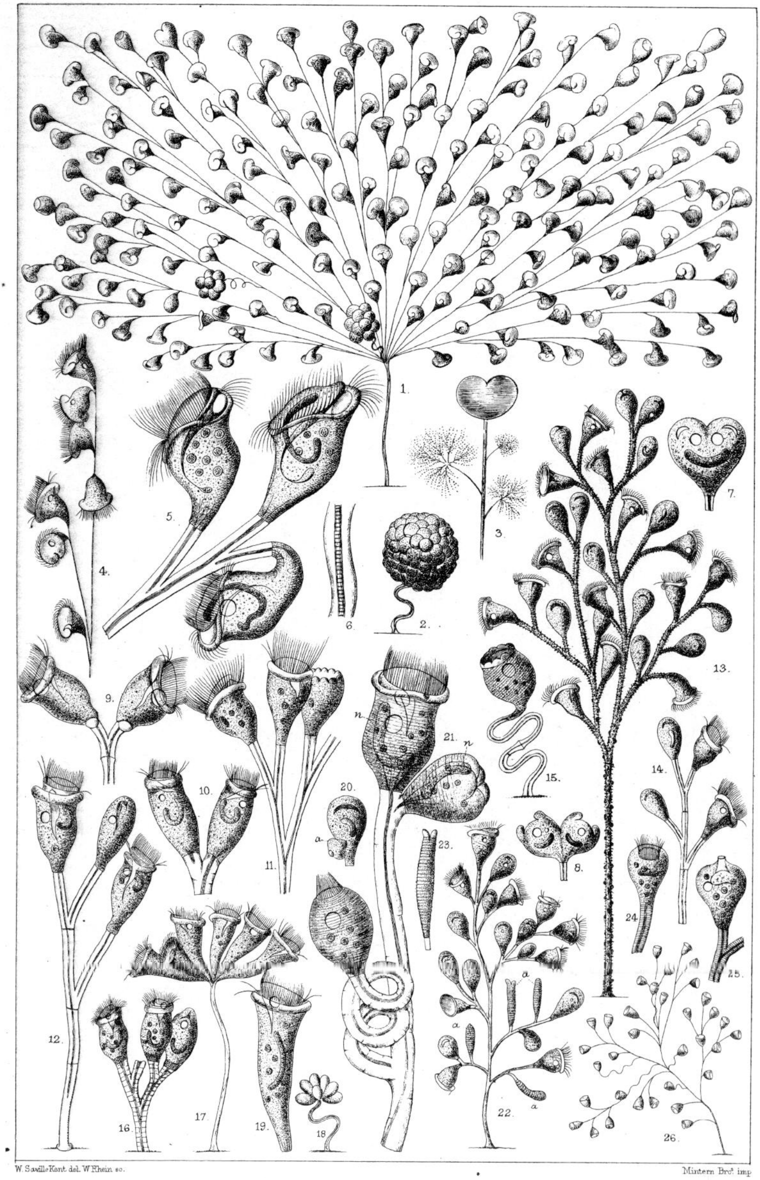

One of William Saville-Kent's illustrations from
A Manual of the Infusoria, 1880-82

Watercolour of Great Barrier Reef echinoderms by William Saville-Kent, 1893

Watercolour of Great Barrier Reef corals by William Saville-Kent, 1893

Emilie Kaye in Sydney, Australia, in 1944

Detail of the mosaic floor in the crypt of St Paul's Cathedral, London, made in the 1870s by inmates of Woking prison

a small, mouse-like creature, with much of the promptitude of the mouse or the lizard, surprised, in disappearing when alarmed. The approach of any strange or unknown face whom she feared might come to spy her out and stare constituted a real alarm for Constance Kent. When anyone went the length of asking, 'Which is Constance?' she had already concealed herself somewhere with wonderful rapidity and cleverness. She was a mystery in every way. It was almost impossible to believe that this insignificant, inoffensive little person could have cut her infant brother's throat in circumstances of such particular atrocity. No doubt there were features in her face which the criminal anthropologist would have seized upon as being suggestive of instinctive criminality – high cheek bones, a lowering, overhanging brow, and deep-set, small eyes; but yet her manner was prepossessing, and her intelligence was of a high order.

Griffiths returned in another memoir to the young woman's ability to conceal herself:

Constance Kent was like a ghost in Millbank; flitting noiselessly about, mostly invisible . . . She spoke to no one, and no one addressed her, the desire to efface herself was always respected, and her name was never mentioned.

In 1877 Constance petitioned Richard Cross, the Home Secretary in Benjamin Disraeli's Conservative government, for an early release. William's former father-in-law, Thomas Bennett, also wrote to Cross on her behalf. Their pleas were turned down. That summer, the Millbank medical officer recommended that Constance be spared cooking duties (these were arduous, and the kitchens gloomy and bare) and instead given needlework shifts. The authorities should consider transferring her to another gaol, he said, as her health was weakening and she would benefit from a 'change of air' – but he did not recommend returning her to Woking, because of 'the great dislike which for some reason or other she entertains to that prison'. She was sent later that year to the female convict prison at Fulham, south-west London, which housed four hundred women.

From cell 29 of Fulham gaol she petitioned Cross again in 1878. In her efforts to win his mercy, she invoked her youth at the time she killed Saville, her contrition, the voluntary nature of her confession, her good behaviour in gaol. She tried to convey what had driven her to murder, in jagged, insistent phrases:

> *the unconquerable aversion to one, who had taught her to despise and dislike her own mother, who robbed that mother of the affection both of a husband and a daughter, the sense of the wrong done to her mother when once discovered became yet more intensified after her death, her successor never alluding to that mother but with taunting sarcasm, she therefore sought to retaliate on its authoress, the mental agony her own mother had endured.*

The petition was refused. She pleaded for mercy again in 1880, in 1881 and in 1882, when she added to the list of her tribulations her failing sight (she had an eye infection) and the 'degrading associations' to which she was subjected in gaol. These pleas were turned down by the new Home Secretary, Sir William Vernon Harcourt, a member of William Gladstone's Liberal administration. The Reverend Mr Wagner wrote letters on her behalf and found other churchmen – such as the Bishop of Bloemfontein – to do the same. Constance unsuccessfully petitioned Harcourt again in 1883, and by 1884 was almost in despair. She had served nearly two decades, she implored him, 'without one ray of hope to brighten a life which since earliest recollection has been passed in confinement, either of school, convent, or prison, while before her now only lies a gloomy future of approaching age after a youth spent in dreary waiting, and heart-sickening dis-appointment, in complete isolation from all that makes life worth living, amid uncongenial surroundings from which mind and body shrink'. Harcourt again marked her petition 'nil'.

Only after serving every day of the twenty-year sentence, on 18 July 1885, was Constance freed.

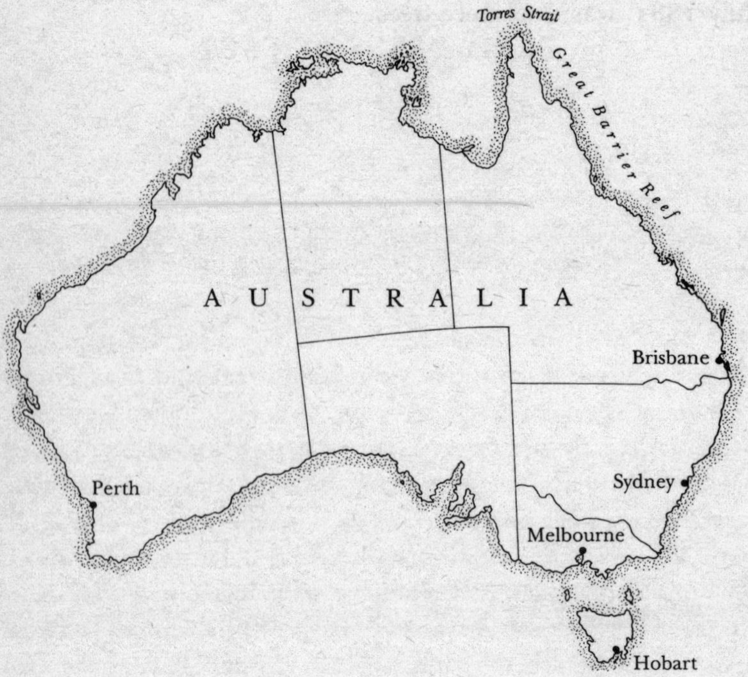
Torres Strait
Great Barrier Reef
AUSTRALIA
Brisbane
Perth
Sydney
Melbourne
Hobart

CHAPTER NINETEEN

FAIRY-LANDS OF FACT

1884–

In 1884 William and his second wife sailed for Tasmania. He had accepted a position as Superintendent and Inspector of Fisheries in the colony, at a salary of £350. He adopted his middle name as part of his surname, and was now known as William Saville-Kent. His half-sister Mary Amelia, now twenty-nine, travelled with them; she had been working as a governess to two girls on a farm in Wiltshire. Two years later they were joined in Hobart, the island's capital, by William's other three half-siblings, first Acland (now twenty-six, until recently a linen salesman in Manchester), then Eveline (twenty-eight – she had been the baby asleep in the Road Hill nursery on the night of Saville's death) and Florence (twenty-five).

William's main tasks in Tasmania were to revive the native oyster industry, which was in danger of being destroyed by over-exploitation and neglect, and to advance the introduction of salmon to the colony's waters. He soon made enemies. His fellow fisheries commissioners complained that he neglected his 'proper duties' to pursue experiments – he had constructed a huge hatchery in his house in Hobart. He was also 'ungraciously only too prone to attribute ignorance to the Commissioners'. William claimed that the Tasmanians had not succeeded in cultivating salmon in their waters at all, only trout. His contract was terminated in 1887.

However tactless William may have been, his talents were noticed elsewhere in Australia. Over the next decade he was given posts as adviser to the governments of Victoria, Queensland and Western Australia. He moved first to the southern city of Melbourne, the capital of Victoria, known in the 1880s as 'Marvellous Melbourne' and 'the Paris of the Antipodes'. His half-brother Acland headed to the goldfields of Victoria in 1887, but quickly fell ill. He died in Melbourne the same year, with William at his side.

William and his wife moved in 1889 to a house on the river by Brisbane, a sprawling, makeshift town that served as the capital of the north-eastern state of Queensland. William adopted two spiny anteaters, 'Prickles' and 'Pins', as pets; though they were shy at first, he wrote, curling away from him under their spikes, after a while they followed him around the house and grounds, or let him carry them, dandled over his arm like lapdogs. He also acquired a pair of fern owls, 'big balls of fluff' with 'gleaming', 'glorious golden eyes', which he adored. William had himself grown a wild, wiry beard that engulfed the lower part of his lean face, leaving all the expression to his high, glinting eyes. His hair lay flat across the scalp, parted in the centre. When out inspecting Queensland's fisheries and oyster beds, he wore linen suits, elasticated boots and a pith helmet.

The 'excessively timid' fern owls, William reported, changed shape according to what they were feeling. They showed 'delightful abandon' before members of the household, but would freeze and shrink into themselves at the approach of a stranger, so that they looked just like sticks. When William came home after a few days' absence, the male bird would puff up in pleasure, extending every feather so that he almost doubled in size. The owls, like the Saville-Kents, had no offspring, but they made an elaborate nest each year. William once slipped some bantam eggs into the empty hollow, and found that the birds sat on them happily, waiting for the chicks to hatch. Three times a day he hand-fed the fern owls with raw beef steeped in water, adding a grasshopper, a beetle or a moth as a treat. To capture the astonishing range of his birds' moods and bodies, he took up photography. A camera, like a microscope, gave its owner extra powers of sight. William could now look for longer as well as more closely, and he could show others what he had seen. He took pictures, enlarged them, studied them with a magnifying glass. With his new instrument, he began to record the extraordinary coral forms of the 1,200-mile-long Great Barrier Reef, which he described as his 'fairy-land of fact' off the Queensland coast.

In 1892 William returned to England with sixty cases of specimens to present to the Natural History Museum and a cache of paintings and photographic prints to show to a publisher. He was accompanied by his wife and the fern owls. The male owl developed a taste for strawberries during its stay in London, and the female for slugs; both were keen on the city's cockroaches.

William Saville-Kent's *The Great Barrier Reef* was published in London in 1893. This beautifully produced volume made the reef famous, and served as the standard reference work for decades. William's silvery photographic plates were reproduced next to written descriptions of the live corals' colours: lemon, myrtle, shrimp pink, apple, crimson, electric blue. The fish he photographed looked like sea monsters, their eyes shining and their scales dark as iron. At the end of the book were colour plates of his paintings of fish and corals, the anemones waving their tentacles, wild and bright.

William sailed back to the Antipodes that year to take up an appointment at the oyster fisheries in Perth, Western Australia. Though the owls went with him, Mary Ann remained in England. Their marriage seemed to have fractured. On a visit to Tasmania,

William stayed with the elderly naturalist and watercolourist Louisa Anne Meredith, and had an affair with her twenty-one-year-old granddaughter.

He returned to England in 1895, though, and bought a house with his wife on the fossil-packed cliffs of Hampshire, about a hundred miles east of the cottage on the cliffs in which he and Constance had been born. William kept Australian lizards in the greenhouse, finches in the study. At Burlington House, London, in 1896 he staged an exhibition of his photographs and water-colours, along with 'some Western Australian pearls of abnormal foundation', reported *The Times*, 'one of these, two inches in diameter, presenting a striking resemblance to a child's head and torso'. He donated two lizards to London Zoo: a frilled lizard and a spiny-tailed monitor. With the first of these he demonstrated that lizards could walk on two legs, which suggested that – as his patron Huxley had argued – these creatures were descended from bi-pedal dinosaurs. The lizards were 'link species' in the evolutionary chain.

William was a great enthusiast for the lumpy, the scaly, the oddities and cast-offs of natural history. In *The Naturalist in Australia* (1897), his second book about the southern hemisphere, he described his love for the baobab tree, with its swollen trunk and spiky crown of branches. He was struck by the tree's 'tenacity of life', he said. It seemed possessed of a freakish creative force. In the bush, he wrote, it was common to see a baobab's trunk 'prostrated, probably centuries ago by some abnormal storm, out of which a fresh tree has reared itself phoenix-like with renewed youth and vigour'. He knew of only one truly dead baobab, he said – it had been struck by lightning, a 'cataclysmic overthrow' as a result of which the tree's 'destruction is thorough and complete'. William took a picture of its blasted trunk, part of which reared above the ruined tree in the shape of 'a weird monstrous bird that has mounted guard and broods like a disembodied spirit over the destruction wrought'.

In 1904 William was lured back to Australia for eighteen months to work for a private company that was trying to transplant and culture pearl oysters. On his return to England he found backers for his own project to cultivate pearls artificially, and then once more headed for the islands of the South Pacific.

Pearls are the only jewels made by living creatures, glowing objects locked in gnarled, primeval cases. In about 1890 William had become the first man artificially to culture half-pearls, or blister pearls; now he was planning to create fully spherical, or 'free', pearls, which took shape deep in the flesh of the oyster. In 1906 he set up a pearl farm on Thursday Island in the Torres Strait, at the northern tip of the Great Barrier Reef, where he developed a method of opening the shell of the oyster without killing the creature within, then slipping a particle of shell into its fleshy folds. The soft oyster would coat the irritant in thin layers of nacre, that eventually formed a prismic, lustrous sphere, the product of shell and flesh. Two Japanese scientists were credited with being the first to create spherical pearls, in 1907, but recent research suggests that William Saville-Kent developed the technique, and perhaps the pearls themselves, before them. He refused to divulge the details of his method to his backers, but agreed to write them down and deposit them in a bank, to be opened in the event of his death.

In 1908 William fell ill and went home to England to die. He succumbed on 11 October to an obstruction of the bowel, the same condition that killed his mother and his first wife. When the investors in his oyster project opened the envelope in the bank, they found nothing intelligible within it – William took the secret of artificial pearl cultivation, with his other secrets, to the grave. His widow, who inherited £166, covered his tombstone at the church of All Saint's, Milford-on-Sea, with coral skeletons. She sold off the rest of his corals, sponges, shells and pearls, and lived alone in their Hampshire cliff house until her own death eleven years later.

Mary Ann and Elizabeth, the two eldest Kent sisters, had moved in 1886 from their lodgings in Regent's Park to St Peter's Hospital, Wandsworth, an almshouse a mile or so from Lavender Hill which housed forty-two people, and had its own chapel, hall and library. Mary Ann died in 1913, aged eighty-two, leaving her estate (worth £129) to Elizabeth. Elizabeth followed her nine years after that, at ninety, bequeathing £250 to a cousin called Constance Amelia Barnes and £100 to her half-sister Mary Amelia, with whom she had corresponded to the end.

Constance Kent had a gift for invisibility – the townspeople of Dinan in the 1860s and the Millbank prison warders in the 1870s had been struck by her ability to merge with her surroundings, to disappear, and in the 1880s she vanished even more conclusively. The public had no idea where Constance went after leaving gaol, and they were not to find out for almost a century.

It emerged in the 1950s that when Constance was released from prison in 1885 the Reverend Mr Wagner took her to stay with a branch of the St Mary's sisterhood that he had established next door to his own house in Buxted, Sussex. Each month she reported to the police at Brighton, about twenty miles away. One of the sisters at Buxted recalled that on her arrival Constance walked 'like a convict, flatly', and had dark spectacles, cropped hair and rough, hardened hands. Her table manners were coarse. She was 'very silent' at first, said the sister, but later talked about the mosaics she made in prison, especially those in the crypt of St Paul's. She never spoke of her family. She told the sisters that she was going to emigrate to Canada and find work as a nurse, under the name Emilie King. This, it turned out, was a half-truth, a misdirection.

In the 1970s it was discovered that early in 1886 Constance sailed for Tasmania with her half-sisters Eveline and Florence, using the alias Emilie Kaye (a homonym of 'Emily K') – Acland had made the crossing a few months before. They joined William and his wife in Hobart. The closeness of these brothers and sisters, who might have been divided by murder, was a reminder of how private, and odd, the emotional life of the family remained.

Constance and William kept a constant and delicate connection for as long as both lived. Constance moved to Brisbane with her brother and his wife in 1889 – she shared a house with them and the shy owls. A year later she went to Melbourne to help look after typhoid victims, and stayed to train as a nurse. She was working as a matron in a private hospital in Perth when William arrived there in 1893. In the mid-1890s she moved to Sydney, which William visited several times between 1895 and 1908. She worked in a lepers' colony at Long Bay, and as matron of an institute for young offenders in Parramatta, on the outskirts of the city.

Constance outlived her brother. In 1911, still using the name Emilie Kaye, she opened a nurses' home in Maitland, north of Sydney, which she ran until her retirement in the mid-1930s. She spent the next decade in rest homes in the suburbs of Sydney. She kept in touch with Mary Amelia's daughter Olive, though Olive did not know that 'Miss Kaye' was her aunt – she thought she was an old friend of her mother and of her aunts Eveline and Florence.* For Christmas 1943 Constance ordered a reference work on birds for her great-nephew, Olive's only child. She sent it to Olive with a letter expressing her disappointment in the book: 'I expected illustrations of nests, eggs etc in a popular form It is a mere bird catalogue.' But at least it was better than most children's books, she added, which were 'grotesque bizarre & hideous . . . all fancy fiction on monstrosities The ugly gollywog has banished the beautiful Fairy.'

When Constance turned one hundred, in February 1944, the local paper pictured her on a sofa, smiling at the camera. The

* Mary Amelia had married an orchard-keeper in Sydney in 1899, and given birth to Olive, her only child, the next year. Eveline, known as Lena, married a doctor in 1888 and had a son and a daughter. Florence never married, and spent her last years living with her niece Olive.

newspaper paid tribute to 'Emilie Kaye', a 'pioneer nurse'. 'Once she nursed lepers,' it announced, oblivious to her deeper past. The King and Queen sent her a congratulatory telegram, and the Archbishop of Sydney called round with a bunch of flowers. Olive attended the birthday celebrations. Emilie Kaye was a 'really wonderful old lady', she reported, 'quite jolly. Everyone seemed fond of her too.'

Two months later Miss Kaye died. In her will she left Olive several mementoes, including a brooch, a gold watch and chain, and two cases, which remained unopened for more than thirty years.

In 1974 Olive and her son made a trip to England. They visited Baynton House, where Olive's mother was born, and learnt the story of the murder at Road Hill. Olive began to wonder whether Emilie Kaye had been her lost aunt, the murderess Constance Kent. Back at home in Australia, Olive and her son cut open the cases that 'Miss Kaye' had left and found in one a daguerrotype of Edward, Constance's older brother, who had died in Havana of yellow fever, and in the other a portrait of the first Mrs Kent.

CHAPTER TWENTY

THE MUSIC OF THE SCYTHE ON THE LAWN OUTSIDE

In 1928, sixteen years before Constance Kent's death, the crime writer John Rhode published a book about the murder at Road Hill House. In February the next year his publisher received an anonymous letter postmarked Sydney, Australia, which began with the instructions: 'Dear Sir, Do what you like with this, if any cash value send it to the Welsh miners to men who our civilization is torturing into degeneration Please acknowledge receipt in the Sydney Morning Herald under Missing Friends.' The letter went on to give a child's-eye view of the Kent family's early life. It was an astonishingly vivid document, about three thousand words long, and it was difficult to believe that it could have been written (or dictated) by anyone other than Constance. In places, it closely matched the letter she wrote to Eardley Wilmot and the petitions to the Home Secretaries, none of which was made public until many years later. Though it made no mention of Saville, the letter from Sydney sought to explain the origins of his death.

According to this document, Constance loved the 'pretty, very capable' governess who joined the Kent household in the early 1840s, and Miss Pratt made 'a pet' of her. But Miss Pratt's arrival soon divided the family. The elder son, Edward, quarrelled with Samuel when he met him emerging from the governess's bedroom one morning. As a result, he and the two older daughters were dispatched to boarding school. When home from school all three favoured their mother's wing of the house, as did William, the youngest, to whom Mrs Kent was 'devotedly attached'. Mary Ann and Elizabeth, according to the letter-writer, were always adamant that their mother was sane. Constance, meanwhile, spent her days in the library with her father and her governess. Miss Pratt 'spoke of Mrs Kent with a sneer, calling her a Certain Person, ridiculing her. Constance was sometimes rude to her mother & would tell the governess what she had said, she made no comment other than a Mona Lisa smile.' Mrs Kent used to describe herself to her children as 'your poor mama', which puzzled Constance.

The household became reclusive, and as the children grew up their friendships were closely monitored. One day Constance and William were tending their plots of earth behind the shrubbery when they were drawn to the sound of 'merry laughter' from the next garden. They looked longingly over the hedge and, though they had been forbidden to play with the neighbours, could not resist an invitation to join in. Their transgression was discovered, and as punishment their 'little gardens' were 'uprooted and trampled down'. Outsiders were not welcome: two tropical birds sent by Edward to his siblings were confined to a cold back room, where they died.

Constance was once encouraged to befriend a girl who lived a mile or so away, but the relationship was not a success: 'after a period of mutual boredom, the girl falsely accused C of trying to set her against her mother'. The accusation was poignant, given that Constance had herself been taught to treat her mother as an enemy.

As Constance grew up, the affection between her and the governess wore thin. Lessons were particularly fraught. If

Constance mistook a letter or word, she was punished for obstinacy.

> *The letter H gave Constance many hours of confinement in a room while she listened longingly to the music of the scythe on the lawn outside, when words were to be mastered punishments became more severe 2 days were spent shut up in a room with dry bread & milk & water for tea, at other times she would be stood up in a corner in the hall sobbing I want to be good I do I do, till she came to the conclusion that goodness was impossible for a child & could only hope to grow up quickly as grown-ups were never naughty.*

The letter from Sydney was written throughout in this loosely punctuated, fevered style, as if the writer were rushing to channel a torrent of memory.

When the family moved to Baynton House, Wiltshire, the letter-writer continued, Miss Pratt punished Constance's fits of temper by locking her in a garret, and the girl delighted in perplexing her gaoler. She used to 'act the monkey' by draping a fur across her chest, climbing out of the window, scaling the roof, sliding down the other side and slipping into a different attic room. She would then return to the room in which she had been confined, unlock the door and let herself in: 'the governess was puzzled at always finding the door unlocked, the key was left in, the servants were questioned but of course knew nothing'.

If imprisoned in the wine cellar, Constance lay on a pile of hay and 'fancied herself in the dungeon of a great castle, a prisoner taken in battle fighting Bonnie Prince Charlie & to be taken to the block the next morning'. Once, when Miss Pratt released her, the girl was smiling, 'looking rather pleased over her fancies'. The governess asked her why.

'Oh,' she said, 'only the funny rats.'

'What rats?' asked Miss Pratt.

'They do not hurt,' said Constance, 'only dance and play about.'

Her next gaol was a beer cellar, where she pulled the spigot off a cask, and after that she was locked in two spare bedrooms that were said to be haunted – on a certain date, a 'blue fire' burned in the grate. If confined in her father's study on the ground floor, she clambered out to climb trees, 'displaying a very cruel disposition by impaling slugs and snails on sticks in trees and calling them crucifixtions'. She was a 'provocative and passionate' child, who longed for excitement, even violence. She would slip away to the woods 'half hoping half fearing, she might see a lion or a bear'.

At boarding school she was 'a black sheep', said the author of the letter, 'resentful of authority', 'ever in trouble', though she had 'nothing to do with the gas escape, which was probably owing to the taps having been forgotten when the meter was turned off'. (The writer's anxiety to clear Constance of the school gas leak is a convincing detail.) Constance gave nicknames to her teachers. One was 'Bear in a bush' for his thick black hair. A minister who took Bible class learnt that he was known as 'the Octagon Magpie' (a reference to the shape of his chapel). Instead of reprimanding her, the minister laughed and 'thinking he might bring some good out of her took some extra pains with her, but seeing the other girls were jealous she gave stupid replies on purpose & so fell from grace'. After this she made an attempt to 'turn religious', but a book by the Puritan preacher Richard Baxter convinced her that she had already committed 'the unforgivable sin' – blasphemy against the Holy Spirit – and so might as well give up on goodness.

The letter claimed that Constance read Darwin as a girl, and scandalised her family by expressing her belief in his theory of evolution. Constance, like William, seemed to find release in the natural world. Animals ran through the letter from Sydney like emissaries of freedom – the lion, the bear, the sheep, the monkey, the magpie, the tropical birds, the dancing rats, even the sacrificial slugs and snails.

After her mother's death, Constance was convinced that 'she was not wanted, everyone was against her', and her new step-mother confirmed this to her. Once, when Constance was home from boarding school, the second Mrs Kent told her that 'only for me you would have remained at school when I said you were coming one of your sisters exclaimed What! That tiresome girl so you see they do not want you'. Constance was inspired to run away to sea with William, said the letter-writer, by reading about 'women disguised as men earning their living and never found out until they were dead'. She persuaded her brother to go with her, and afterwards 'was treated as a bad boy who had led the other astray'.

Constance began to suspect that her mother, whom she had mocked, had never been insane; rather, 'she must have been a saint': 'about her mother there seemed to be some sort of mystery'. The letter-writer explained that Constance slowly came to realise that her father and her governess had been lovers since she was very young. With hindsight, she guessed at the sexual secrets that had been kept from her – her memories were ignited and disfigured by suspicion. As a small child, Constance had 'slept in a room inside that of the governess, who always locked the door between when she came to bed. Mr Kents bed & dressing room were on the other side & when he was away the governess said she was frightened to be alone & Constance had to sleep with her.' Once, in the library, Miss Pratt took fright during a thunderstorm and rushed over to Samuel. He drew her down onto his knee and kissed her. 'O! not before the child,' she exclaimed. Constance was disturbingly entangled in this sexual scene, bearing witness to their intimacies, sleeping in a locked chamber of the governess's room, or taking her father's place in the governess's bed.

Like the heroine of Henry James's *What Maisie Knew* (1897), Constance was a child obliged 'to see much more than she at first understood'. This was how the impulse to detect might begin, in confusion or fear, in an urge to grasp the half-guessed-at secrets of the adult world. Constance read the clues scattered through her early life, pieced together a crime (the betrayal of her mother), identified the criminals (her father and her governess). Perhaps all detectives learn their curiosity in childhood, and remain unusually absorbed by the past.

The letter from Sydney threw out an intriguing suggestion about the Kent family history: the writer remarked that Constance and William had 'Hutchinsonian' teeth; that William had an abscess on one of his legs; and that several of their siblings had died in infancy. Hutchinsonian teeth are notched incisors, identified by the physician Jonathan Hutchinson in the 1880s as a symptom of congenital syphilis. This condition also causes leg ulcers (gummata), and used to claim the lives of many babies. The writer of the Sydney letter was hinting that Samuel's first wife was syphilitic.

Syphilis is an affliction easy to suspect in retrospect, and difficult to prove – Isabella Beeton and her husband, Thomas Hardy and his wife, Beethoven, Schubert, Flaubert, Nietzsche, Baudelaire, van Gogh have all been identified as possible sufferers. The illness was widespread in the nineteenth century – there was then no cure – and was known as the 'Great Imitator' for its capacity to mimic other afflictions, taking on their colours like a chameleon. Since it was usually contracted through illicit sex, its victims hid its existence. Those with the money to buy confidential medical care often succeeded in keeping their secret.

Supposing Samuel caught syphilis in London, the symptoms might have forced his resignation from the dry-salters company and his flight to Devonshire in 1833: the disease manifests itself in painless chancres, usually on the genitals, for the first few weeks, but then produces a fever, aches, and an unsightly rash all over the body. Samuel may have needed to escape from view. If he had 'the pox', his desire for seclusion and secrecy is easier to understand, as is his apparent failure to find another job until 1836.

In the first few months, syphilis is wildly infectious – when Samuel had sex with his wife, the bacteria issuing from the chancres on his body are almost certain to have swarmed through a tiny cut or tear in hers. (These bacteria, which were identified under the microscope in 1905, are known as spirochetes, a name derived from the Greek for 'turning threads'.) The first Mrs Kent would unwittingly have passed the illness on to the babies in her womb. A foetus with congenital syphilis was likely to be miscarried or stillborn, and if it survived birth was typically puny, wizened, feeble, barely able to feed, and prone to die in infancy. Syphilis could have accounted for the several miscarriages that Mrs Kent suffered, as well as the four infants in succession that she saw die. Some children of syphilitic mothers showed no signs of the illness in their youth but grew up to develop notched teeth, bowed legs or other of the symptoms identified by Hutchinson. Perhaps Joseph Stapleton suspected syphilis when he alluded to how a man's 'intemperance' – alcoholic, financial or sexual – could damage his children.

If Samuel had syphilis, he was presumably one of the lucky majority of sufferers who after a year or two showed no obvious further symptoms. But his wife seems to have been one of the unlucky minority who after some years (typically between five and twenty) developed tertiary syphilis, a condition not understood until long after her death: this often manifested itself in personality disorders and then paresis, 'general paralysis of the insane', a steady, incurable deterioration of the brain. As well as explaining her mental illness and frailty, tertiary syphilis could account for her early death (at forty-four) from intestinal blockage – gastro-intestinal problems were among the many possible symptoms, and death usually took place between fifteen and thirty years after the initial infection.

It is tempting to blame syphilis for the similarly early death of the second Mrs Kent, who became paralysed and almost blinded before dying in Wales at forty-six – her symptoms are characteristic of tabes dorsalis, also a manifestation of tertiary syphilis – but she could only have caught it from Samuel if he became re-infected. This was possible. Samuel would have thought himself cured once his chancres and rashes subsided. Mid-Victorians believed that the pox could not be caught twice – a myth that arose because re-infection was not accompanied by lesions or spots.

The evidence is circumstantial and inconclusive. Even the author of the Sydney letter was probably not sure. But if we hypothesise backwards from the Hutchinsonian teeth, the beginning of the story of the Kent family's tragedy may have been a sexual encounter between Saville's father and a London prostitute in the early 1830s. The clue may have ended in the almost invisible world by which William Saville-Kent was so enthralled, in a thread-like, silvery, twisting creature so tiny that it could be seen only through the glass of a microscope.

The connection between syphilis and diseases such as tabes dorsalis and paresis was not recognised until the late nineteenth century, so it is only with hindsight that we can suspect Samuel of causing his wives' ill-health. When he publicised the insanity of the first Mrs Kent, or the paralysis and blindness of the second, Samuel Kent had no idea that he might be leaving clues to the corruptions of his own body.

Strangely, the letter from Sydney in no way cleared up the implausible elements in Constance's confession of 1865, even though the book by John Rhode that provoked the letter had described that confession as 'frankly incredible' and so 'utterly unsatisfactory' that there were grounds for doubting the girl's guilt. 'Her psychology appears so amazing that almost any speculation based upon it is justified,' wrote Rhode. 'It is indeed possible that, in the intensively religious atmosphere of St Mary's Hospital, she conceived the idea of offering herself as a sacrifice, in order to clear away the cloud that rested upon her family.' The person best placed to solve a crime ought to be its perpetrator. As *The Times* observed on 28 August 1865: 'The previous failure of all investigation had shown that the mysteries of the murder could never be unravelled but by the person who had committed it.' Constance had proved an imperfect detective, in her confessions and in the anonymous letter in which she seemed to bare her soul: her solution was flawed. Did this mean she was not the murderer?

The holes in her story left the way open for other theories about the murder, which were formulated in private from the start, and in public once all the main players in the case had died. Long before these, Whicher himself had a theory that could account for the gaps in Constance's evidence. It was never made public, but was outlined in his confidential reports to Sir Richard Mayne.

In his first surviving report, Whicher noted that Constance 'was the only person who slept alone except her Brother, also home for his holidays (and who I have some suspicion assisted in the murder but at present not sufficient evidence to apprehend him)'. Back in London, after Constance had been bailed, Whicher observed that both Constance and William had come home a fortnight before the murder: 'Supposing Miss Constance to be the guilty party and to have had an accomplice, that accomplice in my opinion would in all probability be her brother "William" . . . judging from the close intimacy existing between the two.' Whicher added to this report:

> *as far as I am able to form an opinion that the murder was committed either by Miss Constance alone while in a fit of insanity or by her and her brother William from motives of spite and jealousy entertained towards the younger children and their parents, and I am strongly impressed with the latter opinion judging from the sympathy existing between the two, the fact of their sleeping in rooms alone, and especially the dejected state of the Boy both before and after his sister's*

arrest, and I think there would not have been much difficulty for the Father or some of the relatives to have obtained a confession from him while his sister was in Prison, but under the peculiar circumstances of the case I could not advise such a course.

It would seem natural for William to be 'dejected' after the death of his brother; for Whicher to note it, the form this dejection took must have been peculiar – a turning inwards, a curdling guilt or fear. Whicher made clear the alternatives he discerned: either Constance was crazy, and killed Saville alone; or she was sane, and killed Saville with William's help. From the start, Whicher suspected that William and Constance had planned and carried out the killing together. By the time he left Road, he was almost certain of it.

Whicher believed that Constance, as the older, odder and more determined of the two, had instigated the murder plot, but he believed she had done so on her brother's behalf and with his help. William had the clearer motive for murder: Saville had supplanted him in his parents' affections, and his father often told him that he was inferior to the younger boy. If both he and Constance had plotted to kill Saville, the fact that the plan came to fruition was less surprising: the two children together, isolated and embittered, may have inhabited a fantasy world secured by the other's belief, both imagining that they were acting in defence of each other and of their dead mother. Their resolve would have been strengthened by the determination not to let one another down.

Samuel Kent may have encouraged the police to suspect Constance in order to shield his son. He may have been protecting William when he told Stapleton the story of the children's escape to Bath, twisting the narrative to suggest the boy's sensitivity and the girl's unshakeable nerve. At the time of the investigation, William was often dismissed as a suspect on account of his timidity. Yet Whicher believed that he was capable of taking part in a murder. The press reports of the Bath escapade suggested that the boy had a strong-willed, inventive nature, and his later life bore this out.

Throughout the investigation into Saville's murder many had argued that two people must have participated in the crime. If William helped Constance, this would explain how the bedclothes had been smoothed down when Saville was taken out of the nursery, how Saville was kept hushed as the windows and doors were negotiated, how the evidence was destroyed afterwards. Constance may have mentioned only the razor in her confession because she herself used only a razor, while William wielded the knife. The letter from Sydney avoided any reference to the murder itself; perhaps this was because there was no explanation that could fail to implicate her accomplice.

Several of the stories that drew on the case seem haunted with the possibility that Constance and William were still hiding something. In *The Moonstone*, the heroine protects the man she loves by allowing herself to be a suspect. The runaway brother and sister in *The Mystery of Edwin Drood* share a dark history. The enigma of *The Turn of the Screw* lies in the silence of two children, a brother and sister locked together by a secret.*

Whether William had been her accomplice or simply her confidant, Constance worked at all times to shelter him. As soon as she confessed, she insisted that she had committed the crime 'alone and unaided'. She told her lawyer that she refused to plead insanity because she wanted to protect William, and she tailored her statements about the murder and its motive to the same end. In none of them did she mention him. Though she had complained to her schoolfriends about how he was treated by Samuel and Mary –

---

* Henry James's novella was published in 1898, the heyday of the Sherlock Holmes series. *The Turn of the Screw* runs the detective story backwards, unravelling all its comforts: it refuses to dissolve the mystery of the children's silence; it implicates the detective-narrator in the nameless crime; and it ends, rather than begins, with the death of a child.

the humiliating comparisons to Saville, the way he was made to push a perambulator around the village – she made no reference to this in 1865. She said of her father and stepmother, 'I have never had any ill will towards either of them on account of their behaviour to me,' carefully avoiding the ill will she might bear them on anyone else's account. The answer to the mystery of Saville's murder might lie in Constance's silence after all; specifically, her silence about the brother she loved.

Constance gave herself up in the year before William's twenty-first birthday, when he was due to inherit a £1,000 bequest from their mother. He hoped to use the money to fund a career in science, but was still hampered by the uncertainty and suspicion surrounding the family. Rather than both of them live under the cloud of the murder, Constance chose to gather the darkness to herself. Her act of atonement liberated William, made his future possible.

AFTERWORD

The third chapter of Joseph Stapleton's book on the Road Hill murder is devoted to the post-mortem examination of Saville Kent's body. Among the doctor's many observations about the corpse is a description, in characteristically florid prose, of two wounds on the boy's left hand.

> *But upon the hand – that left hand, that beautifully chiselled hand, hanging lifeless from a body that might, even in its mutilation, furnish a study and a model for a sculptor – there are two small cuts – one almost down to the bone; the other just a scratch – upon the knuckle of the forefinger. How came they there?*

Stapleton's explanation for these injuries briefly, violently, pulls Saville back into view. From the nature and position of the wounds the surgeon deduces that the child woke just before he was killed, and raised his left hand to fend off the knife striking at his throat; the knife sliced into his knuckle; he lifted his hand a second time, more feebly, and the blade grazed his finger as it cut into his neck.

The image makes Saville suddenly present: he wakes to see his killer and to see his death descend on him. When I read Stapleton's words I was reminded, with a jolt, that the boy lived. In unravelling the story of his murder, I had forgotten him.

Perhaps this is the purpose of detective investigations, real and fictional – to transform sensation, horror and grief into a puzzle, and then to solve the puzzle, to make it go away. 'The detective story,' observed Raymond Chandler in 1949, 'is a tragedy with a happy ending.' A storybook detective starts by confronting us with a murder and ends by absolving us of it. He clears us of guilt. He relieves us of uncertainty. He removes us from the presence of death.

POSTSCRIPT

Four months after this book was published, a reader wrote to tell me that she had come across a photograph of Jonathan Whicher. The picture was in the archive of Frederick Bowker, a solicitor with whom Whicher had worked on the case of the Tichborne Claimant, and it was now in the keeping of the Hampshire museums service. When I went to Winchester to look at the archive, I found a second photograph. Both were taken in the early 1870s. They were the first images of Whicher I had seen.

In the full-length portrait, reproduced on page 305, Whicher cuts a jaunty, dapper figure, humorous and self-assured. It is easy to imagine him slipping a stolen wallet from a swell-mobster's pocket with a cheerful 'That'll do!' The photographer has placed him against a screen painted to mimic the interior of a country-house drawing room, with a long window thrown open to the lawns beyond. The detective rests his hand lightly on a high basket of flowers. His air of breezy prosperity is fitting: by 1870 Whicher had been proved right about the Road Hill murder; he had unmasked the Tichborne Claimant as a butcher from Wapping; he had married a well-to-do widow. It was no wonder that he had a spring in his step.

In the other portrait, the head-and-shoulders shot on the opposite page, he is more subdued, nearer to the man Dickens had once described: unassuming and thickset, with 'a reserved and thoughtful air, as if he were engaged in deep arithmetical calculations'. His eyes are gentle, watery, and so pale that they are almost clear. His mouth is set in a wry, sympathetic half-smile. He looks slightly older than in the full-length photograph – the eyes more pouchy, the whiskers more grizzled – though that may be simply because the camera is closer. He is wearing the same clothes, presumably his best set, and the same gold watch and chain, probably those he later bequeathed to his friend John Potter. Something is suspended from a string around his neck: an eyeglass, perhaps.

The photographs were taken during the Tichborne trials, and sold as *cartes de visite*, albumen paper prints affixed to four by two-and-a-half inch cuts of card. They would have cost a shilling apiece, like the dozens of others – of the Claimant, the Tichbornes, the lawyers and so on – that were produced as souvenirs of the case. The close-up of Whicher was printed by the London and Provincial Photographic Company, opposite Charing Cross railway station at the western end of the Strand, while the full-length portrait is marked 'Powell, Charing-cross'.

Sidney Powell had a studio at 38 Chandos Street, across the Strand from the station. He advertised himself as a photographer and optician – a common combination in the mid-nineteenth century – and he seems to have been something of a rogue. He was sued in 1862 for selling pirate photographic prints of Rosa Bonheur's fashionable painting *The Horse Fair*. Seven years later a plainclothes police inspector visited his shop, posing as a customer, and Powell offered him two erotic oil paintings for 100 guineas; these may have been the 'very curious and recherché' cabinet paintings by François Boucher that he had advertised in the *Pall Mall Gazette* the previous year. He then showed his bogus client some obscene photographs, warning him of the need for caution because the police were getting 'very sharp' in finding out dealers in indecent images. At this, the inspector revealed his identity and arrested him. Powell was sentenced to eighteen months' hard labour for peddling dirty photographs, but he was back in business by 1871, when he placed an ad in *The Era* for a memorial portrait 'from life' of Charles Dickens surrounded by twenty-two of his characters, at a cost of two shillings, post free. A year or two after this he photographed Whicher.

Powell's studio was two blocks west of Dickens' former premises in Wellington Street, where the novelist had met Whicher in the summer of 1850. At Dickens' invitation, a group of policemen – Inspectors Field and Walker, Sergeants Whicher, Thornton, Kendall, Smith and Shaw – had gathered one sultry evening at dusk in the *Household Words* offices. In an article that July, Dickens described how he and this 'amicable brotherhood' sat at a round table laid with cigars and glasses, while the hubbub of the hackney-coachmen, river-boatmen and theatregoers of Covent Garden rose through the open windows. Whicher's colleagues urged him to tell the story of how he had caught the famous horse-thief and conman 'Tally-ho' Thompson. 'A man oughtn't to tell what he has done himself,' said Whicher, 'but still, as nobody was with me, and, consequently, as nobody but myself can tell it, I'll do it in the best way I can.' He took a drink of brandy and, 'leaning forward a little, and placing a hand on each of his legs', embarked on an account of his dogged and inventive pursuit of Tally-ho through the pubs and post-offices of England. It was a rattling tale, which ended with the detective arresting the horse-thief in a pub in Northamptonshire, and then sharing a brandy with his prisoner. 'I understand he always praises me up to the skies,' Whicher told Dickens, 'and says I'm one of the best of men.'

Twenty years later, Whicher was again having his image made in a room off the Strand, this time a likeness in pictures rather than words. Again he was in the ascendant. Again his manner was easy, self-possessed, with just a hint of something withheld.

In the same month that one reader alerted me to the existence of a picture of Jack Whicher, another sent me a pair of old photographs of Road Hill House. This correspondent, a solicitor called Richard Rose, had found the pictures while leafing through a box of miscellaneous stereoscopic cards on a market stall in west London. Having heard an adaptation of my book on the radio, he thought that he recognised the name 'Road Hill House' on one of the cards. He bought it for £5 and sent me a copy, enclosing a plastic stereoscopic viewer and an explanatory letter. The two pictures on the card, which are now reproduced in the second plate section of this book, show the back of the building; to the right of each frame is the crescent of windows in the drawing-room, the middle one of which had been found open on the morning of Saville Kent's death. They were the only nineteenth-century photographs of the house I had seen, and – as Mr Rose pointed out – they contained an eerie, suggestive oddity.

A stereoscopic card consists of two almost identical photographs mounted side by side. When looked at through the lenses of a stereoscope, they become a single three-dimensional image. The details in the foreground – the spindly fence and branches in the Road Hill House scene – spring sharply out, lending the picture an illusion of volume and depth. Of all the optical toys of the 1850s and 1860s, stereoscopes enjoyed the greatest popularity: millions of cards were sold, along with thousands of boxes and binoculars through which to view them.

Before sending me the pictures of Road Hill House, Richard Rose had scanned them in to his computer and blown them up so that he could examine them in detail. The photographs on a stereoscopic card were usually taken simultaneously, with a double-lens camera designed for the purpose, but Mr Rose realised that the Road Hill House photographer had used an ordinary, single-lens machine: he first took one image, then slid the camera two-and-a-half inches across his tripod and took another. In most respects the pictures were the same as each other, apart from the minute change of perspective necessary to produce the stereoscopic effect, but there was a difference. 'Between the two exposures, very probably less than two minutes,' wrote Mr Rose, 'something has happened.' In the first shot, the right-hand image, the panes of the middle window are blank, their darkness interrupted only by the reflections of winter sunlight filtering through clouds and branches. But in the left-hand picture, two faces are visible behind the glass. In the time that it took the photographer to adjust the camera for the second shot, a dark, thickly bearded man and another, slightly shorter person had come to the window.

The identity of the figures was mysterious. 'When I first saw them,' wrote Richard Rose, 'they gave me a little shiver, as when M. R. James slips a chilling detail into a story or Peter Quint makes an appearance in *The Turn of the Screw*.'

Since the publication of my book I had received letters about ghosts. Former residents of Baynton House, where the first Mrs Kent died, and of Langham House, as Road Hill House was now known, reported strange sounds and visions: a woman in grey pacing the corridors, a boy sitting on a low bedroom chair, a girl's hands reaching from a wall, a child crying after midnight. The rooms seemed imbued with the Kent family's unhappiness. As Mr Rose's letter reminded me, there are traces of the tragedy in published ghost stories as well. In M. R. James's *The Mezzotint* (1904) a museum curator is sent a print of a country residence similar to Road Hill House: the building dates from the early nineteenth century, has three rows of sash windows and a portico at the front. The curator thinks the drawing very ordinary, but on glancing at it a second time he notices a shape near the frame: 'hardly more than a black blot on the extreme edge of the engraving – the head of a man or woman, a good deal muffled up, the back turned to the spectator, and looking towards the house.' A few hours later he examines the picture again: 'In the middle of the lawn in front of the unknown house there was a figure where no figure had been at five o'clock that afternoon. It was crawling on all-fours towards the house.' To the curator's horror, the print continues to mutate: the next time he looks, a window is open and the creature has disappeared; and then the window is shut and the figure is again on the lawn, stealing away from the house with a child in its arms. At the close of James's story the curator discovers that a century earlier the building in his picture had indeed been the scene of the abduction of a child. The engraving he now owns was made by the lost boy's grief-crazed father.

Like the mezzotint, the stereoscopic card of Road Hill House seems to change on closer inspection, to offer up a secret. The photographs, once magnified, provide a brief, cryptic narrative, a before and an after, two frames from a film. To guess at the meaning of the apparitions at the window, I needed to find out when the pictures were taken, and by whom.

The label on the back of the card reads: 'Road Hill House. Nightingale, Photographer, Trowbridge. Also, post free 2s, a Series of Five Photographs, forming a complete panorama of the whole of the premises.' The Trowbridge census returns of 1861 and 1871 and the town's business directory of 1855 list a William Brookman Nightingale, photographer, actuary and insurance agent. He had a house in Fore Street and a studio in the Parade, and at the time of the Road Hill murder had just turned thirty.

Judging by the trees in his pictures of Road Hill House, which are almost bare of leaves, William Nightingale photographed the property in early winter. Since no year was given on the label, I checked the local newspapers to see if he had advertised the images, and found a notice in the inaugural issue of the *Trowbridge Chronicle, Volunteers' Gazette, and West of England Advertiser*: 'Views of Road Hill House FOR THE STEREOSCOPE On cards 1s large size 2s 6d. WB Nightingale'. The paper is dated 11 May 1861, which means that the photographs were taken in the winter of 1860-61, when the Kents were still in residence.

After printing the pictures in his studio, Nightingale seems to have made drawings from them: the *Marlborough Times* of 15 May reported that 'Mr Nightingale, photographic artist' sold engravings of Road Hill House at the auction held there in April, immediately after the Kents had left for Weston-Super-Mare. The auction took place on a wet, wintry Saturday, the newspaper added; the books were sold first, and then the wine, 'of which a large quantity was "tasted".' Nightingale's prints were inexpensive mementoes of the murder scene – cheaper than the furniture, at any rate, though the newspaper noted that some visitors took their souvenirs for free: they tore sticks off the trees surrounding the house and pulled chunks off the skirting boards inside.

An article in another paper supplied the clue to how Nightingale had come to make these pictures. According to the *Morning Post* of 18 April 1861, Joseph Stapleton's forthcoming book about the murder would 'include a ground plan of the house and several engravings from photographs of the house and grounds which were taken expressly for this purpose.' Stapleton and Nightingale were near neighbours in Fore Street, and the surgeon-cum-author seems to have commissioned the actuary-cum-photographer to provide the illustrations for his work. In May 1861 these pictures appeared, uncredited, in Stapleton's *The Great Crime of 1860*. Two of the images in that book are also reproduced in this one: the floor-plan of the house on page xiv and the bird's-eye view of the premises in the first plate section, which Nightingale presumably constructed from his five-picture panorama.

We know that Samuel Kent authorised the text of *The Great Crime of 1860*, which points to his daughter Constance as the likely killer of his son. It is clear that the photographs, too, were made with Kent's consent: the wet collodion plates used in mid-nineteenth-century photography had to be developed and fixed immediately after being exposed, so Nightingale must have rigged up a darkroom at Road Hill House, either in a tent in the garden or a room indoors. Perhaps Nightingale and Stapleton called on Samuel Kent together in the winter of 1860. While Nightingale went out to take his pictures, the two older men may have repaired to the drawing room to discuss the details of the narrative and, catching sight of the photographer and his tripod on the grass near the river, walked over to the window to watch him at work. Nightingale had already taken one picture from this angle and was preparing for the second, the extra shot he needed to make a stereoscopic card. The blurred, white-haired figure that he inadvertently photographed in the drawing room could be the sixty-year-old Samuel Kent. The bearded man next to him could be their mutual friend Joseph Stapleton, aged forty-six. They were far enough away for Nightingale not to have noticed them as he opened the shutter, nor even later as he developed and printed the plates.

If all this is so, these photographs capture the start of the afterlife of the Road Hill case. The pictures try to fix the house in its time, yet the tiny shift between them opens up another story. The image within the image, the figures looking back at us through the glass, shows two men plotting the first book about the murder of Saville Kent.

Kate Summerscale
London, November 2008

NOTES

PROLOGUE

xix *On Sunday, 15 July 1860 . . . for 1s.6d.* From Whicher's expenses claims in the Metropolitan Police files at the National Archives – MEPO 3/61.

xix *The day was warm . . . into the seventies.* Weather reports in the July, August and September 1860 issues of *The Gentleman's Magazine.*

xix *At this terminus in 1856 . . . excelled at untangling.* From reports in *The Times*, 7 & 12 April 1856; and 3, 4 & 12 May 1858.

xx *Dickens reported that 'in a glance' . . . 'chronicled nowhere'. In* 'A *Detective Police Party', parts one and two, Household Words,* 27 July 1850 and 10 August 1850.

xxi *'the prince of detectives'.* In *Scotland Yard Past and Present: Experiences of Thirty-Seven Years* (1893) by Ex-Chief-Inspector Timothy Cavanagh.

xxi *'shorter and thicker-set' . . . smallpox scars.* In 'A Detective Police Party', *Household Words*, 27 July 1850.

xxi *William Henry Wills . . . of the Detective police.'* In 'The Modern Science of Thief-taking', *Household Words*, 13 July 1850. Dickens probably contributed to the writing of this piece. For details of the journal and its contributors, see *Household Words: A Weekly Journal 1850–1859 Conducted by Charles Dickens – Table of Contents, List of Contributors and Their Contributions Based on The Household Words Office Book in the Morris L. Parrish Collection of Victorian Novelists* (1973) by Anne Lohrli.

xxii *The only clues . . . his eyes were blue.* From MEPO 21/7, Metropolitan Police discharge papers.

xxiii *A Great Western Railway . . . less than an hour.* From *Black's Picturesque Tourist and Road and Railway Guidebook* (1862); *Stokers and Pokers; or, the London and North-Western Railway, the Electric Telegraph and the Railway Clearing-House* (1849) by Francis Bond Head; *Paddington Station: Its History and Architecture* (2004) by Steven Brindle; railway timetables in the *Trowbridge Advertiser* of January 1860.

CHAPTERS 1, 2 & 3

The narrative of these three chapters is drawn mainly from newspaper reports of the testimony given to the Wiltshire magistrates between July and December 1860, affidavits made to the Queen's Bench in November 1860, and the first book about the case, *The Great Crime of 1860: Being a Summary of the Facts Relating to the Murder Committed at Road; a Critical Review of its Social and Scientific Aspects; and an Authorised Account of the Family; With an Appendix, Containing the Evidence Taken at the Various Inquiries*, written by J.W. Stapleton and published in May 1861. The newspaper sources are the *Somerset and Wilts Journal*, the *Trowbridge and North Wilts Advertiser*, the *Bristol Daily Post*, the *Bath Chronicle*, the *Bath Express*, the *Western Daily Press*, the *Frome Times*, the *Bristol Mercury, The Times*, the *Morning Post, Lloyds Weekly Paper* and the *Daily Telegraph*. Some details of furnishings are drawn from newspaper accounts of the auction of the contents of Road Hill House in April 1861.

CHAPTER 3

38 *On a visit to the country . . . house is his castle."'* In *The King of Saxony's Journey through England and Scotland in the Year 1844* (1846) by Carl Gustav Carus.

38 *The American poet . . . privacy of their homes.'* In *English Traits* (1856) by Ralph Waldo Emerson. Quoted in *The English Home and its Guardians 1850–1940* (1998) by George K. Behlmer.

CHAPTER 4

43 *It was still light . . . green as grass*. From weather and crop reports for July in the *Devizes and Wiltshire Gazette*, 2 August 1860.

43 *the railway station's narrow platform*. Rowland Rodway, formerly Samuel Kent's solicitor, was leading a campaign to improve the facilities at Trowbridge railway station. The platforms were dangerously narrow, he argued, there was no raised walkway across the line, and no waiting room. The *Trowbridge and North Wilts Advertiser* of 21 July 1860 reported on the campaign.

43 *Trowbridge had made money . . . muslin cheap*. History of Trowbridge and surroundings from *The Book of Trowbridge* (1984) by Kenneth Rogers; *John Murray's Handbook for Travellers in Wilts, Dorset, and Somerset* (1859); and photographs and maps in the

Trowbridge local history museum. Reports of wool trade in *Lloyds Weekly*, 15 July 1860.

44 *Wine, cider, spirits . . . at the bar*. From an advertisement in the *Trowbridge and North Wilts Advertiser*, 4 August 1860.

44 *'I couldn't do better than have a drop . . . courage up'*. In 'A Detective Police Party', *Household Words*, 27 July 1850.

44 *Jonathan Whicher was born . . . outright villains*. Details of Whicher's family from the St Giles baptism registers in the London Metropolitan Archives (X097/236), and the marriage certificate of Sarah Whicher and James Holliwell. Camberwell's history from the *London and Counties Directory 1823–4*, *The Parish of Camberwell* by Blanch (1875), *Camberwell* by D. Allport (1841) and *The Story of Camberwell* by Mary Boast (1996).

45 *When Jack Whicher applied . . . good character*. Whicher's referees were John Berry, a house painter of 12 High St, Camberwell, later of Providence Row, and John Hartwell, also of Camberwell. From MEPO 4/333 (a register of recruits to the Metropolitan Police) and the census of 1841. Police entrance requirements and procedure from *Sketches in London* (1838) by James Grant.

45 *Like more than a third . . . submitted his application*. The other constables were former butchers, bakers, shoemakers, tailors, soldiers, servants, carpenters, bricklayers, blacksmiths, turners, clerks, shop workers, mechanics, plumbers, painters, sailors, weavers and stonemasons. From *Scotland Yard: Its History and Organisation 1829–1929* (1929) by George Dilnot.

45 *His weekly wage . . . a little more secure*. Police rates of pay from Parliamentary Papers of 1840, at the British Library; for comparative pay to labourers, see 'The Metropolitan Police and What is Paid for Them', *Chambers's Journal*, 2 July 1864.

45 *The 3,500 policemen . . . sixteenth century)*. There was one policeman for every 425 inhabitants of the city. Figures from *Sketches in London* (1838) by James Grant. Nicknames from *The London Underworld* (1970) by Kellow Chesney and *London Labour and the London Poor* (1861) by Henry Mayhew, Bracebridge Hemyng, John Binny and Andrew Halliday.

46 *Whicher was issued . . . sideburns instead*. Details of police uniform from: *Mysteries of Police & Crime* (1899) by Arthur Griffiths; *Scotland Yard: Its History and Organisation 1829–1929* (1929) by George Dilnot; *Scotland Yard Past and Present: Experiences of Thirty-Seven Years* (1893) by Timothy Cavanagh.

46 *At a time when all clothes . . . degree of stupidity.'* In 'The Policeman: His Health' by Harriet Martineau, *Once a Week*, 2 June 1860.

47 *Andrew Wynter . . . neither hopes nor fears.'* In 'The Police and the Thieves', *Quarterly Review*, 1856. Another commentator, James Greenwood, echoed this: 'So long as the common constable remains a well-regulated machine, and fulfils his functions with no jarring or unnecessary noise, we will ask no more.' From *Seven Curses of London* (1869). Both quoted in *Cops and Bobbies: Police Authority in New York and London, 1830–1870* (1999) by Wilbur R. Miller.

47 *Whicher shared . . . King's Cross.* From the census of 1841.

47 *This was a substantial brick building . . . recreation room.* From the John Back archive at the Metropolitan Police Historical Collection, Charlton, London SE7.

47 *All single men . . . publican on the route.* Regulations from: *Policing Victorian London* (1985) by Philip Thurmond Smith; *London's Teeming Streets 1830–1914* (1993) by James H. Winter; and Metropolitan Police rules and orders in the National Archives. Details of a policeman's day from: *The Making of a Policeman: A Social History of a Labour Force in Metropolitan London, 1829–1914* (2002) by Haia Shpayer-Makov; 'The Metropolitan Protectives' by Charles Dickens in *Household Words*, 26 April 1851; and works already cited by Grant, Cavanagh and Martineau.

48 *four out of five dismissals, of a total of three thousand, were for drunkenness.* The estimate of Colonel Rowan and Richard Mayne, the Police Commissioners, given to a parliamentary select committee in 1834. See *The English Police: A Political and Social History* (1991) by Clive Emsley.

49 *Holborn teemed with tricksters . . . burgled houses.* Slang from *London Labour and the London Poor* (1861) by Henry Mayhew et al. and *The Victorian Underworld* (1970) by Kellow Chesney. Thieves acting as decoys from *The Times*, 21 November 1837.

In 1837, the year that Whicher joined the police force, almost 17,000 people were arrested in London, of whom 107 were burglars, 110 housebreakers, thirty-eight highway robbers, 773 pickpockets, 3,657 'common thieves', eleven horse stealers, 141 dog stealers, three forgers, twenty-eight coiners, 317 'utterers of base coin', 141 'obtainers of goods by false pretences', 182 other fraudsters, 343 receivers of stolen goods, 2,768 'habitual disturbers of the public peace', 1,295 vagrants, fifty writers of begging letters, eighty-six bearers of begging letters, 895 well-dressed prostitutes living in brothels, 1,612 well-dressed prostitutes walking the streets, and 3,864 'low' prostitutes in poor neighbourhoods. From *Scotland Yard: Its History and Organisation 1829–1929* (1929) by George Dilnot.

49 *The entire police force . . . June 1838. The Times*, 30 June 1838.

49 *Already the police were familiar . . . an asylum. The Times*, 23 December 1837.

49 *Jack Whicher's first reported arrest.* From *The First Detectives and the Early Career of Richard Mayne, Commissioner of Police* (1957) by Belton Cobb and *The Times* of 15 December 1840.

50 *There had been outrage . . . infiltrated a political gathering.* The agent was Popay, the gathering Chartist – see *Scotland Yard: Its History and Organisation 1829–1929* (1929) by George Dilnot. Peel had assured the House of Commons in 1822 that he was dead against a 'system of espionage'.

50 *Magistrates' court records . . . buy him off with silver.* Court records in London Metropolitan Archive – references WJ/SP/E/013/35, 38 and 39, WJ/SP/E/017/40, MJ/SP/1842.04/060.

50 *The Metropolitan Police files show . . . under two inspectors.* Details of the hunt for Daniel Good and the formation of the detective division from MEPO 3/45, the police file on the murder; *The First Detectives* (1957) by Belton Cobb; *The Rise of Scotland Yard: A History of the Metropolitan Police* (1956) by Douglas G. Browne; and *Dreadful Deeds and Awful Murders: Scotland Yard's First Detectives* (1990) by Joan Lock.

50 *('Dickens later described. . . bags his man').* In 'A Detective Police Party', *Household Words*, 27 July 1850. Thornton was born in 1803 in Epsom, Surrey, according to the census of 1851. He was married to a woman seventeen years his senior, with whom he had two daughters.

51 *Whicher was given a pay rise . . . bonuses and rewards.* Information on pay from Metropolitan Police papers at the National Archives and from parliamentary papers on police numbers and rates of pay at the British Library – 1840 (81) XXXIX.257.

51 *'Intelligent men have been . . . in 1843. Chambers's Journal* XII.

52 *In the London underworld . . . classless anonymity.* The term 'Jacks' is cited in *The Victorian Underworld* (1970) by Kellow Chesney. Detective officers also became known as 'stops', according to *The Slang Dictionary* published by J.C. Hotten in 1864, and as 'noses', according to Hotten's dictionary of 1874. The 1864 edition included some of the London detectives' own lingo: to 'pipe' a man was to follow him; to 'smoke' was to detect, or to 'penetrate an artifice'.

52 *The first English detective story. . .1849.* In *Chambers's Edinburgh Journal* of 28 July 1849. This magazine published eleven more stories by Waters between then and September 1853. The twelve were issued as a book in 1856.

52 *'They are, one and all . . . speak to.'* From 'A Detective Police Party', *Household Words*, 27 July 1850.

52 *George Augustus Sala . . . questioning them.'* From *Things I Have Seen and People I Have Known* (two volumes, 1894) by George Augustus Sala. More recent commentators, such as Philip Collins in *Dickens and Crime* (1962), have seen the novelist's relations with the detectives as faintly patronising.

52 *In* Tom Fox *. . . higher intelligence'.* This collection of short stories – sold for 1*s*.6*d*. – was published in April 1860 and went into a second edition that summer.

53 *In 1851 Whicher . . . fleeing the bank with their loot.* Bank robbery reports from *The Times* and the *News of the World*, June and July 1851.

53 *'The credit for skill . . . Dickens and the like.* Also that year, Charley Field was criticised for the underhand manner in which he caught two men who had tried to blow up the railway tracks at Cheddington, Buckinghamshire. He disguised himself as a match-seller, according to the *Bedford Times*, took rooms in the town and made himself at home in the local pubs, where he would joshingly introduce himself as a 'timber merchant', until he got the information he sought. See *Dickens and Crime* (1962) by Philip Collins.

53 *Like Whicher . . . little finger'.* Literary detectives were inconspicuous and quiet. Carter of the Yard in Mary Elizabeth Braddon's novel *Henry Dunbar* (1864) looks like something between 'a shabby-genteel half-pay captain and an unlucky stockbroker'. The police detective in Thomas Hardy's *Desperate Remedies* (1871) is 'commonplace in all except his eyes'. The narrator of John Bennett's *Tom Fox* (1860) says, 'I always made use of my eyes and ears, and said little – a precept every Detective should lay to heart.' The detective in Braddon's *The Trail of the Serpent* (1860) is mute.

54 *In 1850 Charley Field . . . a lovely idea!'* From 'Three "Detective" Anecdotes' in *Household Words*, 14 September 1850.

55 *The artistry of crime . . . the analytical detective.* The 'Newgate novels' of the 1820s to 1840s were melodramas about fearless criminals such as Dick Turpin and Jack Sheppard. For the ascendancy of the detective hero, see, for example, *Bloody Murder: From the Detective Story to the Crime Novel – a History* (1972) by Julian Symons; *Bloodhounds of Heaven: The Detective in English Fiction from Godwin to Doyle* (1976) by Ian Ousby; *Detective Fiction and the Rise of Forensic Science* (1999) by Ronald Thomas; and *The Pursuit of Crime: Art and Ideology in Detective Fiction* (1981) by Dennis Porter. The shift of focus was described by Michel Foucault in *Discipline and Punish* (1975): 'we have moved from the exposition of the facts or the confession to the slow process of discovery;

from the execution to the investigation; from the physical confrontation to the intellectual struggle between criminal and investigator'.

55 *Whicher, who was said . . . charge of the department.* From MEPO 4/333, the register of joiners, and MEPO 21/7, a record of police pensioners.

55 *In 1858 Whicher caught the valet . . . Essex cornfield.* From reports in *The Times*, 30 June and 6 & 12 July 1858. Investigation into the murder of PC Clark from Metropolitan Police file MEPO 3/53.

55 *In 1859 . . . sued Bonwell for misconduct.* The Bonwell case inspired an extraordinary editorial in the *Daily Telegraph* of 10 October 1859: 'This London is an amalgam of worlds within worlds and the occurrences of every day convince us that there is not one of these worlds but has its special mysteries and its generic crimes . . . It has been said . . . that Hampstead sewers shelter a monstrous breed of black swine, which have propagated and run wild among the slimy feculence, and whose ferocious snouts will one day up-root Highgate archway, while they make Holloway intolerable with their grunting.' Quoted in *Black Swine in the Sewers of Hampstead: Beneath the Surface of Victorian Sensationalism* by Thomas Boyle (1988). See also reports in *The Times* of 19 September to 16 December 1859.

55 *A couple of months before he was despatched . . . rings fall to the floor.* From reports in *The Times* of 25 April, 4 & 7 May, 12 June 1860.

56 *He was 'an excellent officer . . . take on any case'.* From *A Life's Reminiscences of Scotland Yard* (1890) by Andrew Lansdowne.

56 *If Whicher was certain . . . a man to me.'* From 'A Detective Police Party', *Household Words*, 27 July 1850.

56 *He was not above . . . left cheek.* From *Scotland Yard Past and Present: Experiences of Thirty-Seven Years* (1893) by Timothy Cavanagh.

CHAPTERS 5 TO 14

The main sources for these chapters are: the Metropolitan Police file MEPO 3/61, which includes Whicher's reports on the murder, Whicher and Williamson's expenses claims, letters from the public and notes from the Commissioner of the Metropolitan Police; *The Great Crime of 1860* (1861) by J.W. Stapleton; and newspapers including the *Somerset and Wilts Journal*, the *Bath Chronicle*, the *Bath Express*, the *Bristol Daily Post*, the *Frome Times*, the *Trowbridge and North Wilts Advertiser*, the *Devizes Advertiser*, the

Daily Telegraph and *The Times*. Other sources are given in the notes below.

CHAPTER 5

59 *It was another dry day . . . sailed overhead.* Details of birds from *Natural History of a Part of the County of Wilts* (1843) by W.G. Maton; *A History of British Birds* (1885) by Thomas Bewick; *The Birds of Wiltshire* (1981), edited by John Buxton. Weather here and subsequently from local newspapers and from *Agricultural Records 220–1968* (1969) by John Stratton.

59 *In this part of England . . . suffocate it in mud.* From *The Dialect of the West of England* (1825, revised 1869) by James Jennings, and *Dialect in Wiltshire* (1987) by Malcolm Jones and Patrick Dillon.

60 *There were at least four pubs . . . impossible to unravel.* Occupations and businesses from the census returns of 1861. Information on mills from *Warp and Weft: The Story of the Somerset and Wiltshire Woollen Industry* by Kenneth Rogers (1986), *Wool and Water* by Kenneth G. Ponting (1975) and exhibits in the Frome and Trowbridge local history museums.

61 *Samuel Kent was disliked . . . three or four shillings a week.* From a report in the *Frome Times* of 17 October 1860. Joseph Stapleton did not accept that Samuel was unpopular – he claimed that his colleague's 'urbanity and concessory spirit' had done much to popularise 'an obnoxious law'. Elsewhere in his book, though, he said Samuel was victimised by those to whom he was 'personally obnoxious by his faithful discharge of official duty'.

61 *the Temperance Hall.* This was a building erected by the subscription of villagers who were opposed to alcohol, particularly the sale of beer on the Sabbath and the custom of children fetching beer for their parents. The *Somerset and Wilts Journal* reported that many had assembled in the hall on the Wednesday before the murder, while the rain pelted down outside, to belt out Temperance tunes; they were accompanied by the twenty-two members of the Road Fife and Drum Band, with Charles Happerfield, the postmaster, on piano.

62 *A cloth merchant . . . finest houses in the area.* Information on Ledyard from *A History of the County of Wiltshire: Volume 8* (1965), edited by Elizabeth Crittall.

64 *Affluent mid-Victorians . . . in their own quarters.* In *The Gentleman's House: Or How to Plan English Residences from the Parsonage to the Palace* (1864) Robert Kerr advised: 'The family

constitute one community; the servants another. Whatever may be their mutual regard and confidence as dwellers under the same roof, each class is entitled to shut its door upon the other, and be alone.' Quoted in *A Man's Place: Masculinity and the Middle-Class Home in Victorian England* (1999) by John Tosh.

66 *Whicher was familiar . . . the wrong way*. In 'The Modern Science of Thief-taking' by W.H. Wills, *Household Words*, 13 July 1850.

68 *The writers of the mid-nineteenth century . . . cut off'*. From *Mary Barton* (1848) by Elizabeth Gaskell; *The Female Detective* (1864) by Andrew Forrester; and 'The Modern Science of Thief-taking', *Household Words*, 13 July 1850.

68 *One case that turned on such evidence . . . Greenacre was hanged in May 1837*. For Greenacre's capture, see *Dreadful Deeds and Awful Murders: Scotland Yard's First Detectives* (1990) by Joan Lock.

69 *In 1849 the London detectives . . . railway-station locker*. For the Mannings' murder of Patrick O'Connor, see *The Bermondsey Horror* (1981) by Albert Borowitz and MEPO 3/54, the police file on the case.

69 *The detectives . . . steamships*. During the investigation – on 1 September 1849 – the *Illustrated London News* drew consolation from the fact that 'detection is sure to dog the footsteps of crime – that the guilty wretch, flying on the wings of steam at thirty miles an hour, is tracked by a swifter messenger – and that the lightning itself, by the wondrous agency of the electric telegraph, conveys to the remotest parts of the kingdom an account of his crime, a description of his person'.

69 *Whicher checked the hotels . . . against the killers*. Details of Whicher's role in the investigation from MEPO 3/54 and *Dreadful Deeds and Awful Murders: Scotland Yard's First Detectives* (1990) by Joan Lock.

69 *two and a half million copies*. Figure from *Victorian Studies in Scarlet* (1970) by Richard D. Altick.

69 *A series of woodcuts . . . dashing action heroes*. In *The Progress of Crime; Or, The Authentic Memoirs of Maria Manning* (1849) by Robert Huish.

70 *He awarded Whicher . . . £15*. From MEPO 3/54.

70 *The next year . . . the detective had found*. From 'The Modern Science of Thief-taking', *Household Words*, 13 July 1850.

71 *In east London in 1829 . . . her next two children, Saville and Eveline*. As well as *The Great Crime of 1860* (1861) by J.W. Stapleton, this account of the Kent family's past draws on certificates of birth, marriage and death, and documents in the Home Office file HO 45/6970.

CHAPTER 6

79 *Joshua Parsons was born . . . hardy perennials.* Information about Parsons from census returns of 1861 and 1871 and from 'Dr Joshua Parsons (1814–92) of Beckington, Somerset, General Practitioner' by N. Spence Galbraith, in *Somerset Archaeology and Natural History*, issue 140 (1997).

80 *physicians who specialised . . . perfect little devils from birth'.* From 'Moral Insanity', in the *Journal of Mental Science*, 27 July 1881. In *The Borderlands of Insanity* (1875) Andrew Wynter wrote: 'It is agreed by all alienist physicians, that girls are far more likely to inherit insanity from their mothers than from the other parent . . . The tendency of the mother to transmit her mental disease is . . . in all cases stronger than the father's; some physicians have, indeed, insisted that it is twice as strong.' For writings by Savage and Wynter see *Embodied Selves: An Anthology of Psychological Texts 1830–1890* (1998), edited by Jenny Bourne Taylor and Sally Shuttleworth.

81 *an almost naked woman stabbing the boy in the privy.* The idea that the killer had been naked was to recur – the *Western Daily Press* of 4 August 1860 pointed out that near the kitchen door, 'two taps of water could have been made use of to wash away any marks, if the person was nude'.

82 *Objects could regain their innocence only when the killer was caught.* For an account of the way that objects are infused with significance during a detective investigation, and returned to banality afterwards, see *The Novel and the Police* (1988) by D.A. Miller.

82 *the original country-house murder mystery.* The horrible circumstances in which Saville's body was found also played a part in establishing the conventions of this form. The corpse in a detective novel, wrote W.H. Auden in his essay 'The Guilty Vicarage: Notes on the Detective Story, by an Addict' (1948), 'must shock not only because it is a corpse but also because, even for a corpse, it is shockingly out of place, as when a dog makes a mess on a drawing-room carpet'. The classic country-house murder is an assault on propriety, an aggressive exposure of base needs and desires.

82 *'sensitiveness . . . detective faculty'.* In *Villette* (1853).

82 *'reckoned 'em up'.* In 'A Detective Police Party', *Household Words*, 27 July 1850.

83 *'If you ask me to give my reason . . . safe keeping of the swell mobsmen.'* In 'The Police and the Thieves', *Quarterly Review*, 1856. 'Between the detective and the thief there is no ill blood,'

wrote Andrew Wynter in the same article; 'when they meet they give an odd wink of recognition to each other – the thief smiling, as much as to say, "I am quite safe, you know;" and the detective replying with a look, of which the interpretation is, "We shall be better acquainted by and by." They both feel, in short, that they are using their wits to get their living, and there is a sort of tacit understanding between them that each is entitled to play his game as well as he can.'

83 *'That was enough for me'*. In 'A Detective Police Party', *Household Words*, 27 July 1850.

83 *'I could even notice the eye . . . saw him busy.'* From *The Casebook of a Victorian Detective* (1975) by James McLevy, edited by George Scott-Moncreiff, a selection of pieces from McLevy's autobiographical volumes *Curiosities of Crime in Edinburgh* and *The Sliding Scale of Life*, both published in 1861.

83 *The journalist William Russell . . . comparing both'*. From 'Isaac Gortz, the Charcoal-Burner' in *Experiences of a Real Detective* (1862) by Inspector 'F', 'edited' by Waters.

84 *'The eye . . . invisible to other eyes'*. From 'The Modern Science of Thief-taking', *Household Words*, 13 July 1850. When Dickens accompanied Charley Field to a St Giles basement, he noted the detective's 'roving eye that searches every corner of the cellar as he talks'; he described the lanterns carried by Field's sidekicks as 'flaming eyes' that created 'turning lanes of light' ('On Duty with Inspector Field', *Household Words*, 14 June 1851). For a discussion of surveillance and the eyes of the literary detective, see *From Bow Street to Baker Street: Mystery, Detection and Narrative* (1992) by Martin A. Kayman.

84 *He once arrested . . . pick pockets*. From *The Times*, 4 June 1853.

84 *The seemingly supernatural sight . . . theories of Sigmund Freud.* For the fictional detective's ability to read faces and bodies as if they were books, see *Detective Fiction and the Rise of Forensic Science* (1999) by Ronald Thomas.

85 *The standard text on the art of face-reading*. Lavater's essays first appeared in 1789; a ninth edition was published in 1855. See *Embodied Selves: An Anthology of Psychological Texts 1830–1890* (1998), edited by Jenny Bourne Taylor and Sally Shuttleworth.

87 *Coolness was a prerequisite for an artful crime*. Dickens wrote an essay about this: 'The Demeanour of Murderers', *Household Words*, 14 June 1856.

88 *Even before Whicher's arrival . . . previous day's* Daily Telegraph. Letters quoted in the *Bristol Daily Post* of 12 July 1860 and the *Somerset and Wilts Journal* of 14 July 1860.

88 *A bump behind the ear . . . the seat of secretiveness.* From the 1853 edition of George Combe's *System of Phrenology.*

88 *This was probably the same . . . a tiger from a sheep.'* Letter quoted in the *Somerset and Wilts Journal* of 14 July 1860.

CHAPTER 7

91 *The warm weather . . . eclipse of the sun.* From the *Frome Times*, 25 July 1860.

91 *an odd episode that had taken place four years earlier, in July 1856.* Account of the runaways episode of July 1856 from Whicher's reports to Mayne in MEPO 3/61, Stapleton's *The Great Crime of 1860* and local newspaper stories.

92 *In one newspaper . . . sister's affection.'* Probably the *Bath Express* – the piece was reproduced, without attribution, in the *Frome Times* of 25 July 1860 and the *Devizes Advertiser* of 26 July 1860.

93 *Another report . . . at the side'. Bath and Cheltenham Gazette*, 23 July 1856.

93 *'The little girl . . . mode of sitting.'* In the piece reproduced in the *Frome Times* of 25 July 1860.

93 *Emma Moody, fifteen . . . wool workers.* From the census of 1861.

94 *'I have heard her say . . . just the contrary.'* This dialogue is reconstructed from Emma Moody's testimony at the magistrates' court on 27 July 1860.

94 *According to Whicher's reports . . . in my place?'* From report in MEPO 3/61.

96 *'wonted sagacity'.* From a report in *The Times* on 23 July 1860; *'knowledge and sagacity'.* From a letter by Dickens of 1852; *'vulpine sagacity'.* From 'Circumstantial Evidence' in *Experiences of a Real Detective* (1862) by Inspector 'F', edited by Waters.

96 *'sleuthhound'.* In *Shirley* (1849).

96 *'the chase was hot . . . upon the right track'.* From *Recollections of a Detective Police-Officer* (1856) by Waters.

96 *'If any profession . . . ridding society of pests.'* In *The Casebook of a Victorian Detective.*

96 *'a vast Wood . . . being discovered.'* From *An Enquiry into the Causes of the Late Increase of Robbers* (1757), quoted in *The English Police: A Political and Social History* (1991) by Clive Emsley.

97 *In 1847 . . . hummingbird skins.* From reports in *The Times*, 9, 15 & 19 April 1847 and 14 October 1848.

97 *Jack Hawkshaw . . . all his skins.'* 'You detectives,' observes another

character in the play, 'would suspect your own fathers.' *The Ticket-of-Leave Man* was first performed at the Olympic Theatre in Drury Lane, London, in May 1863, and proved a huge success.

CHAPTER 8

99 *'At the back of the house . . . very accessible.'* From testimony given on 1 October 1860, reported in the *Bristol Daily Post*.

100 *Before Whicher's arrival . . . seen traces.'* Testimony of Francis Wolfe on 2 October 1860, reported in the *Bristol Daily Post*.

100 *'An intimate personal knowledge . . . village boys'*. From the *Somerset and Wilts Journal*, 13 October 1860.

103 *'I contrived to elicit . . . very suggestive.'* From 'Circumstantial Evidence' in *Experiences of a Real Detective* (1862) by Inspector 'F', edited by Waters.

103 *'In both we are concerned . . . detective devices.'* From *Psycho-Analysis and the Establishment of the Facts in Legal Proceedings* (1906) by Sigmund Freud.

104 *Smith was a Glasgow architect's daughter . . . hot chocolate*. See *The Trial of Madeleine Smith* (1905), edited by A. Duncan Smith. Henry James quoted in 'To Meet Miss Madeleine Smith' in *Mainly Murder* (1937) by William Roughead.

105 *a kind of heroine*. In *Latter-day Pamphlets* (1850) by Thomas Carlyle.

106 *The dizzying expansion . . . by 1860*. Figures on newspaper readership from *Black Swine in the Sewers of Hampstead* (1988) by Thomas Boyle. The expansion of the press was fuelled by the repeal of the stamp tax in 1855, which ushered in the first penny newspapers the next year, and the repeal of the duty on paper in 1860.

106 *The tailor had educated himself . . . do the same*. Whereas Dr Kahn's anatomical museum was open only to gentlemen, according to advertisements in *The Times*, literate members of both sexes could read the newspapers.

107 *In answer to their questions . . . William to go with me.'* From notes taken by the lawyer Peter Edlin, who was present at the interview, and passed on to the author Cecil Street, who published *The Case of Constance Kent* (1928) under the pen name John Rhode. These and other papers about the case are in an archive assembled by Bernard Taylor, the author of *Cruelly Murdered: Constance Kent and the Killing at Road Hill House* (1979, revised 1989).

107 *As the week wore on . . . body was found.* A partly accurate version of the rumour was reported in the *Somerset and Wilts Journal* of 21 July 1860.

107 *In the evening of Saturday, 30 June . . . wicks needed trimming.* From testimony given by Samuel Kent, Foley, Urch and Heritage in the magistrates' court in October and November 1860.

109 *'Every Englishman . . . closed to the world.'* In *Notes on England* (1872).

109 *Privacy had become . . . or a tea.* For discussions of middle-class domestic life in Victorian England see, for instance, *Family Fortunes: Men and Women of the English Middle Class 1780–1850* (1987) by Leonore Davidoff and Catherine Hall, *The Spectacle of Intimacy: A Public Life for the Victorian Family* (2000) by Karen Chase and Michael Levenson, and *The Victorian Family: Structures and Stresses* (1978), edited by A. Wohl. In an essay in this anthology, Elaine Showalter writes that secrecy was 'the fundamental and enabling condition of middle-class life . . . The essential unknowability of each individual, and society's collaboration in the maintenance of a façade behind which lurked innumerable mysteries, were the themes which preoccupied many mid-century novelists.'

In 1935 the German philosopher Walter Benjamin connected this new privacy to the birth of detective fiction: 'For the private citizen the space in which he lives enters for the first time into contrast with the one of daily work . . . the traces of the inhabitant impress themselves upon the *intérieur* and from them is born the detective story, which goes after these traces.' Quoted (and translated) by Stefano Tani in *The Doomed Detective: The Contribution of the Detective Novel to Postmodern American and Italian Fiction* (1984).

110 *A murder like this could reveal . . . middle-class house.* In an article about the popularity of detective stories, Bertolt Brecht wrote: 'We gain our knowledge of life in a catastrophic form. History is written *after* catastrophes . . . The death has taken place. What had been brewing beforehand? What had happened? Why has a situation arisen? All this can now perhaps be deduced.' Published in 1976 in Brecht's collected works and quoted in *Delightful Murder: A Social History of the Crime Story* (1984) by Ernest Mandel.

110 *A month before the murder . . . oftener, a family'.* *Notes on Nursing* quoted in the *Devizes and Wiltshire Gazette* of 31 May 1860.

113 *In the evening . . . were still green.* Information on weather and crops from the *Trowbridge and North Wilts Advertiser* of 21 July 1860, and the agricultural report for July in the *Devizes and Wiltshire Gazette* of 2 August 1860.

CHAPTER 9

115 *The chairman of the magistrates . . . the services of a detective.* Information about magistrates from *The Book of Trowbridge* (1984) by Kenneth Rogers and the census of 1861.

116 *Shortly before three o'clock . . . no further remark to me,' said Whicher.* From Whicher's testimony to the magistrates later that day.

120 *'It's no use . . . given way.* From 'A Detective Police Party', *Household Words*, 27 July 1850.

120 *Dolly was a clever, energetic man . . . the first police-station library.* From the census of 1841 and *Critical Years at the Yard: The Career of Frederick Williamson of the Detective Department and the CID* (1956) by Belton Cobb.

120 *Dolly shared lodgings . . . sixteen other single policemen.* From the census of 1861.

121 *One of these, Tim Cavanagh . . . a rabbit from a near neighbour.'* From *Scotland Yard Past and Present* (1893) by Timothy Cavanagh.

122 *His colleague Stephen Thornton . . . some of the passengers.* From *The Times*, 18 November 1837.

122 *In 1859 an eleven-year-old girl . . . depraved imagination'.* From the *Annual Register* of 1860.

123 *On Saturday morning . . . schoolfriends.* From expenses claims in MEPO 3/61, the census of 1841 and the census of 1861.

124 *'She has spoken to me . . . deceased child.'* From Louisa Hatherill's testimony at the Wiltshire magistrates' court, 27 July 1860.

125 *While Constance was in gaol . . . taken into custody.* This rumour was reported in the *Bristol Daily Post* of 24 July 1860.

126 *Whicher was careful . . . other policemen.* Fifteen years earlier, in March 1845, Mayne had reprimanded Whicher and his fellow Detective-Sergeant Henry Smith for showing a want of respect to senior officers that was 'most indiscreet and legally unjustifiable'. As it was the first time that any detectives 'had improperly come into collision' with their uniformed colleagues, Mayne let the pair off with a caution, but he warned that any future offence would be dealt with severely. From MEPO 7/7, police orders and notices from the office of the Commissioner, cited in *The Rise of Scotland Yard: A History of the Metropolitan Police* (1956) by Douglas G. Browne.

129 *As for her supposed lover . . . or the Neighbourhood'.* In a note by Whicher on a letter from Sir John Eardley Wilmot on 16 August 1860, in MEPO 3/61.

129 *the fullest version . . . fishing in the river*. Reported in the *Somerset and Wilts Journal*, 13 October 1860.

129 *In the county court the previous month . . . rival dairy farmer*. From the *Frome Times*, 20 June 1860.

CHAPTER 10

134 *A man in North Leverton . . . She fainted*. Account of the Sarah Drake case from reports in *The Times*, 8 December 1849 to 10 January 1850.

136 *In the spring of 1860 . . . the name of her employer*. Reported in the *News of the World*, 3 June 1860.

137 *Alienists detailed . . . cold cunning*. Monomania was a condition identified by the French physician Jean-Etienne Dominique Esquirol in 1808. See *Embodied Selves: An Anthology of Psychological Texts 1830–1890* (1998), edited by Jenny Bourne Taylor and Sally Shuttleworth.

137 The Times *. . . the key to the asylum?'* On 22 July 1853.

137 *It was even suggested . . . puerperal mania*. Stapleton reported this rumour in his book of 1861.

137 *Perhaps the killer had a double consciousness*. For double consciousness and crime, see *Unconscious Crime: Mental Absence and Criminal Responsibility in Victorian London* (2003) by Joel Peter Eigen.

138 *'Experience has shown . . . seemingly irrelevant.'* In 'The Mystery of Marie Roget' (1842) by Edgar Allan Poe.

138 *'I made a private inquiry . . . as a trifle yet.'* Arthur Conan Doyle's private detective Sherlock Holmes adopted the same techniques: 'You know my method. It is based on the observation of trifles'; 'there is nothing so important as trifles' – from 'The Man with the Twisted Lip' (1891).

138 *He asked Sarah Cox . . . within the hour*. From Whicher's reports in MEPO 3/61 and Cox's testimony at the Wiltshire magistrates' court on 27 July 1860.

139 *'When I am deeply perplexed . . . work out my problems.'* From *Diary of an Ex-Detective* (1859), 'edited' by Charles Martel (in fact written by the New Bond Street bookseller Thomas Delf). In a similar passage in Waters' *Experiences of a Real Detective* (1862) the narrator mulls over a case as if assembling a jigsaw or a collage: 'I lay down on a sofa and had a good think; put together, now this way, now that way, the different items, scraps, and hints, furnished me, in order to ascertain how they held together, and what, as a whole, they seemed to be like.'

141 *As Mr Bucket says . . . point of view.'* A detective's greatest weapon, said Dickens, was his ingenuity. 'For ever on the watch, with their wits stretched to the utmost, these officers have . . . to set themselves against every novelty of trickery and dexterity that the combined imaginations of all the lawless rascals in England can devise, and to keep pace with every such invention that comes out.' From the second part of 'A Detective Police Party', *Household Words*, 10 August 1850.

In *The Perfect Murder* (1989) David Lehman observed that 'the detective novel took murder out of the ethical realm and put it into the realm of aesthetics. Murder in a murder mystery becomes a kind of poetic conceit, often quite a baroque one; the criminal is an artist, the detective an aesthete and critic, and the blundering policeman a philistine.' See also *The Aesthetics of Murder: A Study in Romantic Literature and Contemporary Culture* (1991) by Joel Black.

142 *The nightdress was his missing link . . . evolved from apes.* A nightdress that tied a respectable adolescent girl to murder, like the bones that would prove the connection between men and monkeys, was a terrible object, to be feared as much as sought. For the anxieties aroused by the idea of the missing link, see *Forging the Missing Link: Interdisciplinary Stories* (1992) by Gillian Beer. For negative evidence and the nineteenth-century endeavour to decipher fragments, see *Victorian Detective Fiction and the Nature of Evidence: The Scientific Investigations of Poe, Dickens and Doyle* (2003) by Lawrence Frank, and the same author's 'Reading the Gravel Page: Lyell, Darwin, and Conan Doyle' in *Nineteenth-Century Literature*, December 1989.

142 *Dickens compared the detectives . . . new form of crime.* From the second part of 'A Detective Police Party', *Household Words*, 10 August 1850. In the mid-nineteenth century the idea of detection imprinted itself on natural history, astronomy, journalism – any pursuit that could be construed as a quest for truth.

145 *In* Governess Life *. . . destroying the peace of families'.* For the sexual and social uncertainty provoked by the figure of the governess, see *The Victorian Governess* (1993) by Kathryn Hughes.

146 *Forbes Benignus Winslow . . . their children'.* In *On Obscure Diseases of the Brain, and Disorders of the Mind* (1860). An extract appears in *Embodied Selves: An Anthology of Psychological Texts 1830–1890* (1998), edited by Jenny Bourne Taylor and Sally Shuttleworth.

146 *The detective was another . . . sully a middle-class home.* For the

threats to middle-class privacy posed by servants and policemen, see *Domestic Crime in the Victorian Novel* (1989) by Anthea Trodd.

CHAPTER 11

157 *During Whicher's inquiries . . . dreadful crime.'* From the *Frome Times*, 18 July 1860.

158 *The word 'detect' . . . fascination with the case.* See *Domestic Crime in the Victorian Novel* (1989) by Anthea Trodd. In Alain-René Le Sage's *Le Diable Boiteux* (1707), still popular in Victorian England, Asmodeus perched on the steeple of a Spanish church and stretched out his hand to lift every roof in the city, revealing the secrets within. *The Times* in 1828 referred to the French detective Vidocq as 'an Asmodeus'. In *Dombey and Son* (1848), Dickens called for 'a good spirit who would take the house-tops off, with a more potent and benignant hand than the lame demon in the tale, and show a Christian people what dark shapes issue from amidst their homes'. In *Household Words* articles of 1850 Dickens referred to how the demon could 'untile and read' men's brains, as if bodies were buildings, and himself took 'Asmodeus-like peeps' into 'the internal life' of houses from the carriage of a train. Janin's reference to Asmodeus was in *Paris; Or the Book of One Hundred and One* (translated 1832).

158 *'If every room . . . travelling exhibition.'* From *The Casebook of a Victorian Detective*.

159 *Mrs Kent gave birth . . . Acland Saville Kent.* Acland was Mrs Kent's mother's maiden name; Francis, Saville's first name, had been her father's Christian name.

CHAPTER 12

161 *Whicher reached Paddington . . . at number 40.* Information about Whicher's links to Holywell Street from the census returns of 1851, 1861, 1871, 'Police Informations' of 20 January 1858 in MEPO 6/92, and the classified columns of *The Times* of 3 February 1858. 'The tricks of detective police officers' from *The Female Detective* (1864) by Andrew Forrester.

162 *the 'Big Ben' clock . . . giving off a brilliant incandescence.* From reports in the *News of the World*, 17 June 1860.

162 *Dickens visited Millbank one warm day . . . as well as anyone in it.'* From a letter to W.W.F. de Cerjat of 1 February 1861, published in *The Letters of Charles Dickens 1859–61* (1997), edited by Madeline House and Graham Storey.

162 *The part of Millbank . . . rising off the river.* Descriptions of Pimlico from 'Stanford's Library Map of London in 1862', *The Criminal Prisons of London and Scenes of London Life* (1862) by Henry Mayhew and John Binny, and *The Three Clerks* (1858) by Anthony Trollope.

163 *The public entrance . . . to the south the river.* Description of Scotland Yard from prints and maps in the Westminster local history library, and from *Scotland Yard Past and Present: Experiences of Thirty-Seven Years* (1893) by Timothy Cavanagh. In 1890 the Metropolitan Police headquarters moved to a building on the Thames Embankment, which was named New Scotland Yard, and in 1967 to an office block in Victoria Street, which was given the same name.

163 *The letters, addressed to Mayne . . . throughout the month.* Most of the letters from the public are in MEPO 3/61.

165 *In early August . . . employed as a Detective, or what?'* These two letters are in the Home Office file on the case, HO 144/20/49113. Sir John Eardley Wilmot, a married man of fifty with eight children, was judge of the county court at Bristol. He went on to be Conservative MP for South Warwickshire from 1874 to 1885. He was not a very successful advocate, according to the *Dictionary of National Biography*, but in 1881 he helped to win compensation for Edmund Galley, who had been wrongly convicted of murder in 1835. Eardley Wilmot died in 1892.

168 *The public was fascinated by murder . . . the investigation of murder, too. Punch* magazine had satirised 'murder-worship' in 1849. See *Victorian Studies in Scarlet* (1972) by Richard D. Altick.

In an essay of 1856, George Eliot analysed the appeal of Wilkie Collins' stories: 'The great interest lies in the excitement either of curiosity or of terror . . . Instead of turning pale at a ghost we knit our brows and construct hypotheses to account for it. Edgar Poe's tales were an effort of genius to reconcile the two tendencies – to appal the imagination yet satisfy the intellect, and Mr Wilkie Collins in this respect often follows in Poe's tracks.' From a review of Collins' *After Dark* in the *Westminster Review*.

171 *On Tuesday, 31 July . . . piece of pickled pork.'* Account of the Walworth murders from *The Times* of 1, 8, 14, 16, 17 & 20 August 1860 and the *News of the World* of 2 September 1860.

175 *dramatised for the London stage.* In *Vidocq*, by Douglas Jerrold.

175 *The Victorians saw in the detective . . . cast him out.* Many learnt to find these thrills in detective fiction instead. 'Most traditional novels offer some of the pleasures of the keyhole,' observed Dennis Porter in *The Pursuit of Crime: Art and Ideology in Detective Fiction* (1981),

'but apart from various forms of erotica none does so more systematically than the fiction of detection. The secret of its power resides to a large degree in the trick that makes of voyeurism a duty.'

175 *A few voices . . . Whicher's defence.* The *Law Times* was sure that Whicher had identified the murderer and her motive. 'The child was his mother's pet, and *malice against his mother* – a fiendish desire to inflict a wound on her through him – would be a motive neither impossible nor improbable . . . Both of them, brother and sister [William and Constance], entertained very strong feelings of hostility, almost amounting to hatred towards the mother of the child . . . they knew that she had won the affections of their father while their mother was yet living. They had complained of neglect and ill-treatment by her, and of her partiality for her own children.' Since Saville had been taken from his cot by 'a light, practised hand', the journal added, a woman must have been involved in his abduction.

CHAPTER 13

181 *A week afterwards . . . unrestrained crying.'* Account of Youngman's execution from the *News of the World* of 9 September 1860.

183 *On Monday, 24 September . . . quite innocent.* A year later the Home Office, after prolonged wranglings, paid Slack's firm £700 for its work on the case. See HO 144/20/49113.

187 *Mrs Dallimore was a real-life version . . .* The Female Detective *(1864)*. Amateur female detectives also appear in Wilkie Collins' 'The Diary of Anne Rodway' (1856) and in *Revelations of a Lady Detective* (1864) by 'Anonyma' (W. Stephens Hayward). This book's jacket shows the lady detective as a dangerously emancipated, sensual creature. She wears a plump red-and-white ribbon round her throat, a hat piled high with flowers, a fur stole and velvet cuffs. She gives the prospective reader a sidelong gaze while lifting her full black coat to reveal the hem of a red dress.

188 *'the late Edgar Poe'.* Poe had died, aged forty, in 1849. In life, he suffered from alcoholism, depression and episodes of delirium. The critic Joseph Wood Krutch wrote that Poe 'invented the detective story in order that he might not go mad'. *Edgar Allan Poe: A Study in Genius* (1926), quoted in Peter Lehman's *The Perfect Murder* (1989).

190 *'Mr Kent, intriguing . . . disposes of same.'* See *The Letters of Charles Dickens 1859–61* (1997), edited by Madeline House and Graham Storey.

190 *The* Saturday Review *. . . beyond their routine'.* In the *Saturday Review* of 22 September 1860.

191 *The idea took hold . . . minds of our countrymen.'* In *Once a Week*, 13 October 1860. The author pointed out that, by this argument, few murders should take place in sunny southern Europe, which in fact had many violent deaths.

191 *A freak storm had hit Wiltshire . . . Saville Kent had died.* The natural historian and meteorologist George Augustus Rowell gave a lecture on the storm on 21 March 1860 and subsequently published it as a pamphlet, *A Lecture on the Storm in Wiltshire.*

CHAPTER 14

197 *Saunders asked Foley . . . he did not!'* In a letter to *The Times*, Stapleton claimed that a microscope would not have helped determine the nature of the blood on the nightdress he saw. 'I had no hesitation in advising the authorities that the nightdress shown to me . . . furnished no clue to this crime . . . I hoped that this nightdress was withdrawn for ever from public observation. However, Mr Saunders has dragged it from its obscurity again, and, as it seems to me, in wanton and useless violation of public decency and private feeling.' The nightdresses had become the emblem of the Kent family's decency and privacy; to speculate about them was to repeat the violation of their home.

200 *The persistent feeling . . . of the night-dress?').* In *The Road Murder: Being a Complete Report and Analysis of the Various Examinations and Opinions of the Press on this Mysterious Tragedy* (1860) by A Barrister-at-Law.

200 *His colleagues had to conduct . . . leave of absence.* From correspondence in HO 45/6970.

201 *In the last days of November . . . compact of secrecy'.* This letter was not made public until 24 July 1865, when it was published in *The Times*, but it was dated 23 November 1860. A letter Constance wrote that day has also survived, a note in which she thanks Peter Edlin, her lawyer, for 'the pretty pair of mittens and the scarf' that he had given her: they 'will remind me whenever I look at them', she writes, 'of how much I am indebted to the giver'.

CHAPTER 15

207 *At the beginning of 1861 . . . failing to examine Samuel.* Nor was any importance attached to allegations that the jury had been 'packed' in Samuel's favour. Before the inquest opened James

Morgan, the parish constable, and Charles Happerfield, the postmaster, had replaced two of the randomly selected jurors with 'men of judgement'. The two discharged were a tailor (whose wife had asked that he be excused) and William Nutt's father, a shoemaker who lived in the cottages next to Road Hill House. Their replacements were the Reverend Mr Peacock and a prosperous farmer called William Dew, who – like Happerfield – was an activist in the temperance movement.

207 *'You talk of the Road murder . . . may be never discovered now.'* Letter to W.W.F. de Cerjat in *The Letters of Charles Dickens 1859–61* (1997), edited by Madeline House and Graham Storey.

208 *Later that month, Samuel applied . . . cannot be acceded to'.* From correspondence in HO 45/6970.

209 *The Kents instructed . . . dispose of their belongings.* Account of the auction from the *Somerset and Wilts Journal* and the *Trowbridge and North Wilts Advertiser.*

211 *Over the summer the factory commissioners . . . in the Dee valley.* From HO 45/6970. William may have visited Constance in Brittany that summer – according to the Passport Office files, a William Kent was issued with a passport for travel on the Continent on 10 August.

211 *For several months . . . unlikely to attract attention.* Whicher's name appeared in *The Times* of 2 March 1861 when he testified against a man accused of stealing a crate of opium worth £1,000 from the London Dock Company, but this was a case that had been assigned to him a year earlier. The man he arrested was acquitted. Perhaps the jurors were suspicious of the prosecution witnesses – a convict and an opium dealer. Or perhaps, after the Road Hill case, it was Whicher they mistrusted.

211 *Just one was covered in any depth . . . his uncle's will.* Whicher obtained the vicar's address by pretending to be a lawyer – the adoption of a false identity was a common if unpopular detective practice. From reports in *The Times* and a transcript of the trial of James Roe at the Old Court, 21 & 22 August 1861.

212 *In the summer of 1861 . . . since Road Hill.* Account of the Kingswood murder from MEPO 3/63, the Metropolitan Police file on the case; and reports in *The Times*, the *Daily Telegraph* and the *Annual Register* of 1861.

215 *The Kingswood investigation had unfolded . . . a mockery of a detective's skills.* Franz's solicitor offered Dickens an article on the mind-boggling coincidences of the case (see Dickens' letter to W.H. Wills of 31 August 1861, in *The Letters of Charles Dickens*). The solicitor's article was published anonymously in *All the Year Round* the next January.

216 *'If I was not the cleverest . . . of their own accord.'* From 'Bigamy and Child-Stealing' in *Experiences of a Real Detective* by Inspector 'F', edited by Waters.

216 *'I believe that a chain . . . corrupt testimony.'* From 'Circumstantial Evidence' in *Experiences of a Real Detective.*

216 *'The value of the detective . . . what they mean.'* In *The Female Detective* (1864) by Andrew Forrester.

217 *This novel, a huge bestseller . . . terrified of exposure.* It went into eight editions in three months.

219 *'those most mysterious of mysteries . . . London lodgings'.* From 'Miss Braddon', an unsigned review in *The Nation*, 9 November 1865.

219 *In 1863 the philosopher Henry Mansel . . . conjured at Road.* Sensation literature was 'moulding the minds and forming the tastes and habits of its generation', wrote Mansel, 'by preaching to the nerves'. From an unsigned review in the *Quarterly Review* of April 1863. For discussions of the sensation novel, see especially *Black Swine in the Sewers of Hampstead: Beneath the Surface of Victorian Sensationalism* (1988) by Thomas Boyle; *Domestic Crime in the Victorian Novel* (1989) by Anthea Trodd; *From Bow Street to Baker Street: Mystery, Detection and Narrative* (1992) by Martin A. Kayman; *The Novel and the Police* (1988) by D.A. Miller; *In the Secret Theatre of Home: Wilkie Collins, Sensation Narrative, and Nineteenth-Century Psychology* (1988) by Jenny Bourne Taylor; 'What is "Sensational" About the Sensation Novel?' by Patrick Brantlinger in *Nineteenth-Century Fiction* 37 (1982).

220 *Joseph Stapleton's book . . . Rowland Rodway.* It cost 7*s*.6*d*. a copy.

220 *It was as if the domestic angel . . . bloodthirsty ghoul.* Other writers had noticed women's enthusiasm for brutal crimes. Edward Bulwer-Lytton, for instance, argued in *England and the English* (1833) that it was women who showed 'the deepest interest over a tale or a play of tragic or gloomy interest . . . If you observed a ballad-vender hawking his wares, it is the bloodiest murders that the women purchase.'

221 *Stapleton suggested that . . . corrupting sins'.* As a physician, Stapleton would have been familiar with essays like Benedict Morel's *Treatise on the Degeneration of the Human Species*, serialised in the *Medical Circular* in 1857, which argued that the sins of parents were visited on their children in the form of physical weaknesses.

221 *Mansel, too, cited the Road Hill murder . . . and adultery.* In 'Manners & Morals', *Fraser's* magazine, September 1861.

221 *Its influence was evident . . .* Aurora Floyd *(1863).* 'I think of a

quiet Somersetshire household in which a dreadful deed was done,' says the narrator of *Aurora Floyd*, 'the secret of which has never yet been brought to light, and perhaps never will be revealed until the Day of Judgement. What must have been suffered by each member of that family? What slow agonies, what ever-increasing tortures, while that cruel mystery was the "sensation" topic of conversation in a thousand happy home-circles, in a thousand tavern-parlours and pleasant club-rooms.'

In the 1950s the popular historian Elizabeth Jenkins wrote an essay on the ways in which the Kent family story influenced Charlotte Yonge's novel *The Young Step-Mother; Or, A Chronicle of Mistakes* (1861). The stepmother of the title marries into the Kendal family, and faces resistance from a sulky adolescent step-daughter, four of whose siblings have died in childhood. The stepdaughter accidentally knocks unconscious her half-brother, a three-year-old who is 'a marvel of fair stateliness, size and intelligence'. Jenkins subsequently discovered that most of the novel was published in serial form in the first half of 1860, before the Road Hill murder. Her mistake serves as a caution against seeing the influence of Road Hill everywhere; though Jenkins pointed out that the fact that the novel preceded the murder could make the similarities seem stranger still.

222 *The novelist Margaret Oliphant . . . taste or morals.'* From 'Sensation Novels', an unsigned review in *Blackwood's Edinburgh Magazine* of May 1862.

222 *A year later she complained . . . modern fiction'*. In the *Quarterly Review* of April 1863.

222 *bestsellers in 1861. Curiosities of Crime in Edinburgh* and *The Sliding Scale of Life*, both published in 1861 – the first sold 20,000 copies in three months, according to an article in *The Times* in July that year.

223 *'The modern detective is generally at fault . . . low and mean.'* From 'Crime and its Detection', an unsigned article by Thomas Donnelly in the *Dublin Review* of May 1861.

223 *The word 'clueless' . . . in 1862*. The phrase was 'clueless wanderings in the labyrinth of scepticism', according to the *Oxford English Dictionary*.

223 *'a cowardly and clumsy giant . . . who comes in his way'*. Published on 25 October 1863 and quoted in *Cops and Bobbies: Police Authority in New York and London, 1830–1870* (1999) by Wilbur R. Miller.

223 *In the* Saturday Review *. . . middle-class crimes*. In 'Detectives in Fiction and in Real Life', *Saturday Review*, June 1864.

224 *This establishment . . . Anglican Church.* See *Wagner of Brighton: The Centenary Book of St Paul's Church, Brighton* (1949) by H. Hamilton Maughan.

224 *His friend Detective-Inspector . . . in charge of the department.* From the census of 1861, Thornton's death certificate, MEPO 4/2 (a register of deaths in the Metropolitan Police) and MEPO 4/333 (a register of admissions and promotions). The detective division had expanded a little but was still only about twelve men strong, in a force that now boasted some seven thousand officers.

224 *In September 1862 . . . the Tsar's family.* See MEPO 2/23, the Metropolitan Police file of 1862 on aid given to the Russian government to reorganise the Warsaw police. Joseph Conrad's father, Apollo, had been a leader of this insurgency until 1861, when he was arrested and exiled to Russia.

224 *Superintendent Walker.* Walker was with the detectives when they met Dickens in 1850 – Dickens dubbed him 'Stalker'. He was not himself a detective but a member of the Commissioner's office.

225 *On 18 March 1864 . . . 'congestion of the brain'.* See MEPO 21/7, Metropolitan Police retirement papers.

225 *'protracted mental tension'.* From *A Practical Treatise on Apoplexy (with essay on congestion of the brain)* (1866) by William Boyd Mushet.

CHAPTERS 16 & 17

The account in the next two chapters of the events of 1865 is drawn mainly from the *Daily Telegraph, The Times*, the *Salisbury and Winchester Journal*, the *Observer*, the *Western Daily Press*, the *Somerset and Wilts Journal*, the *Penny Illustrated Paper*, the *News of the World* and the *Bath Chronicle*, and from the files MEPO 3/61, HO 144/20/49113 and ASSI 25/46/8. Additional sources are listed below.

CHAPTER 16

227 *On Tuesday, 25 April 1865 . . . Covent Garden.* Weather conditions from reports on the Spring Derby at Epsom, seventeen miles from London, which fell on 25 April that year. After the coldest March since 1845, the Derby was the hottest in years, according to *The Times*, the temperatures higher than the July average.

227 *The Bow Street office . . . discoloured walls. The Builder* of April 1860 reported that conditions in the court were bad in winter,

abominable in summer. Magistrates had been trying to secure new premises since the 1840s. Details of courtroom from *Oliver Twist* (1838) by Charles Dickens and *Survey of London Volume 36* (1970), general editor F.H.W. Sheppard.

229 *Wagner was a well-known figure . . . danger to the English Church.* See *Wagner of Brighton: The Centenary Book of St Paul's Church, Brighton* (1949) by H. Hamilton Maughan and *Aubrey Beardsley: A Biography* (1999) by Matthew Sturgis.

231 *In the course of this examination . . . summoned from Scotland Yard.* Dolly Williamson had married since his return from Road, and now had a daughter, Emma, aged two. Durkin had been in charge of a notorious case of July 1861 that inspired one of the essays in William Makepeace Thackeray's *Roundabout Papers*. A money-lender in Northumberland Street, off the Strand, had opened fire on a new client, Major William Murray of the 10th Hussars, a veteran of the Crimea. Murray fought back and eventually killed his assailant by smashing him over the head with a bottle. It emerged that the money-lender's rage sprang from a secret obsession with Murray's wife.

'After this,' wrote Thackeray, 'what is the use of being squeamish about the probabilities and possibilities in the writing of fiction? . . . After this, what is not possible? It is possible Hungerford Market is mined, and will explode some day.' The eruption of irrational violence could arouse excitement, wonder, even awe – the safety of the world was suddenly blown apart and anything at all could follow. The Northumberland Street crime, which also features in *The Moonstone*, is one of the cases explored in *Deadly Encounters: Two Victorian Sensations* (1986) by Richard D. Altick.

232 *(John Foley had died . . . aged sixty-nine).* His death certificate states that he died of a hydrothorax at St George's Terrace, Trowbridge, on 5 September 1864.

233 *'angel in the house'.* The term is from a poem published by Coventry Patmore in 1854, which describes the self-sacrificial purity and devotion of his wife, Emily.

233 *'Constance Kent, it is said . . . other agency than their own.'* In *The Times*, 26 April 1865. The *Bath Express* was similarly cynical about women's instincts. It argued on 29 April that this crime had a 'finesse of cruelty' of which only a woman was capable. The *Saturday Review* said it hoped that Constance was a 'psychological monster' rather than the embodiment of female adolescence. For attitudes to female killers, see *Twisting in the Wind: The Murderess and the English Press* (1998) by Judith Knelman.

235 *Detective-Inspector Tanner . . . a week at a time.* Tanner retired from the force due to ill-health in 1869 and opened a hotel in Winchester. He died in 1873, aged forty-two. See *Dreadful Deeds and Awful Murders: Scotland Yard's First Detectives* (1990) by Joan Lock.

241 *The Reverend James Davies . . . very wicked young woman.'* From *The Case of Constance Kent, viewed in the Light of the Holy Catholic Church* (1865) by James Davies and *The Case of Constance Kent, viewed in the Light of the Confessional* (1865) by Edwin Paxton Hood.

242 *James Redding Ware reprinted his pamphlet . . . death of her brother.'* From *The Road Murder: Analysis of this Persistent Mystery, Published in 1862, Now Reprinted, with Further Remarks* (1865) by J.R. Ware. The 1862 pamphlet was also published as a short story in Andrew Forrester's *The Female Detective* (1864) – 'Forrester' was a pseudonym, probably an allusion to a family firm of private inquiry agents based in the City of London.

243 *From her cell . . . undeceived on this point.'* Rodway passed the statement on to the press, and it appeared in several newspapers that summer.

244 *Children, he wrote elsewhere . . . the figure of the child.* See *Embodied Selves: An Anthology of Psychological Texts 1830–1890* (1998), edited by Jenny Bourne Taylor and Sally Shuttleworth. 'The moral lesson to be learned is the existence of evil passions in the breasts of even young children,' said the *Medical Times and Gazette* on 22 July 1865 – quoted in *Victorian Murderesses: A True History of Thirteen Respectable French and English Women Accused of Unspeakable Crimes* (1977) by Mary S. Hartman.

244 *Later, Bucknill told the Home Secretary . . . her father and brother.* From a letter of 30 August 1865 in HO 1144/20/49113.

244 *Rodway explained Constance's rationale . . . urged on her behalf.'* From a letter in HO 1144/20/49113.

CHAPTER 17

248 *John Duke Coleridge . . . getting up my speech.'* Coleridge earned more than £4,000 a year, according to the *Dictionary of National Biography*. Diary extract from *Life and Correspondence of John Duke, Lord Coleridge* (1904).

248 *He composed a letter . . . my conviction.'* Correspondence in Bernard Taylor's archive.

251 *As soon as the death sentence was passed . . . A maiden die on the fatal*

tree'. Broadside ballads, in order of quotation: 'The Road Hill Murder Confession of the Murderess', published by Disley, 1865; unnamed ballad quoted in the *North Wilts Herald* of 10 September 1865; 'Trial and Sentence of Constance Kent', also printed by Disley, 1865, and reprinted in Charles Hindley's *Curiosities of Street Literature* (1966). See Roly Brown's article on Constance Kent and the Road Murder, no. 15 in his series on the nineteenth-century broadside ballad trade in *Musical Traditions* magazine (mustrad.org.uk).

252 *A Devonshire magistrate . . . lunacy in the 1840s.* See affidavit from Gustavus Smith, dated 24 July 1865, in HO 1144/20/49113.

253 *On the morning of Thursday . . . slightest emotion.'* Pritchard was hanged on Friday.

253 *(in fact, Willes had decided . . . passed in confession').* Letter from Coleridge to W.E. Gladstone, 6 April 1890, quoted in *Saint – with Red Hands?* (1954) by Yseult Bridges.

258 *Bucknill finished his letter . . . could succumb to insanity.* In a lecture on 'Insanity in its Legal Relations' delivered before the Royal College of Physicians thirteen years later – in April 1878 – Bucknill said more about Constance's motive. The girl had stored up a 'fund of rage and revengeful feeling' against her 'high-spirited' stepmother, on account of the disparaging comments the second Mrs Kent made about Constance's 'partially demented' mother. Constance tried to run away from the stepmother's 'hated presence', but when she was caught and brought home resolved to take vengeance. She thought poison would be 'no real punishment' and decided instead to kill Saville. 'A dreadful story this,' remarked Bucknill, 'but who can fail to pity the depths of household misery which it denotes?' Quoted in *Celebrated Crimes and Criminals* (1890) by Willoughby Maycock.

259 *Forty years later . . . at every pore.'* From 'Fragment of an Analysis of a Case of Hysteria' (1905) in *The Standard Edition of the Complete Psychological Works of Sigmund Freud* (1953–74), edited by James Strachey, Alix Strachey and Alan Tyson. This essay concerned one of Freud's first patients, the eighteen-year-old 'Dora'.

CHAPTER 18

261 *In October 1865 . . . behind Millbank's high walls.* Information on Millbank gaol from *The Criminal Prisons of London and Scenes of London Life* (1862) by Henry Mayhew and John Binny; *The Princess Casamassima* (1886) by Henry James; and the *Penny Illustrated Paper* of 14 October 1865.

262 *In 1866 he married his landlady . . . sheep grazed on the green.* From Whicher's marriage certificate, on which he described himself as a bachelor, not a widower. Hippolyte Taine referred to sheep grazing outside Westminster Abbey in his *Notes on England* (1872).

263 *Private inquiry agents . . . Ignatius Pollaky.* Pollaky had become a successful private detective with offices at 13 Paddington Green, near the railway station. In 1866, according to *The Times*, he broke a ring of white slave traders who were kidnapping young women in Hull and selling them in Germany. A song in Gilbert & Sullivan's comic opera *Patience*, which opened in London in 1881, praised 'the keen penetration of Paddington Pollaky'. He died in Brighton in 1918, aged ninety.

263 *The work was well-paid . . . to divorce her.* From a report in *The Times* of 9 December 1858.

263 *In his new role Whicher took part . . . the Tichborne Claimant.* Account of the case of the Tichborne Claimant from: *Famous Trials of the Century* (1899) by J.B. Atlay; *The Tichborne Tragedy: Being the Secret and Authentic History of the Extraordinary Facts and Circumstances Connected with the Claims, Personality, Identification, Conviction and Last Days of the Tichborne Claimant* (1913) by Maurice Edward Kenealy; *The Tichborne Claimant: A Victorian Mystery* (1957) by Douglas Woodruff; *The Man Who Lost Himself* (2003) by Robyn Annear; and reports in *The Times*.

264 *'It has weighed upon the public mind like an incubus.'* From *The Tichborne Romance* (1872) by A Barrister At Large (A. Steinmedz), quoted in *Victorian Sensation* (2003) by Michael Diamond.

266 *'I daresay you hear me frequently abused . . . Your Old Friend, Jack Whicher.'* Quoted in *Scotland Yard: Its History and Organisation 1829–1929* (1929) by George Dilnot.

267 *Jack Whicher was still living . . . until death.* From census returns of 1861, 1871, 1881, marriage certificate of Sarah Whicher and James Holliwell, and Holliwell's citation for the Victoria Cross.

267 *'It is a very curious story . . . the detective prime?'* Dickens quote from a letter to W.H. Wills – see *The Letters of Charles Dickens 1868–1870* (2002), edited by Graham Storey, Margaret Brown and Kathleen Tillotson. Robert Louis Stevenson letter of 5 September 1868 quoted in *Wilkie Collins: The Critical Heritage* (1974), edited by Norman Page.

269 *In 1927 T.S. Eliot compared . . . fallible.'* From an article in the *Times Literary Supplement* of 4 August 1927.

270 *Henry James characterised . . . works of science.'* From 'Miss Braddon', unsigned review in *The Nation*, 9 November 1865.

270 *In May 1866 Samuel Kent renewed his plea . . . congestion of the lungs*. Papers on Samuel Kent's application to retire on full pay in HO 45/6970. In March the annual report of the factory inspector Robert Baker had referred to the great wrong done to Samuel in the years since Saville's death. An extract from Baker's account of his colleague's trials, including the 'threatened blindness' and subsequent paralysis of Mrs Kent, was published in *The Times* on 24 March 1866. According to her death certificate, Mary Kent died at Llangollen on 17 August 1866 – Samuel was present at her death.

270 *That summer he was awarded . . . common and cruel*. See *The Times*, 9 July 1866.

271 *Through the winter of 1867*. Information about William Kent's life after 1865 from *Savant of the Australian Seas* (1997) by A.J. Harrison. An electronic second edition of this biography, completed in 2005, is available on the STORS website of the State Library of Tasmania – members.trump.net.au/ahvem/Fisheries/Identities/Savant.html.

271 *He gave the name 'retrospective prophecy' . . . a word as "backteller"!' said Huxley*. From the essay 'On the Method of Zadig: Retrospective Prophecy as a Function of Science' (1880). In *Lady Audley's Secret* Mary Braddon described the detective's procedure as 'retrograde investigation'. The American philosopher Charles Sanders Peirce developed his theory of 'abduction', or retrospective deduction, in about 1865. 'We must conquer the truth by guessing,' he wrote, 'or not at all.' For the idea of 'backward hypothesising', see: *The Sign of Three: Dupin, Holmes, Peirce* (1983), edited by Umberto Eco and Thomas A. Sebeok; *The Perfect Murder* (1989) by Peter Lehman; and *Forging the Missing Link: Interdisciplinary Stories* (1992) by Gillian Beer.

272 *'Alone, perhaps, among detective-story writers . . . more essential and more strange.'* From *Appreciations and Criticisms of the Works of Charles Dickens* (1911) by G.K. Chesterton. Chesterton was adapting Job 19: 'For I know that my redeemer liveth, and that he shall stand at the latter day upon the earth' (King James Version of the Bible).

Others have found the endings to detective stories disappointing: 'The solution to a mystery is always less impressive than the mystery itself,' wrote Jorge Luis Borges in the short story 'Ibn Hakkan-al-Bokhari, Dead in His Labyrinth' (1951). 'Mystery has something of the supernatural about it, and even of the divine; its solution, however, is always tainted by sleight of hand.'

273 *He left his money . . . joint executors*. From Samuel Kent's will, dated 19 January 1872 and proved by William on 21 February that year.

273 *In January 1872 Samuel Kent . . . of a stillborn boy.* Biography from *Savant of the Australian Seas* (1997, revised 2005) by A.J. Harrison; *Guidebook to the Manchester Aquarium* (1875) by William Kent; *A Manual of the Infusoria* (1880–82) by William Kent; death certificate and will of Samuel Kent; birth announcement in *The Times*; marriage certificates of William Kent; census of 1881.

275 *In 1875 William's wife . . . obstruction of the bowel.* According to the death certificate, she died in Withington, Manchester, on 15 February.

275 *Jack and Charlotte Whicher . . . fields of lavender.* Lavender Hill information from: *Directory for Battersea Rise and the Neighbourhoods of Clapham and Wandsworth Commons* (1878); *Directory for the Postal District of Wandsworth* (1880); *The Buildings of Clapham*, edited by Alyson Wilson (2000); and *Battersea Past*, edited by Patrick Loobey (2002).

276 *In the summer of 1881 . . . went to his wife.* From Whicher's death certificate, will and probate in the Family Records Centre and the Court of Probate.

276 *After Jack's death . . . executor of her will.* From Charlotte Whicher's will and probate at the Court of Probate.

277 *Williamson was . . . unofficial hours.'* From *Fifty Years of Public Service* (1904) by Arthur Griffiths.

277 *The Chief Superintendent . . . a game of chess.* From *Scotland Yard: Its History and Organisation 1829–1929* (1929) by George Dilnot.

277 *'A Scot, from the crown of his head . . . valuable public servant.'* From *Scotland Yard Past and Present: Experiences of Thirty-Seven Years* (1893) by Timothy Cavanagh.

277 *Field – who by the 1870s was reduced almost to poverty.* In a letter written in January 1874 from 'Field Lodge', his home in Chelsea, he begged a client for £1 that he was owed – he had spent the past four months ill in bed, he said, and his doctor's bill was £30. From a letter in the British Library manuscripts collection: Add.42580 f.219. Field died later that year.

277 *In a notorious trial of 1877 . . . six detective inspectors.* From *Critical Years at the Yard: The Career of Frederick Williamson of the Detective Department and the CID* (1956) by Belton Cobb, and the census of 1881. Wilkie Collins also died in London in 1889, aged sixty-five.

278 *According to a police commissioner . . . harassing work'.* Unnamed police commissioner quoted in *Scotland Yard: Its History and Organisation 1829–1929* (1929) by George Dilnot.

278 *the crypt of St Paul's Cathedral in London.* Most of the mosaic floor in the St Paul's crypt was made by female inmates of Woking prison between 1875 and 1877, according to the St Paul's chapter minute books for 1874–89.

In the early 1870s about 100 women worked in the mosaics department at Woking, earning 1*s* 2*d* a day. They broke waste marble into chips, assembled the chips into decorative blocks and then rubbed them smooth with a piece of York stone. When the Woking convicts' black-and-white mosaic floor was installed at the Bethnal Green Museum in east London in 1872, the prison authorities drew attention to Constance's pre-eminence as a mosaicist. *The Graphic* of 29 June reported: 'We understand that Constance Kent is a clever teacher of this work to her fellow-prisoners.' But two years later her relationships at the gaol had soured. A reporter from the *Daily News* visited the Woking mosaics department in December 1874, to find that Constance was no longer working there. As he left the prison, the reporter saw a row of 'stocking knitters' outside their cells. They rose to their feet as he and the superintendent drew near. 'I noticed a woman of about 30 standing at the end of the row,' he wrote. 'She was full-featured, of sallow complexion, with dark eyes and had her short dark hair pushed back under her cap. She was noticeable amid the crowd, because, whilst all the rest curtsied as the Lady Superintendent passed and looked eagerly for the ever-ready smile of recognition, she, after casting one sharp, angry glance at the approaching visitors, stood sullenly, regarding the floor. 'Who is that?' I asked Mrs Gibson, when we were out of sight and hearing. 'That,' said the Lady Superintendent, 'is Constance Kent, and a very hard subject she is to deal with. She is one of the few women in the prison that I cannot 'get at'.'

A piece by the same journalist published in 1878 suggested why Constance had been removed from mosaic-making duties: 'She had more than once tried to escape, and at the time of my visit was undergoing special punishment having just been detected in carrying out a clandestine correspondence, which she had arranged with great cunning, and was persisting in with singular determination.'

The photograph of Constance in the second plate section of this book was taken at Woking that year.

278 *Major Arthur Griffiths . . . intelligence was of a high order.'* From *Secrets of the Prison House* (1894) by Arthur Griffiths.

279 *Griffiths returned in another memoir . . . her name was never mentioned.'* From *Fifty Years of Public Service* (1904) by Arthur Griffiths.

279 *In 1877 Constance petitioned . . . marked her petition 'nil'.* Petitions and letters of support in HO 144/20/49113.

CHAPTER 19

283 *In 1884 William . . . and Florence (twenty-five).* The information about William and his family in this chapter is drawn mainly from *Savant of the Australian Seas* (1997, revised 2005) by A.J. Harrison. Other sources include: 'Emigration of Women to Australia: Forced and Voluntary', a paper delivered to the Society of Genealogists in London by Noeline Kyle on 31 August 2005; the English census of 1881; and two of William's own books – *The Great Barrier Reef* (1893) and especially *The Naturalist in Australia* (1897).

286 *At Burlington House, London . . . and torso'.* From *The Times* of 11 June 1896.

287 *Two Japanese scientists were credited . . . before them.* The Australian pearl specialist C. Dennis George pointed out that the stepfather of the two Japanese pearl pioneers spent several months on Thursday Island in 1901, and had opportunity to observe William Saville-Kent's methods. George also argued that Saville-Kent succeeded in cultivating whole pearls before he died, and claimed that a string of these were found in the possession of a female vet in Brisbane in 1984; another set is rumoured to be in the possession of a family in Ireland. See *Savant of the Australian Seas* (1997, revised 2005) by A.J. Harrison.

288 *Mary Ann and Elizabeth . . . corresponded to the end.* Information about the Kent family from death certificates and wills, correspondence in Bernard Taylor's archive and research in Australia by A.J. Harrison and Noeline Kyle. St Peter's Hospital is described in *Old and New London: Volume 6* (1878).

288 *It emerged in the 1950s . . . under the name Emilie King.* From *Saint – with Red Hands?* (1954) by Yseult Bridges. Bridges said that she obtained the information first-hand, from a woman who was twenty-two when she met Constance in 1885. When Bridges wrote her book, the story of what subsequently became of Constance was unknown.

288 *In the 1970s . . . Miss Kaye died.* Constance's Australian exile was disclosed in *Cruelly Murdered* (1979) by Bernard Taylor.

The amateur criminologist Ivor Cantle (1919–1980) spent much of his life trying to discover the fate of the Kents and he, too, traced Constance to Australia. He subsequently became friends with Olive and her family.

290 *In her will . . . the first Mrs Kent.* In this will, written in 1926, Constance bequeathed the nurses' home she had established to a fellow nurse, Hilda Lord, and left her money to the Joseph Fels Fund. Fels (1853–1914) was a Jewish-American soap magnate,

social reformer and philanthropist who established model communities for the unemployed and for craftsmen in England and the US. He believed that taxation should be based solely on land ownership. The account of the discovery of the family portraits left to Olive is from correspondence in Bernard Taylor's archive.

CHAPTER 20

291 *In 1928 . . . the origins of his death.* Rhode quoted and discussed this letter in an essay in *The Anatomy of Murder: Famous Crimes Critically Considered by Members of the Detection Club* (1936). The original letter was destroyed by enemy action in the Second World War, but Rhode's typed version survived.

294 *At boarding school . . . gas leak is a convincing detail.)* The gas leak was mentioned in the *Somerset and Wilts Journal* in 1865. Constance was boarding at a school in Bath, according to the newspaper, when 'being offended with her teacher, she deliberately turned on the gas throughout the house, making no secret of the fact that her intention was to cause an explosion'.

294 *The letter claimed that Constance read Darwin.* This was plausible, since *The Origin of Species* received a huge amount of attention when it was published in 1859. There was an impossibility in the letter, though – the author claimed that the young Constance used to shock people by referring to 'La Divine Sara' Bernhardt, but the actress – who was born in the same year as Constance – did not become famous until the 1870s.

295 *Like the heroine . . . absorbed by the past.* In an essay of 1949 the psychoanalyst Geraldine Pederson-Krag suggested that the murder in a detective novel is a version of the 'primal scene', in which a child witnesses or imagines his or her parents having sexual intercourse, and interprets the act as violent. The victim represents one of the parents, the clues represent the nocturnal sounds, stains and jokes that the child observed but only dimly understood. The reader of a detective novel, says Pederson-Krag, satisfies his or her infantile curiosity by identifying with the detective and thus 'redressing completely the helpless inadequacy and anxious guilt unconsciously remembered from childhood'. See 'Detective Stories and the Primal Scene' in *Psychoanalytic Quarterly* 18. In 1957 the psychologist Charles Rycroft argued that the reader was not only the detective but also the murderer, playing out hostile feelings towards the parent. See 'A Detective Story' in *Psychoanalytic Quarterly* 26. These approaches are discussed in *Bloody Murder:*

From the Detective Story to the Crime Novel – a History (1972) by Julian Symons.

296 *The letter from Sydney threw out . . . corruptions of his own body.* Information on syphilis from *Pox: Genius, Madness and the Mysteries of Syphilis* (2004) by Deborah Hayden, and from Alastair Barkley, a consultant dermatologist in London.

Since this book was first published, another story has emerged about Samuel's sexual dalliances in London in the early 1830s: a woman called Josephine Bridges wrote to the author in 2008 to say that she believed that her great-great-grandmother, a wardrobe mistress at a London theatre, bore Samuel Kent a daughter before 1835. This girl, Rosa Kent Fuller, went on to marry Edwin Martin, a carpenter in Iden, East Sussex; their first child was born in the summer that Saville Kent was murdered. The Martins later ran a railway crossing, at which Rosa was run down and killed by a motorist in 1908. She was buried in Iden churchyard.

Josephine Bridges' mother and grandmother had told her that Samuel Kent visited his illegitimate daughter often and treated her well. None the less, Rosa Kent Fuller is listed in the census of 1841 as an eight-year-old 'pauper' living at the West London Union School in Edmonton, Middlesex, an institute for impoverished children from the Strand district of London. Her mother may have been the Mary Ann Fuller, aged 25 or so, listed that year as an inmate of the Strand Union workhouse in Cleveland Street, Fitzrovia. Unmarried mothers were nearly always sent to the workhouse, and the Boards of Guardians set up in London in the 1830s habitually separated poor children from their parents by sending them to schools outside the city.

If Samuel was Rosa's father, Mrs Bridges and her family are the Kents' only known English descendants.

298 *the book by John Rhode. The Case of Constance Kent* (1928).

299 *The person best placed to solve a crime . . . its perpetrator.* In Sophocles' *Oedipus the King*, sometimes cited as the original detective story, Oedipus is both the murderer and the detective; he commits and he solves the crimes. 'In any investigation, the real detective is the suspect,' wrote John Burnside in *The Dumb House* (1997). 'He is the one who provides the clues, he is the one who gives himself away.'

299 *The holes in her story left the way open . . . the main players in the case had died.* In *Murder and its Motives* (1924) Fryniwyd Tennyson Jesse accepted Constance's guilt but lamented that the girl was born into an age unable to understand and accommodate her complex psychology. In *The Rebel Earl and Other Studies* (1926)

William Roughead regretted that the alienists had not recognised that Constance had 'a mind diseased'. In *Saint – with Red Hands?* (1954) Yseult Bridges argued that the true killers were Samuel Kent and Elizabeth Gough, and that Constance confessed in order to protect them. In *Victorian Murderesses* (1977) Mary S. Hartman agreed that Constance probably made a false confession to conceal her father's guilt. In *Cruelly Murdered* (1979) Bernard Taylor proposed that Constance killed Saville, but that Samuel, who was having an affair with Gough, mutilated the body to conceal his daughter's crime and his own misdemeanour.

Among the fictional versions of the story is a scene in the British horror film *Dead of Night* (1945), in which a girl encounters the ghost of Saville Kent in a remote corner of a country house – he speaks of Constance's unkindness to him. Two years later Mary Hayley Bell's play *Angel*, directed for the London stage by her husband, Sir John Mills, so confused audiences with its sympathy for Constance that it closed within weeks and almost ended Bell's career as a playwright. Eleanor Hibbert, who as Jean Plaidy produced historical novels, fictionalised the case in *Such Bitter Business* (1953), under the pseudonym Elbur Ford. Two characters in William Trevor's *Other People's Worlds* (1980) become obsessed by the Road Hill murder, with horrible results. Francis King's *Act of Darkness* (1983) set the story in colonial 1930s India, and had the boy accidentally killed by his sister and his nursemaid when he surprises them in a lesbian embrace. James Friel's *Taking the Veil* (1989) placed the case in 1930s Manchester, and had the boy killed by his father and his aunt-cum-nursemaid after he witnesses them having sex; his teenage half-sister mutilates the body and makes a false confession of murder to protect the father, who has sexually violated her. In 2003 Wendy Walker compressed the story into a book-length poem, *Blue Fire* (as yet unpublished), which used one word from each line of Stapleton's *The Great Crime of 1860*.

299 *his confidential reports to Sir Richard Mayne*. In MEPO 3/61.

AFTERWORD

303 *Stapleton's explanation . . . cut into his neck*. Joshua Parsons, who was in charge of the post-mortem, disagreed with this interpretation of the cuts to Saville's finger. The incisions had not bled, he told the magistrates' court on 4 October 1860, which meant that they must have been made after death, probably by accident. In any

case, he said, he thought the cuts were on the right hand, not the left. His reading of the body supported the theory that the child was suffocated, a finding that Stapleton was determined to disprove. The doctors' dispute returns Saville to the realm of riddle and debate. The image of the live child dims.

303 *'The detective story . . . a happy ending.'* In a letter of 2 June 1949 to James Sandoe. From *The Raymond Chandler Papers: Selected Letters and Non-Fiction, 1909–1959* (2000), edited by Tom Hiney and Frank MacShane. Chandler argued in the same letter that a detective story and a love story could never be combined, because the detective story was 'incapable of love'.

LIST OF ILLUSTRATIONS

SELECT BIBLIOGRAPHY

Further sources are detailed in the Notes

PRIMARY SOURCES

Metropolitan Police, Home Office and court files

ASSI 25/46/8
HO 45/6970
HO 144/20/49113
MEPO 2/23
MEPO 3/61
MEPO 3/53
MEPO 3/54
MEPO 4/2
MEPO 4/333
MEPO 7/7
MEPO 21/7

Newspapers

The Bath Chronicle
The Bristol Daily Post
The Daily Telegraph
The Frome Times
The Morning Post
The News of the World
The Observer
The Penny Illustrated Paper
The Somerset and Wilts Journal
The Times
The Trowbridge & North Wilts Advertiser
The Western Daily Press

Journals

All the Year Round
The Annual Register
Chambers's Edinburgh Journal

Household Words
The Law Times
Once a Week

Books and pamphlets

A Barrister-at-Law, *The Road Murder: Being a Complete Report and Analysis of the Various Examinations and Opinions of the Press on this Mysterious Tragedy*, London, 1860
'Anonyma' (W. Stephens Hayward), *Revelations of a Lady Detective*, London, 1864
Braddon, Mary Elizabeth, *Lady Audley's Secret*, London, 1862
Cavanagh, Timothy, *Scotland Yard Past and Present: Experiences of Thirty-Seven Years*, London, 1893
Coleridge, Ernest Hartley, *Life and Correspondence of John Duke, Lord Coleridge*, London, 1904
Collins, Wilkie, *The Woman in White*, London, 1860
Collins, Wilkie, *The Moonstone*, London, 1868
Davies, James, *The Case of Constance Kent, viewed in the Light of the Holy Catholic Church*, London, 1865
Dickens, Charles, *Bleak House*, London, 1853
Dickens, Charles, *The Mystery of Edwin Drood*, London, 1870
House, Madeline and Storey, Graham, *The Letters of Charles Dickens 1859–61*, London, 1997
Hood, Edwin Paxton, *The Case of Constance Kent, viewed in the Light of the Confessional*, London, 1865
Forrester, Andrew, *The Female Detective*, London, 1864
Griffiths, Arthur, *Secrets of the Prison House*, London, 1894
Griffiths, Arthur, *Mysteries of Police & Crime*, London, 1899
Griffiths, Arthur, *Fifty Years of Public Service*, London, 1904
Hotten, John Camden, *The Slang Dictionary; or, The Vulgar Words, Street Phrases, and 'Fast' Expressions of High and Low Society, etc*, London, 1864
Huish, Robert, *The Progress of Crime; or, The Authentic Memoirs of Maria Manning*, London, 1849
James, Henry, *The Turn of the Screw*, London, 1898
Kenealy, Maurice Edward, *The Tichborne Tragedy: Being the Secret and Authentic History of the Extraordinary Facts and Circumstances Connected with the Claims, Personality, Identification, Conviction and Last Days of the Tichborne Claimant*, London, 1913
Kent, William, *Guidebook to the Manchester Aquarium*, Manchester, 1875
Kent, William, *A Manual of the Infusoria: Including a Description of All Known Flagellate, Ciliate and Tentaculiferous Protozoa, British and*

Foreign, and an Account of the Organisation and Affinities of the Sponges, London, *1880–82*

Lansdowne, Andrew, *A Life's Reminiscences of Scotland Yard*, London, 1890

Mayhew, Henry, *London Labour and the London Poor*, London, 1861

Mayhew, Henry, and Binny, John, *The Criminal Prisons of London and Scenes of London Life*, London, 1862

McLevy, James, *The Casebook of a Victorian Detective*, ed. George Scott-Moncreiff, Edinburgh, 1975, a selection from *Curiosities of Crime in Edinburgh* and *The Sliding Scale of Life*, Edinburgh, 1861

Poe, Edgar Allan, 'The Man of the Crowd' (1840), 'The Murders in the rue Morgue' (1841), 'The Mystery of Marie Roget' (1842), 'The Tell-tale Heart' (1843), reprinted in *Complete Stories and Poems*, New York, 1966

Saville-Kent, William, *The Great Barrier Reef*, London, 1893

Saville-Kent, William, *The Naturalist in Australia*, London, 1897

Stapleton, Joseph Whitaker, *The Great Crime of 1860: Being a Summary of the Facts Relating to the Murder Committed at Road; a Critical Review of its Social and Scientific Aspects; and an Authorised Account of the Family; With an Appendix, Containing the Evidence Taken at the Various Inquiries*, London, 1861

Ware, James Redding, *The Road Murder: Analysis of this Persistent Mystery, Published in 1862, Now Reprinted, with Further Remarks*, London, 1865

'Waters' (William Russell), *Recollections of a Detective Police-Officer*, London, 1856

'Waters' (William Russell), ed, *Experiences of a Real Detective* by Inspector 'F', London, 1862

SECONDARY SOURCES

Altick, Richard D., *Victorian Studies in Scarlet*, New York, 1970

Altick, Richard D., *Deadly Encounters: Two Victorian Sensations*, Philadelphia, 1986

The Anatomy of Murder: Famous Crimes Critically Considered by Members of the Detection Club, London, 1936

Atlay, J.B., *Famous Trials of the Century*, London, 1899

Beer, Gillian, *Forging the Missing Link: Interdisciplinary Stories*, Cambridge, 1992

Boyle, Thomas, *Black Swine in the Sewers of Hampstead: Beneath the Surface of Victorian Sensationalism*, New York, 1988

Bridges, Yseult, *Saint – with Red Hands?: The Chronicle of a Great Crime*, London, 1954

Browne, Douglas G., *The Rise of Scotland Yard: A History of the Metropolitan Police*, London, 1956
Chesney, Kellow, *The Victorian Underworld*, London, 1970
Cobb, Belton, *Critical Years at the Yard: The Career of Frederick Williamson of the Detective Department and the CID*, London, 1956
Cobb, Belton, *The First Detectives and the Early Career of Richard Mayne, Commissioner of Police*, London, 1957
Collins, Philip, *Dickens and Crime*, London, 1962
Dilnot, George, *Scotland Yard: Its History and Organisation 1829–1929*, London, 1929
Emsley, Clive, *The English Police: A Political and Social History*, London, 1991
Frank, Lawrence, *Victorian Detective Fiction and the Nature of Evidence: The Scientific Investigations of Poe, Dickens and Doyle*, New York, 2003
Harrison, A.J., *Savant of the Australian Seas*, Hobart, 1997
Hartman, Mary S., *Victorian Murderesses*, New York, 1977
Hughes, Kathryn, *The Victorian Governess*, London, 1993
Kayman, Martin A., *From Bow Street to Baker Street: Mystery, Detection and Narrative*, Basingstoke, 1992
Knelman, Judith, *Twisting in the Wind: The Murderess and the English Press*, Toronto, 1998
Lehman, David, *The Perfect Murder: A Study in Detection*, New York, 1989
Lock, Joan, *Dreadful Deeds and Awful Murders: Scotland Yard's First Detectives 1829-1878*, Somerset, 1990
Maughan, Herbert Hamilton, *Wagner of Brighton: The Centenary Book of St Paul's Church, Brighton*, Loughlinstown, 1949
Miller, D.A., *The Novel and the Police*, Berkeley, 1988
Miller, Wilbur R., *Cops and Bobbies: Police Authority in New York and London, 1830–1870*, Chicago, 1999
Ousby, Ian, *Bloodhounds of Heaven: The Detective in English Fiction from Godwin to Doyle*, Cambridge, Massachusetts, 1976
Porter, Dennis, *The Pursuit of Crime: Art and Ideology in Detective Fiction*, New Haven, 1981
Rhode, John, *The Case of Constance Kent*, London, 1928
Rogers, Kenneth, *The Book of Trowbridge*, Buckingham, 1984
Roughead, William, *The Rebel Earl and Other Studies*, Edinburgh, 1926
Shpayer-Makov, Haia, *The Making of a Policeman: A Social History of a Labour Force in Metropolitan London, 1829–1914*, Aldershot, 2002

Symons, Julian, *Bloody Murder: From the Detective Story to the Crime Novel – a History*, London, 1972

Taylor, Bernard, *Cruelly Murdered: Constance Kent and the Killing at Road Hill House*, London, 1979, revised 1989

Taylor, Jenny Bourne, *In the Secret Theatre of Home: Wilkie Collins, Sensation Narrative, and Nineteenth-Century Psychology*, London, 1988

Taylor, Jenny Bourne and Shuttleworth, Sally, eds, *Embodied Selves: An Anthology of Psychological Texts 1830–1890*, Oxford, 1998

Thomas, Ronald, *Detective Fiction and the Rise of Forensic Science*, Cambridge, 1999

Trodd, Anthea, *Domestic Crime in the Victorian Novel*, Basingstoke, 1989

Wohl, A., *The Victorian Family: Structures and Stresses*, London, 1978

Woodruff, John Douglas, *The Tichborne Claimant: A Victorian Mystery*, London, 1957

ACKNOWLEDGEMENTS

I am very grateful to Bernard Taylor for directing me to his archive of papers on the Road Hill murder and for allowing me to use the images he gathered – he has been exceptionally generous. Thanks also to Stewart Evans, the custodian of the archive, for his guidance and hospitality, and to Cynthia Yates for being such a welcoming and informative hostess at Langham (formerly Road Hill) House. For help on specific queries, thanks to Joseph Wisdom at St Paul's Cathedral, Susanna Lamb at Madame Tussaud's, Eleri Lynn at the Victoria & Albert Museum, Katherine White at Trowbridge Museum and Anthony J. Harrison in Australia. Thank you to Leslie Robinson for the maps. More generally, I am indebted to the staff of the National Archives, the Family Records Centre, Battersea Library, Southwark Local History Library, Trowbridge Museum, Frome Museum, the London Library, the British Library, the London Metropolitan Archives and the Metropolitan Police Historical Collection.

For the material they have contributed to the paperback edition of this book, thank you very much to Richard Rose, Lesley Grayson, Josephine and Michael Bridges, Gina Sanders, Professor Clyde Binfield, James Fergusson, Eric Jenkins, Gillian Roberts, Christopher Parsons, Michael Yelton, and Gill Arnott of the Hampshire Museums Service.

For their advice and their support, huge thanks to my family and friends, among them Ben Summerscale, Juliet Summerscale, Valerie Summerscale, Peter Summerscale, Robert Randall, Daniel Nogués, Victoria Lane, Toby Clements, Sinclair McKay, Lorna

Bradbury, Alex Clark, Will Cohu, Ruth Metzstein, Stephen O'Connell, Keith Wilson and Miranda Fricker. In the early stages of my research, I was sent to excellent sources by Sarah Wise, Rebecca Gowers, Robert Douglas-Fairhurst and Kathryn Hughes. Towards the end, I had wonderful readers in Anthea Trodd and Peter Parker. My thanks also to PD James for her observations on this case and to former Detective-Inspector Douglas Campbell for his comments about detective work in general.

For putting so much into publishing the book, thank you to Alexandra Pringle, Mary Morris, Kate Tindal-Robertson, Meike Boening, Kathleen Farrar, Polly Napper, Kate Bland, David Mann, Phillip Beresford, Robert Lacey, and the rest of the brilliant people at Bloomsbury. Thank you to my terrific editors at Walker & Co, George Gibson and Michele Amundsen, and to the other publishers who have shown faith in the book, including Andreu Jaume of Lumen S.A. in Barcelona, Dorothee Grisebach of Berlin Verlag, Dominique Bourgois of Christian Bourgois Editeur in Paris, Andrea Canobbio of Giulio Einaudi Editore in Turin, and Nikolai Naumenko of AST in Moscow. I am grateful also to Angus Cargill and Charlotte Greig for their early interest and encouragement. My thanks to the excellent Laurence Laluyaux, Stephen Edwards and Hannah Westland of Rogers, Coleridge & White Ltd, to Julia Kreitman of The Agency, and to Melanie Jackson in New York. Special thanks to David Miller, my friend and agent, for always seeming to understand better than I did what it was that I was trying to do. His contribution to this book is immeasurable. My son, Sam, has already been rewarded (with a trip to Legoland) for being patient while I worked, but I'd like to thank him here for being altogether fantastic.

INDEX

A NOTE ON THE AUTHOR

Kate Summerscale is the author of the bestselling *The Queen of Whale Cay*, which won a Somerset Maugham award and was shortlisted for the Whitbread Biography Award. She has also judged various literary competitions including the Booker Prize. She lives in London.